The Death of
of
Ben Linder

The Death of Ben Linder

The Story of a North American
in Sandinista Nicaragua

Joan Kruckewitt

Joan Kruckewitt (signature)

SEVEN STORIES PRESS
New York ● Toronto ● London

Seven Stories Press
140 Watts Street
New York, NY 10013
http://www.sevenstories.com

In Canada:
Hushion House, 36 Northline Road, Toronto, Ontario M4B 3E2, Canada
In the U.K.:
Turnaround Publisher Services Ltd., Unit 3, Olympia Trading Estate, Coburg Road, Wood Green, London N22 6TZ U.K.

Library of Congress Cataloging-in-Publication Data
Kruckewitt, Joan.
The Death of Ben Linder: the story of an American in Sandinista Nicaragua /
Joan Kruckewitt.
p.   cm.
ISBN: 1-888363-96-7
1. Linder, Benjamin Ernest, 1959–1987—Journeys—Nicaragua. 2. Linder, Benjamin Ernest, 1959–1987—Death and burial. 3. Nicaragua—Politics and goverment—1979–1990. 4. Nicaragua—Foreign relations—United States. 5. United States—Foreign relations—Nicaraguan. 6. Americans—Nicaragua—Death. 7. Engineers—Nicaragua—Death. I. Title.
F1528.22.L56K78   1999
972.845'53'092—dc21   98-55231
                                                                        CIP

9 8 7 6 5 4 3 2 1
Book design by Adam Simon

Seven Stories Press
140 Watts Street
New York, NY 10013
http://www.sevenstories.com

Printed in the U.S.A.

*A portion of the proceeds from the sale of this book will be donated to
the Ben Linder Project/Green Empowerment.*

Frontispiece: Ben Linder on his six-foot multiple-gear unicycle pedaling down the
Pacific Coast, 1980. COURTESY OF THE LINDER FAMILY

In memory of my friends and colleagues Ian Walker and Cornel Lagrouw, who also covered the wars in Central America.

HONDURAS

Río Coco

TEGUCIGALPA
YAMALES
AYAPAL
PUERTO
CABEZAS
LAS MANOS
JALAPA
Río Bocay
SAN JOSÉ DE BOCAY
OCOTAL
WIWILÍ
MT. KILAMBÉ
QUILALÍ
ZOMPOPERA
SOMOTO
PANTASMA
EL CUÁ
SEGOVIA
MOUNTAINS
EL ESPINO
PEÑAS BLANCAS MOUNTAINS
WASLALA
ESTELÍ
JINOTEGA
EMPALME LA DALIA
SOMOTILLO
CHAGÜITILLO
LA TRINIDAD
MATAGALPA
MATIGUÁS
Río Grande de Matagalpa
POTOSÍ
SÉBACO
CHINANDEGA
NICARAGUA
CORINTO
LEÓN
CORN ISLANDS
(ISLAS DE MAÍZ)
Pan American Hwy
TIPITAPA
JUIGALPA
RAMA
PUERTO SANDINO
MANAGUA
Río Escondido
BLUEFIELDS
MASAYA
GRANADA
CARIBBEAN
SEA
MONTELIMAR
PACIFIC
OCEAN
Lake
Nicaragua
RIVAS
SAN JUAN DEL SUR
PEÑAS BLANCAS
SAN CARLOS
0   30   60 km
20   40 miles
COSTA RICA
Río San Juan

TRACY CRO

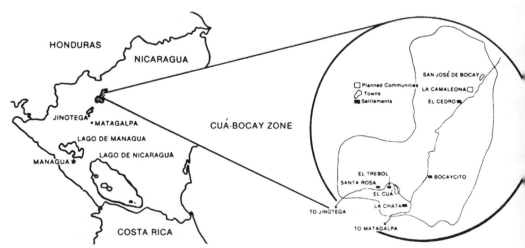

HONDURAS   NICARAGUA

JINOTEGA
MATAGALPA
CUÁ-BOCAY ZONE
LAGO DE MANAGUA
LAGO DE NICARAGUA
MANAGUA

SAN JOSÉ DE BOCAY
LA CAMALEONA
☐ Planned Communities
◯ Towns
▪ Settlements
EL CEDRO

EL TREBOL
BOCAYCITO
SANTA ROSA
EL CUÁ
LA CHATA
TO JINOTEGA
TO MATAGALPA

COSTA RICA

Contents

Acknowledgments

This book was a group project. It could not have been written without the support of hundreds of friends throughout the long years that it took to get published.

The idea came about through a chance encounter in summer, 1987, on the corner of Ashby and Telegraph in Berkeley, California, when I ran into a former U.C. Berkeley classmate, Ted Nace. I was taking a break, visiting Berkeley from Managua, after having had an exhausting year covering the Hasenfus trial, the intense upswing of the war after the U.S. Congress approved $100 million dollars in aid for the Contras, and the death of Ben Linder, whom I knew. Ted suggested that I write an article about Ben.

Back in Managua, Larry Boyd and I discussed the project and, as we began interviewing people, quickly realized that Ben's story merited a book. I wish to especially acknowledge and thank Larry for his hard work during the early stages of the book, especially in the numerous difficult trips we took to El Cuá and San José de Bocay during the war years. I also would like to thank others who did interviews: Jan Howard-Melendez, Bob Malone, Katherine Griffin, Barbara Stahler-Sholk, Millie Thayer, Beth Stephens, Maritza Peña, and members of the Witness for Peace teams.

Each of the tape-recorded interviews was meticulously transcribed, and for this I'd like to thank: Patricia Mulligan, Richard Stahler-Sholk, Ana Julia, Judy Cook, Viviana Fernández, John Kane, Charles Scanlan, Cynthia Downs, and Gregory Jackson.

Journalists Fred Bruning, Eric Scigliano, and John Lantigua generously allowed me to quote from their stories and source material.

Research data, especially CIA documents that became available years after Ben's death, were critical in completing the investigation into his murder. I'd like to thank Lisa Hirshfield for her research at the Data Center in Oakland, California; Peter Kornbluh and Kate Doyle at the National Security Archive in Washington, D.C.; and Michael Ratner and Beth Stephens at the Center for Constitutional Rights in New York. Also thanks to Ed Griffin-Nolan, who allowed me to examine the Witness for Peace documents in Managua, and others who provided original research materials and/or leads: Rebecca Leaf, Jeff Hart, Barbara Wiggenton, Circles Robinson, Lois Wessel, Bruce Petschek, Claire Foster, Piers Lewis, and Richard Bermack.

For years, the manuscript, in its various forms, accompanied me everywhere.

In 1989, I took it to Panama, while covering the U.S. invasion there. In 1991, long after the Sandinistas lost the elections, I left Nicaragua and was sent to Germany, where I worked on the manuscript during a cold, lonely winter in Berlin, while the Gulf War was waged. I returned to Berkeley to finish it, and want to thank all my friends and coworkers at Peachpit Press for their unflagging encouragement and generous support. I'd also like to mention my favorite mechanic, Bob Howard, who made it possible for me to show up there every morning.

In 1993 and 1995, after acquiring more CIA documents, I returned to Nicaragua to gather more information, and I'd like to acknowledge Lillian Hall and Paul Berman, who accompanied me on two of the most harrowing trips into the mountains.

Throughout the years, I had many people read, comment and edit the manuscript. I'd particularly like to thank Kit Duane, James Frey, Sheyla Hirshon, Elizabeth Gaffney, and Kera Bolonik. I also give special thanks to Maile Melkonian for her excellent eye for detail and late-night work sessions.

In Managua, I'd like to thank the former members of CUSCLIN; Ria Reyburn and the Guadamúz family in Managua, especially Doña Quiqua; and Hortencia Obando Torrentes. In the U.S., my deepest appreciation goes to my parents, Charles and Lorraine Kruckewitt, who never knew what I was doing, but always supported me. I would also like to acknowledge Fred Royce, Dee Knight, Jean Carroll, June Carolyn Erlick, Mehrene Larudee, Lou Dematteis, Donna Goldstein, Wendy Monroe for safekeeping my CIA documents, and the staff of Bolívar House at Stanford University (who helped me more than they could imagine).

My deepest gratitude also goes to the Linder family, Alison Quam, Don Macleay, and Mira Brown for their willingness to open their lives and share their memories of Ben. Also, my sincerest thanks must go to my friend, Ted Nace, without whose support this book would never have been published.

Finally, I am grateful to everyone who gave me interviews about Ben, who wrote letters and poems about him, and who supported both the writing of this book, and me, in various ways. You know who you are, and this book is yours too.

Joan Kruckewitt
Stanford, California
July, 1999

Prologue

On April 30, 1987, under a fierce afternoon sun, a funeral procession wound its way through the cobbled streets of Matagalpa, a small city in Nicaragua. The country's president, Daniel Ortega, and his wife, Rosario Murillo, followed the casket, slowly walking arm in arm with two Americans, David and Elisabeth Linder from Portland, Oregon. The Linders' son and daughter, John and Miriam, walked beside them. Oscar Blandón, a hydroplant operator and electrician from the remote village of El Cuá, walked alone, head hidden underneath a baseball cap, a sentinel that never strayed from the casket. Clowns from the Nicaraguan National Circus followed behind, their painted mouths turned downward. Behind them walked thousands of Nicaraguans and foreigners. The funeral procession stretched for more than seven blocks.

In the coffin lay Benjamin Ernest Linder, a twenty-seven-year-old American engineer. While working on a small hydroelectric dam that eventually brought electricity and running water to a village in the middle of Nicaragua's war zone, he was ambushed by a group of Contras, anti-Sandinista rebels financed by the U.S. government. Ben Linder's death made front-page headlines around the world. His life and death were bitterly debated in the United States, on radio and television, in newspapers, and in Congress. Opponents of Washington's policy in Nicaragua called him a "national hero" and a martyr of the left, while supporters of Washington's policy justified him as a "legitimate target" and asked, "Was he a Communist?" President Ronald Reagan, who had earlier proclaimed, "I'm a Contra too," made no comment, but Vice President George Bush stated that Linder was "on the other side."

CBS News correspondent Dan Rather had a very different take on the first murder of an American by the Contras:

> Benjamin Linder was no revolutionary firebrand, spewing rhetoric and itching to carry a rifle through the jungles of Central America. He was a slight,

softspoken, thoughtful young man. When, at 23, he left the comfort and security of the United States for Nicaragua, he wasn't exactly sure what he would find. But he wanted to see Nicaragua firsthand, and so he headed off, armed with a new degree in engineering, and the energy and ideals of youth.

This wasn't just another death in a war that has claimed thousands of Nicaraguans. This was an American who was killed with weapons paid for with American tax dollars. The bitter irony of Benjamin Linder's death is that he went to Nicaragua to build up what his own country's dollars paid to destroy—and ended up a victim of the destruction. The loss of Benjamin Linder is more than fodder in an angry political debate. It is the loss of something that seems rare these days: a man with the courage to put his back behind his beliefs. It would have been very easy for this bright young man to follow the path to a good job and a comfortable salary. Instead, he chose to follow the lead of his conscience.

Ben followed his conscience when he moved to El Cuá, a small village in the Nicaraguan war zone, where he, as part of a team of Americans and Nicaraguans, brought electricity to the town. Ben also delighted farmer's children by clowning and unicycling down the village's one dirt road. Ben knew that the area was dangerous, but for him, the risks were worthwhile. He wrote, "I see the kids and I feel like taking them all away to a safe place to hide until the war stops and the hunger stops and El Cuá becomes strong enough to give them the care they deserve. The pied piper of El Cuá. But I can't do that, and even if I could it wouldn't help the neighboring towns. So instead, I try to put in light, and hope for the best."

This is the story of what drove Ben to take the risks he did.

Chapter 1

Ben Moves to Managua

On a still, hot afternoon on June 11, 1983, some 2,500 graduating seniors filled the gymnasium of the University of Washington in Seattle. Ben Linder, one of the shortest men in line, filed out into the aisle with the engineering students.

Ben's girlfriend, Alison Quam, who was receiving her degree in theater arts, also sat among the graduates. She had a round face, and long, straight brown hair and stood almost a head taller than Ben. In the audience sat Ben's father, tall, big-shouldered Dr. David Linder, and his mother, Elisabeth, whom Ben resembled.

As the line of students moved toward the stage, Ben hesitated. Then, amidst a swirl of black robes, he disappeared out of the gymnasium door.

The engineers moved forward, closing up his space. One by one they walked up a side ramp and across the stage, where they received a diploma and shook hands with the dean.

The ceremony dragged on; then suddenly, from the back of the gym, came a glimpse of black, a whoosh of robes. Ben zipped down the side aisle, riding a unicycle, and resumed his place in line among the graduates. When his turn came to receive his diploma, he zoomed up the ramp onto the stage, arms out, eyes glinting, a wide smile across his freckled face. Friends whistled, cheered, and stomped their feet, and the huge gymnasium rocked with sound. "It was the high point of the ceremony," said Alison. "Not everyone knew him personally, but everybody had seen him riding [his unicycle] around campus." Ben wheeled across the stage, halted in front of the podium, and gently rocked back and forth as he accepted his diploma and shook the dean's hand. He wheeled about to face the crowd and bowed low on the unicycle. The crowd roared.

Two months later, Ben was packing to go to Nicaragua. Sitting in his parent's cheery yellow house in the hills above Portland, Oregon, he sorted his belongings into duffel bags and suitcases: engineering textbooks, notebooks, cotton shirts, jeans, Pepto-Bismol, and vitamins. He packed face paints, magic tricks, and a new, lightweight clown costume bought just for the tropics—a red and yellow striped shirt, red checkered pants, and a bulbous red nose. He packed his unicycle into an odd-shaped crate. His parents bought items for him at hardware shops and drugstores, checking them off from lists he compiled. A steady stream of visitors stopped by to say good-bye and good luck.

Ben had been promised an engineering job in Nicaragua, a Central American country that had only recently emerged from forty-five years of dictatorship. He planned to work there for a year, using his newly acquired engineering skills to help those less fortunate. Alison had just accepted a job in a theater in Indianapolis, Indiana, and promised to wait for him. She believed in Ben's convictions. Although she had never been interested in political causes, during the three years that she and Ben had been together, she always supported his interests.

In August 1983, as his parents drove him to the airport, they worried about him, yet at the same time had confidence in his decision. Ben was an intelligent, careful, levelheaded person. They were also excited for him, wondering what kind of world he was heading into. They promised to visit him in December.

Ben flew to Miami, then boarded the afternoon flight for Managua. As the plane winged south for two and a half hours over the bright blue Caribbean and the green-brown island of Cuba, Ben became increasingly plagued by doubts over his move to Nicaragua.

David and Elisabeth raised their three children, John, Miriam, and Ben, to work for peace and justice, to help others, to question society, and to think independently. During the 1960s, when the family lived in San Francisco while Dr. David Linder worked at Children's Hospital, they often attended protests against the Vietnam War. Elisabeth clutched Ben's little hand. He was spellbound by the spectacle of it all: the banners, the mass of people, the panorama of colors, and the street performers in their white face paint. In 1970 the Linders moved to Portland, Oregon, and became active in the town's small progressive community. They often offered their living room for political meetings and their spare bedroom to visiting activists. Ben learned to form his own political opinions from the family dinner table discussions. "I learned that politics was a perfectly acceptable topic of conversation, even a desirable one, and that questioning was a good thing—questioning anything and everything," he later said.

Ben read books on literature, philosophy, politics, and science fiction. He especially enjoyed the works of Franz Kafka, Jean-Paul Sartre, Mahatma Gandhi, Allen Ginsberg, and Shalom Aleichem. He chose to attend Adams High School, an innovative Portland school, from which he graduated a year early. Ben became a vegetarian because he didn't want animals killed for his benefit. And just before leaving for college in the summer of 1977, he participated in a thirty-eight-hour sit-in against nuclear power at the Trojan nuclear power plant outside Portland. David visited him at the sit-in, bringing sheets to ward off the heat during the day and coffee to fend off the chill at night.

Throughout his years at the University of Washington, and as early as high school, Ben had wanted to work in the Third World. He studied engineering not merely as a natural outgrowth of his mechanical abilities but also because he enjoyed building, creating, and designing, skills that could be useful in underdeveloped countries. While in college during the 1980s, he watched graduating classmates obtain high-paying jobs in defense work at Boeing, Bremerton Naval Shipyard, and the Hanford Atomic Works, none of which appealed to him. Ben said, "I didn't spend five years at the University of Washington, and eleven years in school before that, to go out and build equipment that, instead of working for the benefit of the human race, was working for the imminent destruction of the human race."

Ben wanted no part of any U.S. government-affiliated program with conservative Ronald Reagan in office. In his junior year, he instead became interested in Nicaragua and its new revolutionary government. The leftist Sandinista guerrillas, having overthrown dictator Anastasio Somoza in 1979, proclaimed that they were setting up a new society that benefited the poor. Ben was initially skeptical. "You read in the paper about repression in Nicaragua, you read this, you read that. From the groups on the left you hear how wonderful it is. In '82 I rolled up my sleeves and said, 'I've got to find out about this.'" That summer, he traveled to Costa Rica to study Spanish and twice visited neighboring Nicaragua. Ben didn't see repression. What he did witness was a government committed to helping its people in a "poor, hard country" that needed skilled professionals.

Nicaragua was to leftists throughout the world in the 1980s what Spain was to progressive Americans in the 1930s. Thousands of foreigners were offering their skills in support of the revolutionary Sandinista government in Nicaragua. During his summer visit to the nation's capital, Managua, Ben met a resident Canadian doctor who offered him a place to stay should Ben return. He also met a local engineer from the state-owned utility company who suggested that the electric company would surely welcome a young, committed engineer like him after he graduated.

On the evening of August 14, 1983, Ben's plane landed at the Augusto César Sandino Airport in Managua. A bright sign glowed in the quick-falling tropical dusk: BIENVENIDOS A LA TIERRA DE SANDINO, (Welcome to the Land of Sandino). Passengers descended a rollaway steel staircase onto the runway and into hot and muggy air. Dozens of young soldiers in camouflage uniforms, automatic rifles slung over their shoulders, observed passengers entering the terminal. Nicaragua was a country at war.

Ben passed through customs, where the Canadian doctor met him. They drove into the capital along the dimly lit Northern Highway.

Managua was a squalid city. Wooden shanties lined the main roadway, where buses, battered cars, army trucks, and horse carts vied for space. Pedestrians clogged the roadside, walking, hitchhiking, or waiting at bus stops. Overloaded buses roared by, with passengers clinging to doorways and sitting on roofs. Horses' hooves clattered on paving stones, vehicles honked, unmuffled army jeeps thundered by, fare collectors yelled from buses, and peddlers selling lottery tickets and soft drinks shouted above the din. The air smelled of rotting garbage, decaying fruit, and diesel fumes. Mongrel dogs roamed vacant lots, digging through trash.

The Canadian doctor took Ben to the place that he shared with several other foreigners. The previous upper-class owners had fled Nicaragua when the Sandinistas took power, and the new government confiscated the property. Once stately, the house had deteriorated from lack of maintenance. Outside, chickens ran loose on the scrubby crabgrass, and inside, gaps in the wooden ceiling panels revealed a corrugated tin roof. The bathrooms were stripped of mirrors, showerheads, and other fixtures, and the only furniture was made from packing crates. "It has that richness-gone-to-pot-after-a-revolution feeling," Ben wrote.

Once Ben arrived, though, he felt confused and alone. He wrote, "It is strange; for one and one-half years I've been living for these moments and now I really am here. I kept wondering if I really want to do this.... I feel better, then worse, then better, then worse."

Managua always came alive before dawn. Roosters crowed, *kikikiki*, their calls echoed by other roosters in the neighborhood. Ragged, barefoot boys darted through the streets, shouting the names of newspapers they were selling, *"¡Barricada! ¡Nuevo Diario!"* Solemn-faced girls followed behind, selling hot tortillas out of tubs balanced on their heads. Sturdy women with plump wrists and ankles pushed wooden-wheeled carts down the streets, calling out names of tropical fruits: "Mangos, *sandías, zapotes, mamones, nancites.*" Managua residents did household chores in the cool early mornings, before the relentless sun rose in the sky.

Ben was up before dawn, his confusion and depression of the previous night subsiding. By 8:00 A.M. he was first in line at the bank. Dollars could be traded on the black market at a substantial gain, but Ben would change all of his money and keep his dollars in local banks. As Nicaraguans lined up behind him, Ben must have realized for the first time what it was like to be of average height. At five feet four inches, Ben stood as tall as most Nicaraguan men and taller than most Nicaraguan women.

At the bank, Ben opened an account, a "symbolic act of permanence," and rented a box at the post office. Then he walked to the National Institute of Energy (Instituto Nacional de Energía [INE]), where he had been promised a job. There, Ben filled out an application in Spanish. As he looked around the empty room, he wondered why there were no political posters on the walls. Ben turned in his application, and the receptionist advised him to come back *mañana.*

Ben wandered around the capital. Although Managua had some 800,000 people, the city was a sprawling maze of pockmarked streets, vacant lots, and skeletons of multistoried concrete buildings. It had once been a compact city, complete with a few eight- and ten-story buildings, but on December 23, 1972, an earthquake that measured 6.3 on the Richter scale leveled it. More than 10,000 people were killed, and three-quarters of the city's residents lost their homes. International aid poured into the country, but Somoza pocketed most of the money instead of rebuilding the city. His plundering of international relief aid, and the brutality of his army, the National Guard, led to the increasing withdrawal of international support for his government, and to the growing strength and popularity of the Sandinista guerrillas.

In Managua, symbols of the four-year-old revolution were everywhere. Giant concrete letters on a hill dominating the city's southern skyline spelled out "FSLN," (Frente Sandinista de Liberación Nacional—the Sandinista National Liberation Front).

Buildings were splashed with huge, colorful murals of women picking coffee, doves carrying olive branches, Uncle Sam conquering Latin America, and the silhouette of Augusto César Sandino, the Sandinista hero and namesake, in his wide sombrero and knee-high boots. Billboards promoted vaccination campaigns, adult education, breast-feeding, and the Sandinista militia. Soldiers in green uniforms, both male and female, were everywhere.

The revolution had adorned but not rebuilt the capital. Ben wandered through the earthquake ruins of downtown Managua, gaping at the concrete ruins that served as shelter for poor families. Ragged clothes hung across once ornate entryways, and women cooked over campfires in tiled patios. Friendly, barefoot children approached foreigners, asking for pencils and notebooks for school, and one child showed Ben how to spin a *trompa*, a wooden top. In a letter to Alison, Ben described Managua. "People are very friendly but then push to get onto the bus. There are women cooking food over fires on street corners. The food is sometimes good, sometimes bad— and always deep-fried. It is served on a banana leaf. So what is Managua like? Strange, fun, overwhelming, scary, hot and very much alive." In the same letter he wrote, "It is a crazy city. The buses are packed, the drivers are crazy, and cows graze in empty lots in the center of the city. Trees are being planted, but there is so much to be done. That is the general feeling here, so much to be done."

On his second day, Ben checked on his job application and was told once again to return the following day. He was disappointed. He had expected to start work immediately but knew he had to be patient. In the Third World, paperwork did not move as fast as it did at home. "So why am I here?" he wrote. "Adventure is part of it. Proving myself is also part. Doing good is a very large part. The rest I guess will be known in time."

As the days passed, his patience gave way to exasperation and frustration, as he heard the same thing over and over. "Quizás mañana," (Maybe tomorrow). After checking on his application status, Ben often crossed the street to eat lunch in a rickety green-and-orange-striped diner, open to the air on two sides. He ordered the only food served, *gallopinto* (rice and beans fried together), grated cabbage topped with slices of green tomato sprinkled with lemon juice, and tortillas. Sometimes an unidentifiable meat dish was included. Ben had been a vegetarian for years, and he found himself faced with a dilemma: What to do with the meat? Toss it to the mangy dogs scrounging underneath the table? There were no napkins in which to hide the meat, and throwing food away in the midst of such poverty and hunger seemed arrogant. Ben finally solved the problem, as he explained in a letter to Alison: "I've started to eat some meat. It is hard to do but slowly I'm 'bearing through.'"

In 1983 Nicaragua seemed cut off from the rest of the world to many resident foreigners. English-language newspapers and magazines were not sold in the country, while news broadcasts in English—Voice of America, Armed Forces Radio, and the BBC—could only be picked up on shortwave radios. Ben used his unemployed time to improve his Spanish. He listened to the radio, chatted with strangers, and read articles in *Barricada*, the Sandinista newspaper. Much of the news reported attacks in the countryside by Contras, anti-Sandinista guerrillas supported by the Reagan administration. The more Ben read, the angrier he became, especially because he wasn't helping yet.

On July 19, 1979, when the Sandinistas overthrew Somoza and took over the country, most of Nicaragua—an area the size of New York State, with a population of 3 million people—was not accessible by road. The majority of people lived in the countryside, where only 5 percent of the children completed sixth grade. The average life expectancy was fifty-three years, and the main causes of death were preventable diseases like diarrhea and tuberculosis. Two-thirds of children under five years old suffered from malnutrition. Eighty percent of the country's houses did not have running water, and some 60 percent had no electricity. Most Nicaraguans lived in small shacks with dirt floors, even in the cities.

As Ben wandered around Managua, talking to Nicaraguans in his rapidly improving Spanish, he probably encountered the revolutionary fervor that swept the city, where everyone called each other *compañero*—"companion, comrade, friend." Government workers were paving streets, laying water pipes, and hooking up electric lines. Bus fare and milk were subsidized, and health care and education were free. The school population had doubled, and after a five-month national campaign, the country's literacy rate jumped from 55 percent to 88 percent. In the countryside, the government was carrying out agrarian reform, organizing agricultural cooperatives, granting lands to day laborers, building schools, and starting adult education programs.

Health volunteers went door to door, teaching nutrition and vaccinating against measles and polio. Nicaragua's infant mortality rate fell, making it the lowest in Central America, and in 1983 the World Health Organization (WHO) declared Nicaragua a model for health care in Latin America. This was a complete turn-around from four years earlier, when after four decades of dictatorship by the Somoza family, the country had one of the worst health care records in the hemisphere. Ben wrote to his friends:

> Somoza left the country in shambles. Flat broke. He took everything but the debt. Granted, there are still problems now, but there is a feeling of hope, there is a feeling of building a new country. At times this exuberance leads to false hopes. Many more times it leads to a say in life that has never before been experienced for the majority of Nicaraguans.
>
> It is hard for us to imagine the meaning of a paved street. In Nicaragua there are two seasons—wet and dry. When it is wet the mud is two feet deep. When it is dry the dust permeates everything. Eating becomes like a picnic at the beach, all the food crunches with dust. Slowly more and more streets are being paved.
>
> But that is only the physical benefits. The more important changes are the feelings of being in control. This is in control of walking out at night and not being afraid of being shot by the police, as was the case before 1979. It is establishing control of the neighborhood and the workplace. It is in education, health care and work. This is control. Granted there is still a long ways to go, but people are still fighting. Not fighting against the govern-ment, but rather fighting old habits, old customs and the results of centuries of oppression. Unfortunately, at the borders, the struggle goes on militar-ily. The old enemies keep fighting with more and more U.S. support. It is such a waste. I guess our government knows quite well how to drain an econ-omy through military spending.
>
> Pardon me for speech making, but it is impossible to get a feeling for Nicaragua without a feeling of political struggle.

In the early morning of September 8, Ben was jolted awake by an explosion. He sprang out of bed, fumbled in the dark for his glasses and watch, checked the time, and ran to the window. A second blast sounded, followed by the rat-tat-tat of gunfire coming from the direction of the airport. When the firing stopped, Ben relaxed, assuming that the army was testing its antiaircraft guns.

But later that day he found out that the explosions were a result of the Con-tras' first air attack on Managua. A twin-engine Cessna had dropped a bomb near a communications center, while a second Cessna dropped a 200-kilogram bomb on Managua's airport. The force of the blast knocked the Contra's low-flying plane out of control, and it crashed into the base of the control tower, bursting into flames and killing the pilot, copilot, and a baggage handler.

When Ben learned of the attack, he wrote, "All of this is very bad. In my book of strategy this was a test by the Contras of Managua's air defense." But rather than frighten Ben off, the attack increased Ben's desire "to give it my best shot."

No one seemed interested in Ben's help, however. The INE officials informed Ben that he didn't have the correct visa to work in Nicaragua, and that he needed to be sponsored by an international organization. INE officials suggested that he go to Costa Rica to seek sponsorship and return to Nicaragua with the correct visa. Ben was crushed. He didn't want to spend weeks waiting in Costa Rica for something that might not happen. For the first time since his arrival, he wondered if he might have to sacrifice working at the electric company.

Ben's housemates advised him to use personal connections. This was how things got done in Nicaragua. Encouraged by their stories, Ben vowed to take their advice. "I've just begun to fight," he wrote. He immediately started calling friends of friends, acquaintances, people he had met in the streets, on the buses, in the diners, asking them to intervene for him, to pressure INE to give him a job. They told Ben to keep pushing and be patient. Ben was beginning to realize that persistence could accomplish the seemingly impossible, and that "no" did not necessarily mean "no," but "maybe" or "yes."

Ben was increasingly lonely, though, and missed his girlfriend. He wrote to Alison every two or three days, and she wrote back regularly. He called every other week, although making the call required riding a crowded bus to TELCOR, the state-owned telephone company where the only long-distance public phones were located. He often had to wait an hour or more for his turn. Whenever he heard Alison's calm, soothing voice, words tumbled out of him. He tried to explain what life was like in Nicaragua. He hoped she'd understand and share his enthusiasm, but Ben didn't think he succeeded in conveying his excitement. How could he ever explain the revolution to her? Even the spot where he was standing—a cramped, sweltering phone booth—was so far from her reality, the dappled gold and rust of autumn in Indiana. Ben often felt depressed after speaking with her.

Ben and Alison had met on Halloween in 1978, during Ben's sophomore year in college. He was wearing white face paint, a bulbous red nose, and rainbow socks and was juggling pins with his dormitory roommate, Jim Pittman, outside a campus dance. Alison, a freshman, paused to watch. "This seemed so much more interesting to me than what was happening at the dance," said Alison. Ben caught her eye, smiled, and handed her the pins to give her a quick juggling lesson. "He was very, very friendly, and I instantly took a liking to him. He seemed like somebody you could trust," Alison recalled.

The two didn't see each other until a few months later when they took the same geology course, a class of 700 students. Alison spotted him riding to class on his unicycle and sat down next to him. When Ben took the following year off from school to work repairing office machines, Alison would go to visit him. Ben often invited her to dinner, introducing her to French, Polish, and Mexican food. They were both vegetarians, and Ben frequently prepared elaborate multicourse dinners for her. She in turn helped him develop his clown, "Benito the Fool." Drawn together by their shared love of theater, the two discussed costumes, acting, and the plays they'd seen. Their friendship gradually blossomed into a romance, and they became inseparable. When they graduated, Ben and Alison promised to spend only one year apart. When they said good-bye, they didn't realize how badly they would miss each other.

After two months of waiting to hear about a job, Ben fell into a depression and then became ill. Bouts of vomiting and diarrhea wracked his body, while the oppressive heat sapped his strength. Instead of rising at dawn like most Nicaraguans, he lay in bed until 9:30 A.M. The heat in the cement-block bedroom was stifling, and his sheets were drenched in sweat. Listless and alone, he wandered out to the patio, plopped down in the hammock, sipped a cool fruit drink, and lost himself in books: *The Brothers Karamazov, The Magic Journey, And Also Teach Them to Read,* and *Quixote on a Burro.*

Everything in Nicaragua seemed so overwhelmingly complicated—from riding a bus to speaking Spanish to trying to get a job. His mood fluctuated between elation at being in Nicaragua and despair of ever finding an engineering job. He wrote, "Sometimes I just feel great going with the flow. Other times I think I can actually control myself in it. But there is also that what-in-the-fuck-am-I-doing-in-this-godforsaken-hot-humid-dog-eat-dog-country. My moods swing with the least motion."

When he was depressed, Ben dreamed of being with Alison in the United States, in Portland or Seattle, where life was easier. On the other hand, he dreaded the thought of having to return home without having accomplished anything.

He wasn't sure if he had any choice anymore. He had thought that his job at INE was secured, but after waiting for two months, Ben wondered if perhaps his future as an engineer lay in the States, and not in Nicaragua. He decided that if he still didn't have a job by the time of his parents' Christmas visit, he would reluctantly return "stateside with the folks."

Chapter 2

Clowning in Nicaragua

After Ben's daily visits to INE, he would emerge into the sweltering day, wondering how to spend another afternoon. One day he spotted a patched circus tent pitched in a trash-strewn field near the Coca-Cola plant and the *Nuevo Diario* newspaper office. The tilted archway's faded red letters read CIRCO LIBERTAD (Liberty Circus).

Inside, Ben found acrobats, clowns, and jugglers practicing in a small sawdust-covered ring. Douglas Mejía, the stout head of the circus, noticed the slender, curious foreigner walk in. "We thought he was a tourist stopping by to watch the rehearsal," he said. Ben, however, was studying the performers intently. Juggling and unicycling had been part of his life since high school. His unicycle, a birthday gift from his parents, was his constant companion. He rode it across Seattle to visit friends, to city hall to leaflet against U.S. military aid to El Salvador, across campus to plaster political posters on red brick walls, and through the halls of the engineering buildings as other students gawked at him.

Borrowing the juggling balls, Ben tossed them into the air with aplomb as the jugglers watched in astonishment. As he juggled, Ben explained to a suspicious Douglas that he was an engineer from the United States who was also a clown and unicyclist. Douglas doubted the foreigner knew anything about the circus. Why, thought Douglas, would an American engineer be hanging out with circus performers, uneducated people regarded as lower-class, living in broken, dingy trailers? He decided to test Ben. He wheeled out the circus's most valuable possession, a fragile seven-foot-tall, homemade unicycle.

Ben examined the unicycle with the eye of an expert. In the summer of 1980, he'd owned a six-foot-tall, custom-built multiple-gear unicycle. He pedaled it for some

1,200 miles, from Canada down the Pacific coast toward the Mexican border. Along the way, he teamed up with other jugglers and unicyclists. When he arrived in San Francisco, his friend Nancy Levidow joined him in pedaling across the Golden Gate Bridge. By mid-September, Ben had reached Santa Barbara. When his school term began, he returned to Seattle. "It was such a Don Quixote kind of thing to do," said Seattle juggling friend Dave Finnigan, "because there's no reason to do it. It was a wonderful way for a kid to spend a summer and grow up a bit."

Under the patched Managua circus tent, when someone gave Ben a leg up, he confidently mounted the homebuilt unicycle. He soon found he wasn't able to get a tight grip on the unflared seat, nor was he able to balance on the flat tire. He tottered above the others for a few seconds, then pitched forward into the sawdust. Ben quickly remounted, but again tumbled off. Bored, the circus performers drifted away. One of the jugglers walked across the ring on his hands, while another dropped his pants and peed into the shavings.

Douglas's suspicions were confirmed. The American was not a circus performer.

Disappointed and embarrassed by his performance, Ben wanted to prove to the performers that he was one of them. That evening, he assembled his unicycle. "Well, if I can't stay as an engineer, maybe I'll join a circus," he wrote.

The next day, Ben headed for Circo Libertad on his unicycle, pumping hard along the paving stones of the Northern Highway, holding his hands outstretched to balance himself. Cars slowed to keep pace with him, and through the windows, children pumped their hands up and down, mimicking his pedaling. Ben threw them a wave, clanging the bell on his unicycle. Buses pulled up alongside him, and passengers broke into smiles, gasping and pointing at him.

Ben rode the unicycle underneath the tilted archway of Circo Libertad into the tent. Douglas, his three sons, and seventeen-year-old Carlos, who performed on the homebuilt unicycle, clustered around him, staring at the slick, shining unicycle. Ben circled the arena, juggled four balls atop the unicycle, and then turned sharply, flinging sawdust in the air. "We realized that here was a circus artist in disguise," said Douglas, who now doubted that the American was really an engineer.

Carlos stroked the unicycle, running his hands along its flared seat, and squeezing its sturdy tires, then jumped on top of it, riding it around the ring, smiling. "Off with the wheel to the circus," Ben wrote. "They went gaga."

From that day on, Ben headed for the circus, where he spent hot afternoons practicing with the jugglers, doing "ferocious club passing," making "quick killer throws," learning new hat tricks with a "hot hat juggler," and performing "3-3-10s" with the jugglers. Whenever Ben brought his unicycle, Carlos rode it around the ring for hours, then greased and polished it with a dirty rag. One day he offered to buy it. Ben couldn't bring himself to sell his unicycle, as he had "logged too many miles."

One morning Ben arrived at the circus to find the performers rehearsing a political skit about an upper-class couple against the revolution. The clowns developed characterizations of Contras, Sandinistas, bourgeoisie, and poor people. When Ben asked if there was a role for him, the performers tittered and asked him to play "Tío Sam"—Uncle Sam. He laughed. "I accused them of typecasting," Ben wrote. "We had two rehearsals in the morning and then broke for lunch. Little did I know that those were the only rehearsals I'd have."

After lunch, he squeezed between guitarists and a marimba band in the back of a truck and drove to a park in the working-class neighborhood of Máximo Jerez, where 400 people were waiting for them. "It was a great feeling to be in a pickup truck in a warm Managua night listening to two guitars playing revolutionary songs and just feeling part of the gang," he wrote. While Sandinista leaders spoke, children darted through the crowd, throwing firecrackers and lighting bottle rockets. Afterward Ben and the others performed. "Improvisation is hard, but not impossible, in Spanish," Ben wrote. "A lot of obvious gestures and a basic simple idea. We pulled it off. I didn't feel scared among all those faces."

Salvador Rodríguez, a member of the circus family, was especially pleased by Ben's performance because the crowd had been so impressed with his accent. "After the show, some people asked me how Tío Sam, the clown, twisted his tongue around to speak English," Salvador said. "They had no idea that Tío Sam really was a gringo— but one of our gringos—a good gringo."

A few days later, Douglas took Ben to a circus workshop where Cuban performers were teaching gymnastics, trapeze, acrobatics, mimicry, and juggling. "When Ben showed up, the Cubans were suspicious of him—an American who claimed he was an engineer, an American who hung around but didn't say much," said Douglas. Ben was confused by the Cubans' rapid-fire Spanish and puzzled by their reserved attitude toward him, a strong contrast with the blunt curiosity of

Nicaraguans. Douglas told the Cubans that Ben was a revolutionary, and by the end of the workshop, Ben's wide smile and openness had won them over. Ben wrote, "The teachers are these hot Cuban performers. Most of them studied in the Soviet circus school—one of the best in the world. Maybe this is what Reagan is talking about when he speaks of the USSR-Nicaraguan-Cuban triangle."

After the workshop, the Cubans invited Ben to visit them. He and Jim Levitt, a friend from Seattle, spent a hot, lazy afternoon on the hotel patio, drinking rum with the Cubans, discussing circuses, revolutions, and Cuba's energy policy. Ben was disturbed to find out that the Cuban government was building a nuclear plant and wondered if someday the Nicaraguan government would do the same, instead of developing alternative energy resources.

Even though Ben enjoyed clowning, he was worried that time was slipping away. He still did not have a job. "As of tomorrow I'll have been here 2 ½ months. That is a long time," he wrote. "I like it here and feel very good about just being here. But I'm not giving anything. That is so basic to my existence. It is also something I hope always to keep with me. If I left now I would be richer but I wouldn't have helped out. Maybe part of it is ego gratification but I truly believe that is only a part of it."

At that time, Americans in Nicaragua were not aware of how the Reagan administration was targeting the Sandinista government. Three years earlier, at the 1980 GOP convention, delegates had established the removal of the Sandinista government as a priority. In August 1981, the CIA assembled anti-Sandinista guerrillas, known as the Contras, which included members of Somoza's National Guard, in neighboring Honduras. On the night of March 15, 1982, saboteurs blew up two bridges near the Honduran border. This was considered the opening salvo in the Contra war. The Sandinista government reacted by imposing press censorship, proclaiming a national state of emergency, and restraining political freedoms.

President Reagan signed two CIA findings regarding Nicaragua. The first authorized covert action programs in Nicaragua and Central America, and the second authorized $19 million for weapons and other support for paramilitary groups to attack the Sandinistas. The consequences were immediately felt, for the Contras increased attacks across the country. Contra speedboats machine-gunned the Pacific coast harbor of Puerto Sandino and attacked oil storage facilities on the Atlantic coast, destroying 400,000 gallons of fuel, a month's supply for the entire coastal region. Unidentified planes attempted to bomb the oil storage facilities at the port city of Corinto.

On October 2, Contra forces blew up two transmission towers in the south, cutting electricity lines between Nicaragua and Costa Rica. The Contras destroyed customs posts along the southern and northern borders, and CIA agents blew up the oil pipeline at Puerto Sandino. The CIA requested more weapons for the Contras. Three thousand guns were rushed to the Contras in Honduras. To bolster morale, Sandinista leader Daniel Ortega addressed the nation, calling on Nicaraguans to work together to defeat the Contras. He announced new emergency measures, including rationing fuel and energy, expanding the army reserves and militia, tightening security on economic targets, and enacting new civil defense measures.

Everyone was alarmed by the escalating attacks. Many people feared that the war, which had been confined to the countryside, was now coming to the cities. Foreigners began contacting each other. Between 1,500 and 2,000 Americans, including those affiliated with churches, lived in Nicaragua. Of those, about 300 had permanent jobs in Nicaraguan government organizations. Americans, after the Cubans, were estimated to be the second largest foreign community in Nicaragua.

Americans who supported the Sandinistas began organizing themselves and formed the Committee of U.S. Citizens Living in Nicaragua (CUSCLIN). Every Monday at 6:45 P.M., some forty members of CUSCLIN, which Ben dubbed the "gringo club," met in the government's Human Rights Commission office. Lawyers, doctors, engineers, electricians, computer programmers, concert pianists, translators, tour guides, agronomists, nurses, professors, teachers, and ecologists discussed what they, as Americans, could do to stop the war. After attending his first meeting, Ben wrote, "stronger liberal than radical bent. Good contacts. I'll keep in touch with the group but I don't think I'll get 'involved.'"

At that meeting, Ben met his first American friend in Nicaragua. Dr. Anne Lifflander had just arrived after working in a South Bronx hospital for three years. She had come to practice medicine in a country where the government supported health care, and was looking for a job in a public hospital.

Anne and Ben discussed culture shock and adapting to life in a foreign country. Anne said she could not get used to the men, who made catcalls, hissing like snakes, when she passed them in the street. Ben revealed that it was a shock for him to live in a place where he could not easily communicate with people, and was ready to give up and return to the States. They were relieved to find out that they were both experiencing tremendous mood swings and missed the same things, like the Sunday edition of the *New York Times,* and bagels and cream cheese.

The two of them took day trips to Granada and the small islands in Lake Nicaragua, one of the country's few tourist attractions. They visited Masaya, where Ben had a black leather briefcase made for him. They ate in cheap diners, and Ben persuaded Anne to sample street food from street corner *fritangas,* where big-bosomed women piled greasy fried plantains, cheese, chicken, and unidentifiable pieces of meat on top of rice and beans, then served it on banana leaves. "He'd say to me, 'Which restaurant shall we go to tonight?'" said Anne, "but what he meant was 'Which street corner and which *fritanga?*'"

One evening, Anne invited Ben to her house. She lived with a Nicaraguan family in Máximo Jerez, the neighborhood where Circo Libertad was encamped. In the evenings, neighbors sat in wicker rocking chairs on their porch stoops and gossiped, watched children play under streetlights, listened to the television, and fanned themselves in the soft, humid air. As Ben and Anne walked by, children called out, "Hola Ana." The family that hosted Anne included a woman with several daughters. They recounted tales of fighting Somoza's armored vehicles with fire-bombs made from Coke bottles, rags, and diesel. They told stories of neighborhood kids who, before the revolution, had grown up hustling, selling cold water, shining shoes, carrying groceries for shoppers in the sprawling Mercado Oriental (Eastern Market). Those same kids were now in school, studying, and in Sandinista art and youth groups. The government had built a health clinic in nearby Barrio Riguero, where residents received free medical care.

When Ben returned to the upper-class house he shared with other foreigners, he decided he wanted to live with a Nicaraguan family in a neighborhood like Anne's, to better fit into Nicaraguan culture.

On October 12, U.S.-directed operatives sneaked into the port of Corinto, 110 miles northwest of Managua, and blew up five huge fuel storage tanks. Twenty-five thousand people were evacuated from Corinto while the fire raged for two days, destroying pipes and pump systems, consuming warehouses full of food and medicine, destroying tons of bananas ready for export, and damaging the port's container cranes. Mexican, Colombian, and Cuban firefighters flew in to battle the flames. More than 3.2 million gallons of gas and diesel fuel—a large percentage of the country's fuel reserves—burned, and losses were estimated at $380 million. Using the attack as an excuse, Exxon announced it would no longer allow Mexico, Nicaragua's sole oil supplier, to use its tankers.

As the country was cleaning up from the Corinto attack, former U.S. Secretary of State Henry Kissinger, leading a commission that included Lieutenant Colonel Oliver North, ended a Central American fact-finding tour with a one-day visit to Nicaragua on October 15. The Sandinista government called on Nicaraguans to protest the attack on Corinto, and some 50,000 people demonstrated, chanting and marching through the streets of Managua. Ben joined the demonstrators, taking a turn pushing the wheelchair of Juan Gonzales, a Sandinista soldier who had lost his legs fighting the Contras.

Several days later, the Sandinista-led artists' union staged a protest against the escalating Contra attacks. Dressed in his clown outfit—oversize red-and-yellow-striped shirt, short, baggy, red-checked pants, and straw hat with flowers—Ben joined other circus performers to march through the streets of Managua. Clowns on stilts, carrying a red-and-black Sandinista banner, led the march, while Ben pedaled his unicycle alongside them, clanging the bell and joining hands with dirty, barefoot shoeshine boys. He pedaled up and down the line of demonstrators, circling brass marching bands, pirouetting around dancers, and rocking back and forth beside the army band, whose members smiled and laughed. Ben lent his unicycle to another performer and walked with a group of puppeteers.

"The march was wonderful. Probably the best time I've had yet here in Nicaragua. How do I describe 500 screaming clowns, poets, painters, dancers, a couple of marching bands? Chaotic, anarchistic, fun, revolutionary. I rode from one group to another, jesting, dancing and fooling. Even with the military band. It was so much fun," wrote Ben.

Just days later, Contras swooped down on the isolated village of Pantasma, in the most deadly attack since the war began. The rebels cut off communications so the army did not know about the attack, and militia members—armed civilians—attempted to defend the village. Eight teachers barricaded themselves in the schoolhouse and shot back, but when the shooting ended thirteen hours later, only one teacher was still alive. The Contras overran the village and destroyed the school, the bank, the Agrarian Reform office, the coffee warehouse, the sawmill, and three food dispensaries. They killed forty-six villagers, including three village leaders, whom they lined up against a wall and executed. By the time the army troops arrived, the battle was long over. From the United States, Contra leader Adolfo Calero warned that there would be more Pantasmas soon.

In Managua, Ben continued to spend his afternoons at Circo Libertad, making himself useful by cutting fabric for a new tent or helping Douglas fix the battered public address system. After Ben rewired the system, eliminating squeaks that had plagued the system for years, Douglas began to believe that he really was an engineer.

Douglas invited Ben to eat with his family during lunchtime. Ben often pulled out surprises from his black briefcase. "He always had little gifts for the kids; you never knew what he would bring," Douglas said. Over meals, Douglas told Ben that his circus, formerly called Brooklyn Circus, used to perform throughout Central America before the revolution, but by 1983 war had closed the borders, preventing travel outside Nicaragua. He complained that the government was attempting to control circuses by pressuring the owners to join a government-controlled circus union. At the same time, he was pleased the government was organizing free schools and workshops, trying to make circus performers skilled professionals. Ben was amazed that, in the midst of the Contra attacks, the Sandinista government was promoting circuses. "There are 23 circuses, and a lot of government effort has been put into the circuses, and I just scratch my head," he said. "Here's a country at war, here's a country doing everything it can to rebuild itself, why do they care about circuses?"

In late October, Circo Libertad moved to a vacant lot in Barrio Riguero. When Douglas announced he was changing the acts, Ben asked him if his clown, "Benito the Fool," could perform with the circus. Douglas hesitated, but when his three sons urged him to let Ben perform, Douglas agreed, with some trepidation.

On opening night, the bright lights of the tilted arch beckoned people to the show. Women selling street food choked the tent entrance. They emptied bottles of Coca-Cola, orange, and *rojita,* red soda, into plastic bags, which people carried inside. The smell of grease drifted through the tent, and scratchy salsa music blared from loudspeakers. Anne Lifflander and Jim Levitt bought tickets for twenty cents and took seats next to the sawdust-covered ring.

The circus drew an eclectic crowd. Families with children, groups of young men, couples on dates, uniformed soldiers, and teenagers climbed unsteady wooden bleachers against the back of the ring. Urchins crawled in under the tent. Frail old retired circus performers wandered through the crowd, selling tickets to win ratty stuffed animals.

At Circo Libertad, Douglas and his three sons, known as the Mejía Family Jugglers, were the highlight of the show. Dressed in blue pants and ruffled purple shirts, they emerged under the arch of lights, juggling pins to a salsa beat. The four performers formed a square, tossing the pins high into the air, keeping time to the music. As the salsa beat sped up, the performers threw faster, until the pins became a blur, a single continuous line that whipped back and forth between the jugglers. Suddenly "Benito the Fool" rode his unicycle into the ring, a flash of yellow stripes and red checks, oversize tennis shoes flopping over the pedals.

The jugglers dared him to catch the pins and teased him by tossing them high over his head. Ben screwed up his face into a frown and said in a high voice, "¿Cómo dices?" (What are you saying?). He clanged the unicycle's bell, then charged after the pins, grabbing air as the pins soared above his head. The clown pedaled back and forth across the ring, head swinging side to side as his eyes followed the pins' trajectory from one juggler to another. He lunged after the pins, and the audience gasped, expecting him to tumble into the shavings, but at the last minute he always regained his balance. The jugglers had moved in, encircling Ben, when he reached up and grabbed a pin, then grabbed another. He juggled them, tossing the pins to Douglas and his sons, forming a five-pointed star. Douglas caught the pins, and the five jugglers took a bow and ran offstage.

The crowd stamped their feet, the rickety bleachers crazily swaying, and yelled for more, summoning the clown with the large red nose. They assumed Ben was a regular part of the show. Douglas gently pushed Ben into the ring, where he selected a boy from the first row and juggled the pins around his head. Ben wrote, "The kid smiled. God, what a relief. A big applause. Cloud nine. The lights were bright and I was home."

After the performance, the Mejía brothers slapped Ben on the back and congratulated him. Douglas recalled, "Ben hugged me and said, 'I've performed in the circus and I feel great. How did I do? Good? Bad? Did I make many mistakes?' He felt like the biggest man in history that night." Douglas's mother, the cashier, gave Ben fifty córdobas to buy a snack, and Ben waved the bill in the air, saying that it was the first salary he had earned in Nicaragua.

As Ben and the others disassembled the riggings, he realized that the three brothers were jealous of his bulbous red nose. Ben had bought it in a theatrical prop store in the United States, but no such stores existed in Nicaragua. Ben looked at the other clowns mournfully, pushed down the corners of his face, and cracked a rhyming joke in Spanish: "No hay divisas para narices" (There's no money to buy noses). The clowns laughed.

That evening, Ben wrote his parents about his first job in Nicaragua. "I go to school for five years, I go to some godforsaken country to save the world with my newly acquired skills and what happens? The only work I can do is clowning around. I guess there is some justice somewhere."

Chapter 3

Ben Finds a Place for Himself

On October 25, 1983, Nicaraguans awoke to the news that the U.S. Army had invaded the Caribbean island of Grenada. The invasion set off shock waves in Managua, as many people believed that Grenada was a practice run for a U.S. invasion of Nicaragua. "People don't talk about 'if' there is going to be an invasion," Ben wrote, "but rather what will happen when there is the invasion."

Overnight, Managua became militarized. Billboards sprung up: CADA CASA UNA TRINCHERA DE LA REVOLUCIÓN SANDINISTA (Every House, a Trench of the Sandinista Revolution). Throughout neighborhoods, at schools, child-care centers, and workplaces, residents dug bomb shelters, hacking at the earth with picks and shovels under the torrid sun, faces bright red, hands covered with blisters. Shoppers bought matches, candles, and kerosene as they prepared for blackouts when bombs fell on the capital. TV announcements and newspaper supplements explained how to build bomb shelters, dig trenches, and shoot rifles. The government announced plans to teach civil defense—including fire control and first aid—to high school students.

The army formed militias in most Managua neighborhoods. Circo Libertad hastily disassembled its tilted arch and folded up the tent. The sawdust-covered ring became a practice field for a militia. Potbellied men in shorts, women in curlers, and teenage girls with red fingernails crawled through the vacant lot, clutching old rifles, firing live rounds, faces blanching at the recoil. On the streets, immigration officials stopped foreigners, checking their residency papers. On the bus, in the market, in corner stores, rifles appeared in the hands of civilians. "For Ben and me it was a transformation," Anne Lifflander explained. "Americans are not used to guns, but we had the feeling of being protected. It was a feeling of being taken care of, of learning to get over our fear and suspicion of the armed aspect of Nicaragua."

The year before, the United States had begun carrying out a series of joint military maneuvers with the neighboring country, Honduras, where the Contras had their bases. In November, 2,000 U.S. troops joined the Honduran army in a seaborne assault exercise involving helicopter gun ships, tanks, and artillery in La Ceiba. Five thousand additional U.S. ground troops were dispatched to Honduras. In Managua, Sandinista National Directorate leader Victor Tirado warned that the United States was preparing 25,000 troops to invade Nicaragua. Ortega told journalists that the invasion could come at any moment. In New York, Nicaraguan foreign minister Miguel d'Escoto addressed the U.N. General Assembly, condemning the "Reagan Doctrine," whereby the United States was ready to intervene anywhere it felt its interests were threatened.

Americans in Managua were frightened and confused about what to do if the U.S. invaded. Anne explained, "To be armed or not armed? How should one participate as an American? Integrate yourself with Nicaraguans? March on the U.S. embassy? Go home and do solidarity work?"

Anne had found a job at Monolo Morales, a public hospital. She said that if there were an invasion she would stay to treat the wounded. Ben, however, was still unemployed and didn't know what to do. He told Anne it would be stupid to stay in Nicaragua during an invasion if he didn't have a clear purpose for being there. On the other hand, he didn't want to return to the United States: "INE goes on and on. The war situation gets realer and realer.... Part of my depression has to do with going home. How can I deal with the pettiness of solidarity organizations? They seem like so much BS after being here."

Ben didn't know what to tell his parents. They were planning to visit him at Christmas, and he had asked them what kind of tour they wanted: "Tourist, beach, political meetings, hanging out somewhere, or all of the above?" However, as the political situation worsened, he contacted them again, suggesting they might not want to travel to Nicaragua after all. "The worsening aggression doesn't help build our confidence. And it really is worsening. The country is going into a true preparatory phase. My doctor friend Anne tells me about her hospital. As of last week they are keeping half of the beds open for emergencies."

Walking home from Anne's house late one November night, Ben cut through La Radial, a neighborhood comprised of wooden shanties. He passed a group of people digging a bomb shelter by flashlight, turned back, and offered to help. The Nicaraguans asked him to come back the next day, not expecting him to return.

In the following days, Ben returned to dig alongside three generations of a family, including the stooped grandfather, his forty-two-year-old carpenter son, and his ten-year-old grandson. Evening after evening, they dug an L-shaped ditch, ten feet long, one yard wide, two yards deep, and covered it with layers of plastic, logs, and dirt. With every bucketful of dirt that he shoveled, Ben's commitment to stay in Nicaragua grew. "They are all there working on a project that should never be," he wrote. "My hands are blistered (like most in Managua) and I feel good. I ask people if they are afraid and they say no. When the war comes they will fight for what they know is theirs. I think I too will fight by their side.... The more I'm here the more I generalize to fight for the world."

When they finished the bomb shelter, the carpenter invited Ben to a Sandinista Defense Committee (Comité de Defensa Sandinista [CDS]) meeting. Established in 1979, the committee brought electricity to the neighborhood and laid the pipe for a communal spigot. That evening, men and women met in a cramped wooden shack, gathering near the windows, fanning themselves in the hot night. At the meeting, they put together a first aid kit and devised an evacuation plan for the children in case of invasion.

The carpenter headed the CDS, and he pointed to Ben as proof to the others that Nicaraguans were not fighting against the American people, but against the Reagan administration. After the meeting, Ben accompanied the carpenter on neighborhood patrols. As they walked through the dirt streets, Ben noticed a shrine to a Catholic saint and a monument dedicated to a young man from the barrio who died fighting the Somoza dictatorship. Between the two monuments was a newly built bomb shelter. "Guess it pays to cover all your bases," Ben wrote.

The gringo club held an emergency meeting to plan what to do in the event of a U.S. invasion. Some Americans decided to return to the United States to work with solidarity groups, while others decided to stay, although they worried that the Reagan administration might use their presence as an excuse to invade. The gringo club members did not want to be rescued like the Americans in Grenada, so they decided to publicize their support for the Sandinistas by holding weekly vigils in front of the U.S. embassy.

The U.S. embassy in Managua was considered one of the safest embassies in Central America, and despite U.S. support for the Contras, there was little animosity against embassy personnel; the ambassador, Anthony Quainton, walked the streets of Managua without bodyguards.

On the early morning of November 19, the gringo club and visiting Americans gathered in front of the embassy's iron gates. They unfurled colorful banners and held posters—WE WANT PEACE, DON'T RESCUE US and STOP THE U.S. WAR AGAINST NICARAGUA—while listening to American speakers as they criticized the Reagan administration's claim that the Contras weren't trying to overthrow the Sandinista government but only putting "pressure" on it to stop shipments of weapons to leftist groups.

On the day following the vigil, Ben was delighted to find several letters from Alison in his post office box. Americans in Nicaragua felt that it was a small miracle to get mail, as letters frequently disappeared between the United States and Managua. Often letters were sent to Nigeria instead of Nicaragua, or arrived opened without the letter inside. After reading Alison's letters about the snows of Indiana, the theater season, and how much she missed him, Ben wrote, "I almost started to cry. I love her and miss her terribly. Overlying that is this feeling that I'll stay here and fight. I just want to lie in her arms and watch her smile."

In his next phone call to Alison, he reported that everyone was bracing for a U.S. invasion, that he still didn't have a job, and that he was lonely and depressed. Alison suggested he return. Ben promised to consider it. "I talked with Alison at night," he wrote. "It was so wonderful to hear her voice. I love her so much. It is when I think of her, of us, that I question my staying here."

The next day, Ben sat down to write her a long letter. Before beginning, he mulled over his commitments to himself, to Alison, to his parents, to his country, to working in Nicaragua, and to his beliefs and ethical values. He weighed the pros and cons of leaving. Staying would be dangerous, even life threatening. But he also believed that, as an American, he had a responsibility to stay. His parents taught him to fight for justice, and he believed that the Reagan administration's policies toward Nicaragua were wrong. He made his decision carefully. He would fight for justice and stay, come what may.

Ben wrote Alison a long letter. On the outside of the envelope, he instructed

"Not to be opened unless there is an emergency." When the letter arrived in Alison's mailbox in Indianapolis, she honored his request and put it in a safe place.

On Thanksgiving, Ben's hundredth day in Nicaragua, INE told him that his employment application had been approved, his immigration papers were in order, and he had been given a job working on the piping layout of a large geothermal plant. "It's incredible what connections mixed with persistence can accomplish," Ben wrote. "A contract! My very own contract. Sight for sore eyes. I walked around smiling my Cheshire cat-pleased-as-punch-grin."

That evening, he called his parents in Oregon to report the good news. The next day, he moved his college engineering textbooks into a small office in the main building of INE and tacked up postcards of Sandino, Che Guevara, and a poem written by a friend and fellow engineer, Barbara Atkinson.

INE's main office, a large, sprawling building built around a central courtyard, was located on a busy main street, the Pista de la Resistencia. Several hundred people worked there, and Ben shared an office with six others, including two engineering students, Alvaro and Mauricio, and a Soviet engineer, Larisa.

INE had drawn up a twenty-year plan for electrical development with the goal of decreasing the country's dependence on imported oil. According to the plan, the most important project was the $35 million "Momotombo" geothermal plant. It would decrease oil imports by 1,500 barrels per day, saving about $8 million annually. With help from Italy and Mexico, the plant was being built on a volcano north of Managua, but it had suffered a number of setbacks. Ben heard that three engineers had already left the project that year, "one to the States, one to Costa Rica, and the third to a private company. A combination of INE not paying enough and conservative politics," he surmised.

Ben was assigned to design a program for a three-dimensional flexibility analysis of Momotombo's piping system. "From what I'm learning, the job is excellent. I was thrown into finishing the piping and layout for a 1.2-megawatt geothermal plant. This is much like playing with a $700,000 Tinker Toy set that only has 5 hubs and 10 sticks," he wrote. "This will put me in contact with a lot of work that I really know nothing about. But I'm learning. It feels good to spend days thinking."

Every morning Ben rode his unicycle to work, stashed it in a corner of the office, and was at his desk by 8:00 A.M. with piping diagrams and his calculator in front of him. He was friendly and gregarious, chatting to everyone from the director of INE to the cleaning ladies, and taught coworkers how to ride his unicycle at lunch.

Ben became friendly with the other engineers in his office, including Larisa, who had just arrived in Nicaragua from Russia. She had married a Colombian man, whom she met while studying at a Russian university. After graduating, they moved to Nicaragua to support the revolution. Ben understood her deliberate Spanish, as they talked of their distant homes and the foods they missed. "Larisa and I dreamed of apples from our father's gardens. Strawberries and snow. Its funny that two people from opposite worlds end up in Nicaragua and think the same memories," he wrote.

During Ben's second week of work, the electric company closed early to allow employees to celebrate the Catholic holy day commemorating the Immaculate Conception of Mary. Ben was surprised at how Catholicism, the religion of 90 percent of Nicaraguans, determined the holidays. "No church-state separation law," he wrote.

That evening, Ben strolled along Avenida Bolívar, Managua's main street, where government employees handed out wooden toys, pieces of sugar cane, oranges, and ginger candies in front of newly erected twenty-foot shrines to the Virgin Mary. Among the crowd, young boys lit firecrackers, then darted away laughing as the explosions spooked the crowds. Ben drifted among the people, bewildered by the cultural customs and religious practices. Although he was not religious, Ben had been raised in a culturally Jewish household. Surrounded by the statues of the Virgin, incense, votive candles, and fervent religious songs, he felt different, and more Jewish. "Amazing shrines. Long lines of families waiting for the goodies. I walked around feeling cold and isolated," he reflected. When a boy recognized him as the clown who rode his unicycle at the head of the artists' march, Ben felt better.

Later that night, soldiers and militia volunteers shot off tracer bullets, orange ribbons of color whizzing across the black sky. At midnight, the songs, fireworks, and rockets reached a crescendo as the sky exploded with a dazzling burst of reds, oranges, and whites. When Ben returned to work, he was upset to find a stray bullet embedded in his desk.

Ben frequently wandered around Managua in the evenings, checking out the various family-owned circuses. "The circus is a very warm community for me. I can go and sit and feel part of something," he wrote. However, when he went to the circus, he often thought of Alison. "Evening at Circo Infantil Americano. Very friendly people. It is their warm conversation that makes me feel good. It is what my life is about. If only I could reconcile that with my love for Alison. Well, I guess I can't have everything but damned if I'm not going to try."

One weekend, Ben rode his unicycle to Circo Libertad, which had set up their patched and faded tent on another vacant lot in Managua. Douglas mentioned to Ben that it was Carlos's eighteenth birthday. Ben remembered his own eighteenth birthday, when his parents gave him the unicycle. After thinking it over, Ben hopped off his "wheel," unhooked its bell, pushed it across the sawdust ring, and presented it to Carlos. "Feliz Cumpleaños" (Happy Birthday), wished Ben. Carlos stroked the gleaming chrome, then hopped on the unicycle, forming pirouettes in the ring. Ben explained to his friends in the United States, "All I have left of my unicycle is my bell. You didn't think I could give that away? I guess it was just time to move on."

In mid-December, David and Elisabeth flew to Managua as promised. Ben waited for them in the airport, but the Aeronica flight from Mexico was late, and airline officials were unable to say when the plane would arrive. His parents finally arrived nineteen hours late, exhausted and bewildered, dragging luggage full of hard-to-find items like tea, toothpaste, and deodorant, and a box of donated medicines.

As Ben bundled them into a taxi, Elisabeth remembered her own arrival, as a child, in Mexico. She had been raised in a sophisticated and intellectual Jewish family in Prague, Czechoslovakia. In 1938, on the eve of World War II, she and her brother were sent to England. Two years later the family reunited in Mexico City, where they settled, and Elisabeth learned to speak Spanish.

Ben expected his parents, especially his mother, to adapt quickly to Nicaragua. He allowed them little time to get used to the shortages and to adjust to being in a country at war. Checking into the Hotel d'Lido, David and Elisabeth remarked on the bomb shelter adjacent to the swimming pool. Ben brushed aside their concerns, saying Nicaraguans had to be ready for the worst.

He took them on a tour of Managua that included stops at Barrio La Radial, a CDS meeting, Anne's hospital, and his office. One evening, they went to Circo Libertad. They sat in the front row, and after the performance, one of the jugglers asked Ben to critique his act. Elisabeth was surprised. "I thought, who is this professional juggler who is asking my little kid to critique his work?"

The Linders had not traveled to a Third World country before and were subsequently unprepared for the destitution they witnessed. "I was numbed by the poverty," said David. "People looked bedraggled and poor. I was surprised by how little visible evidence there was of the revolution."

After a few days, David developed heart arrhythmia. In Matagalpa, two Cuban doctors examined him and sent him by ambulance to Managua, where he was shuffled from hospital to hospital as the ambulance attendants searched for a functioning EKG machine. They finally arrived at 4:00 A.M. at Manolo Morales, the public hospital. Anne was not on duty at the time. "It was gruesome," remembers Elisabeth. She was shocked to see two patients in a bed, covered by a single grubby sheet, and dirty bathrooms without toilet paper, towels, or soap.

"I was petrified, I'd never been so afraid in my whole life," said Elisabeth. "It was Christmas Eve, and I didn't know if I would find Ben. I didn't know where he lived, what his address was. There was no phone. The only way I could get hold of him was at work, and I didn't know if he was going to come in on Christmas Eve."

Ben showed up at work in the afternoon, with a hangover from Larisa's party the night before. After receiving his mother's phone call, he took a taxi to the hospital, where he too became alarmed. "Spooky emergency room," he described it. "The stretcher was of the morgue variety." After examining David, the doctors determined that his condition was not serious, but urged him to return to the United States as soon as possible. All flights were booked until after the holidays, however, so Ben spent the holiday with his parents at the hotel, where they gave him a new unicycle as a Christmas present. Overjoyed, Ben wheeled it onto the patio, making zigzags between the swimming pool and the bomb shelter. He wrote, "I'm glad the folks are here. It is good to touch family at the holidays. It is so important that they feel why I'm here."

When David and Elisabeth packed to go home, Ben wrote letters to send with them. "In the States we talk about the feeling of helplessness about war," he wrote in a "Dear Gang" letter, which Elisabeth photocopied and sent to his friends. "Here there is a feeling of continuing on with the struggle. This is a very deep true feeling; everyone from the big woman digging a bomb shelter for her kids, to the students going off for a month or two volunteering to pick coffee, to the 74-year-old man who takes his turn on the revolutionary vigilance block watch, to the mother who goes off with the militia to fight in the mountains. And here I am in the midst of all this. And I feel good. It is relaxing to be in a country where you are fighting on the side of the power structure and not against it."

The Linders left on the first available flight, just after Christmas. "I think Ben was relieved when we left," said Elisabeth. "He hadn't been there long enough to work through the system."

Shortly after his parents left, Ben's older brother John visited him for two weeks, attending an INE weekend workshop with him. Ben felt he couldn't leave work, so he sent John off to pick coffee with friends for a few days. After his parents and brother left, he felt more alone than ever. At the end of his workday, his head buzzing with new ideas, exciting conversations, and insights into the revolution, Ben arrived home ready to talk, but his foreign housemates were often not home. He wanted to integrate himself more into Nicaraguan society, to discuss politics and the revolution with Nicaraguans, but he wasn't sure how to do that.

Then, Ben visited Diana Brooks, a puppeteer he had met at the artists' march. She invited him to her house in Barrio Riguero for the evening. Diana led Ben up a dirt side street and stopped at a faded mint-green and bubble-gum pink house surrounded by a cement wall. Orange and cashew trees hung over the tin-roofed building. A small dog greeted Diana, and a green parrot preened itself on the porch. Wicker rocking chairs and wooden tables crowded the living room, while floor-length cotton sheets hung in the doorways, separating the living room from the other two rooms.

Diana introduced Ben to her mother Ana, who took an immediate liking to Ben. She invited him to sit in a rocking chair on the patio, and served him a sweet purple drink made from the *pitaya* fruits in her backyard. She told him that her husband, Rodolfo, was in a volunteer militia brigade fighting the Contras. Her two daughters and a nephew were picking coffee with student brigades. The Brooks were a Creole family from the Caribbean port of Bluefields who had moved to Managua seventeen years earlier. The family accepted foreigners into their homes. Franklin, Ana's twenty-three-year-old son, was married to a German woman, and they lived a block away with their two children.

As Ana talked, her parrot frequently screeched "¡Viva Sandino!" and "¡Viva el FSLN!" Ana explained that during the insurrection against the dictator, Barrio Riguero was a Sandinista stronghold, a liberated territory during the nights, a battle zone during the days. The *muchachos*—the nickname for Sandinista guerrillas— often posted youngsters, including the Brooks children, as lookouts. With their mouths covered by red-and-black kerchiefs, young men and women hastily erected wooden barricades. Other residents dashed out of the barrio into the main street, stopped cars, covered the road with broken bottles, and passed out pro-Sandinista leaflets. Drivers who attempted to pass the barricades were forced out of their vehicles at gunpoint, their cars doused with gasoline and set afire. When children spied the National Guard's armored cars moving toward the barrio, they yelled, "¡La Guardia!" Sandinistas fired bullets and tossed Molotov cocktails at the soldiers before disappearing into the maze of connected yards, alleyways, and dirt trails of Riguero. Soldiers smashed the barricades and ordered residents to clean them up.

The *muchachos* hid in houses, flattening themselves on dirt floors, while Somoza's soldiers combed the area, opening fire at shuttered houses, leaving arcs of bullet holes along cement walls.

In the evenings, when the soldiers retreated and the curfew took effect, residents of Barrio Riguero poured out of their houses. The Somoza government had cut off electricity to the neighborhood. By the light of flashlights, candles, and kerosene lamps, families pried up *adoquines*, octagonal paving stones manufactured by a Somoza-owned factory, and built sturdier barricades to seal the barrio's entrances once again. Neighbors knocked holes in wooden fences between yards to provide new escape routes. Hidden pistols emerged from houses as students, gas station attendants, mechanics, bus drivers, and secretaries transformed themselves into *los muchachos*. The Brooks children collected batteries, cigarettes, bread, and milk, and delivered them to the *muchachos*, who crouched behind the barricades, clutching old pistols, .22 rifles, shotguns, military carbines, and M-1 rifles, each with only a few bullets. During the night, the Brooks children helped make Molotov cocktails by stuffing sand, gasoline, and rags into Coca-Cola bottles. Their green-and-pink home became a refuge for *muchachos*.

Often, National Guard patrols dumped the bodies of young men in front of the barricades before dawn, and the Brooks family would awaken to the smell of decomposing corpses. The half-naked bodies, with torture marks on legs and backs and red-and-black kerchiefs around the necks, were a warning to the *muchachos*. Unbeknownst to Ana, her oldest son, Franklin, secretly typed FSLN leaflets and fliers on his high school's typewriter. If he had been discovered by the National Guard, Franklin could have lost his life, or endangered the entire family.

In June 1979 the Sandinistas launched their final offensive, and Barrio Riguero descended into chaos. Snipers shot from corners. Burning tires smoldered unattended in the streets, the thick, black, acrid smoke a warning for all to stay away. During periods of calm, residents scurried to scrounge food and haul water. As the offensive lengthened and June turned into July, Somoza lost control over many areas in the capital, and National Guard pilots dropped 500-pound bombs on Managua's eastern neighborhoods, reducing entire blocks to rubble. When they ran out of bombs, pilots dropped drums of gasoline that exploded into flames when they hit the tin roofs. The wind off the lake blew the sickly sweet smell of death over Barrio Riguero.

On July 17, hemmed in by the approaching guerrillas, Somoza dug up the bodies of his father and brother and fled to Miami. Two days later the Sandinistas rode triumphantly into Managua.

The following spring, the oldest children left for the mountains to teach reading and writing in the Sandinistas' literacy crusade. Franklin was sent to the eastern jungles beyond the mining town of Siuna. Ana also taught literacy at home in the barrio.

Ana reminded Ben of his own mother: open, approachable, interested, dynamic, a ball of energy. With seven adults sharing three rooms, the Brookses' house had to be noisy and crowded. That night, when Ben returned to his house, he wrote, "Their house is an amazing jumble of revolutionaries. It felt good to be there, but I'm glad to have my house to come home to." When Ben visited the Brookses' home a second time, Ana greeted him warmly, treating him like one of the family. Diana knew that Ben was lonely and suggested to her mother that Ben live with them for a while. Four family members were away, and to her, the house seemed empty.

Ana hesitated. She liked Ben, but she worried about allowing him to move into the house without her husband's permission. On the other hand, Ana reasoned, Ben seemed well mannered and trustworthy, and if there was a problem, he could always move out. When Diana told Ben of her mother's decision, he forgot his reservations about the hectic life at the Brookses' and jumped at the chance. "It should be interesting," he wrote. "I'm submerging myself into political Nicaragua, hook, line and sinker."

Chapter 4

Life with the Brooks Family

Ben moved his red suitcase, daypack, briefcase, unicycle, and juggling pins into the Brookses' three-room house. His new housemates included Ana, her two daughters, a dog, a cat, the parrot, a squirrel, and "a strange rodent-type animal that I'm told will later on serve as dinner meat," wrote Ben. The cement-block house had a tile floor and thin plywood room partitions that stopped a foot short of the ceiling. After Ben unpacked in his tiny room, he hardly had space to move. "My New House," he wrote. "My room is right next to the kitchen, separated by a half wall, curtains and a curtain door. Needless to say, privacy isn't a maximum. To make matters more interesting, the one table is also the ironing board. But then I realized that everyone else is sleeping in the same room. I'm glad it isn't permanent and I'm glad I'm here."

Ben felt immediately comfortable at the Brookses' house. Ana often initiated lively political discussions around the dinner table, which reminded Ben of mealtimes at his parents' home in Portland. At home, his outspoken siblings dominated the conversations, but here, Ben was the center of attention.

However, he found it difficult to live with a poor family that struggled to put food on the table. The main meal was usually rice and beans. There were never leftovers, and the household frequently ran out of milk, sugar, and coffee. Running water was intermittent, so Ben hauled water from a barrel in the yard and bathed himself out of a bucket. Toilet paper was a luxury, and he soon learned the purpose of newspaper strips hanging in the outhouse.

Ben worked hard to fit in. He copied Ana's body language, waving his index finger in the air to signal "no," rubbing his thumb and fingers together to indicate money, pointing with his lips. He learned to give directions Nicaraguan style, where addresses are based on the movement of the sun; east was up, *arriba*, and west was down, *abajo*. He copied Ana's Spanish, dropping the *s* at the ends of words and peppering his conversations with *chocho, vaya pues,* and *hijo de la gran puchiga,* local versions of "wow," "OK," and "son of a gun."

"I had just learned the expression '*Sí hombre*' [Yeah, man], and I was going around saying it," said George Moore, a New York artist who lived in Managua. "And Ben said to me, 'No, George, you've got to say, '*Sí, hom*.' He was proud of his command of the language. He sounded like a guy from a working-class barrio." As his Spanish improved, Ben grew more ebullient and gregarious, and his coworkers exploded with laughter when slang flowed from his mouth. "He didn't just want to speak Spanish," said his colleague, American engineer John Kellogg. "He wanted to speak Nicaraguan."

Ben frequently used body language to express emotions, often greeting friends with a silent, exaggerated bow or a grand sweep of a nonexistent hat. He put his middle finger and thumb together to signify "yes;" for "no," he looked away, or gave a stonewall expression. When he disagreed with someone, he looked past the person, pursed his lips, nodded, rocked back and forth slightly, then quietly presented a well-stated argument.

The Brooks household awoke at 6:00 A.M. "He had lots of energy—he couldn't sit still," said Ana. He shared the family's breakfast: coffee, bread, and, when available, eggs and milk. "Ben ate everything," said Ana. "We teased him about where he put it because he was so skinny!" By 7:30 A.M., Ben was out the door, pedaling to and from work on his unicycle.

Ben often rode by a small corner park a few blocks from the Brookses' house that was dedicated to Bill Stewart, an American television correspondent killed by Somoza's National Guard. In the hot afternoons, the park was full of boys spinning tops or playing baseball with a plank for a bat. Young mothers with infants on their laps sat on benches in the shade of yellow-flowering acacia trees. Along the edge of the park, *nancite,* mango, and *zapote* trees bore fruit. A grizzled old man in a faded plaid cap swept the leaves, while teenage couples, escaping hot, cramped row houses, cradled each other on the ledge of a cement monument. On the monument lay a plaque that read: "In memory of Bill Stewart. He did not die in a strange land, and we will cherish his memory because he is part of Free Nicaragua."

Ana fussed over Ben, reheating rice and beans for his dinner, asking him about work, about his ride home. One day, Ana recalled, he returned home trembling and pale, as a bus had nearly sideswiped his unicycle. "He told me, 'I almost got squashed like a cockroach.'"

On weekends Ben helped Ana with the chores that her husband used to do: take out the trash, replace washers, and tighten leaky pipes. He repaired her iron and, much to her dismay, insisted on ironing his own clothes. He climbed into the highest branches of the guava tree to pick ripe fruit, and Ana would make him a guava drink while he read in the hammock slung between the guava and cashew trees in the front yard. When Ana left at 4:00 A.M. to visit her two daughters picking coffee in the mountains, Ben got up with her to send along his own care package: vitamins, iron pills, and antidiarrhea tablets.

Ana missed *el viejo*, "the old man," as she called her forty-four-year-old husband. She hoped Rodolfo's militia unit would return from the mountains soon, but she also worried that he might kick Ben out of the house.

Ana was constantly in motion. Because of water rationing, she usually rose before dawn to fill the barrel in the backyard with water before it was turned off. She cooked the day's rice and beans, took the bus to the market, cleaned the house, and washed laundry by hand in the cement basin in the backyard. In the evenings, she often attended CDS meetings. When she took Ben to a meeting, she introduced him as *el payaso*, "the clown," and Ben volunteered to perform at community events.

Ben was soon asked to participate in a neighborhood vaccination campaign sponsored by the CDS. The next afternoon Ben met at the neighborhood's Popular Culture Center. It was the first of many such performances. "Every several weeks I end up clowning for some neighborhood function," Ben wrote. He usually began his act by applying greasepaint in front of the children, then he and the other performers jumped into the back of a pickup truck. The truck circled the dusty streets, broadcasting through a loudspeaker, urging parents to bring children to the clinic to get vaccinated against tetanus, typhoid, and measles.

Sometimes Ben hopped onto his unicycle and pedaled behind the truck, tooting a high-pitched whistle. Ragged children, accustomed to homemade toys like slingshots, tire rims, and spinning tops, had never seen anything so delightful, so entertaining, and so magical as the clown. Children emerged from doorways to chase him, giggling wildly, reaching out to touch the unicycle, to touch him, to yank his striped shirt. Dina Redman, an American friend from San Francisco, remembers seeing him one time in Barrio Riguero: "Hundreds of kids were chasing him; he looked like a dog with flies chasing him. He had this terrified look on his face because kids were so excited they were trying to pull him off his unicycle. I've never seen someone riding a unicycle so fast; his eyes were bugged out in terror."

In Seattle, Benito the Fool had worn a dark heavy overcoat against the rain and had often played the straight man. In Managua, *Benito el Payaso* wore dazzling colors and entertained people so that they could forget their problems, if even for a few minutes. In a country ravaged by scarcity, Ben's jokes became as sparse and simple as Nicaraguan's daily struggle to survive. His clown was caring, gentle, and unthreatening. He never made anyone the butt of his jokes. He played word games with children, asking them to guess names and numbers, and always encouraged them with a zany smile, even when they answered incorrectly.

Neighborhood performances were often sporadic and unplanned. "Driving around lost," Ben jotted. "Find the place. We drove through the barrio with the PA system on the jeep. I got on the hood and waved to the people. Back to the CDS. They left me for 45 minutes with a pile of kids. It is hard to keep them occupied. But it is one hell of a lot easier than in the States. There is a wonderful lack of inhibitions."

After performances, Ben returned to the Brookses' house, dehydrated, exhausted, and too tired to talk. Ana plied him with fruit drinks, and in the evenings they dragged wicker rocking chairs onto the porch, hoping for breezes in the warm, sultry darkness as they watched neighbors stroll by, bathed in the glow of streetlights.

Even though he was physically exhausted, Ben loved clowning. "It does wonders for my sanity after sitting at a desk all week," he wrote.

In January, Ben's unicyclist friend Nancy Levidow visited from San Francisco for two weeks. She arrived in Managua with suitcases filled with donated juggling clubs, clown noses, makeup, duct tape, juggling rings, and balls. Ben had asked her to collect as many circus props as possible, since "they don't even have tennis balls to practice with." When her tour bus pulled into the parking lot of the Hotel Ticomo, Ben was waiting for her. "He was so gracious and so welcoming—it felt like coming to the home of a loving friend. He was glowing about Nicaragua," said Nancy. They spent five hours talking politics.

Ben told her about the Cuban circus artists' workshop, about the circus school the Sandinistas had started, and about plans for an international exchange where foreign performers would teach in Nicaragua. He said that the Sandinista government was making mistakes, but was learning from their errors. "This was when everything was flowering. Ben was so enthusiastic about the revolution," Nancy said.

Before Nancy could even unpack, Ben said he had scheduled performances for two birthday parties, a refugee center, and a children's camp. Nancy was timid about performing in a foreign land, but Ben's excitement was infectious.

A few days later, after a torrential downpour, they performed at a center for Salvadoran refugee children. In a back room, Ben put on his striped shirt and checked pants, painted his face, strapped on his red nose, and emerged into the muddy yard, pedaling his unicycle, one hand balancing a cake in the air. "It was a huge cake, with disgusting green icing, the kind you buy in market stalls," said Nancy. However, to the refugee children, the cake looked delicious, and they stood riveted, fascinated by the red nose and the green cake. Ben pedaled the unicycle over the uneven ground, stumbling over roots and stones, diving and weaving, the unicycle wheel spinning loosely in the mud. He slid to a stop, leaned forward, then backward, then slid into a turn, while the children kept their eyes fixed on the cake, following his hand up and down. Ben charged the wall, slid, made a U-turn, and careened toward the children, who scattered and ran away screaming. "Most of the children had never seen a unicycle," said Nancy. "It was a sorrowful thing to see the kids get so excited. They responded so strongly to this little amount of stimulation; a clown seemed so extraordinary there." Ben cycled to a table and smoothly lowered the green cake. Celia Contreras, an Ecuadorian who organized the event, cut the cake and, using banana leaves as plates, served the children tiny pieces. As the children stuffed green frosting into their mouths, they kept their eyes on Ben's red nose.

Just before Nancy returned to the States, Ben and she presented their donations to the Nicaraguan National Circus. The Nicaraguan clowns were overjoyed to receive a batch of bulbous red noses.

During the beginning of 1984, the Contras escalated attacks. Gunmen on "piranha" speedboats launched from a mothership stationed in international waters sped into the Pacific coast towns of Potosí, Montelimar, Puerto Sandino, and San Juan del Sur, raking the piers with machine-gun fire.

Mines soon began exploding in Nicaraguan harbors. The Contras quickly claimed credit for this, while in Washington, the Reagan administration denied involvement. By the end of March, mines in the harbors had killed two Nicaraguans, injured fifteen sailors, including five on a Soviet oil tanker, and damaged or destroyed nine vessels, including a Dutch dredger and ships from Panama, Liberia, and Japan as well as several Nicaraguan fishing boats. The Sandinista army and local fishermen tried to clear the mines by dragging a deep-sea net between two fishing boats.

On April 6, the *Wall Street Journal* revealed that the CIA had mined the harbors. Reagan administration officials immediately attempted to defend the mining. As one U.S. official said, "If the country whose ports are being mined is considered responsible for some kind of aggression, in this case support for guerrillas in El Salvador, then mining is considered an act of self-defense just like any other use of force." Jeane Kirkpatrick, U.S. ambassador to the United Nations, responded to charges that the United States violated international law: "We cannot permit . . . ourselves to feel bound to unilateral compliance with obligations which do in fact exist under the [U.N.] Charter, but are renounced by others. This is not what the rule of law is all about." President Reagan said, "Those were homemade mines that couldn't sink a ship. I think that there was much ado about nothing."

However, the *New York Times* called the mining "illegal, deceptive, and dumb," and compared it to German U-boats torpedoing neutral shipping in 1917. Arizona senator Barry Goldwater, chairman of the Senate Intelligence Committee, called the mining a violation of international law. "It is an act of war," he wrote to William Casey, director of the CIA. "For the life of me I don't see how we're going to explain it." The House and the Senate voted to censure the Reagan administration for mining the harbors without notifying the congressional intelligence committees of their actions.

World leaders condemned the mining, including U.S. allies France and Canada, who rebuked the United States. The United Nations Security Council debated the mining for four days. The Nicaraguan government brought suit at the U.N. International Court of Justice against the United States for "using military force and intervening in the internal affairs of Nicaragua in violation of her sovereignty, territorial integrity, and political independence." On the eve of Nicaragua's application, the United States declared that for the next two years, it would not recognize the court's jurisdiction regarding events in Central America.

Americans in Managua fired off angry letters to congressmen and asked friends, solidarity organizations, and church groups to protest the mining. At work, Ben found a way to express his allegiances: he joined the company militia, which had been organized to defend INE if the United States invaded Nicaragua or the Contras attacked Managua.

Luis Mendoza, one of the INE militia leaders, noticed Ben one Saturday morning when he showed up to militia practice in the parking lot wearing hiking boots. The INE militia was comprised of technicians, security guards, gas station attendants, and a few engineers, and Luis led them through a series of jumping jacks, knee bends, and push-ups. After Ben showed up to a few practices, Luis gave him a uniform of olive-green pants and a shirt and advised him to wear tennis shoes. Surprised that militia practices were like gym classes, Ben asked Luis if they would ever practice with guns. Luis said the guns were locked away in the main building, ready if needed.

Although he didn't tell the gringo club that he had joined the militia, Ben was proud of his participation and thought that joining up was crucial to his acceptance by hard-line Sandinistas within INE. Ben enjoyed the camaraderie.

In addition to his involvement with the militia, Ben always volunteered to clown at company activities. On Secretary's Day, hundreds of employees and their families watched as he and Diana Brooks performed Ben's original act, "The Life of Sandino as Seen by a Juggler." "All INE got to know him and love him," said coworker Jaime Merizalde. Ben wrote Alison, "It is fun to have such an absurd skill."

Since Ben did not have a supervisory position at work, he was eligible to join INE's Sandinista union. He told a friend he joined because he enjoyed the contradiction of being an engineer and a member of a labor union. Some internationalists believed that, since they were foreigners, they should not voice opinions, but Ben felt differently. At union meetings, he often made suggestions, protested, and sided with the workers. However, after long speeches and heated discussions where union leaders described government policies, explained the latest shortages, and promised to examine complaints, nothing ever changed significantly.

As time passed, Ben grew more critical of the union, coming to realize that it did not fight for workers' rights but instead unquestioningly supported Sandinista policies. Union leaders encouraged members to join the militia and pro-Sandinista organizations. They justified all Sandinista actions by saying that, until the war ended, civil rights had to be suspended, wages had to be controlled, and strikes had to be forbidden.

Ben told friends that he was frustrated by this trickle-down structure, but understood it. While he realized political rights were limited and wages low, he thought that the Sandinistas sincerely wanted to improve conditions for workers but were impeded by the war. He felt that everyone, including workers, had to make sacrifices. When the government printed a cartoon supplement in the newspapers urging Managua residents to grow vegetables in empty lots, Ben and gringo club member Millie Thayer planted a garden next to the INE gas station pumps. He wanted to add homegrown vegetables to supplement INE's bland cafeteria lunches. His parents and the Portland, Oregon, solidarity group sent seeds, and Ben invited INE employees and gringo club members to a volunteer workday, where they planted beets, carrots, and cabbages. The Nicaraguans advised Ben that the garden had to be watered daily, until the rainy season began in May.

A month after Ben moved into the Brookses' house, Ana's daughters Nereda, nineteen, and Mirna, seventeen, returned from picking coffee in the mountains. They were delighted to find an American living in their house. They joked with him, teased him, hopped onto his unicycle, attempted to juggle, and proudly introduced Ben to their shy, giggly girlfriends. But of the Brooks girls, only Diana learned to juggle. She frequently performed with Ben at workshops organized by Maria de Zuniga, an American who directed the Center for Health Information Services (CISAS), a health education organization. Ben, wearing his checkered pants and huge, floppy tennis shoes, pushed a wheelbarrow into the room, loaded with fruit and vegetables, with Diana perched precariously on top. "Whenever the clown appeared, everyone's enthusiasm picked up," said one of the organizers, Costa Rican Ana Quirós. Ben and Diana juggled tomatoes, carrots, potatoes, yucca, cheese, and eggs, while quizzing the audience.

Shortly after the two younger girls arrived home, sixteen-year-old Alfredo, Ana's nephew whom she had adopted, returned from picking coffee. He had just spent three months living in farmworker's barracks, sharing one room with fifty others, and arrived home to find Ben in his bedroom. Instead of complaining, Alfredo squeezed a cot next to the bed, happy to share his small space. Shy and gangly Alfredo soon taught Ben slang he learned in the mountains, and they often wandered the streets of Barrio Riguero together, eating at *fritangas* and talking politics.

Ben teased the Brooks family, calling them *chachalaca*, "crazy people who talk too much," while Ana called him *el gringito flaquito*, "a skinny little gringo," and a *payaso barato*, "a worthless clown." Ben noticed many Nicaraguans had beards, and when he attempted to grow one, the Brookses joked about the scraggly reddish brown hairs sprouting from his chin, saying his beard looked like a soccer team: eleven on each side. When the neighborhood suffered one of its frequent blackouts, the family gathered around a candle, and Ana quipped, "It's Ben's fault—he flipped the wrong switch today."

Ana and the girls also teased Ben about his appearance. He never paid much attention to his clothes and usually dressed in faded jeans, hiking boots, and rumpled cotton shirts, with a calculator and various pens in his pocket protector. He usually had a frayed green daypack over his shoulder and clutched his now battered black briefcase. Because they couldn't afford new clothes, the Brooks teenagers' clothes were also faded and worn, but they never left the house without ironing their clothes, even their jeans. Although they didn't understand English, they preferred T-shirts emblazoned with sayings like "Party Animal." They listened to American music and sang along to Michael Jackson, Stevie Wonder, and Madonna. They breakdanced at parties, and questioned Ben about American teenagers.

Ben's humor and easygoing nature helped him to adapt, to accept the confusion and disorganization of Nicaraguan society. Unlike many foreigners, he cheerfully accepted ambiguities and last minute changes. Like a wide-eyed child, he delighted in the unknowns, such as the excitement of never knowing where a bus would take him, whether a person would keep an appointment, or if there would be food in the house for breakfast.

But when the three teenagers returned home, the house became crowded, noisy, and hot. The television blared all the time. Someone always had a radio on full volume. The parrot squawked, the dog barked, visitors stopped by unannounced and stayed for hours. Ben wanted to be part of the family, yet he wanted his independence too. "He was trying to be the responsible son in the family," said Nancy, "but also exercising his right to be independent, and maintain parts of a normal American lifestyle."

Sometimes, when the noise and bustle of the Brookses' house became overwhelming, Ben found solitude in a Chinese diner, where he sipped beer, read, wrote letters, and updated his journal.

After an evening alone, Ben plunged into family activities again, including accompanying Ana to the neighborhood Catholic church, Santa María de los Angeles. The church was a traditional gathering place for Sandinistas since the 1970s, when the priest began biblical study circles and started Christian Base Communities, teaching his students that by sharing the lives of the poor, they could liberate them. Going to church in Barrio Riguero was social and political as well as religious. Life-size murals glorifying the revolution, mixing Sandinista and biblical symbols, decorated the interior walls. In sermons, Father Uriel Molina usually discussed the war and invited parishioners to voice their thoughts. Ben enjoyed the meshing of Christianity and the revolution: "It is amazing to see the man in robes talking about us as being sons of Sandino and Carlos Fonseca as well as God. But he pulls it off."

On weekends, during harvest season, the church organized volunteer cotton-picking brigades. One Saturday night Ben and the others sat on the church steps, joking, gossiping, and drinking rum as they waited for the bus to take them to the fields. Saturday night drifted into Sunday morning before the bus finally arrived, and after a three-hour trip, deposited them in the cotton fields. Ben did not enjoy the agricultural work, describing the cotton as "puffy white balls that are boring as hell after ten minutes." For him, the most enjoyable part of the weekend was Sunday afternoon, when Father Molina said mass in a banana grove and everyone picnicked beneath banana fronds.

Just as Ben was comfortably integrated into the family, Ana told him that her husband was returning home on Valentine's Day, after a six-month stint with the militia. Ben knew that Ana had allowed him to move in without Rodolfo's permission, and he worried that he might have to move out.

Before Rodolfo arrived, Ana scrubbed the house from top to bottom and stocked up on food at the market. Ben followed her from stall to stall, carrying the groceries in a burlap bag through the sweltering heat, while Ana bargained for meat that lay on the white tile counter, covered with flies.

On February 14, the Brooks family rose early and took the bus to the Roberto Huembes market to welcome home Rodolfo's militia unit. Ben stood apart from the family and watched as a thin, bearded, weather-beaten man dressed in camouflage stepped out of the returning crowd and hugged his wife and daughters. Ben snapped photographs of the homecoming. "I introduced Ben to my husband," said Ana. "I said, 'This is Ben. He is staying at our house. He's a friend of Diana's.' But Rodolfo stood staring at Ben. He didn't say anything. So I said, 'It's just for a little while.' But I knew it was a lie, because Ben had already become part of the family."

Upon his return, Rodolfo reestablished the rules of the house. He made Ana quit patrolling the neighborhood with a pistol. She was upset, and complained to her daughters and Ben, but never said anything to Rodolfo. She continued attending CDS meetings, but when she arrived home, Rodolfo questioned her about who was there and what was said. The Brooks daughters began arriving home earlier in the evening, although Diana, who had recently become involved with a Cuban doctor, spent more time away.

Rodolfo did not say much to Ben. He sat on the patio, drinking rum, as neighbors and relatives stopped by to welcome him home. He never talked about his experiences in the mountains. Ana hovered over him, feeding him huge plates of *gallopinto*, fried plantains, meat, and chicken, which Rodolfo gulped ravenously. Ana sent the youngest daughter from store to store, searching for eggs for Rodolfo's breakfast, sugar for his coffee, and oil to fry meat.

A week later Rodolfo returned to his job as head of the lottery's internal audit. The pay was low, and Rodolfo struggled to feed his large family. Shortly after sunrise, he fought the crowds to board an early bus to work. In the evening he returned home, irritable and exhausted. Through half-closed eyes, Rodolfo wearily watched Ben return from INE, pushing his unicycle through the living room on his way to Alfredo's room. Ben always said hello, but Rodolfo barely acknowledged him as he silently ate dinner in front of the TV, watched the news, and fell asleep. Ben worried that it might only be a matter of time before Rodolfo kicked him out.

Riding home from work one day, Ben spied the grizzled old man sweeping Bill Stewart Park. Ben hopped off his unicycle to talk to him. The seventy-nine-year-old man, Ricardo Gonzales, lived in a green and orange corner house facing the park, and had witnessed the killing of the American Bill Stewart.

Stewart, a thirty-seven-year-old ABC Television correspondent based in Miami, was sent to Managua in June 1979 to cover the fall of the Somoza dictatorship. On the morning of Wednesday, June 20, Stewart, his translator Juan Francisco Espinosa, driver Pablo Tiffer, cameraman Jack Clark, and soundman James

Cefalo left the Hotel Intercontinental to check out the northeast neighborhoods, which Somoza's troops had bombed and rocketed the previous day. Journalists had heard rumors that many civilians had been killed. Their blue Mazda van, marked with "TV" and *"Prensa Extranjera"* (Foreign Press), slowly drove through Barrio Riguero, maneuvering around the remains of barricades, broken pieces of wood, tin, and shattered bottles. Tires burned in the middle of the deserted streets, filling the air with thick black smoke.

At one corner of Barrio Riguero, Bill Stewart and Juan stepped out of the van with raised hands and flashed a white flag and press credentials. They approached a roadblock manned by a fifteen-member unit of the National Guard. Ricardo Gonzales peeked out the shuttered window. When a soldier motioned Stewart to the ground, the TV crew began filming. Stewart lay on the ground, hands outstretched, holding up his press card. The soldier kicked Stewart in the ribs, then lowered his M-14 rifle. He leveled the gun barrel at Stewart's head and shot him behind the right ear. Stewart's body jerked in the air. The soldier turned toward Juan, led him away, and shot him in the head.

In the van, Jack Clark had kept his camera running. Somoza's soldiers did not know the incident had been filmed.

Ricardo saw the two bodies lying in the street in pools of blood. Gonzales's neighbor, a woman whose front door was less than ten feet from Stewart's body, wanted to bring the body into her house but was afraid to step outside because Somoza's soldiers had surrounded the neighborhood.

Somoza's soldiers approached the van. The TV crew hid the film, and Pablo convinced the soldiers that the crew was from Channel 6, the pro-Somoza television station. He agreed to obey their order and say that Stewart died in crossfire. The soldiers allowed the TV crew to pick up Stewart's body, and the van sped away, leaving the translator's corpse in the dirt road. Ricardo watched in horror as starving pigs gnawed on the man's feet before the National Guard hauled the body away.

That evening, the footage was smuggled out of Nicaragua. The United States aired the film of the execution across the nation. President Jimmy Carter called the killings "an act of barbarism that all civilized people condemn." The murder of Bill Stewart caused American public opinion to turn against Somoza, accelerating the collapse of his regime.

A month later the Sandinistas came to power and built the small park in Bar-

rio Riguero in Stewart's memory. However, as time passed and the Sandinista government slashed the municipal budget, city employees stopped maintaining the park,
and it became shabby and forlorn. Ricardo watched as weeds sprouted, trash piled
up, and the grass withered. He decided that he would take care of the park.

Ben, moved by Ricardo's initiative and dedication, thought that it should be
recognized. Together with Nancy Hanson, an American Catholic nun, he convinced
the gringo club to buy Ricardo a shovel, broom, and machete. The Americans put
Ben in charge of paying him a monthly stipend.

Whenever Ben wheeled by on his unicycle, Ricardo was delighted to see him.
He told Ben how the grass would not grow in the shade, how the trellis was rotting and needed to be replaced, how the dripping faucets needed new washers, and
how the drunks ripped out his *calala* seeds. The local drunks who hung out at the
park taunted Ricardo, calling him old and feeble, warning him that the Americans
were going to fire him and hire a younger man. Ben assured Ricardo that this was
untrue, realizing that this responsibility was now the highlight of the old man's life.

At the Brooks house, Rodolfo watched how Ben chatted incessantly, joked
with Ana and the girls, and arose early every morning to go to work, then returned
home physically tired and emotionally exhausted, just like him. Rodolfo observed
Ben as he cheerfully performed errands for Ana.

Finally, Rodolfo began talking to Ben. They discussed politics. Ben told him
that he had always been a political activist, that he had been jailed for demonstrating against nuclear power, and that while at the university, he had demonstrated
against the draft, and Reagan's policies in Central America. "Ben said Ronald Reagan was crazy, and shouldn't get involved in the problems of countries like
Nicaragua—countries that want to live in peace," said Ana.

One night, Ben arrived home late to find Ana sleeping in his little room after
a fight with Rodolfo. Ben quietly wrapped himself up in a sheet, lay down on the
tile floor, and went to sleep. In the morning, Ben joked about the incident with
Ana but didn't mention it to Rodolfo. The older man noted this and was satisfied
that Ben knew his place.

On weekends, Rodolfo relaxed. Dressed in shorts and a scoop-neck T-shirt,
he played chess on the shady patio during the hot, still afternoons, pouring himself generous tumblers of rum. He eventually invited Ben to join him. Although

Ben was never much of a drinker, he enjoyed drinking with Rodolfo. "Over many games of chess and more bottles of rum, we have become friends," Ben noted. "A Saturday afternoon might start with several small bottles of Flor de Caña [rum]. He'll start the conversation with a light drinking question like 'and what effect will increased interest rates have on Latin America?' And from there the conversation goes on. That is until we have lost the train of thought in the last bottle."

Nicaragua has only two seasons: dry and rainy. The dry season begins in November, and as each month passes, the weather grows hotter, more torrid, and suffocating. Then the May rains arrive, bringing relief and beginning the cool, invigorating six-month rainy season.

In Managua, the winds made the dry season bearable. Winds stirred the dust around, blowing it into houses, settling it on newly mopped tile floors and on wicker rocking chairs, and coating people with a fine, brown film. By March the winds had stilled and the sun became excruciatingly hot, a pulsing yellow-white orb that beat down mercilessly. The Brooks had only one small fan, and their tin-roofed house was sweltering. "The weather here is getting hot," Ben wrote. "Shower in morning, shower after work, shower before bed to cool off. But I like the flow in and out of the house as if walls don't really exist."

Easter Week was always one of the hottest times of the year. Activity in the country ground to a halt. Shops and markets closed, offices locked their doors, traffic stopped, and housewives shut their doors against the infernal heat and clinging dust. Men padded about the house in scoop-necked T-shirts, shorts, and rubber thongs. Nicaraguans who could afford it went to the beach for a week.

Ben spent the first part of the week with Alvaro, an engineering student, and three of his friends at Ometepe, an island in the middle of Lake Nicaragua. "It was a wonderful four days of bullshit, reading, attempting to climb a mountain, dancing and walking around," Ben wrote. "It is very relaxing to travel with Nicaraguans. They can strike up conversations about whatever and carry them on as I usually peter out after '¿Cómo estás?' It was very nice to be with my peer group; engineering students, early 20's and political. In many ways I feel out of place, although well accepted, in many of the circles I move in. But this was a very welcome change. The conversation moved from communism, to heat transfer, to love lives, to the girl that just walked by, and then back to the dynamics of Nicaraguan politics."

When Ben returned to hot and dusty Managua, where Catholic traditions dominated the week, he felt alienated. Church bells rang at all hours, calling the faithful to mass, where vendors crowded church steps selling vials of red liquid that they called Christ's blood. On Good Friday thousands of Catholics paraded through downtown Managua, holding umbrellas to shield themselves from the fiery sun, stopping along the way to perform the stations of the cross. The Brooks girls spent long hours praying in the neighborhood church. Ben was invited, but he politely declined.

Looking for a friend who could understand how he felt, Ben wandered over to visit Anne. They talked about how they felt more Jewish during Easter Week, a strange sensation for them because they both came from nonpracticing Jewish families.

When Ben was growing up, David and Elisabeth celebrated both Jewish and Christian holidays, lighting a menorah, decorating a Christmas tree. The celebrations were family get-togethers, though, not religious feasts. The Linders raised the children in a milieu that emphasized ethics embedded in their heritage.

Of the three Linder children, Ben had been the only one to express interest in his Jewish heritage. As a child in San Francisco, he attended Hebrew school, where he learned Jewish prayers and customs. When the family moved to Portland, eleven-year-old Ben again signed up for Hebrew school but dropped out after a few weeks, because, Elisabeth said, "the school promoted Zionism. Ben came home from Hebrew school talking about Zionism, and his brother blew up!" John, a member of the Young Socialist Alliance, told Ben that Zionism was unacceptable and wrong.

In high school, Ben read the stories of Yiddish writer Shalom Aleichem and hung a print of Marc Chagall's *Old Jew* over his bed. During high school, after John and Miriam had moved out, Ben bought matzo during Passover, which he shared with his father.

"I think Ben actively wondered more about our parents than John and I did," said Miriam. "He lived at home for five more years, and knew them as an adult. I know that he thought about them, and their history, and how the fact that they are Jewish had determined so much about the way their lives are." Ben mulled over how his mother's religion had determined her flight from Czechoslovakia and made her a refugee in Mexico. "For Ben, it's who he was," said Anne, "the ethical basis for everything he did. We both came from nonreligious Jewish families, where being Jewish was very important. We were brought up with similar values: that being Jewish is caring about others who are fighting against oppression. And I think even more so in his family, because his mother had so recently come over from Europe."

During Easter Week, Ben and Anne decided to celebrate Passover. Anne wanted to have a serious religious celebration, to recite the prayers and ask the four questions, but Ben envisioned the dinner more as a social occasion, to enjoy a good meal with close friends. They improvised the traditional seder plate with foods from the market: stuffed cabbage, hard-boiled eggs, a cow bone instead of a lamb's shank bone, tortillas instead of matzo, parsley for bitter herbs, and *charoseth* made with mangos instead of nuts and apples. They invited Jewish Americans from the gringo club—Ricky Weiss, Ruth Warner and Moisés, her Nicaraguan husband—as well as other Americans, Maria de Zuniga and Ani Wihbey, a Catholic nun. Lacking a Haggadah to guide them, they recited the Passover story from memory, and Ben recounted the heroism of Jews in the Warsaw ghetto during World War II.

After the seder, Ben felt as if he was among friends in Nicaragua.

Chapter 5

El Cuá

Ben puzzled over his piping diagrams, arriving early at his job in the INE office, working late to meet deadlines, often returning to the office after Monday night gringo club meetings. His officemates routinely handed in reports late. Ben was disturbed that the other engineers did not take their work as seriously as he did.

Since piping layout was new to Ben, he didn't know if he was doing the job correctly. He had hoped he'd be working with skilled engineers who could guide him, but was disappointed to find few experienced engineers at INE. He grew even more disillusioned when he called up the handful of engineers listed in the phone book and found that almost all of them had left the country.

Looking for advice, Ben frequently turned to his officemate Larisa, who in turn sought his advice about her project. Larisa was working with Swedish engineers to develop a small hydroturbine that could be manufactured in Nicaragua. During the 1970s the U.N.'s development program had financed studies of seven small hydro-electric plants, of which only one was built, in the mountain village of El Cuá, 145 miles northeast of Managua. The 100-kilowatt hydroplant, which would provide the electricity for the town for the first time ever, was slated for completion by the fall.

The project intrigued Ben. The village was immortalized by a song by Sandinista songwriter Carlos Mejía Godoy, "Las Campesinas del Cuá" (The Peasant Women of El Cuá). The revolutionary lyrics told of an incident in the early 1970s, when Somoza's National Guard rounded up, jailed, and tortured a group of women in El Cuá, accusing them of collaborating with the Sandinista guerrillas. The women were imprisoned in La Chiquita, the El Cuá jail, while their husbands were tied to the avocado tree outside. In an attempt to make them confess, the soldiers raped the women and forced them to watch the torture and murder of their husbands, some of whom were dropped alive from planes. The women refused to talk.

When Bertil, an English-speaking Swedish engineer, arrived to work on the El Cuá hydroplant for six weeks, Ben was thrilled because Sweden boasted many hydroelectric plants, and Swedish engineers were considered the best in the field. Ben diligently translated Larisa's slow, deliberate Spanish into English, carefully selecting the correct technical terms, often pausing to look up words in the dictionary. Bertil impressed Ben with his vast knowledge and experience, and Ben asked his advice on graduate studies. Since many European countries generated energy with alternative systems that could be used in the Third World, Bertil encouraged Ben to apply to graduate school in Europe. Ben wrote Peter Stricker, a fellow engineer in the United States;

> I'm musing on graduate school in 1985 or 1987. There are only a few details to be worked out—when, where and why. "Where" is a big question. I'm thinking about Europe: England, Sweden or Italy. These are fantasies but then again Nicaragua once was only a fantasy. Why—if I could figure this out the other two should come relatively easily. Really 'why' has to do with my plans for my life (or at least the 15-year plan).
>
> I also want to do my part in making this world a better place. There is such a shortage of engineers like you and me that want to do good it would be a shame to waste that feeling in a meaningless job. What are the possibilities in the States these days? Are there any interesting alternative energy possibilities?

By the second week, Ben's admiration for Bertil had faded. He came to realize that while Bertil was a professional in the sense of being a highly paid consultant, he had no interest in improving people's lives in Nicaragua, and no interest in the revolution. Ben was especially irritated by his conservative politics. "He is nice enough and very smart. He is also part of the asshole international engineers. 'South Africa is a nice place, good food and climate ... if you don't look around.' He actually said that. I don't think I'll talk politics with him."

Ben soon grew resentful of Bertil because even though Ben was an engineer who had specialized in hydropower, Bertil never asked his advice. Ben also disapproved of his lengthy breaks with Larisa, their extended lunches, their continual tardiness, and their double standards (they became furious when Nicaraguans did the same things). He thought they didn't respect Nicaraguans, nor heed local customs. "Larisa and Bertil work in a very fast, pushy, and basically contrary to Nicaraguan manner," he wrote.

When Bertil and Larisa had to repeat earlier work, Ben thought they were making sloppy mistakes because they were in a hurry and didn't care about the project. "I don't think Larisa is a very good engineer, and playing second fiddle as the translator is a pain in the ass," wrote Ben. He was sure that he could do a better job if only they'd allow him to work on the project.

Just after Easter, Ben was sitting at his desk when he heard that Bertil was making his first field site visit at the El Cuá hydroplant. Upset that no one had invited him, Ben asked his supervisor, Fritz Morlock, if he could go. Morlock said the truck was already full, but Ben insisted he wouldn't mind riding in the truck bed. Two hours later, without even a change of clothes, he sat in the back of the truck, clutching his black briefcase, bumping along the road north.

They drove up the Pan-American Highway, turned northeast onto a narrower paved road, then crossed the wide, fertile Sébaco Valley. The mountains loomed in the distance, a chain of unbroken conical ridges, successively higher, darker, a purple-black *cordillera* that was a source of shelter, revolution, and death. In the 1930s the mountains sheltered Augusto Sandino while U.S. Marines hunted him throughout the country. In the 1960s and 1970s the mountains hid Sandinista guerrillas again, but by the 1980s, it had become the domain of the Contras. When Nicaraguans talked about traveling to the northern mountains, they often whispered about going *adentro*, "within," disappearing into unknown, dangerous territory.

The engineers spent the night in Jinotega, where the paved road ended, and the next morning continued up a twisting dirt road into the mountains. An hour after leaving Jinotega, the truck passed through Pueblo Nuevo, a small town comprised of wooden stores and brick and board houses, stopping at a wooden guard shed where a soldier dropped a rope strung across the road. The war zone began in Pueblo Nuevo. There were no more villages until El Cuá, two hours away. The dirt road narrowed.

The ride to El Cuá was always beautiful. Travelers rounded hairpin turns, passing thick-stemmed ceiba trees, scarlet-flowered flame-of-the-forest trees, cornfields, and bean patches. They sailed past farmers stabbing the dry dirt with hoes, wearing frayed baseball caps shielding their faces, their arms leathery and brown from the sun, and barreled across steel bridges, spanning streams that were barely a trickle during the dry season. Frequently women stooped in the water, pounding ragged shirts on the rocks, while naked children bronzed by the sun scampered at the river's edge. The road passed wooden ranch houses with red-tiled roofs, and pastures where long-horned Brahma cattle grazed, white egrets perched on their backs. The sun beat down relentlessly, and travelers were covered with a fine, red dust.

Farther north, waterfalls plunged down rock cliffs, and the air was heavy with the damp, mossy smell of new growth and rotting logs. The road twisted past pine trees dripping with Spanish moss, groves of bamboo, banana trees, and rows of glossy-leafed coffee bushes. Low clouds drifted through the valley, breaking occasionally to allow glimpses of mountains clad in rain forests.

Three hours up the dirt road, the truck rounded a bend into a small valley. El Cuá, with its 2,000 residents, was strung along one dirt road. Unpainted wooden shacks with tin roofs and sagging porches lined the road. Banana trees sprouted between some houses, and flowers bloomed in old ammunition boxes with Cyrillic writing on the sides. Patched jeans and camouflage uniforms dangled on barbed wire hung across the yards. Along the length of the town flowed the El Cuá River.

The town itself sprawled outward from a scrubby plaza, at the center of which stood a brick monument, bearing the inscription; "In memory of our heroes and martyrs of El Cuá, July 19, 1983, Year of the Struggle for Peace and Sovereignty." Nearby, soldiers lounged next to mortars surrounded by sandbags.

"It's a war zone," Ben said about El Cuá. "You come into town and you have the feeling of being in a military outpost, and of going back a hundred years in time. But, the most striking thing you see is the military presence. Most men you see are carrying arms; they are members of the militia or the army. There's a whole siege mentality."

The two-story army headquarters dominated the town. It was surrounded by barbed wire, trenches, and sandbags. Soldiers in camouflage manned the wooden gatehouse, cradling machine guns, floppy *cachorro* hats shielding their eyes, red and black scarves around their necks. Their eyes often lazily followed wide-hipped farm women padding through the dust, buckets of river water on their heads.

A newly built health clinic and a long, narrow schoolhouse flanked the plaza. The town had no electricity, no running water, no sanitation system, and no industry. It had one or two vehicles, a few one-room stores, several diners that also served as bars, a coffee warehouse, a tiny Catholic chapel and a Protestant church, and one frayed pool table in a dirt-floor shack.

During the dry season, El Cuá was always hot and dusty. At noon, the dirt road was often deserted. Mongrel dogs with protruding ribs sprawled under spindly trees. A score of mules and horses were tethered nearby. The stench of urine mixed with rotting garbage and horse manure pervaded the village.

But El Cuá's squalor was relieved by vivid splashes of color. Ceiba, mango, and avocado trees and wild yellow hibiscus dotted the town. Between the shacks, crimson and purple bougainvillea cascaded over front-yard fences, and ten-foot high poinsettia trees lent a year-round festive air. Hills crisscrossed by corn patches and bean fields surrounded the village, and beyond towered the shimmering silhouettes of peaks, including Mount Kilambé, the highest in Nicaragua.

The visitors drove to the hydroplant, two miles north of town, where the fifty-year-old husky, gray-haired foreman, Rigoberto Gadea, greeted them. Rigo showed them the operator's house, an empty three-room brick bungalow with a tin roof and an indoor bathroom, the only flush toilet north of Jinotega. The hydroplant, or the "powerhouse," a small square brick building, stood about a hundred yards down the hill. A pipe diverted water from a six-foot wide stream, the Río Esperanza, through the powerhouse.

In 1980 INE had used Swedish assistance and financing to hire subcontractors to build the hydroplant, slated to be completed by July 1981. The money evaporated, the plant was never finished, and INE resumed control of the project. Workers built a small dam 800 meters up the mountain, and constructed a cement canal to the powerhouse. Badly designed and weakened by erosion, the canal had collapsed and been rebuilt twice. It led to a 150-meter pipe where the water fell almost vertically to the powerhouse as it turned a turbine to create electricity. In front of the plant, workers had erected a light pole with a transformer, and they put up four more poles and hung streetlights in town, installing two miles of lines from the town to the plant.

After four years of work, the hydroplant was still not functioning. "The history of El Cuá is a sad one," wrote Ben. "In 1981 a badly designed partially complete 100KW unit was partially installed, including a very shiny wire through the center of town. Then the engineer left. Then the project went to other engineers. Then they left."

The generator and the governor, two of the three machines needed to produce electricity, were already installed. The generator was manufactured in the United States and donated by the United Nations, while the governor, which controlled the speed of the turbine, had been built in 1929 and donated by Sweden. The third machine, a small two-by-two-foot turbine, had been produced in a Managua machine shop and was sitting in pieces on the floor of the INE office in Managua.

While translating, Ben got to know Rigo and his crew of eight local farmers. Most of them had only a first or second grade education, and all of them had worked on the project from the beginning.

In the evening the visitors ate rice, beans, and tortillas at a makeshift diner in someone's living room. The visitors ate with the few government employees, usually professionals from cities who were assigned to El Cuá. Rigo introduced the visitors to the others—doctors, teachers, and administrators—as the town's future.

Twilight always descended fast in El Cuá. At sunset, loud, insistent black *zanate* birds filled the trees with a cacophony of calls. Hibiscus plants closed their petals. White jasmine blossoms perfumed the night air. By 6:00 P.M., the town was dark.

The visitors stayed in a bunkhouse next to the plaza, a wooden building partitioned off by thin plywood into four fifteen-foot-square airless cubicles where government employees lived.

That evening, Ben and Rigo sat on the bunkhouse porch, sharing shots of rum with Carlos, the town doctor, who lived in one of the cubicles. The street was dark and silent, except for the Disamar saloon, which had lights powered by a noisy generator. Ben summed up his initial impressions of El Cuá:

> It has a dusty main street, a fleabag hotel, a bar complete with its usual evening brawl. The houses have a post out front to tie the horses. . . . The town is basically one street. A few bars/eating places, houses and that's it. But now it is also a military post. There are trenches around the town. There are several mortars in the central square; there are defense posts all around the town and every third person is in green and armed. The people are very friendly. In some ways I feel like I'm in the land that time forgot. There are no cars here. Light is from kerosene-wick lamps except for the 3 Colemans that I've seen. Everyone from the littlest kid to her mother to her grandmother rides around on horses. The most common machine is the AK-47 which is the standard issue automatic military gun. I think at least 80% of the people here know how to use one; I make up part of the 20% that heads for a ditch. The deeper the better. But I feel comfortable here.

As soon as Ben saw the hydroplant, he wanted to work on it. He envisioned the tangible benefits it would bring to the village, and it fit his understanding of what the revolution was all about. He wrote his parents that he longed to work on the El Cuá plant. "I'm the secret weapon. Mom—how does electrification of the Pueblo sound to you?"

El Cuá had been carved out of the wilderness by Ezekiel "Checo" Rivera, an illiterate farmer born in Jinotega in 1904. Leading a pack mule, Checo and a friend set out north from Jinotega in 1945, searching for unclaimed fertile land. They cleared their own path with machetes until they came to a river valley a two-day mule ride from Abisinia. Checo fell in love with the valley inhabited by deer, wild pigs, ocelots, jaguars, raccoons, tapirs, and monkeys. Jungle trees teemed with parrots, toucans, macaws, and the national bird, the *guardabarranco*, with its foot-long indigo-and-emerald tail feathers. Checo claimed a lush piece of land on level ground next to the stream, built a wooden shanty, and planted his farm: bananas, beans, and corn.

The area was already known as El Cuá. Some said the name originated from the word *guano,* a leafy tree, under which the priest said mass because he refused to preach near any buildings that sold liquor. However, Checo believed it was an Indian name, from the *jabalines*, wild pigs that ran through the river valley, pawing, digging, rooting, and snorting "cuá, cuá, cuá."

In Jinotega word spread fast about the new settlement, and soon other pioneers moved in to buy river-bottom land from Checo. Wealthy entrepreneurs discovered that coffee thrived in the cool, fertile mountains and planted large coffee plantations in the 1950s. "There was one plantation that had three million coffee trees," said Checo. "Everywhere you looked there were coffee trees. Nothing but coffee for miles and miles." Soon landless peasants settled on the plantations, sharecropping, and working for meager wages during the coffee harvest.

As El Cuá prospered, the bishop of Matagalpa visited Checo, requesting a piece of land to build a Catholic church. Checo donated a parcel. A circuit-riding priest took up collections, bought an electric generator, and imported a shiny bell for the church tower. El Cuá became a regular stop on the missionary circuit, and visiting clergy made the arduous trip by mule to baptize children, hear confessions, perform weddings, and say mass.

The coffee harvest had to be packed out on mules, and El Cuá's isolation hampered its economic growth. In the 1960s growers carved a road out of the wilderness to Jinotega. Tractors plowed much of the undergrowth, but manual labor was plentiful and cheap, so most of the work was done by hand. Workers labored for three dry seasons. During the rainy season, the tilled trenches turned into an impassable bog. In the 1970s the Somoza government graded and sanded the road, hauling out precious nogal, cedar, and mahogany wood, but the road remained unpaved, and only four-wheel drive vehicles could reach El Cuá.

After several days of work, the engineers returned to a sweltering Managua.

By Monday morning Ben was back in his air-conditioned office, staring at his piping diagrams, wondering what to do next. He kept thinking of El Cuá. He remembered the advice of his college juggling partner, Dave Finnigan, who had worked on development projects in the Philippines: "Go to the village." Dave told him that the development of poor Third World nations began on the local level. "You work with a national program, but first you start in the village; then you build a country," he said. More than ever, Ben wanted to trade his piping diagrams for the hydroplant.

April melted into May, when the heat and humidity in Managua became unbearable. Not a breeze blew. Leaves drooped. The thick jungle grass in Managua's vacant lots turned brown and scrubby. The little fan in the Brooks house continuously whirred. Ben was homesick for the rainy, cool springs of the northwest. He wrote a friend at the University of Washington, "May in Seattle. The fun in the sun days should be beginning when you read this. The days when you really need to escape mechanical engineering and walk down to a boat on the lake. Down here I'm waiting for rain. We are just finishing up the hot season and a bit of rain should cool things down nicely."

The first rains of the year always arrived in May. The rainstorms came from the mountains, sweeping down over the lake. A slight breeze blew in from the north, strengthening to a fierce wind, which whipped up dust, sent plastic bags skipping through the air, shook palm trees from side to side, and scattered newspapers through empty lots.

From the mountains, lightning exploded. The horizon melted, as sky and earth united into a dark gray. The first raindrops initially pinged down on tin roofs, then suddenly increased, thundering down. Residents quickly shuttered windows. Pedestrians and street vendors scurried to shelter under eaves and doorways. Drivers pulled off the road. The thirsty trees lifted their dry limbs toward the sky. Streams of water cascaded off roofs, rushing into roadways, turning dirt streets into muddy rivers, sweeping along branches and trash. *Aguacero*, Nicaraguans called it, an avalanche of water.

Then the rain stopped. The sun came out. Drivers pulled back onto the roads, pavement steaming from the rain. The earth smelled like newly baked bread. People emerged, laughing, refreshed. The trees sparkled. The humidity was gone. The May rains had arrived, ushering in a new time of growth.

It was during this season that Ben accompanied Bertil back to El Cuá. By May the rains had turned the road into a quagmire, and their four-wheel drive vehicle slowly plowed uphill through the mud, losing traction. On hills, farmers were scattering seeds from buckets tied to waists, and children aimed slingshots at birds to prevent them from eating the seed and new shoots.

During the rainy season, the lush jungle around El Cuá provided cover for increased military activity by the Contras, who swooped down from their bases in Honduras to set up ambushes along the lonely dirt mountain roads. By spring of 1984, passengers traveling mountain roads dreaded seeing charred vehicles lying in the weeds, lines of bullet holes along their sides. Scattered shards of glass dotted blackened spots in the road where vehicles had been set afire. When drivers spied the remains of an ambushed vehicle, they sped away, wondering how many people had been killed.

At the hydroplant, Rigo told the engineers from Managua that he was shorthanded due to planting time, and introduced them to two shy locals, twenty-nine-year-old Oscar Blandón, and twenty-one-year-old Federico Ramos.

Rigo, Oscar, and Federico had all worked on the hydroelectric plant since construction began in 1980. Oscar and Federico cleared the land with machetes, dug holes to put in posts, hauled sand and rocks for the foundation, mixed and poured concrete for the canal and dam, laid bricks for the powerhouse and the operator's bungalow, and helped assemble the plant's machinery.

As Ben worked with Oscar and Federico in the afternoons, he noticed how eager they were to learn mechanical skills. "It is amazing to us, being from the States, the lack of experience people have," Ben wrote. "While most men in the U.S., and now more women, have used a wrench, most people in El Cuá have never even seen one."

In the evenings Rigo and Ben often sat on the porch of the bunkhouse, sharing a bottle of rum. Rigo had seen many engineers come and go and doubted that electricity would ever come to the town. Ben described Rigo, who had a wife in Jinotega and a sweetheart in El Cuá, as "draftsman, surveyor and a bit of everything, including womanizer." Rigo never finished his engineering courses at the university, but he was, as Ben wrote, "one of those people that know a bit about everything and are essential on a job in the outback."

Rigo told Ben about the village, and about an old man who owned the red-and-black house on the edge of town. Cosme Castro had fought some fifty years earlier with the Sandinista hero, Augusto César Sandino.

Sandino was born in 1895 in a dirt-floor hut in the village of Niquinohomo, outside Managua. His mother was a day laborer. He never knew his father. Sandino worked on the Guatemalan banana plantations of the United Fruit Company, and later in the Mexican oil fields, where he met union organizers and socialists. There he developed his own ideology, a populist social policy that included land reform and workers' and farmers' cooperatives. When he returned to Nicaragua, he became a general in the country's Liberal Army.

In 1927 the U.S. government sent the marines to Nicaragua "to protect American lives and property" and guarantee order during national elections. After the U.S.-backed candidate, General José María Moncada, won the presidency, English-speaking Anastasio Somoza García became his personal aide. The marines created and trained the National Guard, and Somoza was eventually appointed the director. He turned the National Guard into his private army, and the Somoza family ruled Nicaragua as a fiefdom for the next forty-five years.

In the late 1920s Sandino demanded an end to fraudulent elections, and the withdrawal of the marines. His demands went unanswered, and he launched a guerrilla war from the Segovia Mountains, leading a peasant and miner army that never numbered more than 1,000. He adopted a red-and-black flag and the slogan Patria Libre o Muerte (A Free Country or Death). Somoza called him a thief, a pillager, and a bandit, but his own men called him the Hero of the Segovias and San Digno, "Worthy Saint." Before going into battle, Sandino always stuck a jungle flower into his cowboy hat.

Sandino's magnetism attracted many barefoot farmers, including Cosme Castro, then a skinny teenager in the mountains above El Cuá. Armed with a machete and a knife, Cosme followed Sandino across the country to Puerto Cabezas to steal rifles, to the Bonanza mines to seize dynamite, to the rolling hills of Chontales, and back north into the jungle to elude the U.S. Marines.

Sandino situated his headquarters at El Chipote, an impenetrable mountain peak fortified with trenches and tunnels. When the marines detected his hideout, Sandino and his men fabricated human decoys out of hay and vanished into the mountains. His followers, organized into small, fast-moving patrols, operated in sympathetic territory where farmers supplied them with food, shelter, and information.

In the early 1930s, as the United States slid into the Great Depression, American public support for foreign military intervention waned, and in 1932 President Herbert Hoover withdrew the marines from Nicaragua. In February 1933 Sandino and the Nicaraguan government negotiated a truce allowing Sandino's followers to set up agricultural cooperatives in the Segovia Mountains. Sandino disbanded his barefoot army.

On the night of February 21, 1934, after Sandino left a dinner with Anastasio Somoza García to finalize the truce, Somoza's soldiers assassinated the leftist leader in an empty field in Managua. Early the next morning, National Guard troops attacked Sandino's agricultural cooperatives, massacring some three hundred men, women, and children. Survivors scattered into the mountains, including the young Cosme. The Somoza family dynasty ruled the country for the next several decades. They responded to all popular demands for reform with repression.

In 1961, a group of disaffected Nicaraguans met clandestinely in Tegucigalpa, Honduras, and organized the Frente Sandinista de Liberación Nacional, the Sandinista National Liberation Front, to overthrow the Somoza dictatorship. The small group of revolutionaries hid in the isolated, rugged mountains of the Cordillera Isabelia, east of El Cuá, where they launched a prolonged popular war. Half a dozen Sandinistas would secretly visit farmers to explain their struggle. Some farmers believed that Sandino had been reborn in the fledgling guerrilla group, which shared its meager medicine and food supplies with the farmers and gained their trust. The farmers drafted relatives and friends until the movement had a chain of supporters throughout the mountains.

In the 1970s the National Guard launched an offensive against the rebel bands, establishing command posts in San José de Bocay, Bocaycito, and El Cuá, where the Guard ordered residents to clear a weed-choked field for a runway but never used it. They activated military operations from the rural command posts, sweeping the mountains, mobilizing patrols on foot, helicopter, truck, and canoe. When soldiers detected guerrillas, they surrounded them. If the rebels slipped away, the Guard accused nearby farmers of supporting them, and imprisoned civilians. American missionaries in the mountains reported systematic cases of torture: soldiers beat civilians, extracted teeth, used electric shock, raped women, and disfigured men to extract information from them. Hundreds of farmers were imprisoned, were tortured, and disappeared. In order to break up the foci of guerrilla support, the National Guard forcibly relocated farmers out of many areas and torched their houses and fields.

Although most villagers had no contact with the Sandinistas, a few farmers near El Cuá, including Cosme Castro, fed them and acted as couriers. In 1979, when the Sandinistas came to power, they rewarded Cosme's long devotion to their cause by giving him a parcel of land on the edge of El Cuá.

In 1983 the Contras attacked El Cuá, overran the edges of town, and damaged Cosme's newly built house. He rebuilt it, defiantly painting it red and black. Cosme said, "If the Contras attack again, they'll know where to find me." Of all the houses in El Cuá, Cosme's shack was a beacon, and a target.

As Ben and Bertil left El Cuá, Ben knew he wanted to meet Cosme.

In Managua, as Bertil and Larisa continued working together, Bertil rapidly learned enough Spanish to communicate with her, so Ben was released from translating duties and returned to his piping diagrams. Ben planned to request a transfer to the El Cuá project after Bertil's short contract expired.

As Ben talked with his coworkers, he was surprised to learn how much their status had deteriorated after the revolution. Before 1979, engineers at the electric company had held privileged positions as skilled, educated professionals in a society of unskilled, uneducated people. They were respected. Engineers owned houses surrounded by walls in upper-class neighborhoods, and had maids and chauffeurs. Engineers' children attended private schools, and their families took vacations in Costa Rica, South America, and the United States.

After the revolution, the Sandinista government indexed a pay scale, and with increasing inflation, engineers' salaries plummeted to about $70 per month. Engineers, especially new ones, could no longer afford the previous luxuries. Like all government employees, from directors to janitors, their salaries were augmented by subsidized products distributed at work—beans, rice, oil, sugar, toilet paper, and soap. Many engineers resented their new, lower status, and left the country to work elsewhere.

To a certain extent, Ben could empathize with his coworkers' frustrations. They had few resources and even fewer opportunities for advancement. There was only one engineering university in the country, which was ill-equipped, its professors badly paid and poorly trained. They assigned little homework. Learning was by rote, and there was scant opportunity for design work, creative thinking, or innovation. At their jobs, engineers had no access to trade journals, magazines, reference books, or even skilled, experienced engineers of whom to ask advice. Most INE jobs were not demanding, and almost all of the original design work was contracted out to foreign consultants, which added to Nicaraguan engineers' resentment of their foreign colleagues.

Ben understood that his coworkers were angry, but he didn't understand their indifference toward their jobs. He wondered if some engineers were purposefully delaying projects, and further wondered if the CIA might have planted people in INE to sabotage the revolution. "Engineers down here seem to be as conservative as in the States. I must admit that I had higher hopes," Ben wrote. "That is definitely one of the negative aspects of working here at INE. I find it a royal pain in the ass. These engineers bitch about not having all of the comforts of 'before' without any comprehension of what life was like for the great majority of Nicaraguans. But at least here I can argue back. It's very nice to be able to talk politics knowing that the government is on my side."

"I found out why there aren't any political posters in the office. It is because there aren't any political people. I've been thinking about that a lot. I guess I came here as 'B. Linder, Engineer for the People,' only to find engineers with their heads up their asses just as everywhere else."

He was usually diplomatic at the office, but at a dinner party with a U.S.-trained local engineer, a supervisor at INE, Ben stridently criticized the company's inefficiencies while the Nicaraguan winced at the table. "You could tell he was thinking: Who is this kid who just came down from Oregon, and he thinks everything is a matter of 'can do' if you get the right kind of technology," said the host, George Moore.

Ben thought that young engineers, who had been teenagers during the insurrection, would be the revolution's strongest supporters. Over lunch in the INE cafeteria, Alvaro and Mauricio, engineering students in his office, told Ben that the "FSLN betrayed its supporters" by not keeping its promises, so therefore they felt no obligation toward the Sandinistas. Ben defended the Sandinistas, lecturing the students on their duty to defend the revolution. He wrote, "We were going at it. Here was the gringo explaining nationalism to the Nicaraguans. Quite disgusted, I asked, 'And in July '79, where were you? Did you take up a gun? Build a barricade? Bring food to a combatant?' The answers—'no.' I then told them that the Frente had made no promises to them and walked away."

After bad days at work, Ben rode home on his unicycle, clutching his briefcase, pedaling over the bumpy paving stones of Barrio Riguero. Children ran out of their houses, moving their hands up and down as if they were juggling, waving, and calling out to him, "¡Adíos cirquero!" (So long, circus man!) Ben told a friend that when he cycled home from a hard day at work, "all worried and mad," the children who chased him made him feel happy. "Everybody talked about this little man with his engineer clothes on and his briefcase riding on a unicycle," said friend Dina Redman. "It was the strangest thing they had ever seen."

Ben cultivated friendships with coworkers, and analyzed the power relationships at INE, determining who was helpful and competent, who was an obstacle and inefficient, who was pro-Sandinista, and who was antirevolutionary. "Ben told me that 90 percent of our work in Nicaragua is social," said Jamie Lewontin, a machinist from Boston. "He said that only 10 percent is technical—and that's dessert."

When Ben arrived in the office, he greeted all the secretaries by name, asked about their children, and invited them to his clowning performances. One of the INE secretaries was known for causing needless bureaucratic problems for foreigners, but Ben constantly flattered her, praising her work, her dress, her manners, and eventually won her over. She would do anything for him.

On June 2, 1984, Ben arrived at work to find Larisa upset and frightened upon her return from El Cuá. Ben described her account: "When they got there, several soldiers ran up to them, looking shocked to see them. This was at 9:00 A.M. At 5:00 A.M. the Contras [had] started to attack. Several trucks had been burned on another road into town. When the people from the office got out of the car they could hear gunfire." Unsure of what to do, they waited at the deserted plant. Rigo was nowhere to be seen. Two hours later, after the Contras had pulled back, Larisa and the other engineers jumped into the vehicle and drove straight back to Managua. "The outer perimeter of defense, about one mile radius from town, held off the attack until 11:00 A.M., when the Contras retreated. My friend that had shown me around when I was there was at the plant when the attack occurred. He wasn't to be found afterward. I haven't been able to find out anything more. It is very sobering. It makes the war so very much realer."

When the Soviet embassy found out about the Contra attack near El Cuá, they forbade Larisa to return. At about the same time, Bertil's six-week contract ended, and he left Nicaragua. INE decided that it was too dangerous to continue working in El Cuá, and suspended all trips to the hydroplant. Ben's plan to ask for a transfer to the El Cuá project disintegrated, and he reluctantly turned back to the piping diagrams.

Chapter 6

Little Ant, the Clown

On June 1, 1984, in their biggest offensive to date, the Contras attacked Ocotal, a town of some 20,000 residents near the Honduran border. They destroyed the sawmill, the radio station, and several silos, killing fifteen townspeople and wounding thirty-four.

After the attack, a farmer outside town found a comic book manual called the "Freedom Fighter's Manual" slipped under the door of his wooden hut. Filled with drawings on how to sabotage factories, government buildings, and offices, it advocated tossing tools down storm drains, damaging office equipment, short-circuiting electrical systems, cutting telephone lines, opening faucets, clogging toilets, and firebombing government buildings. Another pamphlet, which became known as the "Assassination Manual," recommended the "selective use of violence" and advocated "neutralizing" government officials, community leaders, and Sandinista supporters. Both pamphlets were written by the CIA and distributed to the Contras.

In response to the Contra's escalating attacks, the Sandinista government issued a massive call-up. Ben returned to the Brooks house to find Ana and the girls crying. Seventeen-year-old Alfredo had received a draft notice. Ben wrote, "The attacks on the borders are better and better organized and increasing. In the next three months, 10,000 boys, 16 to 20 years old, will volunteer or be drafted. From the high school where the kids in the house study, all of the boys from the equivalent of the 10th, 11th, and 12th grades will be going."

Although all the fighting occurred in the countryside, the city was also affected by the war. "The tension grows here in Managua," Ben wrote to his parents. "It is augmented by shortages of soap, eggs, toilet paper, and toothpaste. All of this leads to a personal tension. I sometimes just want out."

Ben was more expressive in a letter to Alison. "These last months have been very tense. The periodic shortages are frustrating and require an additional thinking on top of the day-to-day. The constant fighting for a place, not just a seat, but a place [on the bus], is a shitty way to start the day and a frustrating way to end it. Superimposed with these day-to-day realities is the constant threat of a U.S. invasion. It isn't the feeling of an immediate threat we felt in November but rather the feeling of probable invasion."

In July, the CDS prepared to celebrate the fifth anniversary of the Sandinista revolution. July 17 was Día de la Alegría, "Happiness Day," the anniversary of Somoza's flight from Nicaragua. Ben dressed as Benito the Clown. At 9:00 A.M. he picked his way through the Eastern Market, where the stench of urine wafted from dark corners. Fat, broad-shouldered women in wide-brimmed hats and frilly aprons sat behind mounds of mangos, pineapples, tangerines, and squashes, arguing loudly as they absently chased flies away from cut watermelons.

Ben climbed the rickety stairs to the second-story office of the Centro de Cultura Popular (CCP), the People's Culture Center. He wrote, "The offices are in the only two-story building in the market. I looked out over the gray and orange of the maze of rusting zinc and cardboard roofs, over the fields which used to make up downtown Managua before the earthquake and out over Lake Managua. It all seemed so fragile, so vulnerable."

In the market stalls below, musicians played two guitars and a marimba. As a crowd surrounded them, Ben observed, "Several of the big fat market women vendors started to dance. Everyone was laughing and clapping. It was beautiful to see these 20 to 30 women—who have known only a very difficult life—laughing."

When Ben descended the stairs in his clown outfit, children mobbed him, and he galloped off. "Amongst the smelly stalls and staring faces I jumped and spinned, leading a small parade of kids to a piñata." Afterward Ben juggled at an INE party and performed for the July 19 Sandinista Youth organization.

On July 19, just before dawn, CDS organizers began blowing whistles throughout Managua neighborhoods. Trucks with loudspeakers circulated the barrios, blasting the Sandinista hymn over the PA system, urging supporters to celebrate the anniversary of the Sandinista revolution.

In the thin morning light, tens of thousands streamed out of their houses, gathering at community centers, offices, and factories to march to the Carlos Fonseca Plaza. Members of the July 19 Sandinista Youth organization, red-and-black bandannas knotted around their necks, chanted "Patria libre o morir," (A free country or death) and "Queremos la paz," (We want peace). Ben joined the pro-Sandinista coworkers in the INE parking lot.

Some 150,000 people streamed into the plaza. Ben wrote his parents, "People marched from all ends of Managua to a new plaza. It was filled up. A sea of people with the red and black flags flowing over them." Soldiers in camouflage climbed onto each other's shoulders, making human pyramids. The soldier at the top of the pinnacle waved a Sandinista flag. Ice-cream vendors clanged bells as they pushed white handcarts through the crowd. Revolutionary songs pumped through the PA system. People shielded themselves from the blistering sun with newspapers.

In front of the stage, soldiers stood at attention, guarding two glass cases that held the military equipment of Carlos Fonseca and the tattered flag of Sandino. Onstage, Sandinista leaders filed out in green fatigues and straw peasant hats. Speaking slowly and firmly, Commandant Daniel Ortega told the crowd that the Contras were escalating attacks, but elections for president and the national assembly would still be held in November 1984. In preparation for the elections, he said, restrictions were being eased on the current state of emergency. Ortega reminded the crowd of General Augusto Sandino's speech, in which he said that if he died before Nicaragua was free, they should send the ants to tell him the news. Ortega motioned toward the tens of thousands overflowing the plaza. "Sandino, here are your ants to tell you Nicaragua is free." The crowd cheered, as a half-dozen cannons fired twenty-one times, their shots echoing across the lake, the smell of gunpowder drifting over the square.

Among thousands of dusty and tired celebrants, Ben trudged home, mulling over Ortega's speech. To honor Sandino, he decided to change the name of his clown, to Hormiguito, el payaso—Little Ant, the Clown. "And so now I'm the little ant to tell Sandino that Nicaragua is free," decided Ben, "the little ant that goes to the barrios where before the kids had no hope of health or education, and now even the clowns come to visit them."

When Ben returned to the INE office the next day he found Mauricio and Alvaro depressed and angry. They had just been drafted. Ben's roommate Alfredo was to depart in the same thousand-man contingent as the engineers. As he prepared to leave, Ben gave Alfredo his pocketknife and some córdobas, while Alfredo presented Ben with his gray peasant shirt which he had worn during the literacy crusade. "Alfredo goes off to war. He is just a kid and like so many kids he goes off. I don't know what to say. I gave him a chunk of money and told him to go have a good time with his girlfriend. It was the best I could do. 'Patria Libre o Morir' (A Free Country or Death) is a lot easier to say in Managua. A big difference here is that the leaders have put their lives on the line only a short while ago. And now thousands of kids are doing the same."

On Wednesday morning, Ana hid in the bedroom, crying. Her son left for the army base, and Ben accompanied the family to the sendoff of Alfredo's contingent, the Julio Buitrago Brigade. Dressed in new green uniforms, one thousand young men stood under the hot sun, in formation, stoic and unblinking. Ben saw Alfredo there, "looking so young in his green uniform with the creases of factory folds. He had one arm around his girlfriend and with the other wiped his eyes with his new green cap. He tried to be such a man."

As Alfredo was getting ready to leave, a woman was being dragged out of the crowd. Ben saw she was having what looked like epileptic convulsions. He wrote;

> I went over to see if I could help. It was better than watching the mothers and sisters cry and feeling my own tears starting to come. I ended up trying to keep the girl from bashing her head on the concrete. A nurse had appeared and was directing the show. Afterwards I asked her what it was. Her diagnosis was of convulsions caused by the emotional shock of her brother leaving, the last reaction to a situation out of her control.

Even though the military situation was tense, and an invasion by the United States was a constant threat, Ben told friends that he was living a life that he wouldn't trade for anything. He was excited to be living in a society that was being rebuilt.

A few days later, Hormiguito made his debut. Ben performed in an eighty-member artist brigade that accompanied election officials registering people to vote. A pickup truck, followed by a bus with the performers, wound its way through the dirt roads of Managua. Wearing his red nose, Hormiguito climbed onto the hood of the truck and waved to the children, who clogged the windows of houses.

When they saw him, they dashed into the street, pursuing the truck. The vehicles halted, and performers and musicians streamed out of the bus, banging drums, strumming guitars, playing marimbas. "We jump out of buses in a neighborhood and start the parade. Drums beating, dancers in folkloric dress dancing, singers singing and clowns clowning. The kids poured out of the streets as we went by. It was beautiful to see the smiles come over people's faces." Performers filled the street, bobbing from shack to shack, inviting everyone to the local school. Children followed the clowns, streaming toward the school; women shuttered windows, snatched up babies, and followed the children. At the school, clowns tossed juggling clubs through the air, and teenagers performed folk dances while officials registered voters.

For four days, election officials registered voters across Nicaragua. In the countryside, farmers rode mules for hours out of the mountains to register to vote in small villages, meeting friends and relatives they had not seen for months.

But all was not peaceful. In Tapasle, a village outside Matagalpa, Contras killed seven unarmed men, castrated them, and slit their throats. One had his skin scraped off his face.

In Washington State, on a warm, sunny June day in 1984, Mira Brown graduated from Evergreen College with a degree in alternative energy systems, and prepared to go to Nicaragua. A short, intense, powerfully built woman, Mira's round face was framed with long, brown hair and a thin braid traveling down the length of her back.

After the graduation ceremony, a friend pressed a small piece of paper into her hand. Mira read the note: "Benjamin Linder, mechanical engineer, working on small hydroelectric projects in Nicaragua, Post Office Box 3155, Managua." The friend had copied the address from one of Ben's "Dear Gang" letters.

When Mira arrived in Managua a month later, she enrolled at Casa Nicaragüense de Español and moved into Máximo Jerez, a working-class barrio. There she lived with a Nicaraguan family headed by a female Sandinista organizer in a state-owned textile factory. Mira immediately became involved with the Sandinistas, attending CDS meetings, going to demonstrations, and accompanying the head of the family on weekly *vigilancia revolutionaria* patrols through the neighborhood.

Mira planned to give slide shows on alternative energy projects in Nicaragua when she returned to the United States, so she visited a hand-cranked rope pump project near Estelí. Back in Managua, she set up a meeting with Ben.

Armed with a long list of names and phone numbers inside his black briefcase, Ben met Mira at the diner across from INE. Ben considered meeting with Americans visiting Nicaragua as part of his job; Ben also enjoyed explaining how to catch a bus, get a visa extended, or differentiate between uniforms. He had written an informal visitor's guide.

Ben formally introduced himself to Mira and immediately quizzed her on her political background. Mira had been interested in Nicaragua since 1978, when she moved into a collective household of activists who cheered when the Sandinistas overthrew Somoza. She explained she had come to Nicaragua to support alternative energy projects and study Spanish. Mira told Ben that their conversation was one of the few times she had spoken English since her arrival.

Satisfied with Mira's political credentials, Ben told her that the government was interested in developing alternative sources of power—especially hydro and geothermal—because Nicaragua was importing all of its oil and had little foreign exchange to pay for it. Mira took copious notes. When she asked if there were alternative energy projects that had been affected by the war, Ben told her that the El Cuá hydroplant had been put "permanently on hold" after the Contras attacked outside the town.

Mira was immediately interested in the hydroplant because it exemplified a good alternative energy project. Ben explained the technical aspects to her, and Mira pressed on. Who would operate it? As Mira became more garrulous and insistent, Ben became more formal. Her buoyant enthusiasm made him draw back.

At the end of the meeting, Ben gave Mira a list of contacts and encouraged her to continue her material aid campaign. Mira told him she was thinking about working in Nicaragua.

During the 1980s, U.S. solidarity groups sent Americans to Nicaragua on two- to eight-week-long tours and work brigades. They included Architects and Planners in Nicaragua (APSNICA), which constructed houses; Ventana, which supported the arts; Mothers in Solidarity with the Nicaraguan People (Madre), which aided mothers and infants; the Nicaragua Exchange, which sent Americans to pick coffee; sister city projects, which twinned Nicaraguan and U.S. cities; and construction brigades from all over the United States. American groups brought donations and built day-care centers, schools, clinics, community centers, and warehouses throughout the country. When visitors left, they frequently became activists in the States, writing letters to Congress, speaking at church and community groups, and even taking to the streets, protesting the Reagan administration's policy toward Nicaragua.

One such group, TecNica, organized visits of skilled technicians, including engineers. When Ben heard about TecNica, he paid them a visit in Casa San Juan, a cozy hotel behind the campus of the Catholic University.

TecNica's goal was to teach Nicaraguans technical skills in order to make the country self-sufficient. The American university professors who founded TecNica in 1984 believed that foreign technicians, consultants, and businesses made locals dependent on skills and technology from the First World. Foreign consultants often organized projects and operated the equipment, but never taught their skills to Nicaraguans. Several times a month, TecNica delegations comprised of engineers, accountants, welders, machinists, lathe operators, printers, computer programmers, and other professionals arrived in Managua to teach courses or work with government institutions.

Ben made friends with the TecNica staff and began taking delegations on tours of machine shops. "If the volunteers didn't have the right kind of machines to work with, he knew where to find them in Managua," said TecNica staff member Shelley Sherman. Ben soon earned a reputation as a serious, dedicated engineer who knew how to get things done, and the TecNica staff invited him to address delegations, a role that he relished, because he got a chance to scope out new talent for INE. Ben spoke to volunteers about differences in technology, education, and ways of dealing with shortages. "He explained how things would shut down because of the lack of a simple spare part or technical know-how," said TecNica employee Barbara Wiggington.

During his presentations, Ben was self-confident and assured. When others argued loudly, he sat back, and when he finally voiced his opinion, he spoke with quiet authority. Volunteers leaned closer to hear him.

After TecNica volunteers had worked at their jobs for a while, they were invited to talk about their jobs. Ben always asked them tough questions: How is the project going to be maintained and repaired? Is it appropriate, and is it going to create an improvement in the life of the people? Is this project going to create a local elite that is going to take advantage of the project's existence?

In spite of his hard questions, Ben was respected and liked by most TecNica volunteers. They admired his slang-filled Spanish and the fact that he lived with a Nicaraguan family, worked in a government institution, and had arrived in Nicaragua alone, without any organizational backing, and found a job. They marveled at how he fit in, how easily he got along with Nicaraguans. They found him easy to talk to and easy to confide in, especially on their doubts about the revolution. He was realistic, straightforward, and jokingly wry about the country's problems and the revolution's shortcomings, unlike other starry-eyed, dogmatic internationalists.

Ben began using the delegations as "pigeons" to bring down items needed at INE. When delegations arrived on Saturday nights, Ben and other Americans who lived in Nicaragua waited at Casa San Juan for U.S. deliveries. "They were so delighted to get the packages," said TecNica organizer David Creighton. They tore into boxes of books, tools, mail, and spare parts like children on Christmas morning.

When delegations were not in town, Ben would eat and drink with TecNica staffers, advising them on how to circumvent bureaucracy and make TecNica more effective.

Ben and the staffers discussed political security and vaguely wondered if the CIA was using TecNica to place spies in government institutions. TecNica staffers tried to screen the volunteers, and enlisted Ben to help. When John Kellogg, a U.S. engineer, applied for a job at INE, Ben questioned him. "He called me on the phone and wanted to know who I was, what I was doing, and the extent of my solidarity activities in the U.S.," said John. "I had the impression he was forty-five or fifty from the way he talked; the tone of his voice struck me as being middle-aged."

TecNica allowed Ben to sift through the résumés. One hot evening, thumbing through a new packet of résumés, he came across an application from a female engineer, Rebecca Leaf, from Winchester, Massachusetts, a 1982 MIT graduate. Ben plucked out her résumé, believing a female engineer would make a nice addition to INE.

Although Ben had many friends in Nicaragua, he wished Alison could be with him. He played mind games, shortening the months mathematically, reducing the time until he'd see her again. In a letter to her, he re-created a walk across

Seattle that they had taken many times, where they ended up on a bench with their arms wrapped around each other on Magnolia Boulevard.

Ben knew that he was becoming more immersed in Nicaraguan politics, and he wondered how it would affect their relationship. At the university, when Alison accompanied Ben to teach-ins or protests, he always had to explain the issues, the movements, and the political splits. He loved Alison, but his commitment to politics was a part of him that he was not sure she could ever understand. "I'm very sad at the idea of us not being able to communicate what is so fundamental to my existence," he wrote. "It scares me."

Ben worried that his deepening commitment to the revolution might create a rift with her. He knew that they were on different paths, and that eventually both would have to compromise. He didn't agonize over it, though, because he believed their lives would merge. It was just a matter of time before they got back together, either in Nicaragua, in the United States, or in another country. He was considering graduate school in Europe. "England would be nice because of the language. Sweden sounds beautiful and has a lot of interesting energy work going on. Would you be up to leaving the country in '85? Being with you is the most important thing for the future."

When Ben and Alison parted, he'd told her he would return in August 1984, after working one year in Nicaragua. However, by spring of that year, he decided to finish his INE assignment, which he estimated would take another year. Alison had just been accepted to a one-year internship in costume design at Yale. He wrote that he would visit in the summer of 1984 and return to Nicaragua for another year. Alison wrote back, saying that she understood, but was not pleased. As summer neared, he wrote again. He had decided to postpone his visit until Christmas, because "if I saw you in July or August I couldn't bear to be away from you for another year."

When Alison heard this, she was very upset. Ben hastily reassured her. "I've thought a lot about what I'm doing here and why. But it is often hard to come to an answer. It often seemed that my love for you was being sacrificed for my revolutionary work. But this isn't true. They complement each other .... My dear Alison, I love you. It is our love and our actions that are stronger than death." Then he made plane reservations for December.

In a letter to Peter Stricker, one of the few men in whom Ben confided about his love life, he wrote that in the summer of 1985, he and Alison planned "on forming our life together. And once more we return to 'where.' 'Why' is very clear."

Members of the gringo club became upset by President Reagan's renewal of old charges against the Sandinistas in the fall of 1984. "The Sandinistas seem always to have been anti-Semitic," alleged Reagan. "After the Sandinista takeover, the remaining Jews were terrorized into leaving." On another occasion, he claimed that Sandinista anti-Semitism was "one of the reasons that we must give assistance to those in Central America who are fighting totalitarian anti-religious forces." In Managua, the U.S. embassy carried out an investigation but found no evidence to back Reagan's charges. U.S. ambassador to Nicaragua, Anthony Quainton, concluded in his report; "The evidence fails to demonstrate that the Sandinistas have followed a policy of anti-Semitism or have persecuted Jews solely because of their religion."

Ben knew Alison had heard Washington's charges of anti-Semitism and wrote her, "One of the more common lies about Nicaragua is anti-Semitism. This comes about from two simple facts. 1) Of the few Jews in the country, several were close associates of Somoza and left after the revolution, and 2) the Nicaraguan government takes a very vocal anti-Zionist position. This isn't very surprising as Israel supported Somoza with arms and continues to support Honduras, Guatemala and El Salvador in their repression.... Therefore we are planning an ecumenical Yom Kippur service."

He heard that a rabbi lived in Estelí. He hitchhiked there to find him. Michelle Costa, an American who ran the Spanish language school, directed him to the house of an eighty-one-year-old Polish man named Wosk, who greeted Ben at 8:00 A.M. with a half-empty bottle of rum. He invited Ben in, offered him a banana and a glass of Coca-Cola, and told him that he had never finished his studies to be a rabbi but had sent all his sons, who were doctors and engineers, to the United States or Israel. "As we talked I realized that Jews have a lot in common," noted Ben. But he also realized that the old man, an anti-Sandinista and a Zionist, would not mesh with Father Molina, a liberation-theology priest, and the Sandinista-supporting Americans who would be attending the service.

On October 5, almost two hundred Americans—Jews, Catholics, Protestants, atheists—observed Yom Kippur, the Jewish Day of Atonement, in an outdoor ceremony under a thatched roof. A female cantor from Berkeley, California performed the service. Ben was very touched by the event, and wrote in his journal:

> When justice burns within us like a flaming fire, when love evokes willing sacrifice from us, when, to the last full measure of selfless devotion, we demonstrate our belief in the ultimate triumph of truth and righteousness, then your goodness enters our lives; then you live within our hearts, and we through righteousness behold your presence.
>
> The bush is burning, but the Voice has not yet spoken aloud; we can only feel, guess, hope; we cannot yet hear. But it may be that we must act in order to hear.
>
> I'm working in El Cuá. It is ... the reality of the war. Zelaya province is falling under Contra control. They are killing children.
>
> I've asked myself what is my path. I've asked myself about my love for Alison and my family. I've asked myself about my love for my people. But we must act before we hear.
>
> I must not cower from the task ahead. In Nicaragua I was shown the trail ahead. Tonight I vow to set forth upon that trail.
>
> That is not to forget my love for Alison nor for my family. It is in our love that I find the strength to carry on. I must have the strength not to ever forget them. If I forget them, then how can I love my people? If I forget the love for my people, how can I love those which are so close? Great is the eternal power at the heart of life; mighty the love that is stronger than death.

That day, Ben prayed for the first time in his life.

That same autumn, Congress bitterly debated Contra aid. Democratic congressmen accused the Reagan administration and the CIA of breaking U.S. laws by mining Nicaraguan harbors and producing the "Assassination Manual." Administration spokesmen denied they had broken the law or were trying to overthrow the government of Nicaragua. They still claimed that the administration supported the Contras to interdict arms shipments from Managua to the Salvadoran guerrillas, and to stop Nicaragua from exporting revolution. Republican congressmen accused the Democrats of being soft on communism. U.S. ambassador to the U.N. Jeane Kirkpatrick endorsed the Contra aid, saying, "We certainly do not condone or advocate passive acquiescence in a new totalitarianism in this hemisphere."

On October 10, 1984, the U.S. House and Senate passed the Boland Amendment, which terminated U.S. assistance to the Contras. Carefully worded, the amendment read; "During fiscal year 1985, no funds available to the Central Intelligence Agency, the Department of Defense, or any other agency or entity of the United

States involved in intelligence activities may be obligated or expended for the purpose of which would have the effect of supporting, directly or indirectly, military or paramilitary operations in Nicaragua by any nation, group, organization, movement, or individual." In theory, all aid to the Contras was prohibited.

To mark the first anniversary of the Grenada invasion of October 25, 1983, Ben wrote a play with the gringo club about Ambassador Kirkpatrick, one of the main architects of the Reagan administration's policy toward Nicaragua. In the northern Nicaraguan mountains, a Contra squad called "Jeane Kirkpatrick" had recently been in the news after ambushing a milk truck and kidnapping the driver.

They performed the play in front of the iron gates of the U.S. embassy at the weekly Thursday morning vigil, while some two hundred people, mostly American internationalists, gathered to watch. Behind the backdrop, Ben changed into his clown costume and his bulbous red nose, exchanging his hiking boots for floppy, oversize tennis shoes. George Moore dressed as Kirkpatrick, depicting her as a school-marmish witch. She screeched and bellowed, thrusting a broom at small Central American countries that cowered prostrate before her, while she demanded that the U.S. Marines invade Nicaragua. With his face smeared with black, white, and red greasepaint, Ben emerged as a marionette representing Honduras, with an actor as Uncle Sam hovering over him, pulling the strings. Just as the U.S. Marines were about to invade Nicaragua, performers representing American internationalists threw a bucket of cold water (labeled *solidarity*) at Kirkpatrick, who, like the Wicked Witch, melted away. The crowd cheered.

That fall, Ben asked his parents to send him an absentee ballot for the U.S. presidential elections. Ronald Reagan was running for re-election against Democratic challenger, Senator Walter Mondale. About the same time, campaigning began in Nicaragua for president, vice president, and the ninety-member Assembly in the first elections to be held since the Sandinistas overthrew the Somoza dictatorship. Overnight, billboards for political parties sprouted, and walls were emblazoned with Sandinista red-and-black paint slashes and their campaign slogan, "Seguimos con el Frente" (Forward with the Front). Some 450 international observers and 600 journalists flooded Nicaragua for the electoral campaign.

Six political parties were competing in the election, and foreigners were surprised to find themselves at the center of a political controversy. Virgilio Godoy, presidential candidate of the Liberal Independent Party, had this campaign slogan: "Get the foreigners out of Nicaragua." He accused internationalists of stealing jobs from Nicaraguans, eating Nicaraguans' food, and interfering in government decisions.

It was true that in 1984, tens of thousands of foreigners blanketed Nicaragua, constructing schools, building health clinics, teaching classes, picking coffee and cotton, working in the most isolated, smallest villages. Some foreign professionals—engineers, agronomists, doctors, and teachers—filled the jobs of skilled Nicaraguans who had left the country. Foreigners from eastern bloc nations, such as the USSR, Bulgaria, and East Germany, were paid salaries from their own governments, lived together, and generally worked in the cities. Foreigners from western countries either earned high salaries from their governments or nongovernmental organizations and enjoyed a higher standard of living in Nicaragua than they did in their own countries, or arrived in the country independently, earned córdobas, and barely survived on their meager wages. English speakers dubbed the internationalists "Sandalistas," as they often dressed in loose, hippie clothes and scuffed sandals, while the Contras called them *sapos de los piricuacos*, "frogs of the rabid dogs,"—Sandinista pawns, Communist dupes.

Some foreigners were natural linguists, quickly grasping the culture and fitting easily into Nicaraguan society. Others never learned Spanish or made Nicaraguan friends. Some were open and humble, while others were condescending and righteous to Nicaraguans, professing they knew what was best for the country. Some Nicaraguans welcomed the foreigners and their skills, while others were resentful of their mobility, opportunities, and dollars, and the fact that they chose to live in poverty.

Ben was bothered that the presence of internationalists had become an election issue. Were they unwanted? Were their skills and efforts not appreciated? What did they think about internationalists at INE? "I asked around among the conservatives, liberals and revolutionaries that I know. Where is this coming from?" he wondered. "They said, 'We don't know, Ben. We're glad you're here,' which made me feel good. People on the street realize there just plain aren't enough professionals. Some people are amazed. They say, 'What are you doing here from the U.S.? We hear everyone in your country supports Reagan.'"

As election day neared, the campaigning turned violent. Rowdy *turbas*—Sandinista mobs armed with sticks, stones, and steel bars—broke up election rallies.

Arturo Cruz Sr. moved from Washington, D.C. to run as the presidential candidate of the Coordinadora coalition, a coalition of opposition parties, but in a deliberate tactic to de-legitimize the elections, he withdrew from the ballot, citing unfair campaign practices.

Fearing the Contras would disrupt the elections, the government mobilized army troops around the country. Nevertheless, the Contras ambushed a truck caravan delivering ballots to San José de Bocay.

On November 1, the FSLN closed its campaign with an outdoor rally in front of Lake Managua. Dressed in his clown costume, pedaling his unicycle, blowing a small trumpet, and waving a plastic Sandinista flag, Ben joined some 300,000 Sandinista supporters streaming toward the evening fiesta. Sandinista followers wore red-and-black T-shirts and paper hats and carried banners.

Daniel Ortega, the Sandinista presidential candidate, gave a somber speech about the possibility of U.S. intervention and exhorted everyone to vote. He asked his supporters if they were willing to defend Managua against an invasion, and the crowd roared, "¡No pasarán, no pasarán, no pasarán!" (They won't cross [the borders]!).

After the speeches, Nicaragua's most popular reggae band, Dimensión Costeña took over the stage, playing their hit, "The Banana Song," to a dancing crowd. Ben danced on his unicycle, dashing in and out of the crowd, pirouetting, and rocking to and fro in time. He cycled close to a young, very thin, short-haired woman, a graceful dancer. He shot out his hand to catch hers and swayed back and forth on the unicycle while she moved her hips to the music. The crowd moved back, giving them space, then circled around them, shouting "¡Eso!" and "¡Viva el payaso!" (Long live the clown!). Suddenly firecrackers began to explode, and a man wearing a bamboo frame shaped like a bull charged the crowd, and the thin woman retreated. Ben grabbed her hand and led her behind the band to a quiet, safe spot. The thin woman thanked him and introduced herself as Marlene Rivera, from Colombia. Ben tooted his toy horn in acknowledgment. After the firecrackers stopped, they continued dancing until Chile, as her friends called her, had to leave. "He touched his eyes with his two forefingers, and made a sound, 'pipipipi,' like he was sad."

Around 4:30 A.M. on November 4, election day, the FSLN party activists, many of whom had stayed up all night, began yelling "¡Viva Sandino!" and paraded house to house, banging on doors, singing, waking households with Sandinista serenades.

Ben accompanied Ana to her polling booth, where voters waited in long lines that snaked around mango trees. Nicaraguans were solemn that day. Ben had to write a report on the elections for U.S. solidarity groups. Election officials handed voters two large ballots, one for presidential candidates and another of party slates for the National Assembly. Both ballots had names and symbols of each party, and a circle below where voters were to make an *x*. Inside the booths, behind long curtains, Nicaraguans marked ballots, deposited them in huge boxes, then dipped thumbs in indelible red ink so they could not vote again. "The whole process went fairly smooth given that it was the first time it was ever done," Ben commented. In other parts of the country, however, eleven polling booths never opened because of threats by the Contras. Near El Cuá, six election officials were killed,

After the votes were counted, Ortega won the presidency, with 63 percent of the vote, but the U.S. State Department quickly dismissed the elections, declaring them a "farce" and "a lost opportunity." The U.S. National Security Council dismissed them as "false, Soviet-style elections."

On November 6, Ronald Reagan was re-elected president. That evening, as millions of Americans watched election returns, CBS-TV interrupted its coverage to report some unnamed Washington official's claim that a Soviet ship was delivering the Sandinistas a shipment of advanced Soviet MiG fighter jets. The sophisticated combat planes, U.S. government officials warned, were a provocation to Nicaragua's neighbors, and Washington would not tolerate them.

The Nicaraguan government denied the allegation and accused the United States of preparing international opinion for direct military attacks against their country. Reagan administration officials countered by citing "cratologists," box experts who claimed they could determine the contents from their shapes. When a Soviet freighter was unloaded, it was found to contain Soviet-built Hind helicopters, a powerful new armament for the Sandinista army.

American warships were dispatched to prowl the Nicaraguan coastline, and U.S. troops suddenly began unannounced military maneuvers in Honduras. U.S. SR-71 reconnaissance planes circled Nicaragua, taking photos of military bases and troops and frightening residents with their sonic booms. In the port town of Corinto, the Sandinista army fired antiaircraft guns at an unidentified low-flying plane. Ben wrote to Alison, "Reagan's re-election is bad news. He is making a big stink of the supposed Soviet MiGs. Remember the Maine and the Gulf of Tonkin. The small things that are used as an excuse for U.S. invasions."

The U.S. actions revived fears of a Managua invasion, and officials placed the Sandinista army on alert. Civil rights were once again suspended. Tanks rumbled through the streets and dug into positions at strategic points around the capital. Army officials mobilized neighborhood militias. Managua residents cleaned out bomb shelters, which had become clogged with trash in the year since they had been built. Factories and offices held air-raid drills. Fifteen hundred Cuban teachers working in the countryside were sent back to Cuba, never to return, for fear they would become targets for the United States. Hundreds of high school students planning to pick coffee in the mountains were ordered to remain in Managua to defend the capital, if necessary. Residents drew up evacuation plans and organized rubble-clearing brigades, preparing for the carpet bombing of the capital. Nicaraguans stayed inside, closed doors, shuttered windows, and braced themselves for what would come.

At the United Nations in New York, Nicaragua called for an urgent meeting of the Security Council. In Managua, Ortega held a news conference in the International Press Club. As he denied that his government was receiving MiG fighter jets, a U.S. SR-71 spy plane flew by, sounding a sonic boom and rattling the water glasses. The journalists laughed nervously.

"My dear Alison, I'm not sure how to tell you this," Ben wrote. "The situation is 'deteriorating' to use the diplomatic word. Reagan, it appears, is engaging in a war buildup. Nicaragua is preparing its defense." He told her he was aware of her concern but that he needed to stay. "One day we'll sit in front of the fireplace and think back on these days."

Chapter 7

Working in El Cuá

At the end of 1984, in spite of the tense political situation in Nicaragua, Bertil returned from Sweden on another short-term contract. With decreased Contra activity around the plant, INE resurrected the El Cuá project. The Soviet embassy still forbade Larisa to travel outside Managua. Ben volunteered to help, but was not needed. Disappointed and hurt, Ben reveled in the chaos and disorganization of the project. "Bertil speaks almost no Spanish, Larisa speaks bad Spanish, Morlock and Bertil don't get along, Morlock has too much other work to do, Larisa is leaving for vacation for two months to the Soviet Union, and Bertil leaves in two and a half weeks. Morlock and I came back from the geothermal project only to find Larisa, Bertil and the three students loading up the equipment on the back of a truck to send to El Cuá. I saw the disorganization and chuckled to myself thanking heaven that it wasn't my project." He clearly envied their challenging assignment.

A few days later, Morlock realized that some of the equipment sent to El Cuá was needed in Managua, and Ben, seizing the chance to work on the project, volunteered to retrieve it. Ben wrote his parents, "After Larisa's [last] trip to El Cuá, the Soviet Embassy told her that in no way can she go back up there. That means I'll get to take her place, I hope. It might seem crazy but please don't worry."

Accompanied by a driver and a mechanic, Ben traveled to El Cuá in an unmarked INE jeep. Along the roadside, next to charred vehicles, they passed lines of white crosses, one for each of the ambush victims.

At the plant, Ben, Rigo, and his crew sorted tools, working at a relaxed pace. When Ben began checking off tasks on a list compiled by Larisa, he realized that she was unnecessarily repeating Bertil's work.

In the evenings Ben sat on the bunkhouse stoop, looking out across the River Cuá to the hill beyond where the army had set up mortars and heavy artillery. Ben wrote, "I feel very good here. The mountains that surround the town are stunning. Evening mist going into a sheer rock face in the distance. Today there was a double rainbow with one end towards the plant. A good omen."

As dusk fell, the town's civilian residents, militia men with AK-47 rifles slung over their shoulders, trudged to guard posts at the town's perimeter. Teenagers wearing oversize camouflage shirts and rubber boots awkwardly carried guns and struggled to keep up with their fathers.

Ben wrote Alison, "When I got to El Cuá I realized that no one had any idea what they were doing. Bertil hadn't done shit to keep track of the project, Larisa didn't know what was happening and Morlock was busy. So there I was, the youngest and least-paid engineer, in a beautiful part of the world with the calm of dusk bouncing down a dirt road with the errors of my elders. Really, I've ended up running the show."

Carlos, the town doctor, frequently wandered out of his cubicle in the bunkhouse and joined Ben, passing him a bottle of rum. Carlos told Ben he had gone to medical school in Mexico. He set up practice there, made money, and enjoyed the good life, but eventually, as Nicaragua disintegrated into war, he felt guilty about abandoning his country, and returned home "to find himself in El Cuá," wrote Ben.

Carlos was the only doctor in town. Before doctors had arrived in the valley, farmers bought pills and brews from traveling medicine hawkers or visited traditional healers, who used home remedies. Due to poor nutrition, sanitation practices and health care, it was common for mothers in the area to have lost three, four, or five children, who often died before they were one.

In 1979, after the revolution, the first doctors in El Cuá held consultations in farmers' homes. Soon they built an eight-by-three-yard shed that served as a clinic. In 1981 West German doctors arrived, bringing the region's first ambulance. They raised funds from local farmers and coffee growers and converted the town's jail, known as La Chiquita, into a health clinic. The avocado tree in front of the building, where prisoners used to be tied, now shaded a porch where mothers lined up with sick children.

The Sandinista Health Ministry restructured the rural health care system, basing it on *brigadistas*, or volunteers from local villages. At workshops in El Cuá, nurses taught *brigadistas* preventive medicine. When *brigadistas* returned to their isolated hamlets, they hiked from farmhouse to farmhouse, carrying bright orange coolers full of measles and polio vaccines. They inoculated children and treated families for malaria, tuberculosis, leishmaniasis ("mountain leprosy"), worms, diarrhea, whooping cough, and respiratory diseases. Since 68 percent of the region's children under five suffered from malnutrition, *brigadistas* also taught families to eat fruits and vegetables when available. Eventually, three Nicaraguan doctors were assigned to the Cuá/Bocay region, where they looked after some 33,000 people.

In 1983 a group of Contras assassinated West German doctor Albrecht Pflaum in Zompopera, thirty miles southwest of El Cuá. As a result, the other West German doctors were whisked out of the area. That same year the Contras ambushed and burned El Cuá's only ambulance and began kidnapping and killing *brigadistas*, easy targets as they hiked along trails with their bright orange coolers. *Brigadistas* became afraid to leave their hamlets, and vaccination campaigns were canceled. In 1984 a measles epidemic swept through the mountains north of El Cuá, killing weak, malnourished children.

Many of the medical problems in El Cuá stemmed from the residents' lack of education about sanitation. People defecated in fields or between houses. In a town of 2,000, there were only four latrines, some of which emptied raw sewage into the nearby river, while children scooped up drinking water downstream. Carlos told Ben that two children had died from worms that year, while many others had succumbed to diarrhea and other preventable illnesses. He was training a village woman as a health volunteer to teach sanitation.

The constant tension of the war also led to emotional and psychological problems. Some children were almost catatonic, traumatized by seeing parents and teachers kidnapped or shot. When Contras passed isolated farms, they often kidnapped men. The wives left behind were petrified that the Contras would return to abduct them.

Although they were rarely seen, the Contras were never far away. Residents of El Cuá were often jolted awake at night by bursts of machine-gun fire in the distant hills. Townspeople froze, sucking in their breaths, waiting to hear if the gunfire would come closer, or fade away. The militia men rushed to fortify the guard posts.

One morning Ben stopped by the health center, and Marilú Reyes, a short, energetic, dark-eyed nurse, showed him the clinic, one room with a few bare cots lit by candles and kerosene lanterns. Medicine was stored in the diesel-powered refrigerator. Outside, thin mothers with even thinner children lined up to see the doctor. The children's stomachs were bloated with parasites, their skin darkened by perpetual malaria, their bodies covered with flea and horsefly bites, and their eyes hollowed by chronic malnutrition. Most did not own shoes. Chiggers burrowed into their feet, keeping them awake at night. Ben made faces to amuse them, but some of the children were so malnourished and listless that they did not respond. "I see the kids," Ben wrote, "and I feel like taking them all away to a safe place to hide until the war stops and the hunger stops and El Cuá becomes strong enough to give them the care they deserve. The pied piper of El Cuá. But I can't do that, and even if I could it wouldn't help the neighboring towns. So instead, I try to put in light, and hope for the best."

While there, Ben also met Casilda de Rizo, the principal of the town's only school. She managed the three-room building that educated some two hundred first-through fourth-graders, and taught morning and afternoon sessions. She often invited Ben for coffee at her small, neat, black-and-white cement-and-wood house on the plaza. There Ben met her husband, Octavio, a lieutenant in the army, and performed magic tricks for their four small children.

Casilda had arrived in El Cuá just before the revolution in 1979, a new bride and one of four teachers in the Cuá/Bocay region. Every day, on her way to the schoolhouse, she walked past the National Guard post, sneaking glances at Somoza's soldiers. "One day in 1979, right in front of the school, a guardsman used his bayonet to cut off the ear of a long-haired teenager," said Casilda. "They suspected men with long hair of being guerrillas. The children were at recess and watched everything; the guardsman yelled at me to get the kids out of there!"

After the revolution, Casilda helped coordinate hundreds of *brigadistas* on a five-month literacy crusade, teaching farmers to read and write. One of the earliest anti-Sandinista groups killed a teacher near San José de Bocay.

Following the crusade, Casilda worked with the Sandinista Ministry of Education, opening thirty-eight new schools in the mountains around the region. Casilda was still one of the few teachers from the area.

Like the health system, the new educational system relied on volunteers. Teachers instructed *promotores*, who in turn taught adult education classes in their small hamlets. Casilda helped set up adult classes, and in the evenings, farmers huddled around Coleman lanterns or smoky kerosene lamps, grasping pencils between leathery fingers, awkwardly tracing the alphabet.

The Contras soon began targeting teachers, whom they accused of spreading Communist propaganda. By 1984 they had killed five teachers and kidnapped more than forty others in the area. Teachers were pulled out of the countryside, and many schools that Casilda had just opened were closed.

Ben liked to hear Casilda's stories about her early days in El Cuá and often visited her in the evenings or on weekends, following his typical workday; as he described to Allison:

> Up at 5:30 A.M. We are in the mountains and there is a chill to the morning. Rigoberto would have been up for half an hour and already bathed in the very little stream behind the house. It is really little more than a trickle that fills a big pot that we dip a washpan into. I drag myself out of bed and wash up.
>
> 6:30 and we drive to a farmhouse half hour from town. Coffee, rice, beans and tortillas. Usually sour cream and a dry salty cheese. Off to the plant to work. It is filled with frustrations as things don't fit or don't work. Today was trying, as a lot didn't work. What I would have given to come home and disappear from the work in your embrace. Instead I took my second bath of the day in the small chilly stream which passes by the project. Lying in the cool water cleanses away much of the frustrations. But there is more work ahead.

At noon, the work crew returned to the farmhouse to eat rice and beans, or meat if a neighbor killed a cow. They continued working until 4:00 P.M., when Ben often took a bath in the cement canal of the powerhouse. At 6:00 P.M. they returned to the farmhouse for dinner, then hurried into town as darkness fell. Ben spent the evening talking and often drinking rum with Rigoberto and Dr. Carlos. By 10:00 P.M. he was asleep on his cot.

As Ben spent more time working on the hydroplant, he realized that Bertil's shoddy design work meant many of the parts specifically ordered from the Managua machine shop were the wrong size and had to be remade. Each change delayed the work by days. Every engineer who had worked there "either welded something to it or drilled a hole" in the generator. Excited about the chance of succeeding where his predecessors had failed, Ben began thinking about staying in Nicaragua longer. He missed Alison, but he wished she would want to join him in Nicaragua.

As Ben prepared for his return to Managua in the INE jeep, Rigo warned him to be careful driving back.

"I'd be lying if I said that there isn't anything to worry about. There is. But please don't worry too much. Trust that what I do, living in Nicaragua, isn't stupid—dangerous perhaps, but not stupid," Ben wrote to his parents.

When Ben returned with the vehicle full of parts and tools, and a detailed list of jobs to be done in El Cuá, Morlock was impressed by his efficiency. A few weeks later, he sent him to the plant again.

When Ben returned to El Cuá, the town seemed strangely silent. "I drove down the main street and, looking at the health center, I saw the ambulance was pulled off to one side, and it didn't have any tires," Ben noted. The white Toyota loaded with medical supplies had been in a caravan with two trucks taking food to a coffee plantation when it was machine-gunned by the Contras, wounding two people, and killing Marilú, the nurse. News of Marilú's death made Ben feel the reality of war for the first time since he began working in El Cuá. "She was full of such life and happiness," he remembered sadly.

One day, a local plant employee named Oscar asked Ben to take photos of his children. Ben followed him past the whitewashed buildings of the La Chata cooperative, down a muddy path lined with coffee bushes to El Golfo, a town of one-room wooden houses strung along a valley. Oscar lived in a ten-foot square shack, with his wife Hilda, their two children, and his mother-in-law. A corn-milling machine was attached to a homemade table, and clothes hung from a rope stretched across the room. The only bed was a board with a thin mattress pushed against one wall. A glass-fronted frame held baby photos.

Oscar was born on a farm outside Estelí, where his family grew corn and beans, and he learned to ride a mule before he could walk. After second grade, Oscar left school to swing a machete in the fields alongside his father.

When Oscar was a teenager in the 1970s, Estelí was a hotbed of clandestine Sandinista activity. Somoza's soldiers were suspicious of all young men who were not in the National Guard and frequently beat Oscar with their rifles, accusing him of supporting the guerrillas. Oscar's brother, a twelve-year-old shoeshine boy, aided the Sandinistas by distributing flyers, which he hid in his shoeshine box. When the National Guard killed him, Oscar said, he joined the guerrillas because he wanted to avenge his brother's death. "I saw that, for the National Guard, being young was a crime," he said.

In 1978 Oscar and another brother melted into the mountains with the Sandinista guerrillas. They traveled by foot, mostly at night, dodging National Guard patrols. They moved fast, going days without food, and finally set up camp in the mountains near Zinica. Oscar fell ill with dysentery while his brother returned to the cities to help launch an offensive. He was later killed in the Estelí takeover.

After regaining his strength, Oscar joined a guerrilla column that stayed in the mountains, attacking guard posts in small villages. In early July 1979 his column entered El Cuá. The three guardsmen in town had already fled, leaving the door of the jail unlocked. The guerrillas torched El Abejón, a bar and brothel run under the auspices of the National Guard. Residents of El Cuá flocked to the dirt road to welcome the fighters. By the next morning, the guerrillas had gone south for the takeover of Jinotega.

When the Sandinistas came to power, Oscar joined the border guards. He quickly tired of military life and quit after just one year. When a friend told him about a job building a hydroelectric plant in El Cuá, he signed on, leaving his wife and four children behind in Estelí. He met Hilda, "stole" her at age sixteen without her mother's permission, and began another family in El Cuá.

After spending time with Oscar, Ben wrote, "He's very smart and will probably end up being the operator of the plant. But his life is hard. The Contras operate close to his house, the army puts pressure on him, and life is expensive. He deserves better. So many deserve more than this shitty world has to offer. 10–20 years of peace and this country could put itself together. But with this damned war what is there?"

While working at the plant, Ben also got to know twenty-one-year-old Federico Ramos, one of the men who had worked on the project from the beginning. Oscar and Federico had met Bertil and Larisa, but Ben was the first foreigner with whom they became friends. "He never treated us like a *patrón*, like he was the engineer and we were his helpers. No, we all shared the work, and we were treated as equals," said Oscar.

As Oscar and Federico began to trust Ben, they began to discuss politics and social conditions in the countryside. Federico said that, before the revolution, his family, like almost all other poor families, worked on large haciendas during the harvest seasons, picking coffee for cash. They worked dawn to dusk for low pay, and were often fed tortillas and beans, since plantation owners considered rice a luxury. Ben recalled how Oscar and Federico described the brutal conditions, and how desperate peasants were to earn cash:

> For this cash they sold themselves to the coffee barons. "Sold" is the only way to describe it. To simply say "worked for" doesn't describe the slave-like work and the subhuman living conditions.
> This is the key to understanding the historical violence of underdevelopment. It is a much deeper, more painful, violence than that of mortars, guns and helicopters. I see people shitting upstream from where others get drinking water; I see people taking water out of the center of the river because it is "cleaner." The other day I saw the mother of five kids using her feet to wash the corn for the day's tortillas, the same feet which walk around the kitchen where the pig, the dog and the kids all sleep. The littlest three kids all have the distended stomachs of parasites with malnutrition. But it is more than just health. Hours a day women carry firewood and water. Why are there so few oxen? Were people so much cheaper than animals, especially women? Why were relatively well-planned water systems put in for the coffee processing, but not for people? Was coffee and the money it made that much more important than the lives of so many children? Education wasn't "needed" for the mozos [day laborers], neither was health care, nor shoes (except for the men in the fields), nor a house which offered the basics for a dignified life. All that I wrote about are part of the violence of Cuá/Bocay. Violence which year after year repeated itself. The effects are still deeply woven into many people's lives and habits.

Ben believed that the revolution was slowly improving social conditions in the countryside, but progress was hampered by the war. He was reminded of the war's constant presence when the director of the huge Central American Hydroelectric Plant, Aldo Rivera Rodríguez, was ambushed and killed by the Contras twelve miles north of Jinotega. His wife and another passenger were wounded.

Ben returned to Managua just as the Contras escalated attacks against coffee pickers in the northern mountains. On November 14, along the road to El Cuá, the Contras attacked the government coffee farm of La Sorpresa, killing seventeen people. The Contras put guns in the peasant's mouths and pulled the triggers. The stomachs of pregnant women were sliced open with bayonets. The next day, six government officials and a local journalist died in another ambush.

On December 4, the Contras attacked a truckload of volunteer coffee pickers, employees of the government-owned telecommunications company (TELCOR), northeast of Estelí. The Contras overwhelmed the eleven militia members accompanying them and bayoneted the wounded. They stripped the bodies of boots and clothes, and poured diesel fuel on the truck and set it afire, burning seven civilians alive, including a taxi driver and a five-year-old child.

Two days later, in Estelí, the twenty-two dead were buried. As the funeral procession wound from the cathedral to the cemetery, dozens of taxis followed the caskets, blowing their horns in a sad, slow cadence.

In spite of the attacks, Americans who supported the Sandinistas continued to stream into Nicaragua in 1984. In December, just as the first group of some six hundred American volunteer coffee pickers arrived, Ben left the country for Christmas vacation. He arrived at Kennedy International Airport in New York, where Alison was waiting for him. They had been apart for seventeen months.

When Alison first saw Ben, she noticed he was tan, thinner, and had grown a sparse beard. His brownish-reddish hair was bleached. In spite of the physical changes, he was the same Ben that she remembered, as he teased her and asked a dozen questions about her life at Yale. Ben stayed in her dormitory, ate at the cafeteria, and attended classes in costume construction and mask making, like old times.

However, in the days that followed, Alison noted how Ben had changed. He now ate meat, ravenously devouring pot stickers, tempura, chicken, roast beef, and steak. He was more serious and determined, and at the same time restless and uneasy.

While Alison studied for final exams, Ben took the train into New York and wandered around, gazing at the store windows crammed with consumer items, watching the crowds, and visiting Rockefeller Center's Christmas tree. He sat for an artist who wanted to paint his portrait in Washington Square Park and was taken aback when she asked for money. "He showed his culture shock through his vulnerability," said Alison.

In a radio interview, Ben described his feelings about flying in from a country in the throes of war. "[In Nicaragua] we try to do so much with so little," he said, while "the intense commercialism and waste in the U.S. ... it was shocking. I just looked at the [Rockefeller Center Christmas tree] lights and said, 'This is pretty,' but somehow felt very, very removed from it. To feel so removed from this country which I love so much was rather shocking to me. It seems so sad that we waste so much. When you think of how much good could be done in Nicaragua and other countries of the developing world. There is so much that could be done here at home. The people of New York go hungry at the same time that millions of dollars are spent on the Christmas tree—it just isn't right."

While in Manhattan, Ben also visited some engineering firms and organizations, with hopes of convincing them to donate textbooks to Nicaragua, but "he only found closed doors," according to Alison. Ben returned to Yale depressed, telling Alison that no one wanted to help Nicaragua, that everyone believed the "Teflon president," Ronald Reagan, who referred to Nicaragua as "the enemy," and Daniel Ortega as "a tinpot dictator."

Alison told Ben she was considering another year at Yale. He good-naturedly said he would look into options for engineers in the area, or consider graduate school. But he also revealed that he was working on an interesting project in Nicaragua, and might stay there for another year. "He told me (and he would always say this) 'I need one more year to accomplish what I need to accomplish,'" said Alison.

During Christmas vacation, they flew to Seattle to visit college friends and planned their future. Alison promised to spend the following summer with him in Nicaragua, and Ben promised her that by summer, 1986, they'd be living together.

He went on to Portland, Oregon, during an unusually cold winter. The city was covered in snow, and the whole family gathered at the Linders' yellow house nestled in the pines for Christmas. Ben talked politics with his brother John, and stationed himself in the kitchen, frequently opening the refrigerator to survey the cheeses, cold cuts, and leftovers. Elisabeth could not remember the last time Ben ate meat, and was surprised to see him "go crazy over a pot roast."

Elisabeth also noted that her son seemed distant. He met with friends doing solidarity work, but he didn't phone his old high school group. He seemed uninterested in local events and alienated from his own culture.

To Ben, these concerns seemed petty. Although he enjoyed the comforts of his parents' house, he was anxious to return to his world. He borrowed Elisabeth's car to shop for tools, mechanical parts, and baseball caps to take back with him. He set up a whirlwind schedule of meetings, running from radio shows to church groups to solidarity committees, always talking about Nicaragua.

David and Elisabeth were well-known community activists, and Ben asked if they could get progressive friends to adopt Barrio La Radial, where he had helped dig a bomb shelter. "Ben said to me, 'Can't you get your neighborhood to establish a sister neighborhood project with a barrio?'" said Elisabeth. "They wanted to get bricks to build a wall; and I said, 'No way!' and he said, 'Why not?'; but I'm not a good organizer, and I couldn't even conceive of how we would talk people into anything like that."

David and Elisabeth worried that he was frittering his time away in Nicaragua and becoming "culturally strange." He talked about people they didn't know and places they had never seen. They supported his projects and beliefs, but they were relieved when he told them he was considering graduate school and returning to the United States.

Ben received a letter from Alison just before flying back to Nicaragua. He reread it several times, stared out the window of his childhood bedroom, and began to cry. Finally, he wrote her back:

> I wish you were here. So many times in Nicaragua I dreamed about getting off the plane and seeing you. It was even better in real life than the dreams. December will always go down as one of the high points in my life. I'm beginning to dream about meeting you in Nicaragua.
> I missed you, still do, so much that every time I wasn't talking to someone I'd think of you, seeing you at the airport in New York, riding up to New Haven, being in your arms, walking around town, sitting in the costume shop, and just *being* with you.

He described his inability to concentrate, how he packed his schedule with meetings and needed the stimulus of other people to stop from being depressed in the States. Portland no longer *felt* like home.

In mid-January, 1985, just days after Daniel Ortega was sworn in as president, Ben flew back to Nicaragua. On the Aeronica plane the stewardess announced, "We are about to land in the free territory of Nicaragua. Please fasten your seat belts." The plane swooped low over grayish Lake Managua, flew along a mountain ridge, and eased down over sprawling wooden shanties. To a visitor arriving from the United States, Managua looked small, sparse, and poor.

The three daily flights from Miami all arrived around dusk at Sandino Airport. Passengers emerged from the plane into the muggy evening and descended a rolling staircase onto the tarmac. "The last several days in the States I felt a cramp of nervousness in my stomach," Ben wrote. "Then, as I got off the plane in Managua, the hot wind washed over me and I was home. The tensions of being in the States all faded away. I was back in my town."

As soon as he could wrangle permission from INE, Ben left for El Cuá, where he enjoyed "feeling the old familiar bumps in the road." After smiles, handshakes, and backslaps with Rigo, Oscar, and Federico, Ben entered the powerhouse while the others waited outside, wearing the baseball caps he had given them. On the workbench was a note, clumsily hand-lettered in English: "Wellcome back Ben. We continued to work." Ben's eyes clouded with tears as he realized that none of the other foreign engineers who had worked on the project had ever returned. "I was so touched," he wrote.

The village buzzed at the height of harvest season. "Everyone is either picking coffee or sorting out the bad beans from the good. It's amazing the amount of time that goes into a cup of coffee," he observed. Farmers led strings of pack mules out of the mountains, hundred-pound sacks of coffee berries slung over their backs, and waited in long lines in front of the coffee warehouse. There, government workers sorted, weighed, and bought the beans. Farmers cashed checks for their harvest and spent most of the money immediately, buying lacy dresses, jeans, plastic sandals, powdered milk or candy for children, and shiny machetes and black rubber boots for themselves. In the evening, the roar of the Disamar saloon's smelly diesel generator filled the night while farmers drank rum shots and stumbled home.

As Ben was working in the powerhouse one day, a soldier arrived on a motorcycle with a note from the army lieutenant, asking if he could borrow their pickup. There were only three vehicles in town, and a band of Contras had been spotted a few miles away. As the soldier drove off in the INE pickup, he told the crew to defend the hydroplant if the Contras were chased that way.

Rigo, Ben, and the crew huddled in the powerhouse, discussing what to do. They didn't have guns, so they couldn't defend the plant, or themselves. Cannons and howitzers boomed from the mountains. The crew heard the swoop of multiple rocket launchers, the tense silence as the projectiles flew toward their targets, then the chilling fall, as deadly shards blanketed an area the size of a football field. The crew ran out of the powerhouse, leaving the turbine in pieces on the floor, and scouted the ridges around the plant, looking for Contras, not finding anything. On the dirt road below, truckloads of soldiers, reinforcements from Bocay, zoomed by.

When the shooting ended, Oscar hiked into town, returning with the news that fifteen Contras had been killed, and the Army had won the battle. Three of the corpses were laid out in the plaza.

Ben had never been so close to a battle before, and his reaction was typical of an adventurous twenty-five-year-old. Exhilarated by his first brush with war, and pleased that the Sandinistas had won the battle, he wondered, "What is it all about? Here I am in the middle of a goddamned war building a hydroelectric plant. I like it up here."

Within a few days, however, Ben's enthusiasm was tempered after visiting Casilda's house, where a huge black bow hung above the door. Inside, he found Casilda's four young children strangely silent and Casilda, eyes ringed with dark circles, dressed in black. Her husband Octavio had been ambushed by the Contras near Pita del Carmen while delivering food. Octavio, who was an army lieutenant, jumped out of the truck and returned fire, but after an hour of fighting, he was among the five people killed.

When the road was safe to travel, Ben returned to Managua, relieved to be back in the capital.

In February 1985 Evergreen graduate Mira Brown returned to Nicaragua as a mechanic with the first donated shipment of bicycles from the Bikes not Bombs organization. She met Ben again at the diner across the street from INE. Since she last saw him seven months ago, she had gotten hepatitis A, recovered, put together a slide show, and showed it across the United States. She had also organized the Nicaragua Appropriate Technology Project (NICAT), a solidarity group that financed technology projects in Nicaragua.

Mira thought Ben would be pleased but was taken aback when, instead of praising her, he launched into a lecture. "He talked about how outsiders affect the development policy by making arbitrary choices about what needs aid and what doesn't," Mira said.

However, when Mira confided that the real reason she had returned was to hunt for a job, he was more supportive, and offered to circulate her résumé around INE, telling her he'd pressure the employment office to get her a work visa. Mira was sure that Ben's help would land her a job.

Ben returned to El Cuá in February. The crew was shorthanded, with one worker drafted, and two others ordered by the government to pick coffee. Ben, Rigo, and Oscar puzzled over a thirteen-inch vibrating pipe on the penstock and a sticky valve. "Each success leads to new problems," he noted. "Yesterday's work was a success. That meant that today we moved one step further. But that introduces new problems which have me completely confused. I have no idea what the solutions are. It's hard at times like this." Ben knew the others were counting on him to solve the problems, but he also felt that it was impossible to accomplish anything on his short trips to El Cuá. "What I'd give to stay up here for a good month or two. Often when I'm here I think of how nice it would be to just build a little house and disappear into this small mountain village," he wrote.

Alone in El Cuá, Ben's thoughts often turned to Alison. He could not wait until she came to spend the summer with him. He wrote, "It will soon be between the 28th of Feb. and the 1st of March—sounds like our anniversary to me. Oh boy!! For five years, I've enjoyed the warmth and compassion of our love. Thank you my dearest of friends."

The next time Ben returned to Managua and called his parents, they asked him about a *New York Times* article by Stephen Kinzer about two teachers who were killed on the road to El Cuá. The two women, nineteen and twenty-two years old, had volunteered to teach in the war zone and were returning to their assignments when the Contras attacked their jeep. Ben said he had heard about it, and assured them they should not worry.

Ben tracked down Morlock and asked him if he could work on El Cuá full-time. Bertil was gone, and Larisa had not yet returned from vacation. However, Morlock advised him that the piping layouts for Mount Momotombo were important, and El Cuá would have to wait. Ben knew El Cuá was not a priority for INE, since it was a small project in a dangerous area that would only benefit some 2,000 people. He knew that INE needed its few skilled engineers to maintain the electrical power grids in the cities, but he did not understand why Morlock insisted that he work on Mount Momotombo, the huge geothermal project outside of Managua. While Ben found the project interesting, he wondered how serious Morlock was about the Momotombo project. In spite of his supervisor's motives, Ben wanted to do a good job, so when he heard that an engineer who specialized in piping was in Managua on a TecNica delegation, he rolled up his drawings and took them to Casa San Juan. The piping specialist took one look at the plans and ripped apart all the work Ben had done for the last nine months. When Ben walked out of Casa

San Juan with the new piping diagrams, he was devastated. He had never studied piping; he had studied hydroplants. *That* is what he should have been working on.

After that incident, Ben became more determined to work in El Cuá. When he heard that a group of Swedish engineers were examining an old hydroplant in Diriamba, an hour's drive from Managua, he sent for the El Cuá crew to come down to work with them. Rigo, Oscar, and Federico, who had never been to the capital, left on the next public transport truck.

The El Cuá crew worked alongside Swedish engineers on the Aguacate hydroplant, which had been shut down many years before. After working on the Aguacate plant for a week, Rigo, Oscar, and Federico agreed that putting together the El Cuá plant would be easy. Ben wondered if and when he would be able to work with them on the project.

Chapter 8

A Decision about Alison

While Ben was stuck in the INE office in Managua, his spirits were buoyed by the arrival of another American engineer, Rebecca Leaf. Rebecca was given a job planning and supervising the maintenance of power plants. In her assigned division, she was the only person with a degree in engineering.

Rebecca was older than many of her colleagues, with a distinguished shock of gray in her short black hair. When she was in her twenties, Rebecca had worked as a potter and returned to college at age twenty-eight, graduating from MIT in 1982. That same year, she visited a friend in Nicaragua and decided to work in the Third World, but wanted to get experience working as an engineer in the United States first. When she began job hunting, she recalled, "I was appalled that the only offers I got for the first six months of my job search were for military contract work." She refused to work on military applications and finally found a job developing a new ceramic for heat exchanges at a company that worked with metallurgical and power companies. After three years there, she submitted her résumé to TecNica.

On her first day at INE, Ben questioned her on hydraulic governors and politics, and they realized their common interests. "We had an affinity based on the fact that we had gone through the same process of thinking about engineering and came up with same ideas of what we wanted to do; the type of training we wanted and how we wanted to use it, which created an instant bond between us," said Rebecca.

She fervently plunged into her job, but was dismayed by INE's shortage of trained personnel and lack of technical books, engineering papers, journals, and access to information, and shocked by her coworkers' incompetence. She complained that no one planned ahead or thought about long-term consequences. Ben explained that part of their job was to change the "patch and fix" mentality, which was a result of colonialism and underdevelopment.

Rebecca felt overwhelmed. Blackouts frequently occurred in the capital, and she felt under constant pressure, never knowing when the next oil shipment would arrive or when replacement parts would be found. Her job seemed to her a losing battle, especially when INE announced electricity cuts to each sector of the capital for four hours a day.

Ben listened sympathetically. He taught her the importance of networking and trading; how a person with cement would repair a house for someone who could repair his car. "Ben was very gregarious," said Rebecca. "He'd meet an engineer from some factory at a party, and before the party was over he would know everything that was going on in that factory. He constantly had his feelers out."

One evening after work, Ben and Rebecca heard drumbeats as they walked through Barrio Riguero. A *gigantona*, a ten-foot-tall puppet with a person inside, danced and whirled in the middle of the street. Two drummers and a poet, who accompanied the *gigantona*, knew Ben and stopped to talk. He introduced them to Rebecca. The giant puppet bowed formally, and the poet stared at Rebecca, taking in the gray shock of hair over her forehead. He paused as the drummers beat out a hypnotic rhythm, and the giant doll rolled, dipped, and danced. The poet sang,

> *Esta mujer que anda allí*
> *tiene el pelo mal pintado.*
> *Piensa que es bonita*
> *pero parece un coco pelado.*

> This woman who comes wandering by
> has had a terrible haircut.
> She thinks it looks pretty
> but it looks like a peeled coconut.

Rebecca and Ben laughed, as the dancer, drummers, and poet snaked down the street, followed by screaming children.

Rebecca was looking for housing, and Ben arranged for her to stay with the family of Franklin Brooks, the oldest son of Ana and Rodolfo. Ben frequently dropped by the house, which was a block away, inviting Rebecca out to *fritanga*, beer, or the circus, but Rebecca often preferred to stay by herself.

In the winter of 1985, President Reagan introduced a bill in Congress asking for $14 million in military aid for the Contras. At a news conference, Reagan revealed that he felt the Contras were "the moral equal of our Founding Fathers and the brave men and women of the French Resistance." He believed the Sandinistas had imposed a "brutal dictatorship" and planned "to turn Central America into a Soviet beachhead of aggression that could spread terror and instability north and south, disrupt our vital sea lanes, cripple our ability to carry out our commitments to our European allies, and send tens of millions of refugees streaming in a human tidal wave across the border." Before the vote, eight U.S. Congress delegations visited Nicaragua on fact-finding tours.

In Honduras, the U.S. Army stepped up joint military maneuvers with the Honduran army. U.S. soldiers built or enlarged eight airfields, including an 8,000-foot all-weather runway at the new U.S. Army headquarters at Palmerola. The runway was capable of handling any military plane, including jumbo C-5 and C-141 transport planes and jet fighters. The Nimitz aircraft carrier and the battleship Iowa "showed the flag" off the Nicaraguan coast. The National Security Agency installed sophisticated electronic eavesdropping posts on Tiger Island, near northwestern Nicaragua, and the 1,200 U.S. troops stationed in Honduras were augmented by rotations of state National Guard units, who constructed more roads and military bases. Some 6,600 marines and paratroopers staged an amphibious landing and air assault. Tank exercises were conducted near the Honduran/Nicaraguan border. In the densely forested mountains near the Contra camps on the border, Sandinistas and Contras clashed during five days of heavy fighting.

Meanwhile, in the United States, the FBI admitted conducting more than a hundred "interviews" with U.S. citizens returning from Nicaragua but denied "harassing" Americans, even though FBI agents visited TecNica volunteers at their jobs, and many travelers to Nicaragua were audited by the IRS upon their return.

Americans who objected to the Reagan administration's policies toward Nicaragua were alarmed by the increasing hostile rhetoric emanating from Washington. They began circulating the "Pledge of Resistance," a church-inspired campaign that enlisted tens of thousands of Americans to carry out acts of civil disobedience if the United States invaded Nicaragua.

In Nicaragua, Sandinista officials, worried about the Reagan administration's escalating threats, stationed tanks around Managua. One tank halted in front of the INE office, parked next to the diner. Young soldiers crawled out, dug ditches and emplacements, and hung a plastic tarp from a tree to shade themselves.

On April 24, 1985, troubled by reports of Contra atrocities and human rights abuses, the U.S. House of Representatives rejected Reagan's request for $14 million in military aide, but the Senate later approved $38 million in "non-lethal" aid, which included food, boots, and uniforms. The bill gave the CIA power to administer the aid and to provide intelligence information to the Contras. After the House rejected his request, the president announced a trade embargo against Nicaragua on May 1, claiming that the country's actions "constitute an unusual and extraordinary threat to the national security and foreign policy of the United States."

In Managua, INE employees heard a special bulletin on Radio La Voz de Nicaragua, and were confused about what the embargo meant. Nicaragua sold 70 percent of its exports—including most of its coffee, shellfish, cotton, and beef—to the United States. Likewise, Nicaragua imported most of its machines, repair parts, agricultural tools, and electrical equipment from the United States. If all trade ended, where would the country get spare parts? The embargo also banned Aeronica, Nicaragua's only airline, from landing on U.S. soil, ending flights to Miami the very next day.

Within weeks, U.S.-manufactured equipment and parts became almost impossible to find, as panicked Nicaraguans hoarded mechanical parts and emptied shelves in hardware stores. The embargo's effects were felt immediately. In the countryside, teachers could no longer get burners for Coleman lanterns and were forced to switch to smoky diesel lamps. In the cities, mechanics were unable to find repair parts for Ford and Chevrolet cars, John Deere tractors, and Bluebird buses. "Instead of designing a piece of equipment, I have to first go out and look for screws ... see what spare parts I can buy. Then I have to go to the shop and see what drill bits they have. Then I design my piece; there's a very definite limitation due to the embargo, the shortage of foreign currency and the general economic crisis in Central America," wrote Ben.

Some U.S.-manufactured spare parts were imported through Panama, but the most important conduit for sneaking parts around the embargo was U.S. solidarity groups. However, when they sent packages through the mail, boxes often arrived opened in Managua, often with contents missing, and resealed with red tape that read: "Opened by U.S. Customs for Export Examination." Boxes arrived from Miami with "Death to the Revolution" scribbled on them.

U.S. customs officials began searching Americans traveling to Nicaragua, seizing luggage they suspected of breaking the ban. When NICAT sent a water quality laboratory, officials in Miami confiscated it. Mira wrote, "Customs said he had to search luggage, looking for 'electronic equipment,' opened the black bag the water lab was in, said it looked like electronic equipment and he took it. Told [the person that] he could pick it up at the airline counter when he returned in two weeks. Of course it wasn't there." Journalists were not immune. *Washington Post* stringer Nancy Nusser had to call the State Department before customs officials in Miami allowed her to take her laptop computer with her to Nicaragua.

The Reagan administration also pressured European and Latin American governments to stop aid to Nicaragua, and Washington officials canceled loans from multilateral lending agencies to Nicaragua. Shortages in Managua worsened.

That spring, Ben began receiving fewer letters, and even his *Juggler's Magazine* arrived irregularly. Feeling estranged from Alison, his family, and friends in the United States, he encouraged his brother and sister to write, then scolded them when they didn't. "John and Miriam. If the best you can do is a shared postcard you should be ashamed." When Ben received a letter from his father telling him that Miriam had decided against visiting Nicaragua, and John was unsure of how to relate to "a more grown-up Ben," he was saddened. Nicaraguan families treated even the most distant relatives like brothers and sisters. He thought of how he barely knew his relatives. He didn't want a gulf to open between him and his family. "As I plan my life away from the U.S. I wonder about its cost," he wrote. "I'm finding? putting? myself away from my family, but not because I want to be away. That is a cost. This year and next I'm willing to pay, but in ten years?"

At least Ben still had Alison. He sent her a series of letters, describing what they'd do when she spent the summer in Nicaragua, but day after day, his glass-fronted post office box remained empty. Ben told himself that she was probably busy with her classes.

In late May, the dry heat finally broke. The rains began, the city became green again, and Ben thought of El Cuá. Neither Bertil nor Larisa had returned to Nicaragua, and the Swedish engineers at INE expressed no interest in continuing the work in El Cuá. Ben was the only one interested, and after much arguing, he convinced his supervisor to allow him to return.

That spring, the Contras began to use a new weapon in the countryside: land mines. Supply planes airdropped Claymore land mines, and during the nights Contras buried them in dirt roads, or concealed them in puddles. Activated by pressure or trip wires, each land mine hurled 700 shards, killing or maiming everything within 800 yards.

When Ben showed up at the El Cuá hydroplant, Rigo and Oscar were surprised to see him. After the land mines began exploding, most people became afraid to travel, and traffic had dwindled.

Ben soon realized after a few days that the turbine needed a metal part. Rigo suggested they have it made at a state-run agricultural mechanization school south of Matagalpa. The next morning they joined a line of vehicles stopped at a roadblock in town, waiting to leave El Cuá, while an army patrol swept the road with metal detectors, searching for land mines. When the patrol found nothing, army officials waved the line through. The first vehicle in line dodged the puddles, while those behind followed the lead's tire tracks. Passengers nervously scanned the road ahead.

Five hours later, Ben and Rigo drove to the school off the highway near Chagüitillo, which sat on six acres of land and was housed in the confiscated two-story brick house of a former Somoza senator. Wrecks of Soviet-made Belarus tractors towed there after an attack by the Contras littered the fields. As part of their studies, students would repair or salvage parts from them.

Rigo and Ben were directed to one of the teachers, a twenty-seven-year-old American machinist named Don Macleay, who was leaning over a lathe with a small piece of metal, demonstrating to a student. Lean and tall, Don had piercing tawny eyes with matching brown hair, and had grown up on U.S. military bases in Japan, Panama, and the States. He became a machinist/millwright in Canada, and an organizer in a trade union there. He learned Spanish by working with Chilean refugees who fled the Pinochet dictatorship in the 1970s. When Don was laid off in 1982, he came to Nicaragua to teach mechanics and machinery.

Don remembered that first meeting. "This short little Yank comes in here, yakking at me in bad Spanish, all puffed up and kind of punchy," said Don. "This cynical Nicaraguan, standing about half a foot taller, comes marching in behind him; a Mutt-and-Jeff combination."

Ben and Rigo asked if he could make a small metal part with specific dimensions. Don told them he could make it, but they should return for it in a few days. He invited them to have coffee in his small wooden house, where Ben spied a complete set of Aerolite passing clubs, enough for two jugglers. The two Americans ended up in a field, tossing the clubs back and forth. As they made smooth, neat arcs, Rigo stared in disbelief, confused at seeing two professionals, an engineer and a machinist, perform a lowly circus act.

In New Haven, deep in spring snow, Alison was busy sewing costumes for the university's theater productions. Week after week, she postponed answering Ben's letters. He wrote her fervent letters about the revolution every three or four days. He always ended by expressing his desire to kiss and hold her again. The letters were not exchanges; rather, they concentrated on his life in Nicaragua. She wasn't captivated by his political cause, or eager to test herself in adversity. She did not share his passionate desire to be of help in the Third World. She still loved him, though, and she finally wrote.

Alison's letter was waiting for Ben when he returned from El Cuá. Ben knew school was ending and hoped that she'd be coming to Managua by July 7, his birthday. But her letter revealed that she would not be spending the summer with him as planned. She'd been offered a staff position at the Yale costume shop as a cutter-draper.

Ben was crushed. He had to talk to her, to convince her to come. He strode over to the long-distance phones and stood in a long, slow line. When Ben finally heard the sound of Alison's voice, she confirmed what she had written: "There is a great job at Yale ... maybe starting at the end of August." The line buzzed and crackled, voices fading in and out. Ben protested, saying that she had to come, he missed her, he had to see her, they had to talk face to face. She only offered a maybe.

Ben stumbled home. After six years of envisioning a life with Alison, he realized for the first time that they could be growing apart. He admitted, "Unfortunately, our interests, and their pursual, lead us to different places. Neither of us seems ready to compromise. We need to talk about it. It's hard." Ben had to consider "how much I was willing to give for the revolution. Not necessarily in Nicaragua, or even in the U.S., but rather in the scheme of the world." Was he willing to give up his girlfriend? She had been waiting for him for two years and didn't want to wait any longer. Was it time to leave Nicaragua?

He sought his parents' advice. "I have been doing a lot of soul-searching about who I am and what I'm doing. I like doing useful work in terms that I define. I enjoy knowing that the 8–5 day I just put in will serve some good and that it, and myself, are recognized for it. I like the hydroelectric work; [the technology] is also applicable around the world and perhaps that is the most important."

Ben knew he wasn't ready to return to the United States. He wasn't homesick, and had visited the States only to spend time with Alison and his family. He wrote, "I'd be very unhappy in the States just to be there and not moving forward."

At the same time, he worried that if he remained in Nicaragua, he might lose touch with his own country. "There is a whole world out there. There are many battles to fight. There are few engineers who are willing to go to these countries. But after several countries and several years of advanced studies in Europe, I'll become a stranger to the U.S. I'll be unemployable in all but a few companies—but most importantly I'll be a stranger."

Ben knew that staying in Nicaragua might also adversely affect his engineering career in the United States. "I want to be reasonably sure that I'm not going to want to cross the bridges that I may well burn." He knew that working for the Sandinista government—one that the Reagan administration labeled "Communist"—would be a black mark on his résumé. He wrote, "Given my plans of where I want to work, and the worsening political climate in the U.S., my return, if there is one, will be more and more difficult for emotional reasons—but also legal ones. There is a good possibility that where I work now will be classified as training centers for international terrorists. This also goes for the people I associate with."

Ben knew it was not too late to return, find a job, and patch up his relationship with Alison. Yet that would mean giving up the El Cuá plant. Which relationship was stronger?

Ben was the only engineer in the country willing to work on the El Cuá hydroplant. If he stayed another year, he thought, he could train Nicaraguans to operate and maintain the plant. "I think that by June '86, the small hydroplant will become a major energy source—even without Ben Linder."

He sought advice from Maria de Zuniga, an American woman who had moved to Nicaragua as an assistant director of the Peace Corps in the late 1960s. In 1970 she moved to Waspán, a Miskito Indian village on the Coco River, where she supervised health projects. She married a local, had two children, and began organizing cooperatives, literacy programs, and Christian-based communities in the small settlements that dotted the river. Maria experienced the corruption and brutality of the Somoza regime, and over time, she became convinced that change was only possible through armed struggle. In 1975 Somoza's National Guard labeled her a "subversive," and deported her. She went to Guatemala and returned to Nicaragua in July 1981 to establish Centro de Información de Servicios de Salud (CISAS), a health training organization.

Maria had adopted Ben into her family and often invited him to her neat tract house in Barrio Linda Vista for weekend brunches of banana pancakes and homemade *ayote* bread. He frequently spent his Sundays swimming at Lake Jiloá with her family, and never missed clowning at the children's birthday parties. She advised him to seriously consider the decision and follow his conscience, and warned that if he stayed in Nicaragua he would be choosing a life full of challenges, hardships, and sacrifices. Given the increasingly hostile accusations from the Reagan administration and the growing funds for the Contras, Maria warned that economic, social, and political conditions in Nicaragua were going to deteriorate. Daily life would become harsher for everyone. Ben wrote, "Maria tells me to have courage, yet she is scared. From her I realize that I must continue on with my work here— and in other countries. It is from her that I also see what a high price the struggle demands."

More than ever, Ben wanted to discuss his future with Alison. Angry and distraught over Alison's indecision, Ben began looking at other women as romantic possibilities for the first time since he moved to Nicaragua.

On July 7, 1985, Ben's twenty-sixth birthday, Ana Brooks threw him a birthday party. Maria de Zuniga, Dr. Anne, Rebecca, and friends from INE crowded into the Brookses' house, sipping rum, eating guacamole, dancing to salsa, rock, and the Maypole dance from the Atlantic coast. "Ben was inexhaustible," said coworker Luis Mendoza. He danced wildly, swinging partners across the floor. "All the women sat down, exhausted from dancing, and Ben would go over and grab the hand of someone to keep on dancing." He juggled his clubs, desperately trying to have a good time. Something was missing from the party: Alison.

Throughout the summer of 1985, the Contras increased attacks across the country. They cut the main highway from Managua to Rama, the easternmost town on the paved road, stopping vehicles, robbing occupants, kidnapping government workers, and attacking agricultural cooperatives and villages.

Before dawn on August 1, Don Macleay was startled awake by the sound of gunfire. He threw on a pair of pants, grabbed his AK-47, and ran out the door, alongside a jumble of teachers and students scrambling to their assigned posts. Don crouched behind the school's cement water tank, peering into the darkness in the direction of the shots. An explosion rocked the ground, and the water tank swayed. The Contras had blown up the main bridge on the Pan-American Highway, two miles from the school.

In a series of coordinated attacks that involved some 2,000 troops, the Contras attacked La Trinidad, a small town located in a jagged mountain valley along the Pan-American Highway, seventy-seven miles north of Managua. Contras swarmed into the town, shooting machine guns and rocket-propelled grenades, yelling, "¡Somos los cachorros de Reagan!" (We're the sons of Reagan!).

La Trinidad's militia fought back, but the Contras quickly overran the town. The Contras rocketed and destroyed the police station, TELCOR, and the health center. They threw up roadblocks on the highway, searched vehicles, burned several cars and a bus, and set fire to a warehouse, destroying 400,000 pounds of rice and beans. After looting and ransacking the stores, they gathered in the main square, drinking soft drinks and beers.

At the mechanization school, Don and a few students stood guard behind the water tank, "hoping to living hell that the Contras were not going to come because we were not going to be able to beat them off." Suddenly, from the south, Don heard a distant hum, an ominous rhythmic thudding. Several Hind Mi-24 helicopters screamed in over the horizon, just skimming the treetops, their bellies heavy with rockets. The rotor blades thundered above Don as the helicopters zipped through the Sébaco Valley, intent on an aerial counterattack. These Sandinista gun ships swooped down into La Trinidad. Tail gunners swiveled the machine guns, and bullets pounded the earth. The Contras had never seen such powerful machinery, such thundering speed and sound. They panicked, scattered into the mountains, and retreated northward. The helicopters, shrieking and whirring, bore down on them, chasing them into open ground, pursuing them over barren mountains. The rotor blades' force bowed grasses and trees before them, exposing the men, some of whom froze, petrified. Dipping low, the Mi-24s pointed their deadly noses as rockets whined and crashed into the earth. The ground shook, the earth exploded.

By late morning foreign journalists arrived at La Trinidad to find the bodies of Contras laid out in the main square. Government officials estimated that sixty-seven Contras, eight Sandinista soldiers, and three civilians had been killed. It was the first time the Sandinista army had used the Soviet-made "flying tanks" in battle, and the helicopters quickly turned the war in the Sandinistas' favor.

After a series of letters and phone calls to Alison, Ben's hopes soared when he convinced her to visit for two weeks. He checked out the National Theater school, hoping she could work there, further hoping she'd stay. He talked to friends in the circus about her designing new costumes, even though there was a shortage of both fabric and money. And he enlisted his friend George Moore, a painter from New York, to tell her about the art scene in Managua.

He organized their itinerary: they would spend the first night in a hotel, a few days at the Brookses' house. They would go on a jungle cruise, ride a boat to Bluefields to visit the Brookses' relatives, and then fly to Corn Island, a honeymoon paradise of white sand beaches, crystal water, and graceful palm trees, where they could swim and snorkel. Most importantly, they could spend time together and make a decision about their future.

Ben was nervous about her visit, though. He wanted another American woman around to whom Alison could relate. He begged Nancy Levidow, who was in Nicaragua on a short-term artist delegation, to prolong her trip.

In late August, an enthralled and bubbling Ben greeted Alison at Augusto Sandino Airport. Although happy to see him, she was quiet and withdrawn, overwhelmed by the crowd of men surging forward to grab her suitcases and the ragged boys pushing newspapers in her face. The sight of so many men and women in camouflage unnerved her.

As planned, they spent their first night together in a hotel, then stayed with the Brooks family, who welcomed her like a daughter. Alison was uncomfortable traveling by river to the Atlantic coast. In the last two months, the Contras had twice attacked the Bluefields Express. Dr. Anne had been aboard during one of the attacks, and attended the seventeen wounded. Ben assured Alison that, since the attacks, the Sandinistas had beefed up security precautions. They rode a crowded bus seven hours down the pock-marked highway to Rama, and boarded the Blue-fields Express. The boat chugged languidly down the murky Escondido River, escorted by fishing boats loaded with soldiers pointing their rifles into the dense vegetation. Passengers joked nervously, fingering bullet holes in the boat's wooden sides.

In Bluefields it rained constantly. Though the Brookses' relatives were friendly and hospitable, they lived in a small, crowded house. The town smelled like sewage. Ben and Alison couldn't go swimming in the polluted water. They could not go to Corn Island because of a bureaucratic snafu; Alison had written "costume maker" as her profession on her visa to enter Nicaragua, and wrote "tailor" on her applica-tion to visit Corn Island. Immigration officials were disturbed by the discrepancy, so Alison could not get the permission to continue on her trip with Ben. The cou-ple flew back to the capital.

Alison was invited to meals at the houses of Maria de Zuniga and George Moore. Alison appreciated the dinners, and listened to the hosts' descriptions of the artistic community in Managua. She described her new staff position at the Yale costume shop, and spoke of the directors she admired and the plays that were planned for the coming season. At the end of the second week, Ben and Alison traveled to the half-moon beach at San Juan del Sur. They spent a few days drinking Victoria beers, eating shrimp and red snapper at beachside stands, and walking hand in hand along the beach. Ben told her about the plant in El Cuá.

As they talked, Alison realized what she had suspected all along was true: Ben was deepening his ties to Nicaragua instead of cutting them. Alison believed that Ben loved her, and wanted to be with her, but felt he was more devoted to his work in Nicaragua than to her. "I began to realize that he had committed himself to work-ing on the El Cuá project," Alison said, "and it probably wasn't going to take a year, but much longer."

Alison and Ben were both serious about their jobs. During her visit to Man-agua she realized that for Ben, "engineering in Nicaragua was certainly more than just work; it was his life, it was something that he brought all of himself to. And because we both had this mind-set about work, we understood we couldn't be together."

During those days on the beach in San Juan del Sur, Alison was hurt and resentful; she had waited so long for them to be together, and Ben had always promised to return to the United States. Ben was devastated because he was losing her. But he also realized that he had chosen Nicaragua over her. "We decided that although we loved, and love each other, the time had come to let each other go," he wrote. When Alison left for Connecticut, they parted as friends. She promised to write, but she didn't know if she would.

Alone in Managua, Ben retreated to the greasy Chinese restaurant, a place he had not been to since his first confusing days in the capital. Sitting alone, drinking beer, he glanced wistfully at the couples jamming the restaurant, holding hands, laughing and happy. Ben was reflective:

> Back at the Chinese Dive. Alison has come and gone. And now, what future am I building? It all sounds so good when I talk about the international struggle as compared to national struggles. But it's hard to be alone mainly on days like today where the shit is coming down all around me and I don't have anyone to talk to. It was so nice to see Alison and have her hug me and then listen as I told her of the day's problems.
>
> I don't want to be alone. It's sad and hard and not my style. Perhaps it is fine for some people but not for me. I look at the young lovers on the street and remember my first years, alone at the university.
>
> I'm more unsure of what to do now more than anything else.

Suddenly he was faced with the prospect of dating. "What is that? Do the dinners that I've had with various female friends now suddenly become 'dates'?" he wondered. "Should I actively try to 'find' someone? I'm not sure how to go about 'dating' in Nicaragua."

Ben wrote his parents, "Now that I'll be here for nearly one year more I'll talk to the house about staying on. I'd be happy to stay there and I think they would too. So as you can see I'm planning to be here until May or June of '86."

Chapter 9

Electricity Comes to El Cuá

On September 19, 1985, an earthquake measuring 8.1 on the Richter scale rocked Mexico City, killing more than 7,000 residents. Some 3,000 buildings collapsed, and tens of thousands were left homeless. People from around the world sent aid, and internationalists in Nicaragua planned a "solidarity fair" to raise money, where groups from each country sold traditional foods: Danes made paté; Colombians, *sancocho*, a thick soup; and Brazilians, *caipirinhas*, rum drinks with sugar and lemon.

The gringo club, including Ben, agonized over what traditional food Americans could sell that used local ingredients. Green salad? Cabbage was plentiful, but the few small heads of lettuce in the markets were always old and wilted. Popcorn? Not unless someone brought kernels from Miami. Finally the committee agreed to make "apple pie." Since apples were no longer imported, they had to use green mangoes. The gringo club scoured markets and stores for flour and butter, but the only flour available was packaged in hand-tied plastic bags and yielded a score of bugs. Cake tins were nonexistent, so Ben borrowed pie pans from Ria Reyburn and Don Reasoner and managed to find butane gas for the oven, even though most people had run out of gas months ago and cooked on single electric burners.

At the solidarity fair, the "apple pies" sold out as soon as they were displayed. In the auditorium, internationalists performed traditional dances, and gringo club members danced a sloppy but spirited Virginia reel. Ben, in his clown costume, roamed from room to room, tossing balls in the air and juggling fruit. Chile, a bone-thin Colombian woman, and her friend Sonia watched him pedaling his unicycle through the hallways, followed by a gaggle of children. At the end of the day Ben returned to the gringo club's booth to pick up the pie pans, but they had disappeared, and Ben, unable to replace them, humbly apologized to the Americans from whom he had borrowed them.

In the fall of 1985 Ben met with Mira, who had moved back to Managua after getting a job at INE. She rode her bicycle every day to an INE branch office and sat in a drab and windowless cubbyhole with air conditioning that heaved hot air. She covered the walls with colorful revolutionary posters, newspaper clippings on biogas buses in China, and photos of women from around the world.

At INE, Mira prepared a study of "Lorena woodstoves." Before the revolution, the United States' congressionally funded Agency for International Development (AID) financed a study that determined the Lorena woodstove—comprised of mud and sand mixed with fiber and water—to be the most efficient option available locally. Sixty Lorena stoves were constructed, but over time their fire chambers had enlarged, their burners widened, and heat and smoke escaped around the edges of the pots until most of them became unusable. Because the AID money had been cut, follow-up studies were never done, but Mira was reevaluating the stoves, examining their efficiency, social acceptance, and technical problems.

Mira wanted Ben's advice. She had a theoretical background in alternative energy projects, but she lacked field experience and feared that Ben would dismiss her as a "technical tourist." When she explained her INE job, Ben nodded approvingly and advised her that, since the woodstoves she was to inspect were in the war zone, she should travel there in unmarked INE trucks. "'Do you think they have unmarked trucks?' I asked him, and he said, 'Are you crazy? Do you think I'd go up to El Cuá in a truck with INE written on it. No way!'"

Mira also told him that NICAT wanted to "adopt" the hydroplant in El Cuá. He immediately dismissed the idea. Mira didn't understand his reaction, but she tried to explain it in a letter to NICAT members. "He told me that he's feeling very sensitive about 'his territory' and doesn't want a lot of people around telling him how to set up hydro there. His explanation is that he's just gotten to a point where he can try out some of *his* design ideas. This doesn't make total sense to me, but I think he's particularly sensitive on this issue because he still doesn't have El Cuá running. I don't think there is any small hydro operating anywhere in the country now."

In the meeting with Ben, Mira also suggested that a NICAT team from the United States visit Nicaragua to inspect old hydroplants for possible reactivation.

Ben believed an inspection team would only be useful if it were comprised of locals working alongside Americans, and he suggested NICAT should instead be "info" gofers, to do research, photocopy information, and make phone calls. They could also acquire badly needed parts like O rings, which were impossible to find in Nicaragua since the embargo. Mira gladly agreed.

Ben confided to his parents:

> Basically I guess I'm happy although usually by 6:00 P.M. after work I'm tired and frustrated. At work I spend all day running around dealing with problems and assholes. Typically asking to borrow a wrench to take to El Cuá, practically on my knees, and then one hour of paperwork to do it. Sometimes there are rays of hope. Yesterday a guy whom I've seen around gave me a ride from one of our buildings across town to another. As we were driving he started to talk about how grateful he is to the internationalists that are in Nicaragua and how important our work is. I thanked him and told him of the frustrations of people not wanting to help out in general; of the person who didn't want to lend me a wrench. Very honestly he said that that was planned and intentional.

Later that month, Ben convinced his supervisor to allow him to return to El Cuá on the condition that he did not take an INE vehicle. Overjoyed, Ben told Dr. Anne Lifflander, who had recently moved back to the United States; "I am finally going back to my mountains. Hopefully, in November, I will be able to finish [the hydroplant]. I wish you'd be here for the inauguration party in El Cuá. I think it will go down as one of the high points in my life."

Before leaving for El Cuá, Ben visited Casa San Juan to seek technical advice from U.S. TecNica volunteers there. David Creighton saw Ben and engineer John Kellogg talking. "Gradually Ben's chair started pulling closer to John's chair, and soon they had their papers and pencils out and their heads together, quite an unmatched pair; John a six-foot-plus championship volleyball player, and Ben, quite the opposite," David observed. "The two of them had their heads together all night playing around with different ways of doing things and there was curiosity and satisfaction going on between them."

One of the volunteers was explaining how to test a hydroplant's output when Mira wandered in and hovered over Ben. She asked him if he had ever done anything like this before, and he replied no. "Has anybody in Nicaragua ever done anything like this?" she asked, and he said he had talked to one man who had talked to someone else who had done something similar. That was the closest they got to anyone who had firsthand experience. Mira wanted to join him in El Cuá to watch the test, but Ben refused. He didn't want an audience.

A few days later, Ben rode the public transport truck all the way to El Cuá, hiked up to the plant, and was shocked to learn that Federico had suddenly quit. Oscar refused to tell him why, so Ben hiked past El Golfo to the valley of gray clouds, where he found the former worker in his corn patch. Federico was apologetic, and explained that he had to return to farming to feed his family.

Later, Oscar told Ben the real story. In October, he said, a group of Contras headed by Encarnación Valdivia—known as Tigrillo, "Little Tiger"—kidnapped Federico's slight, quiet, sixteen-year-old sister, Jacinta. Tigrillo, who weighed less than a hundred pounds and stood less than five feet tall, had a swaggering walk, a tough manner, and was feared throughout the province. He interrogated Jacinta about Federico, Rigo, Oscar, and others who lived in El Golfo, asking if they carried guns, if they were *piricuacos*, "Sandinista rabid dogs," or *sapos*, "toads," spies for the government. Jacinta said she rarely spoke to them, and her husband didn't allow her to leave the house. Tigrillo threateningly suggested that they stop working on the plant because he "didn't want anything to happen to them."

Jacinta was held by the Contras for two weeks, during which time she followed them through the mountains, hiking through dense jungle. In the evenings she had to cook whatever food they found. During the nights, the men fought over her.

At one point, the band spotted a Sandinista army patrol and ran off to set up an ambush, leaving Jacinta behind in an abandoned farmhouse to prepare dinner. They didn't think that a woman alone would have the courage to escape. But as soon as they disappeared, Jacinta ran down the trail in the opposite direction, finally emerging onto a dirt road, where she flagged down a vehicle. By that evening she was back in El Golfo, where she told Federico the Contras had put the hydroplant workers on their death list.

When Ben heard the story, he stopped trying to convince Federico to return. He had always suspected that the hydroplant's workers were targets, and now he was sure of it. "Scared isn't the word, but neither am I whistling by the graveyard," he wrote his friends back home. "There is an ever present tension that I feel. I'll be jumpy and out of sorts for no reason. An anomaly in the routine increases the pressures.... It's the feeling of the whole world pulling at me."

In the evenings, after a full day of work, Ben tried to relax:

I'm sitting on the stoop of the house where the two of us from INE stay in El Cuá. It's Friday afternoon. There is one street in town which makes the stoop a wonderful place to watch the world go by as the cool evening breeze picks up. Since I started writing, a group of school children came by pulling on their teachers' hands, then several campesinos [peasants] on horses, a couple of soldiers off on patrol, and just now the kids came running by after being let out of school. In front of the house, across the street is a field, then the river Cuá, then up on the little hill across the river are several mortars and heavy artillery.

That is what is so strange for me. In the midst of intense country calm with thick green hills of coffee, bananas and corn, the war goes on. . . .

After spending many hours of soul searching yesterday I finally began to understand my life in El Cuá. It is intense. At first I thought it was peaceful, but now I see that it has an intensity which blanks out everything else.

Ever since I left home I keep finding myself challenged and being unsure if I can meet the challenges. Somehow I do but it is always so hard. Will I keep doing this to myself? Probably I will. Who knows why.

In times like this I always think of my unicycle trip [down the Pacific Coast]. It was almost abandoned when Brian told me I had to do it. And I did. Relatively speaking it was easier than this. I know that I'll get the project going. I really do. What is hard is the intensity of it all. The beauty mixed with the war, the abundant land and the poverty and myself, also a contradiction with the land.

One weekend, Sergio, a lanky fifteen-year-old from El Golfo, along with several friends, took Ben hiking in the jungle through a maze of lianas, bamboo, pine, cedar, mahogany, laurel, and breadfruit trees, where iguanas flopped on thick branches. The waxy pink and white petals of the *sacuanjoche*, the national flower, scented footpaths with vanilla. The teenagers picked tangerines and other fruits from trees Ben had never heard of. In the jungle, hikers often rested from the shimmering heat under thick-limbed ceibas, the silk-cotton trees sacred to Mayans. Cicadas hummed a constant high-pitched sound, and howler monkeys roared from treetops. Black *zanate* birds, loud and insistent, mocked the hikers from the tangled canopy. "It was incredibly pretty and amazing" wrote Ben. "Green on green on green."

Back at the plant, he puzzled over the pipe that carried water out of the dam. It was prone to violent shaking as the water knocked against its sides. With Rigo and Oscar observing him, Ben replaced several parts, but the pipe continued vibrating. Frustrated by his inability to solve the problem, Ben confided in his friend Peter from Seattle:

> I'm writing from my favorite godforsaken corner of Nicaragua. Here I am where I was last year at this time, fighting to get this 100KW mini-hydro in. Everything goes wrong. Every piece of metal has a story of how it would fit one day but not the next. I've never seen such bad luck. Yesterday I came back to my room in town, took a large slug of rum and lay back in the hammock and thought about my karma. I just lay there, and wondered about my role on this earth. I finally decided that this really is what I'm here for, like it or not, and that I just have to keep fighting.

Because of pressures at work Ben found that his moods swung from feeling in control to feeling lost and isolated. When things went wrong, Ben became depressed until he figured out a solution. After several days of puzzling over the vibrating pipe, Ben remembered Don Macleay and decided to ask him to look at the plant. One Sunday afternoon, Ben grabbed his daypack and briefcase and plopped down on the bunkhouse stoop to hitchhike out of El Cuá: "Hopefully a truck will come by later today. No one knows. I sit on the porch and wait. I feel like I'm waiting for the stagecoach." With only a few vehicles in town, gas rationing, and the chance of encountering Contras or a land mine, traffic was sparse. The sun reached its zenith, sucking all color out of the countryside. Finally, in the late afternoon, a vehicle passed by, and Ben squeezed in.

Ben located Don and proposed a quick trip to the plant, but the mechanic declined the opportunity. Don was about to leave for Italy to join an old girlfriend. He was burned out, tired, and dissatisfied with most of the projects he had worked on in Nicaragua.

Ben asked him to reconsider. The hydroplant was special; it was a project that would immediately benefit the town's residents. It was a "hands-on" project, and locals would eventually take over. Don's expertise was needed to solve a problem no one else knew how to fix.

Don thought about it. He could see the immediate benefits of electricity— from refrigerated medicine to cold beer. He strongly believed in teaching locals new skills. But he also knew the plant was in a dangerous area. After witnessing the battle of La Trinidad, he was reluctant to enter a war zone again unless he could defend himself. Don proposed a deal. He would make one quick trip to El Cuá on the condition that he be in charge of both the plant repair and self-defense. Ben agreed.

Soon afterward, Don recruited Freddy Cruz, a burly, twenty-five-year-old Nicaraguan machinist. Don also wanted to invite his girlfriend, but Ben refused.

When the other man insisted, Ben suggested that she ride the public transport truck up to El Cuá like all the Nicaraguans.

Late in the afternoon of November 19, Ben, Don, and Freddy left Managua in an unmarked red INE jeep with a roof rack welded out of pipes. They joked all along the Pan-American Highway as they zoomed past young soldiers in camouflage, hitchhiking on the side of the highway, rifles hanging down their backs, floppy hats pulled low against the sun. In Sébaco, barefoot boys chased after the vehicle, thrusting muddy onions and carrots through the window. The jeep climbed the narrow highway, the valley's dusty browns giving way to green hills. They spent the night in a cheap pension in Matagalpa and divided up jobs at the plant over dinner.

The next day, in front of the government office, they loaded up the jeep with tools, a generator, gasoline, vegetables, bread, and a 55-gallon drum of diesel fuel. As they were about to drive off, Don emerged from the office with a camera dangling around his neck and two AK-47 automatic rifles slung over his shoulders.

When the INE driver saw the guns, he refused to leave. Ben feared that they'd make themselves targets if they carried guns. Don and Freddy insisted the guns were for self-defense, and refused to go to El Cuá unless they were armed. Don reminded Ben that he was in charge, and that ambushes happened all the time.

In the end the driver settled the argument, saying that guns were prohibited in INE vehicles. Don looked at the loaded jeep and at the sun sliding toward the horizon. He returned the two guns to the office, climbed into the jeep, and ordered the driver to step on it.

The jeep rattled up the twisting dirt mountain road, passing hills covered with spindly banana trees, squat, shiny-leafed coffee bushes, burned jeeps and troop carriers. They arrived in town after dusk, "about the time you start shitting your pants," Don said. As Ben pointed out the houses of people he knew, Don was thinking that El Cuá "looked pretty squalid. Just some plank houses strung out along a dirt road." The next morning, they drove to the plant to meet Rigo. Don immediately felt a kinship with Rigo. They were both from the working class, were self-trained, and appreciated machines. "Rigo and I were like mind and soul," said Don.

Freddy took the turbine casing apart and packed the seals to stop leaks, while Ben and Oscar worked on the governor. Rigo inspected the canal and intake pipe above the plant. In the powerhouse, Don gently ran his hand along the turbine, the generator, and the governor, stroking them, pulling levers and gears, fiddling with gauges, tightening screws. He disconnected the generator, examined it, ran the turbine, then reconnected it.

Don was always happiest when his hands were smeared with grease. He loved the feel of machine parts in his hand, the cold, clean feel of steel, every angle, every joint having a use, so ordered, so structured, so logical; one part fitting into another part to create an understandable, useful object. He had always taken apart and reassembled any machines he could find.

At lunchtime the crew drove to El Golfo, where Rigo arranged for them to eat meals at the house of Julia and Rosa Amelia Chavarría, two widowed sisters renowned for their cooking. Before the revolution, the women were among the richest landowners in the area. They owned the most impressive house in El Golfo, had bank accounts in U.S. dollars, and sent their children to Catholic boarding schools and on vacations to the United States. Their 140-acre farm included 35 acres of coffee, as well as banana, orange, and lemon trees.

After the sisters' husbands died, their children had moved away, and then the revolution began. They could no longer find employees to work for them as the peasants joined cooperatives, received their own land, or were scared out of the area by the Contras. Now their two-story house had rotting floorboards, holes in the walls, a leaky roof, and a sagging upstairs porch. A daughter in Los Angeles, California, had invited Julia and Rosa Amelia to move in with her, but the women refused to leave their coffee farm.

The crew parked the jeep in the muddy front yard, next to abandoned pieces of rusting coffee-processing machines and rotting lumber. Fifty-year-old Julia, a short, slight woman with gray streaks in her long black hair, always greeted visitors from the front stoop, chickens and turkeys clustered around her ankles. She led visitors into a dark and spare room, walls blackened from years of smoky kerosene lamps.

The diners in El Cuá only served beans and rice, but the widows prided themselves on their fare, where lunch might consist of buttery cheese-filled squash, eggs covered in salsa, avocados, sour cream, and homemade cheese. In the kitchen, an outdoor lean-to with a packed dirt floor, the older sister, Rosa Amelia, leaned over the "stoves," two huge stone and cement fixtures with an open fire. Neighbor children in tatters ran in and out as she worked, mixing with the chicks and piglets. "I feel like I'm stepping back a hundred years in time," Ben commented.

After lunch, Ben would often entertain the kids by juggling lemons from a tree in front of the house. Rigo teased Ben that he was more interested in spending time with children than with adults.

Before the revolution, the widows employed fifteen full-time workers who respectfully referred to them as *las patronas*, the bosses. When a worker's child fell ill, the *patronas* called the doctor, or took the child to a hospital in the city. If the little one died, the *patronas* furnished the coffin, bought new clothes for the burial, supplied the flowers, and paid the priest. Most workers were illiterate, and there was no school near the farm, so the worker's children remained illiterate and maintained the legacy.

After the revolution, the sisters could not hire enough men to maintain their farm, and the farm deteriorated. New labor laws enacted after the revolution forced the widows to pay workers the minimum wage for the first time. In addition, they had to sell their coffee crop to government agencies at fixed prices. Their income dropped. When Ben met them in 1985, the widows only employed five permanent workers, including their adopted fifteen-year-old grandson, but the five men could not keep up with the chores.

During the harvest season, the sisters hired entire families to pick coffee. At lunchtime, berry-stained children, women in ragged knee-length skirts over slacks, and men in pants mostly made up of patches streamed out of the hills, dragging eighty-pound burlap sacks bulging with red berries. The coffee pickers dropped their sacks on the porch, stamped rubber boots to loosen the mud, silently acknowledging visitors with gap-toothed smiles. Women untied wicker baskets dangling from their hips and followed the men to the widows' kitchen, where they ate beans and rice while standing around the stove.

As evening approached, Don suggested that everyone spend the night at the plant so they could test-run the turbine. Since no one disagreed, Ben and Don continued working in the powerhouse, eyeing the spinning turbine long after the sun set. At one point they noticed the jeep had disappeared and were irked that the others had gone for dinner without telling them. When no one returned after two hours, they realized they had been left behind at the plant. Each angrily blamed the other. "I was extremely outraged, and also frightened," remembered Don. "Ben and I weren't talking. It was too late to do anything—the sun had set, the car had gone, the plant was running, we had a mobile generator powering some heater units, we had a small fire going, there was water rushing, and we were making lots of noise."

There were no weapons of any kind at the plant. They didn't know what they would do if the Contras attacked, but decided to rotate guard duty through the night. Don took the first watch, hiding himself in the coffee bushes above the plant. Halfway through the night they traded, but as dark slipped into the light of early morning, Ben abandoned his guard post and crawled off to sleep in the brick bungalow.

The next morning they held a meeting with the crew. The Nicaraguans were embarrassed about the incident and consented to sleep at the plant if the army assigned militia to guard it. Lieutenant Osmar Talavera, the head of the nearest army post, recommended that the crew begin carrying guns. Freddy and Don concurred, while Rigo, Oscar, and Ben protested.

Like most INE employees, Rigo never carried a gun. He saw himself as a civilian without any political affiliation. One time, a group of Contras stopped his unmarked jeep but then waved him on. Rigo believed it was because he was not carrying government employee identification and he was unarmed. And even though Oscar had fought with the Sandinista guerrillas, he now disagreed with the government over many issues, and worried that carrying a gun would mark him as a sympathizer.

Don, on the other hand, felt strongly that they should be prepared. "I didn't like it; it made me feel sick, but I just understand that's how it works," he said. Don argued that the Contras target you whether you are armed or not, so you might as well be able to defend yourself. Ben believed that the Contras had no reason to kill him, as he was merely a civilian engineer. Don responded that the rebels considered all government employees to be targets, regardless of their unmarked vehicles, civilian clothes, or refusal to carry guns. "The graveyards of Nicaragua are full of civilians who went around unarmed, thinking they were immune," he said.

Ben argued that the Contras wouldn't knowingly kill an American because it would cause a political uproar in the United States. Bullets didn't distinguish between Americans and others, countered Don. He reminded the crew about Dr. Albrecht Pflaum, whose frantic waving of his West German passport and pleading for mercy did not prevent the Contras from shooting him at point-blank range. Don refused to sit in the bungalow, cowering, while Nicaraguans risked their lives to defend his.

Ben didn't want Nicaraguans to risk their lives for him. On the other hand, if he carried a gun, he worried what other Americans would say, what the press would write if they ever found out, what his parents would think, and if it would jeopardize his U.S. citizenship. Weighing the issues carefully, he hesitantly decided to arm himself. This convinced Rigo, Oscar, and even the INE driver. All agreed that the guns were only for self-defense.

Soon thereafter, they drove down to the army post, where a soldier handed each a heavy Soviet-made AK-47 rifle, and a clip of ammunition, and scribbled their names on a scrap of paper to keep a "record" of who possessed weaponry. At the plant, Don cleaned and oiled his AK-47, admiring its sleek machinery. Oscar and Freddy disassembled theirs, comparing them to Oscar's old rifle when he fought as a guerrilla, and Freddy's small pistol during the insurrection.

Ben held his gun gingerly, away from his body, frequently checking the safety, pointing the barrel toward the ground, keeping the ammunition separate. He told friends that if he had to shoot the gun, he feared he wouldn't be able to pull the trigger. He hoped he would never have to find out.

Later that day, six militia men—too young or old to have had combat experience—arrived at the plant. Dressed in threadbare camouflage and rubber boots, they carried an assortment of old weapons. All were farmers from La Chata cooperative, working the fields by day and rotating militia duty at night, guarding the coffee fields, the main road, and now, the hydroplant. The men trudged to a ridge above the dam, where they lashed together tree branches and banana leaves into a lean-to, to shelter against the rain.

Don's girlfriend, Jenny Broome, a lanky, blue-eyed biologist from California, met up with the crew shortly thereafter. They showed her the facility, explaining how the hydroplant worked. "Everyone was laughing and happy—there was an air of anticipation," said Jenny. Oscar fished a water snake out of the canal, draped it over a branch, and chased Freddy, who ran alongside the canal, laughing. Jenny snapped photos, including one of Ben with his gun, which angered him. He made her promise to destroy it.

Don and Freddy redid the packing boxes and tested the governor, the regulating system, and the automatic water control. As everything worked smoothly, Don announced it was time to hook them together, to see if they could produce electricity. The crew gathered in the powerhouse: Rigo at the control panel, reading the meters; Ben next to the governor, watching the gauges; Jenny in the doorway, with her camera; and Don at the valve. As Don turned the valve, water rushed through the penstock and into the turbine. The belts took hold, and the machines strained, grinding slowly. The whine of the turbine and generator increased, becoming louder, more powerful, as the whir of machines filled the powerhouse. The crew looked up as the two dusty lightbulbs began to glow faintly until bright light flooded the room.

"I was readjusting levers, checking ballbearings, and looking at the machine," recalled Don, "and then I looked up and saw Ben running up to everybody and shaking their hands, and Rigo dancing around with his footboard, and the other guys dancing and looking at the water going through the canal. Well, they'd been out there anywhere from two to four years trying to get this project done, and they just could not believe that they had electricity in El Cuá!"

Jenny recalls, "It was too loud to talk, but people were jumping around and yelling: 'We did it! After four years, there is light in this place.' Even though it was only enough power to light two light bulbs, it really meant a lot after so long. Ben was really happy—it was his day."

When they checked the gauges, the power level was solid and unwavering. Don, Ben, and Jenny sprinted up the hill to the brick bungalow, where the other three light bulbs glowed just as brightly. They flicked the lights on and off. Don plugged an electric drill into a wall socket, drilling holes into scraps of wood, while Ben hooted over its whine. The machinist rigged a wire from the wall socket and made espresso. The entire crew sat on the slope watching the water rush by in the canal, listening to the comforting, steady hum of the generator.

That night, Ben wrote in the hydroplant's logbook:

Friday, Nov. 22, 1985
Hour: 4:35—Pipe to the turbine was opened.
    4:36—Light!

And he wrote in his journal:

Written by the light of the generator. Today for the first time the plant is running. Tomorrow the governor will be hooked up and we will run the final test. I'm really amazed by the whole mess. Don has been truly wonderful in his work and being supportive of what seems my feeble attempts. But it is coming together. In the midst of it all I sit with my gun at my side.... The plant is generating. I was pleased as could be. My first project. A solo flight without ever having flown with someone. Don stepped into it to pull out of the dive and straighten out the flight.

That night, Don and Jenny slept in the powerhouse, while Ben and Freddy, too excited to sleep, sat outside debating whether or not the noise and the lights were attracting the Contra's attention. Freddy suggested they check on the militia but couldn't locate the guard's lean-to. Too afraid to call out in the dark, they ran down to the powerhouse, where they shook Don and Jenny awake. "Ben told us he was worried," Jenny said. Don told him to go back to sleep.

Ben was still anxious: "Tonight I went up to the penstock to see if anyone was on guard. Finding no one I drove into town, lights off, guns out the windows, bullets in the chambers. For rather strange reasons, many dealing with small town politics, the army has been resistant to giving the project more than six militia men from La Chata."

The sleepy-eyed army commander told Ben that the guards were farther up the ridge. Ben and Freddy returned to the plant and roused Don, who grumpily accompanied them up the hill. There they located the lean-to and found the militia men snoring blissfully, guns strewn about the ground. Don was furious. He grabbed one of the rifles, aimed it toward the sky, and pulled the trigger. A burst of gunfire exploded into the air. The militia men jumped up, feet tangling in their hammocks. "'Hey *compas*, the Contras are over there. Get up!'" yelled Don. The sixth guard, on duty, came crashing through the jungle, rubbing his eyes. "We saw a shadow on that hill over there, we didn't know what it was, and so we fired off our guns," Don told him.

Ben noted in his journal, "One militiaman on guard and five asleep. I must admit I wasn't very pleased with their combat readiness and spelled it out to them. Here is a gringo engineer telling them that they are fucking up on guard duty. All very strange."

The next morning, an army officer drove up to the plant and handed the crew a note from Lieutenant Talavera. It cautioned them not to approach the militia at night because the guards might confuse them with the enemy and shoot. The crew thought the note was hilarious.

That afternoon, when the crew ate at the widows' farmhouse, Rigo sensed that the sisters were nervous. He instructed the crew to leave their guns in the jeep.

Over lunch, the conversation drifted to politics. The widows recalled fond memories of the Somoza government, of those "better times" before the revolution. El Cuá residents spread rumors that the sisters slipped food to the Contras, and perhaps even gave them information on the army's movements. The Contras were never far from El Golfo, and gunfire and mortars were often heard nearby. Nevertheless, the women claimed they had never seen a Contra.

Freddy distrusted country people, and as he listened to the widows praise former dictator Somoza, he worried that they knew he was a Sandinista. When he bit into their tortillas that day, his teeth crunched against something hard, leading him to suspect that the sisters had slipped ground glass into his food. When the women left the room, Freddy whispered that they had poisoned his tortillas and were trying to kill him. Don and Ben only laughed. Later, Freddy squatted among the coffee bushes, sick with diarrhea. On the way back to the house, he noticed Contra slogans painted on a back wall: MUERTE A LOS PIRICUACOS (Death to the Sandinista rabid dogs) and VICTORIA AL FDN (Victory to the FDN—National Democratic Front, the Contras).

On the fourth day of work, Don decided to test the generator and the turbine by using salt water as a dummy load, which mimics an electrical system, instead of lights and appliances, to consume electricity from the generator. No one was sure how to run the test.

They filled two blue 55-gallon drums with water, placed them next to the main pole, connected cables from the generator to steel panels inside the barrels, and added salt. "That was the most critical day. The test was both delicate and dangerous," Rigo said. Ben ladled salt into the barrels while Rigo opened the valve, and as the water heated, it bubbled and splattered inside the barrel. Don climbed a ladder and watched the kilowatt meter attached to the pole. He told them to "crank it up" to about 60 percent capacity.

Ben ladled more salt into the water, and the load on the generator increased. As the gauges shot up, Don ordered Ben to throw in more salt. He dumped several handfuls of damp salt into the barrels, but Don needed more, so Ben tipped the metal can and poured a continuous stream of salt into the boiling liquid. The current rushed up the arc of salt, giving him a shock. Ben's body convulsed. He fell backward, dropping the can into the barrel, and collapsed onto the ground. "Ben was the color of death," Rigo said. Oscar ran to Ben's side and shook him by the shoulder. After a moment, Ben stirred. Recovering from the stun, he insisted that they continue.

They boiled the water for two hours, testing the high-voltage wires and transformers. The crew took readings and plotted a graph. Don climbed a ladder to check the fuse box on the main pole and discovered that one of the fuses was blown. He dispatched Oscar to borrow a replacement from a pole near La Chata cooperative.

At sunset on November 25, they finished running the tests, and Don reconnected the plant to the four streetlights in town, the only part of the village that was wired. "At that time it became a question of 'Do we go to bed or do we finish?'" remembered Don, and everyone agreed to pursue the goal of turning those lights on. They lashed the ladder to the roof rack, tied open the jeep's back doors in case of an ambush, loaded the vehicle with wire, tools, and rifles, then jumped in. Don climbed onto the roof rack, clutching the metal rungs with one hand, his rifle with the other, while Rigo stayed behind. He wanted to flip the switch at the plant. They synchronized their watches to 9:00 P.M. If all went well, the power would be switched on in half an hour.

With the headlights off, Ben drove toward El Cuá, navigating by the moon. In the village, the only light came from the Disamar saloon. The crew parked in the plaza, and set the ladder on the roof rack, while Don ascended the pole to the transformer. Lieutenant Talavera wandered out from the army post, and a few farmers from the saloon sauntered over to watch.

Ben and the others clustered at the bottom of the pole, staring at the cold lightbulb, its silhouette visible in the moonlight. The farmers lit cigarettes, waiting. At the plant, Rigo waited until 9:30 P.M. to open the valve. Water rushed through the pipes, and the machines turned and whirred smoothly.

In town, the crowd watched the lightbulb flicker, darken, strengthen to yellow, darken again, finally settling to a dim glow. People couldn't even see one another's faces. The crew stared at the feeble light. Disappointed and confused, they wondered why it was not as strong as the light in the plant. The onlookers snorted. Everyone knew that INE had been working on the project for five years, and yet the town still did not have electricity.

Measuring the flow with the voltmeter, Don suddenly realized that "the voltages were strange, and I looked up and realized that the transformer was not wired." The transformer was disconnected, and the lightbulb was running on an inductive current.

Ben sent the driver back to the plant to tell Rigo to turn the system on again in two hours. The crew drove to a light pole near the Protestant church, where Don disassembled the transformer, then duplicated the connections on its counterpart in the main plaza. Freddy bought a case of beer at the saloon, just as the bartender shuttered the windows and turned off the noisy generator. The town fell silent. Everyone, except for the crew and a few soldiers on guard duty, had gone to bed.

At the foot of the lightpost, Freddy and the driver paced, waiting for 11:30 P.M. Ben shone his flashlight on the bulb, then on his watch. Oscar shifted his weight on the roof rack, steadying the ladder. Don, at the top of the ladder, roped himself securely to the pole, his lit cigarette the only glow in town.

Back at the plant, Rigo watched the second hand sweep around his watch. "At eleven-thirty I was to charge the line, but I gave them an extra couple minutes, in case they were still working. At eleven-thirty-two I let the electricity flow, and that was when the lights came on; strong, white light; a success!"

Don and the crew were waiting in town. "And then the lights came on and we had pandemonium." The lightbulb cast a glow over the road, the bright, clear light shining over the health center, bathing the red jeep in jagged rays, shimmering and bouncing over the plaza, illuminating the crew's upturned faces. Freddy hooted and screamed. Ben cheered, galloping down the road to check the three other streetlights. Oscar jumped off the jeep to follow Ben, leaving Don dangling on top of the pole. They splashed through puddles, oblivious to the danger, their cries floating out above the black mountains where the Contras waited in the dark.

Two of the other streetlights burned brightly, while the third, in front of the FSLN office, flickered uncertainly. Nevertheless, Ben was jubilant. "Ben said to me, 'Well, little brother, we have a machine, a machine to give light, a machine to give a future to everyone in El Cuá,'" said Oscar.

The crew barreled back to the plant, where Rigo was waiting for them with a box of tracer bullets that he had saved for years, in anticipation of just such a day. He counted out thirteen bullets for each person. "These are bullets of happiness, of celebration," he said, "because, for us, it was a success—for me, five years of work, for Ben, almost two years." The crack of rifles filled the air as the tracers arched across the valley, a line of red against the black sky.

On the ridge, the militiamen heard the shots and ran through coffee bushes to the powerhouse. "They arrived running down the hill, yelling, 'What happened? What's going on?'" Don remembered. "And we said, 'There's light in El Cuá.' They weren't too impressed. They thought the Contras had arrived." As they turned to climb back up the hill, the last guard arrived. "He asked 'What happened?,'" Don said, "and the first militiaman said to the second 'Nothing important. Go back to sleep.'"

Everyone thought the lights seemed to make the plant safer. In the power-house, Rigo and Oscar stared at the machines, then at the two glowing lightbulbs on the ceiling. "They'd been out there from two to five years trying to get this pro-ject done, and they could just not believe that they had electricity in El Cuá," said Don. "It was very emotional. We were very charged up, very happy with ourselves, and very scared."

At the brick bungalow, Freddy passed around beers, then dangled the case in the canal to keep the extras cool. The crew toasted each other, clicking bottles together. "Ben said he felt like a father when his first child has been born," Rigo remembered. "'My baby,' he called the plant."

Ben spent the night in the powerhouse, hovering over the turbine and generator:

November 25, 11:32—the lights went on in El Cuá. I was excited, joyous and amazed. We were back in the operator's house drinking beer while Oscar played the guitar in a yellow slicker. Days of staying up late had had an effect on all of us. I sat there looking at the table. Beer bottles, a pot of coffee, tools, guns. The whole image had a beauty of a team putting its all into an effort—and doing it. El Cuá is working.... I've spent many tor-tured hours wondering what the solution was. As it turned out it wasn't a new nut and bolt or other such gadgetry but rather a skilled mechanic named Don from Canada. A rather crazy sort but an excellent mechanic and very smart. He keeps a running dialogue of historic fact and good insight into politics and people. I just listen to him as he jumps around from off tidbit to interesting observation. Without him the plant wouldn't get done. Every-thing seems so fragile. One person can make all the difference.

In the morning, Don took a photo of the crew in front of the powerhouse, wide grins on their faces. Freddy was in the middle, one hand holding the plastic pole used to throw the switches, and the other hand flashing a victory sign.

Don, Freddy, and Ben drove into town and checked the lightbulbs, which con-tinued to burn brightly. They ordered Cokes at the Disamar saloon, plopped down on a wooden bench in the shade, and overheard a woman gossiping with the storeowner. "This woman was bitching," said Don. "She said, 'First, they told us they were going to turn the lights on by Christmas of last year; then they said in July for the anniversary of the revolution; then they said by the end of the year.' And she was upset that we just did it—like that—without waiting for a special day to turn it on." Don, Ben and Freddy, sitting anonymously against the wall, exchanged looks and stifled their laughter.

   That evening, Ben worried about overtaxing the machines and spent the night in the powerhouse monitoring the gauges. He pulled a cot next to the control panel, and wrote his family: "I wish you all could see the project. I feel rather proud.... Everything feels so far away from here. The folks in Point Arena, Miriam in San Franciso and John in New Orleans. Even Managua seems far away as the nights here in El Cuá are cold. Sweet dreams as I sit here watching the gauges."

Chapter 10

The Next Goal—San José de Bocay

News of the hydroplant's success preceded Ben's return to the INE office in Managua. His coworkers enthusiastically congratulated him, slapping him on the back and shaking his hand profusely. Ben strutted through the dim halls of INE, smiling broadly, giving credit to Don, Rigo, Oscar, and Freddy. "He looked like a child that had just received the latest toy," said coworker Luis Mendoza. Even politically conservative engineers who rarely spoke to Ben complimented him, and the minister of INE, Emilio Rappaccioli, sent letters of congratulations to him and his crew. "We were the victorious group," said Don. "We had just done what no one else had. I got more job offers in that week than any time that I lived in Nicaragua."

"When the plant went on line, there was a little celebration with us," said Don, "but there was also a little bit of a shock wave that went through INE and the government, as people were wondering why the fuck we finished in two weeks what hadn't been done in two years ... and they said it just that way, with words in Spanish just as vulgar."

Charlie Whitaker, one of the officials in charge of development in the Matagalpa/Jinotega region, was impressed by the Americans' initiative. He invited them to celebrate at his house in Matagalpa, where he poured them straight shots of Flor de Caña rum, toasting them repeatedly.

Charlie told them he wanted to implement a long-range development plan that encompassed education, potable water, and electricity spanning El Cuá to the village farther north, San José de Bocay. Hydroplants would supply electricity to appropriate technology projects in the villages, including sawmills, machine shops, and carpentry shops. Each village would build a potable water system, and locals would be trained to operate and repair all the systems. The project included promoting education and health care; building latrines, town dumps, and bridges; and reforesting denuded areas. The effort would coordinate with several government ministries to draw financing and recruit skilled people. Charlie wanted a highly skilled eight-man team to run the project. He proposed Ben as project leader, Rigo as second in charge, and Don as advisor.

Ben was elated at the news. He downed his drink in one gulp, shook hands all around, and poured everyone another drink. Don hunched down in his chair, not saying a word.

Late that night, Ben stumbled back to his hotel. "Drinking, tired and high on it all," he reflected. "Charlie tells me I'm heading up a select team of eight to develop El Cuá/Bocay. Rigo as #2. Don as advisor. Into the big time. It is probably the most exciting and challenging task I've ever taken on. What is so good about it is that we will be working as a team. Finally I'm not taking a job on solo."

The next day, after his head cleared, Ben found Don and told him he was ready to begin work immediately. Don, however, said he wasn't interested. He was leaving for Italy.

Most engineers dreamed of working on an open-ended team project, each member sharing skills with others. To Ben, this was more responsibility than he could ever imagine having in the United States. He argued with the machinist, telling Don this was a chance where they could make a difference, but Don refused to stay. During the three years he had worked in Nicaragua, he had seen too much waste, greed, and corruption. He was tired and had other plans for his life, though he grudgingly acknowledged that he was proud of the El Cuá plant.

Ben was insistent. As a team, they could bring a decent standard of living to the farmers, to the poor people who were hardest hit by the war, he argued. They could teach them the skills to break the cycle of poverty. That was what the revolution was all about, and they had an unequaled chance to participate in it.

Don hesitated. He knew that not only were there smart, willing, and capable locals who could be trained to work, but also that the next hydroplant would be easier to install. "I was amazed at how simple the technology was," he said, "and how much benefit you could get out of a very small investment. I thought it had more to do with developing Nicaragua than [with] puttering around a school. It's the countryside that makes this country tick; this is an agrarian nation."

But he also knew that the sluggish government bureaucracy was a nightmare. There would be endless delays, and he did not plan to wait around. Don didn't want to begin another project until it had full government support.

Still, he was tempted. His airline ticket was round-trip, and the dates could be changed. Mulling it over, he told Ben that he would help draw up the plans. If Ben got government approval, and salaries for Don and the rest of the team, he'd return from Italy to help on the project.

Ben was thrilled that Don had finally agreed to work with him. "Most development people would cringe at putting a machine shop in El Cuá," he conceded. "I think if Don wasn't doing it I'd cringe also. But then again, without Don, El Cuá wouldn't be working." Around this time Ben wrote Peter Stricker in Seattle, informing him about the El Cuá hydroplant and telling him that he was no longer interested in going to graduate school. He had decided to stay in Nicaragua for several years to continue his work.

Don and Ben threw themselves into planning the "El Cuá/Bocay Integrated Development Project," consulting with Rigo, Charlie, and a group of government officials, who, according to Ben, were "all young and very sharp people." Don and Ben stayed up late, working in the Casa de Gobierno (Government House). They drank sugary black coffee as they hunched over desks, writing plans and timetables and arguing over priorities.

Both agreed that the most important aspect of the project would be to educate and train local residents. "We realized how ridiculous it was to be putting electric light in people's houses when those people didn't understand electricity, had no knowledge of repair work, and were all dying of diarrhea," said Don.

First, they planned to build the mechanic's shop, so work would no longer come to a standstill for lack of proper equipment. Eventually, the mechanic's shop would also produce the turbines and other components for the three additional hydroplants to be built in the valley.

Oscar and Rigo would train locals to operate and repair the hydroplants. The newly skilled would train other locals. In twenty years, Ben estimated, there would be a marked increase in the technical ability in the area: "The idea is not just to put electricity into a town. That is easy and can happen anywhere. The important thing is to also deal with the social-technical problems that go with it."

Development meant not only bringing electricity, or piping in water to a dirt-floor shack, but actively involving people in their own betterment. Development consisted of changing centuries-old ways of thinking—raising grass-roots awareness about basic rights, teaching local processes by which these could be ensured, and giving the people confidence to do it themselves.

But the Cuá/Bocay area was a war zone. To a certain extent, the Contras and the Sandinistas were fighting over the farmers' loyalty. Ben and Don thought that the Sandinistas would win the farmers' support with the benefits of the revolution: electricity, education, and health.

Where would they find skilled personnel to train the locals? Almost all technicians, engineers, mechanics, machinists, surveyors, and other necessary personnel lived in cities. Ben and Don doubted they could persuade such people to move to a war zone, but perhaps they could convince internationalists to work on the project. They believed the Contras were targeting Nicaraguans but not Americans. Ben felt that Americans had a particular responsibility to work in war zones to demonstrate that not all Americans supported the Contras.

Don, Ben, and the local government officials drew up an outline and a budget for the project. Charlie Whitaker and other Matagalpa officials promised government financing and technical support. But when Don left to pack for Italy, Ben began to worry. Lying on a bed in Matagalpa, he could hear the pop of firecrackers and the high-pitched songs of Purísima, the feast of the conception of Mary. He flashed back to his first Purísima, a few days after starting work at INE, two years earlier. Since the beginning, INE had often seemed like an enemy, fighting him at every turn. INE funds had been slashed, like those of all government ministries, as more than 60 percent of the national budget was now directed toward fighting the war. Basic items were no longer imported but arrived in the country as donations. The Soviet Union was sending lightbulbs, potatoes, and lard. In spite of Charlie's fervent promises, Ben knew he should not count on the government. He would have to solicit funds from nongovernmental organizations and solidarity groups. But how to go about it? Ben hit upon the idea of making a video of the El Cuá hydroplant project. He would send it with Don to raise money in Europe. "Next step—video. Essential. I'm running fast. I love it."

Looking for transportation for a quick visit to El Cuá, Ben remembered that his friend George Moore owned a jeep. Ben frequently stopped by George's sprawling red-tiled house in Barrio Bolonia to unwind, take a hot shower, or drink an imported beer from the "Diplo," the hard-currency dollar store. George and his wife, journalist Alice Christov, coddled Ben, often inviting him to stay for red snapper or lobster dinners. Ben entranced them with stories about El Cuá. Ben invited George to visit El Cuá, and he enthusiastically accepted.

Early one December morning, George picked up Ben, along with Barbara Wigginton and Jeff Hart, amateur videomakers from Oregon living in Managua. Barbara remembers that Ben "tried to play down the danger to get us to do the footage. He had a way of making things sound exciting, so you'd end up saying you'd help."

George drove his red jeep out of Managua before dawn, and by 8:00 A.M. they were in Jinotega, where they picked up Rigo, who kissed his wife good-bye. Outside Jinotega, the paved road ended. George hunkered down over the steering wheel, casting his eyes ahead, and thought of the dozens of ambush stories he had read about in *Barricada*. He hoped the Contras would not target people from the country that was bankrolling them.

When they entered El Cuá, they saw hundreds of black plastic tarps covering the hills: a Batallón Ligera Infantaría (BLI), a light hunter battalion of several hundred soldiers. Ben explained that their presence ensured the safety of El Cuá. George looked at the black dots on the hills, not feeling reassured by a group of seventeen-year-old-boys guarding the town.

George was surprised to find the plant comprised only of one small brick building. He looked at the thick jungle and the few scraggly militia men rocking back and forth in hammocks. "I thought, it would be so easy to blow this plant up," he said.

Since they only had a few hours of sunlight left, Jeff quickly videotaped the powerhouse, pipe, canal, and dam. Ben tested the governor, turning the plant on and off, and George noticed how the engineer interacted with locals. "Ben had a good relationship with Oscar and Federico," said George. "It was not patronizing. He wasn't the gringo; he was just a regular guy."

Jeff wanted to interview someone who spoke English. Ben wanted Oscar and Rigo to be the stars of the video, but he reluctantly agreed to narrate. "He put emphasis on the plant being built by and for Nicaraguans," said Barbara. On camera, Ben predicted that in a few months the whole town would be electrified, although no houses were connected to the plant yet.

At dusk a light rain fell, and George drove into town, where ramshackle hovels stretched out along the one muddy road. Rigo kissed his girlfriend hello as barefoot boys led caravans of mules through town, each loaded with burlap sacks full of coffee beans to be taken to the ENCAFE warehouse.

Across the street, farmers stood in long lines at the bank to cash checks they had just received for their coffee crop. Young soldiers wandered around, blank-faced, toothbrushes in the front pockets of camouflage uniforms, plastic rosaries dangling from their necks. Mangy dogs wandered the muddy road.

George found the village smaller and more destitute than he had expected. "El Cuá seemed to me to be the loneliest place to live," he said. None of them had ever seen a place so desperate.

The guests ate rice and beans in a diner. The rain began throbbing so loud they couldn't hear each other talk. After dinner, they sat on the bunkhouse porch, drinking rum mixed with grapefruit juice. Night fell, and as sheets of rain pelted the black tarps, George felt sorry for the soldiers huddling under the wet plastic.

A soaking-wet man stumbled onto the porch, held his hand out to George, fell against him, and declared how happy he was to have Americans in solidarity with Nicaraguans in El Cuá. His breath stunk of a vile homebrew. As George sidestepped the man's fetid breath, Ben whispered that the drunk was one of the town's schoolteachers. "He seemed like Li'l Abner," said George. "The place was full of degenerated hicks. And I thought, These are the people Ben deals with? I don't envy him."

The engineer shook the man's hand, patted him on the back, and convinced him to continue walking down the road. "Ben was not idealistic about the place," said George. "He made cracks about the people and said, 'This one is a joke.'"

Except for four streetlights and a few lanterns in houses, the town was dark at night. In the hills above El Cuá, soldiers' campfires flickered. Ben advised his visitors that they should sleep with their boots near their beds in case they had to flee during the night. "When night fell, you could feel the tension, like the Contras were moving around," Jeff said. "It was time to go into the house and be quiet until morning." The guests unrolled sleeping bags on the floor, while the flame of the kerosene lantern threw large shadows on the walls.

Jeff, Barbara, and George tossed and turned throughout the night. They were sick with diarrhea, but didn't want to run through the mud and dark to the nearest outhouse. George wondered if the soldiers were getting soaked from all of the rain. "I thought, I would not want to live in the boondocks—I don't care whose revolution it is," he said, wondering how Ben could stand it. He appeared so easygoing, so unfazed, and so cheerful. Indeed, he seemed to thrive on the hardships.

At 4:00 A.M. George was awakened by the thump of heavy leather boots hitting the ground. He struggled out of his sleeping bag and wandered to the porch. There he spied soldiers marching in formation up the muddy road. El Cuá was slowly waking up. Roosters crowed nearby, answered by cocks from the other end of town. Farmers on horses clip-clopped by, their hooves tossing up mud.

In the thin light, George watched a steady parade of people—like a religious pilgrimage—march down to the river, carrying toothbrushes and towels draped over their arms. "I felt like I was in the hall, watching everyone on their way to the bathroom," he said. Along the river, every resident staked out his own spot to bathe. Despite the rigorous moral code of modesty among farmers, women washed themselves in bras and panties, while a few yards away teenaged soldiers, clad only in underwear, averted their eyes.

Rigo, who rose before 5:00 A.M., had already bathed. Ben and the visitors splashed their faces with water from a washbasin. The radio was blaring *Puño en Alto* (Fist in the Air), an adult education program, at 5:30 A.M. The visitors were eager to leave, but they had to wait until the army finished patrolling the roads for land mines. Meanwhile, Ben gave them a tour of the health center. As visitors walked through the clinic, twenty-five-year-old Juana Gonzales, the cleaning woman, mopped the floor behind them, her long, black hair pulled into a ponytail, swinging back and forth, keeping rhythm with the mop. Each year, nurses and doctors from Managua left the clinic after working their required one-year stint, but Juana, the only local, always stayed on.

When army officers told the visitors it was safe to leave, George slammed the jeep's gas pedal to the floor, looking forward to a long shower, a decent meal, and a night of undisturbed sleep in his own bed. In Matagalpa, George dropped Ben off with the video stowed inside his black briefcase. Ben checked into a cheap pension, where he soothed a cold with a bowl of chicken soup. The overcast sky and blustery wind outside reminded him of Oregon. "I'm caught up and keep going," he wrote. "I've got a room in a hotel and I feel like a traveling businessman. But what a strange industrial development in an isolated mountain village in a war zone in some Latin American country. But it is more than that. It is a program which has a strange completeness that few people would understand."

Ben gave Don a copy of the video to show in Europe to raise funds for the project. Don reminded Ben that he had to sort through the bureaucracy before he returned. Don remembered, "He said that he would send me a telegram in Europe; red—forget it; yellow—your choice; green—you're obliged to come because it's on and we're depending on you to handle the education and machine-tool end of it."

On December 2, the Contras shot down an Mi-8 Sandinista army helicopter with a SAM-7 surface-to-air missile, killing all fourteen soldiers aboard. "It is the first time such sophisticated equipment is being given to terrorists," a Nicaraguan Foreign Ministry statement said. "This represents a dangerous escalation in the [Reagan administration's] mercenary war against Nicaragua." President Ortega harshly condemned the attack, saying that "the United States is stimulating a wave of international terrorism and leaving the way open for anybody to use truly dangerous weapons. The United States is demonstrating that it does not want a peaceful solution to problems in Central America." He warned that the use of ground-to-air missiles could unleash a wave of terrorism that endangered both civilian and military aircraft, and called for an urgent meeting of the U.N. Security Council. Nicaragua recalled its ambassador to the United States. Secretary of State George Shultz denied that the United States had supplied the Contras with the missiles, but praised the downing of the helicopter, saying it was "fine" and that he was "all for it."

That Friday afternoon in Managua, government offices closed early, and INE workers, carrying banners and placards, joined the demonstrators, including many internationalists, who jammed the streets. They marched to the U.S. embassy to protest the downing of the helicopter. Some 30,000 people rallied in front of the U.S. embassy, while a cordon of Sandinista police surrounded the front gates, keeping the demonstrators twenty yards away. Marines in riot gear watched the crowd from the embassy rooftop. American journalists spotted novelist Graham Greene among the Nicaraguan protestors.

Sonia Campos, a representative of the Frente Patriótico de Madres (Patriotic Front of Mothers), a group of women whose sons were fighting in the war, addressed the crowd: "I say to Reagan, to the Pentagon, that while they give those missiles to the Contras, we are giving our sons to defend this land."

As the quick tropical dusk fell, demonstrators sang the FSLN hymn:

Adelante marchemos compañeros,
avancemos a la revolución,
nuestro pueblo es el dueño de su historia
arquitecto de su liberación.

Combatientes del Frente Sandinista
adelante que es nuestro porvenir,
rojinegra bandera nos cobija,
¡Patria Libre, Vencer o Morir!

Los hijos de Sandino
ni se venden, ni se rinden,
Luchamos contra el yanqui,
enemigo de la humanidad."

Let's march forward, compañeros,
advancing to the revolution,
our people are the owners of their history,
we're the architects of our liberation.

Fighters of the Sandinista Front,
our future is to go forward,
a red and black flag brings us together,
A free country, victory, or death!

The sons and daughters of Sandino,
never sell out, nor give up.
We'll fight against the Yankees,
the enemy of humanity.

The demonstration ended after the song. People disbanded, scrambling to get home, eat dinner, and watch the evening soap operas on TV. That night, Mira worked late at the INE building. Sometime after dark she wheeled her bicycle through the dim, deserted halls to her home, where her housemate Mirna, a Sandinista activist told her about the demonstration in front of the U.S. embassy.

Mira couldn't believe she had missed the protest. After watching the news, she wrote:

> I think most people at that demo ... like many Nicaraguans, believe that
> it is just a matter of time until the U.S. invades Nicaragua, outright. I was
> not at the demo (everyone left work to go to it, leaving me working alone
> in my office, unaware.) I was really upset when I realized what had hap-
> pened—I have to get myself better integrated into the communications net-
> work in the office. I ache with regret that I didn't go, and find myself feeling
> angry at people in general for not having told me!

Because of a shortage of farmhands, the government mobilized state workers to pick coffee every harvest season. Spurred on by radio jingles "a cortar el rojito" (to cut the little red ones), 120 INE secretaries, receptionists, cleaning women, chauffeurs, librarians, bus drivers, night watchmen, technicians, and engineers had left for the mountains to pick coffee for three months.

On Christmas Eve, friends of the INE workers picking coffee gathered in the parking lot to visit their colleagues. Ben, with his briefcase and unicycle, squeezed into the back of a troop transport truck, among musicians and soldiers. As the caravan pulled out of the parking lot, musicians began beating their drums. "We left Managua loaded with enthusiasm," said Francisco Chavarría, an INE employee and musician.

The caravan snaked north, while musicians passed guitars to soldiers, who strummed and sang, calling out "¡Feliz Navidad!" (Merry Christmas!) to farmers walking along the road. After Jinotega, the dirt road wound through steep hills and crests hidden by the mist. The travelers unfurled plastic tarpaulins over the backs of the trucks before the rains beat down on them. The trucks continued north for two hours to La Sorpresa, a state-owned coffee farm where seventeen people had died in an attack by the Contras a year before. Trenches ran behind the faded white-washed bunkhouses, and bomb shelters lined the cookhouse.

When the trucks pulled into the muddy yard, the foreman blew a cowhorn. Farmhands and INE workers streamed out of the mist, some wearing camouflage uniforms, rifles, and leather ammunition belts strapped to their chests, carrying baskets brimming with red coffee berries.

INE coffee pickers surrounded the caravan, warmly greeting coworkers, enveloping relatives in hugs. Some visitors hardly recognized their friends and relatives, their faces withered and browned by the sun, their bodies significantly lighter. Ben distributed powdered milk, soap, animal crackers, and hard candies, while women served cauldrons of shredded chicken with vegetables and rice to hungry INE coffee pickers. They had been surviving on rice, beans, and tortillas three times a day.

Afterward, INE employees were praised for their work on the farm at an official ceremony. As the musicians struck up a revolutionary song, Ben emerged from behind a bunkhouse in his clown costume, riding his unicycle, struggling to keep his balance in the mud. "The whole place fell apart," said Francisco Chavarría. Children stampeded after him, dodging and screaming when he turned abruptly to charge them. The farmhands were mesmerized. "They had never seen a clown," said Jaime Merizalde, an INE coworker. "For them, it was something from another world." Ben pedaled past the trenches, disappearing behind the bunkhouses as scores of ragged, barefoot children chased after him. After a few minutes he reappeared, breathless and spattered with mud, and dismounted from his unicycle, as the children surrounded him, gingerly touching his red nose, running their fingers along the cycle's spokes.

Darkness fell quickly, and the foreman blew the cowhorn again, signaling everyone to prepare for the night. Militia men hurried to their posts in the hills, where they loaded rifles, counted out ammunition, and divided night watches. An occasional flashlight beam sliced through the darkness.

Ben's coworkers found space for him and other visitors in a dank bunkhouse, where coffee pickers slept on hard wooden platforms stacked two or three high. INE coffee pickers jokingly warned the visitors to watch for tarantulas, scorpions, biting ants, and Contras. Exhausted after the day's work, coffee pickers quickly fell asleep, while visitors lay awake as rats ran across the rafters, dogs barked, and babies cried in the night.

Before dawn on Christmas Day, the cowhorn sounded. Francisco and Ben scrambled out of their bunks and slipped down the muddy slope to the communal kitchen. Stout-armed women who had been awake since 3:00 A.M. palmed tortilla dough onto a griddle while toddlers with distended bellies clung to their dresses. Militia men with rifles gathered around the cauldron of boiling coffee, wishing the women a Merry Christmas.

Suddenly, a loud blast shattered the morning, the warning siren of a Contra attack. It blasted again. Militia men scattered to the trenches. Women scooped up toddlers and dashed for the bomb shelters. Francisco ran after the women, Ben following behind. As they pushed into the dark, narrow opening of a bomb shelter, they were hit by an overpowering stench; coffee pickers had been using the bomb shelters as latrines. Human excrement covered the ground. "We all crammed in there,"

Francisco said, "and Ben started laughing. 'Damn,' he said, 'this is really a joke—the bullets aren't going to kill us but the shit sure will.'"

As the siren wailed, the shelter became so crowded that it was hard to breathe. Everyone waited for the sound of gunfire, the boom of mortars, but as minutes passed, the only sounds were the muffled sobs of toddlers and the sniffling of older children. As more time passed, everyone relaxed.

Finally, the head of security came by and told everyone the siren had been a false alarm. As they emerged from the shelter, Jaime told Ben that La Sorpresa used to have a hydroplant to clean the coffee crop, but it had never been connected to the bunkhouses to provide electricity for the farmhands. Ben examined the old rusty turbine and the cracked pipes. Before joining the caravan back to Managua, Ben added La Sorpresa to a list of coffee farms as a possible site for future hydroplants.

In February 1986, after repeated requests, Ben was finally transferred to Pequeñas Plantas, the small INE hydroplants division at Montoya, where Mira worked. After Ben moved into the office, his corner resembled a junkyard.

When Mira discovered that Ben had been transferred, she began seeking his advice about her cookstove report and running workshops, among other things. Ben responded pleasantly, but her questions were endless, and he began to lose patience. When he started avoiding her, Mira realized that she needed a pretext to talk to him.

After a few weeks, Ben's attitude toward Mira softened. The government hadn't responded to his numerous requests for tools, personnel, and financial support for the Cuá/Bocay project, and he decided to ask Mira for help from NICAT. She was happy to help. Ben also asked her to find information on fish production, so that he could raise and sell fish in El Cuá to boost the children's protein intake.

Mira wrote a detailed letter to Gordon Scott, the head of NICAT in Bellingham, Washington, describing the pivotal role that NICAT could play in the project, and asked him to collect résumés of skilled technicians to volunteer.

However, in spite of Mira's unconditional support for the El Cuá project, NICAT members in the U.S. wondered about the safety of their volunteers and asked her if the Cuá/Bocay project would be a target. Mira wrote back:

> Any development project in the Sixth region [Jinotega province] is a potential Contra target. This is the nature of the war the U.S. is funding here. Unable to gain the popular support necessary to hold territory, the Contras are left only with the option of hit-and-run terrorism and economic sabo-

tage. Their attacks on development projects are multi-purposed: 1) to continue the devastating effects on the Nicaraguan economy, making daily life more and more difficult for all Nicaraguans, thus contributing to a general weariness and some erosion of support for the Sandinistas, 2) to prevent people from participating in development projects out of fear for their lives and families, thus distancing Nicaragua from its goal of participatory development, and 3) to prevent the 'benefits of the revolution,' i.e. the benefits of development in the interests of the people, rather than in the interests of the multi-nationals, from reaching parts of the campesino population and reinforcing their support of the revolutionary projects.

In Barrio Riguero, Rebecca Leaf suddenly found herself living alone when Franklin Brooks received a scholarship to study in Cuba. Rebecca asked Ben if he wanted to share the house with her, and he quickly agreed, since the Brookses' house was overflowing with people. After living there almost two years, he missed his privacy.

When Ben told Ana Brooks he was moving out, the tears rolled down her fat cheeks. She made him promise that he would visit, and helped him carry his belongings to his new house, one block away.

In the new house, Rebecca and Ben divided the chores. Ben often cooked dinner, using whatever food he found in the refrigerator: potatoes with onions, cream, and cheese, a salad of cucumbers, tomatoes, and dill, a dessert of ice, milk, bananas, and rum thrown in the blender. Ben always ate his meals on the far side of the kitchen table, because, as Rebecca recalls, "He told me that it was self-training from El Cuá—he sat facing the door in case something happened."

On weekend mornings, Ben often dashed around the block, filling a burlap sack with eggs at one corner store, bread at another, then experimenting with foods. During the weekends Rebecca and Ben cleaned house and hand-washed laundry in the cement basin in the backyard. "He occupied all the basins and then never got around to cleaning them for weeks at a time," said Rebecca. "That was my only complaint as a housemate."

Ben's enthusiasm, unbridled optimism, and sharp, dry wit ameliorated Rebecca's perpetual reserve, although she made it clear to him that she was not interested in discussing love lives, or gossiping. Rebecca was more comfortable discussing turbines and generators than politics or feelings, and since she enjoyed discussing work, Ben often brought her to TecNica meetings. Soon she began relying on TecNica volunteers for information, books, and technical advice.

On February 25, 1986, President Reagan asked Congress to authorize $100 million, including $70 million in military aid and $30 million "non-lethal aid" for the estimated 20,000 Contra troops. The aid request included $3 million for the Contras to establish a human rights commission. Since the Contras had such a loathsome human rights record, some human rights experts believed this money would be used to cover up their human rights violations. Aryeh Neier, America Watch's vice president, said that $3 million would make them "the world's second-best funded human rights group" after Amnesty International.

For the next month, in preparation for one of his toughest policy showdowns with Congress, President Reagan and his administration forcefully lobbied the Democrat-controlled Congress to approve Contra aid. Secretary of State George Shultz, Assistant Secretary of State Elliott Abrams, and White House Chief of Staff Donald T. Regan appeared on network news programs. The White House communications director, Patrick J. Buchanan, wrote in the *Washington Post's* opinion page, "With the vote on Contra aid, the Democratic Party will reveal whether it stands with Ronald Reagan and the resistance—or Daniel Ortega and the Communists."

On March 18, timed to coincide with President Reagan's push for Contra aid, the State Department issued a report charging the Sandinistas with "ever greater repression of their own people to maintain their hold on power." In a nationally televised address from the Oval Office, President Reagan pleaded for Contra aid as he raised the specter of communism sweeping northward to America's doorstep. Condemning the Sandinistas as an "outlaw regime," he said that they posed a direct threat to the United States, and that halting communism and international terrorism in Nicaragua would serve as a historic test of his presidency. "For our own security, the United States must deny the Soviet Union a beachhead in North America," he said, lest there be a possible "Soviet ally on the American mainland only two hours' flying time from our own borders." He said that the aid was vital to national security to get rid of the "malignancy in Managua" that may spread and become "a mortal threat to the entire world."

Reagan dismissed his critics' demands for serious negotiations with the Sandinistas: "Desperate Latin peoples by the millions would begin fleeing north into the cities of the southern United States, or to wherever some hope of freedom remained." He called Nicaragua a "command post for international terrorism" and said it provided weapons and training to radicals in at least a dozen nations in

Latin America, persecuted and tortured religious leaders, and was a center for the international drug trade.

In the Democratic response to the presidential address, Senator James Sasser of Tennessee said there was no disagreement that Nicaragua "must never become a base for Soviet military adventurism in this hemisphere ... but our disagreement is with the means the president has used to achieve these goals." Sasser added, "Our concern is that the president is seizing military options before he has exhausted the hope of a peaceful solution."

The House of Representatives bitterly debated the Contra aid proposal. When some administration officials questioned the loyalty and patriotism of President Reagan's opponents, some legislators resented the administration's tactics and hardened their position against Contra aid. Democrats troubled by the lack of a coherent policy said this reminded them of the confusion that led the nation into the Vietnam War. Representative Lee H. Hamilton, Indiana Democrat and chairman of the Select Committee on Intelligence, warned, "This Contra war has isolated the United States, not Nicaragua. This proposal will lead us to further escalation, to more bloodshed and to stalemate. There are better alternatives than an expanded war."

On March 20, 1986, the House of Representatives voted 222–210 to reject the $100 million aid package. President Reagan termed the House defeat a "dark day for freedom.... This vote must be reversed." After his defeat in the House, Reagan shifted his lobbying efforts to the Republican-dominated Senate, which still had to vote.

One day in mid-March, Ben appeared at Mira's door in the INE office, toting burlap sacks bulging with grapefruit and avocados from El Cuá, to invite her to his house. When she arrived, ready to work, Ben served her a grapefruit daiquiri and a big bowl of guacamole. Mira was surprised to see Ben acting as host and, for the first time, felt that he welcomed her company. Sipping a daiquiri, Ben chatted about INE and his family in Portland, telling her that he had a close relationship with his parents and wanted to tell them about El Cuá. "He said to me, 'What would you say if I sent a letter saying that here we are in the truck with bullets in the chamber, ready to shoot, with people out in front on foot looking for mines?'" Startled, Mira looked at him, since she had no idea that El Cuá was that dangerous. "I told him, 'No, of course you can't say that to your parents.' But, inside myself, I was shocked, thinking, 'Is that how it really is up there?'"

Semana Santa, Holy Week of 1986, a Nicaraguan holiday, began in March, one of the hottest months of the year. Shops and offices closed for the week. Newspapers stopped publishing. Radios stopped broadcasting news. Because of a shortage of cooking oil, women used lard to cook the traditional holiday foods—*almíbar*, fruit preserves, and dried fish. A shipment of donations had just arrived from the USSR, and there were rumors that it was whale blubber instead of lard.

In the mountains, firefights between the Sandinista army and the Contras increased as both sides took advantage of the dry season before the May rains turned the jungle into a bog. Two Sandinista army battalions, backed by rocket barrages, made a lightning thrust some thirteen miles across the Honduran border into El Paraíso province, where they attacked the main Contra training bases in the Las Vegas salient. Casualties ran high on both sides. In the 1,500-worker textile factory where Mira's Nicaraguan housemate worked, three workers had family members killed that week.

In Tegucigalpa, the Honduran capital, American officials ordered a Honduran press spokesperson to denounce the incursion, but Honduran officials, wary of getting involved further between the Sandinistas and the Contras, remained silent. In Washington, the Reagan administration announced that Nicaragua had invaded Honduras. Opponents of Contra aid accused Washington of exaggerating the raid to garner support for the Contra aid bill in the Senate. On Monday, March 24, U.S. officials met with Honduran president José Azcona Hoyo, pressing for a public complaint against Nicaragua, and suggested that if Honduras did not ask for U.S. help, future monies to Honduras could be jeopardized. Since 1979, U.S. military assistance to Honduras had increased from $2.3 million to $67.4 million. The Honduran armed forces chief, General Humberto Regalado, responded by calling the U.S. embassy to ask for assistance in transporting troops to the border. On Tuesday, Azcona sent a letter to Reagan backing the request, thus complying with Washington's wishes but also embarrassing his own country, as he was acknowledging that the Contras used Honduran territory as their base. Azcona then left for the beach, where he could not be reached for comment for the rest of the week. The Reagan administration ordered $20 million in emergency funds sent to Honduras, including air defense weapons, ammunition, training, emergency spare parts, and armaments for helicopters. U.S. pilots used fourteen U.S. helicopters to airlift more than 500 Honduran infantrymen to near the Nicaraguan border. Six hundred U.S. troops were dispatched to Honduras, and further U.S. troops were put on alert.

In Managua, INE was closed throughout Holy Week, so Mira attempted to work in her small rowhouse. Unable to concentrate in the hot, cramped rooms, she wandered over to Ben and Rebecca's house. She wrote, "I sat sipping grapefruit daiquiris at Benjamin's, and he mentioned that things were pretty tense just now in the States." She had been so busy working on her cookstove report that she hadn't been aware that the Sandinistas had invaded Honduras. Mira missed President Ortega's news conference, but she knew Ben and Rebecca had listened to it on the radio. She wrote in her journal:

> Apparently [Ortega] was asked directly three times if Nicaraguan troops had entered Honduras. He said no, they hadn't invaded; that Honduras had lost its sovereignty in those areas because they had allowed them to be controlled by Contra forces armed by the U.S; and that the Contra training camp destroyed was the camp in which Robelo, Calero, and other Contra chiefs had held a press conference and had claimed that they were in a 'liberated zone' inside Nicaragua, and that the U.S. and Honduras had always insisted that all the Contra camps were in Nicaragua.
> I drank another daiquiri and giggled about it all.
> Yup, looks like Nicaragua 'invaded' Honduras.

On March 27, 1986, by a vote of 53–47, the Republican-dominated Senate approved President Reagan's request for $100 million in aid to the Contras. Reacting to the vote, President Reagan said the vote was "sure to send a profoundly reassuring signal to the freedom fighters in Nicaragua and to Nicaragua's threatened neighbors," and called the Sandinista offensive in Honduras "a slap in the face to everyone [in the House] who voted against aid" to the Contras. Senator Jim Sasser said the vote was "certainly no mandate for the president's policy.... It's time to agree on where we're going in Central America before we find ourselves with United States troops on the battlefield and the body bags coming home once again." Since the bill had already been defeated in the House of Representatives, it did not pass into law. President Reagan vowed that he would get the House of Representatives to approve it.

In Barrio Riguero, Ben and Rebecca discussed how the money, if approved, would affect people in the countryside. "We thought Americans were immune from attack," said Rebecca. "We thought that the Contras were not selecting Americans as targets because of the political consequences it might have."

But they did realize that attacks on foreigners had been increasing. The first to be kidnapped was thirty-two-year-old Regine Schmemann, a West German biologist, who was seized by Misura, a Miskito Indian Contra faction, on June 14, 1985. She was held for twenty-one days and forced to march through the jungle to Honduras before being released. In August 1985 a Contra group led by Edén Pastora captured twenty-nine Americans from the ecumenical religious group Witness for Peace, who were on a peace vigil on the Río San Juan, the river border between Costa Rica and Nicaragua. The Contras kidnapped everyone aboard the boat, including the Witness for Peace members, fifteen international journalists, and the nine-member Nicaraguan crew. Pastora called the Witness of Peace members "wolves in sheeps' clothing," held everyone for twenty hours, then released everyone unharmed. In February 1986 a twenty-nine-year-old Swiss agronomist, Maurice Demierre, a member of Brothers without Borders, and a very observant Catholic, was giving a ride to a group of villagers who had just finished an Easter procession when the Contras detonated two Claymore mines under his truck, then sprayed it with machine-gun fire. Demierre and four Nicaraguan women were killed in the ambush.

Working in the war zone brought up another sensitive question that Ben and Rebecca often discussed: whether foreigners should carry guns. Ben told her he had carried a gun for one week, but had returned it to the army when he left El Cuá. Likewise, Ambrosio Mogorrón, a forty-four-year-old Basque nurse from Spain, was a pacifist. One of the first health workers to arrive in San José de Bocay after the revolution, he frequently stuffed his knapsack with dentist's tools, pliers, knives, antiparasite medicine, antibiotics, and painkillers, then disappeared into the mountains for days, pulling teeth, dispensing medicine, giving shots, and assisting at births. He trekked to isolated areas where Nicaraguan health workers were afraid to go. Self-taught in epidemiology, he studied leishmaniasis (mountain leprosy), a fly-borne disease that causes skin lesions. Ambrosio wore civilian clothes and never carried a gun. He was well-known throughout the Cuá/Bocay valley, and in 1985 the Sandinista government awarded him the José Benito Escobar Medal for his work.

On the other hand, Yvan Leyvraz, a red-haired Swiss internationalist who worked for MINVAH, the Ministry of Housing, building houses in the war zone, never left town without a rifle. Yvan often consorted with Sandinista officials and army officers, traveled in military caravans, wore camouflage uniforms, and draped bullets, bandolier style, across his chest.

When Franklin Brooks returned from Cuba, Rebecca moved into a boardinghouse, where she was charged rent in dollars. Ben moved back in with the Brooks family, but after living in the quiet house with Rebecca, he longed for more privacy and stability in his life. "When he came down to Managua from El Cuá, he wanted to have a place to wash up, to have a key to open the door, to have a place that was his," said Rebecca. "We both had a bit of money and were both tired of shuffling around from one house to another," so they decided to pool their money, buy a house in a working-class neighborhood for $1,000, then fix it up.

They recruited Tom Kruse, an American architect, to examine a house they found for sale, a $500 shanty with a dirt floor and a tin roof full of holes, but built in the shade of a huge, spreading mango tree and within bicycling distance of INE. Tom peered through the window slats, knocked on the plywood, shook the door, measured the shanty with a tape measure, and pronounced that, with many improvements, the shanty could be upgraded to a house.

Ben and Rebecca began negotiating with the owner, but upon research they found that there was no clear title. Soon afterward, when Rebecca rode by the shanty on her bike, she found out that the owner's cousin had moved in.

A short while later Ben and Rebecca found another house for sale, a wooden row house with two small bedrooms, a large living room, and an attached kitchen. A tangle of vines sheltered the front windows from the fiery sun; there was a front porch onto which they could pull out rocking chairs during the hot, sultry evenings, and an enclosed backyard with several cement washtubs. The house was in the working class barrio of Monseñor Lezcano, a neighborhood that bubbled "with a feeling of life and activity," Rebecca said. Row houses were interspersed between mechanic's shops, carpentry shops, car repair shops, hardware stores, and corner groceries. In the mornings, boys sold newspapers, and horse carts jangled by. Women sold fruit drinks out of their living room windows, and in the evenings set up *fritanga* stands on street corners. Children crowded the streets, tossing wooden tops and chasing after tire rims. Ben and Rebecca felt at home in the barrio and began negotiations for the house with the vines on its windows.

Whenever Ben went to El Cuá, he turned on the plant, but he turned it off when he left. Ben's actions greatly irritated thirty-eight-year-old Captain "Miguelito"

Castro, the head of the Sandinista Front, whose office was one of the few buildings in town to be wired to the plant. Captain Miguelito was eager to have electricity twenty-four hours a day, but Ben told him that was impossible until Oscar was fully trained. In reality, though, Ben didn't want to operate the plant around the clock until he was in El Cuá to monitor the machines.

The Captain, as everyone called him, was a short, burly, soft-spoken man from the area; he had been raised on his family's cattle farm in Bocaycito, north of El Cuá. He began collaborating with the Sandinista guerrillas in 1972. Since he knew all the families in the region, he organized a network of Sandinista collaborators in the Jinotega Mountains. He knew the mountain trails and the isolated hiding places, and often visited Cosme Castro's guerrilla camp, high up in the rocky ledges of Peñas Blancas. He fought in the first offensive in Estelí in 1978, where he took a bullet in his left arm. After the revolution he held various government positions, and in April 1984 he was appointed political secretary of El Cuá, at which point he moved with his wife and their four children to the family farm north of town. The Contras had often tried to ambush him, twice destroying his vehicles, but each time he escaped unharmed, thus earning the nickname El Brujo, "the Warlock." Unfazed by Contra threats, he often barreled up the lonely mountain roads to his farm in his new green Toyota pickup.

Miguelito had only a few years of schooling and read haltingly, mouthing the words. He puzzled over maps. Nevertheless, he was the most powerful man in town. He called public meetings and gave orders to both military personnel and civilians. Everybody obeyed him.

As soon as the plant began functioning, the Captain brought up a refrigerator from Jinotega and stocked it with beer. Whenever the plant was turned on, one naked lightbulb bathed the Captain's office. In the evenings, he often played his radio/cassette player, listening to romantic ballads, merengue, and *cumbia* on cassette tapes, or tuned in to Radio La Voz de Nicaragua. Army officers, Sandinista officials, and other government workers naturally migrated toward the Captain's brightly lit office, smoking, laughing, drinking, and playing cards. But whenever the hydroplant was turned off, the Captain's office remained dark and silent. Government officials hurried to eat dinner before night fell.

One sweltering day in April, the Captain dispatched a jeep of soldiers to the plant and ordered Oscar to turn on the plant that evening. Oscar nodded, but he was worried; Ben had told him never to turn on the plant without him there. On the other hand, the Captain was in charge of the town.

That evening, Oscar slipped on his rubber boots, unhooked his machete from the wall, slung a burlap sack over his shoulder, and disappeared into the jungle to cut wild plantains.

Later that night, Captain Miguelito invited Mario Acevedo, a local official, and Yvan, the Swiss internationalist, for drinks in his office. Tall and rugged, with a full beard and wild, curly, uncombed red hair, Yvan downed shots of rum, joked about women, and acted blasé about the Contras. He spent winters teaching skiing in Switzerland, and summers building houses in resettlement cooperatives in the Nicaraguan war zones. He blazed his pickup along mountain roads, whipping around hairpin turns, loading the truck with farmers hitching rides, wearing out one pair of shock absorbers after another. High-ranking army officers and Sandinista government officials always welcomed him with backslaps and shots of rum whenever he appeared in their villages.

When the electricity didn't come on that evening, Yvan and Mario drove up to the plant, where they found the hydroplant locked and Oscar gone. Yvan and Mario forced open the lock to the powerhouse, surveyed the turbine, generator, and governor, and found a manual in English. By the light of a flashlight, Yvan flipped through it, looked at the diagrams, and followed the step-by-step instructions to turn on the machines, using a pipe wrench to force open the valve to the dam. The machines began chugging, and the Captain's office was alight.

That evening, the Captain held a party late into the night. Just after dawn, Oscar returned home and turned off the hydroplant.

When Ben found out about the break-in, he was furious, and angrier yet when he realized that the valve to the dam had been damaged, and that the plant had been run without the automatic on. Ben marched into town to confront the Captain, who, outraged, told him it was a military priority that the town have electricity twenty-four hours a day.

Ben knew that he should have had the plant running around the clock, but he was reluctant to turn it on until the government approved the Cuá/Bocay project and he could move to El Cuá full-time. As the months dragged on, and he received no word from the government, Ben began to worry that they might never approve it. He knew that INE favored large-scale centralized projects because they affected more people and were more economical than smaller projects, which were expensive in terms of time, manpower, and resources for the amount of energy they produced. He wrote his parents:

> Much of my life has been up in the air since December. I've been wait-ing for a final decision on the Cuá-Bocay project. Things go around and around in circles without apparent end or direction. Meetings lead to other meetings, lead to reports being rewritten, and at the end of this, other meet-ings. The largest block in the process, especially my part in the project, is INE, or, more exactly, the vice-minister of INE's refusal to give full INE support to the project. There are a number of reasons why he doesn't want to involve INE. I think the primary reason is a lack of commitment on his part—to take the risks—(our part) of working in the war zone. There are basic decisions we all make as to the importance of our work as individu-als in relation to our ideals. Given a self-centered set of ideals, work is very important for self-advancement, the case of the vice-minister. For him the Cuá-Bocay project is 'just another hydro project' that could be put in a much more comfortable place where his picture could be taken with someone from the Swedish Embassy and another two-year donation could be agreed upon. Unfortunately that is a possibility, but not in El Cuá or Bocay. Meanwhile we lost the opportunity to do the necessary survey work in the dry season.

Ben had seen plans evaporate and international grants lost because of inertia by officials. He began to panic that the El Cuá project would slip through his fin-gers. He knew of only one person who was ready to work, and who could guar-antee the project's success: Don. Ben talked to Charlie about his fears. They knew that Don was counting on Ben to work through the bureaucracy, set up the infra-structure, and get government approval, but they decided they couldn't wait any longer. They sent the "green light" to Don in Europe.

In Europe, Don's reunion with his Italian girlfriend hadn't worked out, and as he mulled over what to do next, he often thought of Nicaragua. Italian newspa-pers reported the Contra aid votes in the U.S. Congress, and heavy fighting between the Contras and the Sandinista army. Don's European friends, who were involved in solidarity groups, often asked him about Nicaragua, and while Don worked on the El Cuá video, converting it to PAL format to fit the European video system, he often cited the hydroplant as a Sandinista success that benefited the poor. When Don received Ben's telegram, he gladly made reservations to fly back to Nicaragua, planning to give the Cuá/Bocay project a year of his life.

Chapter 11

Don Moves to El Cuá

Don returned to Managua in April 1986 and appeared at Ben's office early the next morning, still suffering from jet lag. Don sensed Ben was nervous, and after one conversation, found out why. The Cuá/Bocay project was no further along than when he had left five months earlier. INE had not given final approval: funds and tools had not yet been allocated, and there was no personnel assigned to the project.

Don was furious. He flew out of Ben's office in a rage. Don decided that he had two options: give up on El Cuá and return to Europe, or throw himself into the project to make the plan a reality. "The only thing that could keep the project alive," said Don, "was to keep the activity going in the field." He stuffed a few belongings into a daypack, caught the bus to Jinotega, where he hopped the 6:00 A.M. public transport truck to El Cuá, and by afternoon had moved into a vacant cubicle in the bunkhouse. Carlos, the town doctor who used to live there, had suffered a mental breakdown, and had been transferred after taking his clothes off in the middle of town.

Don introduced himself to Captain Miguelito, handing him letters of recommendation from Sandinista officials. Don understood relationships in a small town, and knew that the project's success depended on his relationship with the Captain.

Don offered the Captain an unfiltered cigarette, and they both lit up. The Captain eyed Don cautiously as he told him about his many years working in Canada, and the mechanic's shop he planned to build in El Cuá. He also revealed his plan to connect the entire town to the hydroplant.

The Captain's first question to Don was whether the electricity would be on twenty-four hours a day. Don thought that it would. Pleased by the answer, the Captain decided that he could work with Don.

When Don left the Captain's office, he had an AK-47 rifle dangling from his shoulder. In El Cuá, all officials and most government employees were assigned guns, loaded and ready. Government workers and many locals also had camouflage uniforms because they belonged to the militia. Don wanted a uniform also, but no one had one large enough for him.

Back in his cubicle, Don examined the gun, running his hand over the barrel, clicking the safety on and off, unloading the ammunition, and squeezing the trigger. He counted the clips and clicked one in, then pulled it out, quickly jamming another one in. He dismantled the rifle, piece by piece, wiping off the grease, then reassembled the gun, hearing the satisfying click as he slipped the clip into the holder.

With his rifle dangling from his shoulder, Don trudged up the hot, dusty road, ready to hitchhike, but not one vehicle passed. After hiking the two miles to the plant, Don decided he had to get a car.

At the plant, Oscar was surprised and pleased to see Don, especially when he found out that he was there to stay. After examining the machines, which ran flawlessly, Don instructed him to run the plant twenty-four hours a day.

In Managua, Ben realized that Don was angry with him and knew that he had to take immediate action. Ben gathered the few maps of Jinotega province he could find, took the public transport truck to El Cuá, and knocked on Don's bunkhouse door, ready to plan their next steps. Together they examined the maps, trying to discern if the streams had a strong vertical drop and year-round head flow to support a hydroplant. Since the maps were old and not to scale, they realized they'd have to build a weir—a notched dam—to measure the water flow. Ben and Oscar planned to erect it in El Cedro cooperative to acquire dry-season data before the rainy season began in May, while Don would remain in El Cuá to oversee the plant.

As Ben prepared to leave, Don asked him if he would carry a gun. El Cedro cooperative straddled a Contra infiltration route between two mountains, where hundreds of Contras, coming from bases in Honduras, passed by on their way into central Nicaragua. In the past three years, the Contras had attacked El Cedro cooperative twice, killing seventeen members. Don reminded Ben that he would be working outside the coop, walking the same mountains and fording the same streams as the Contras. After discussing the situation, Ben and Oscar decided to arm themselves, but wear civilian clothes.

Ben and Oscar picked up AK-47 automatic rifles from the Captain, who arranged a ride for them to El Cedro in an army jeep. As they left, he warned them to be on the alert for the Contra troops, who had been sighted in that area. They clutched their rifles, scanning the road for land mines, as they imagined ambushes and discussed what to do if the Contras opened fire on them. Ben wrote, "How often have I written about survival? Here I am riding around the war zone of Bocay with a loaded gun on my lap. Every curve scares me. I know that one of these times I won't be lucky. From one of the cornfields a burst of machine gun fire will rip through the side of the jeep. Will I keep myself together to roll out of the jeep? If so, what will I do? Will my legs be so shot up that I won't be able to seek cover?"

After an hour of tense driving, the jeep crested a hill, then descended into the valley where El Cedro huddled. Shacks were strung along the road, home to 271 people. Jagged trenches surrounded the settlement.

The land on which El Cedro was built had originally belonged to a Somoza supporter who fled to Honduras after the Sandinistas came to power. In 1982 nine families, many of whom had worked for years as day laborers on the farm, formed a cooperative on the farm. On August 10, 1983, the Contras had ambushed the public transportation truck near El Cedro, killing fifteen of the eighteen passengers. To defend themselves, the cooperative organized a militia, using knapsacks made of feed sacks, rubber mud boots and World War II–era guns—Garands, Baycetas, and hunting rifles.

In December 1983, the Contras had launched an offensive in the Cuá/Bocay valley, and on December 16 Kaliman—"Superman," a Contra leader—and his group opened fire on El Cedro with their automatic weapons. They quickly overpowered the coop militia. El Cedro's residents fled into the hills, and an hour later the Contras had occupied the coop, looting the warehouse, ransacking houses, pitching clothes, radios, blankets, and mattresses into the mud outside. Kaliman kidnapped the nurse and set fire to the health center, the warehouse, several houses, two trucks, and the coop's only tractor. Seven coop members and five Contras died in the attack.

Families rebuilt the coop, but on June 9, 1985, the Contras attacked again. By this time the El Cedro militia was armed with AK-47 automatic rifles, and the fighting was fiercer, but the El Cedro militia once again withdrew. The Contras overran the cooperative, killing eleven people and kidnapping eight others. They burned all sixty-one houses and torched the health center, the warehouse, and the Protestant and Catholic chapels. They killed all the chickens, pigs, ducks, and dogs, and slaughtered nearly a hundred cattle, a significant blow for the coop.

After each attack, some families had fled El Cedro for the relative safety of El Cuá and Bocay, while other families who lived in isolated farmhouses in the mountains, afraid of being kidnapped by the Contras, abandoned their farms to join El Cedro cooperative. Included among the cooperative population were four war widows and six women whose husbands had disappeared with the Contras before they moved to El Cedro. Six of the nine men who formed the cooperative were killed by the Contras.

The war had touched every family in El Cedro. With each Contra attack, residents mourned their losses, buried their dead, and rebuilt their houses, but the attacks sapped morale. After every attack El Cedro's residents became sadder, more resigned and hopeless, unable to think or initiate action.

By 1986, coop residents were overwhelmed with fatigue and fear. The women's empty eyes reflected pain and powerlessness. The community was comprised primarily of parasite-laden children, women, and old men. Children played "bowling" using rocks and bullet casings collected from the ground. They chased each other though the gutted timbers of burned-out houses. Many of El Cedro's residents, like Sorida Blandón, mother of seven children, had grown up in the war. "I have known war since I was fifteen years old. I lost my father and my four brothers in war before the [Sandinista] triumph. The National Guard came one night and bound them together with barbed wire and took them away ... they were pushed from a plane. After that my mother would not eat or drink and she died. In the attack on El Cedro two of my sons had their eardrums ruptured. I would have to go to Jinotega [five hours away] to learn if they can be treated. But I am afraid to leave my family because in case there is another attack, I would want to be with all of my children."

When Ben heard the history of the coop and saw how dispirited its residents were, he wondered how they managed to continue working. "Somehow the corn and beans are planted, grown, and picked. There is so much more that could be done—except for the war. If it only ended ... but it goes on. There is so much work to be done. But, bit by bit, I must remember that I can't do it all. I'll do my bit."

Ben and Oscar met the cooperative's president, who assigned Sergio and Luis—experienced construction workers and good marksmen—to work with them. The four men, all carrying rifles, hiked out of El Cedro, following the stream, looking for a steep drop to build the weir. Every morning, hiking to the weir, they passed armed farmers in the fields, who kept one eye on the horizon and the other on the cornfield. Throughout the days, the wooden weir slowly took form.

In the evenings Ben sometimes wandered by the government-run "Farmer's Store," which was supposed to sell cooking oil, soap, salt, sugar, boots, machetes, and other products at subsidized prices, but the shelves were bare. Because of ambushes by the Contras, private transport truck owners stopped transporting goods to El Cuá and the more northern settlements. The government was organizing convoys of eighteen-wheel trucks, but the caravans had stopped running when the Contras were spotted near the road, and no supplies arrived for weeks at a time. Families had to survive on what they grew: corn, coffee, beans, and plantains.

Ben also visited the nurse at the health center. After a Contra attack, the health center was always the first structure to be rebuilt, but even so, three or four children died from malnutrition and preventable diseases every year. One of the few sources of protein was *cuajada*, a hard, salty cheese. When the rainy season ended, the coop's bony cows stopped producing milk, and when supply caravans stopped running, resident's meals were reduced to black coffee and tortillas three times a day.

As dusk fell, weary women dropped their voices to whispers. The tin-roofed coop hunkered down in the valley as darkness enshrouded it. Militia men donned rain ponchos and rifles, stuffed clips of ammunition into chest pouches, and hiked into the rain, joining croaking frogs in the hills. Militia men squatted in the jagged muddy trenches above the settlement, waiting.

On the last day of April, a militia member spotted a group of several hundred Contras on a nearby ridge. That night, Ben wrote:

> Tomorrow is May Day. We have been advised that the Contras might attack tonight or in the morning. The sunset is beautiful. How do I feel? Somehow with the sunset and the unusually warm weather I feel calm. But tonight I'll sleep with my boots on. Scared! Of course. Tonight I may be in a battle. 500 on one side and 100 on the other. And here I am. One day the road is "clean." The next day we can't work as the Contra might attack. I asked one of the guys, Sergio, the carpenter, if he ever is scared, "No, es vivir o morir." (No, it's either fight and live or surrender and die.) So very simple.

During the night, gunfire from automatic weapons growled down the valley. The thump of mortars could be heard in the distance. Shadows flitted by, and militia men nervously fired warning bursts of tracer bullets. Coop members rotated guard duty, but many militia men, too nervous to sleep, stayed awake throughout the night as they aimed rifles into the darkness, straining to hear the first shot, the first rallying call to the trenches.

Around 4:00 A.M., the most likely time for an attack, word went down the line, "Ponéte chiva," (Be ready, get tough.) Militia men struggled out of hammocks, loaded extra clips of ammunition into chest pouches, released the safeties of their guns, and crouched in the trenches. They stared into the darkness, which gradually gave way to the first red streaks of the new day. Chickens fluttered to the ground from tree limbs where they had roosted during the night. The sun rose. Ben wrote, "Well, it looks like the Contras aren't going to attack." From the coop kitchen drifted the sound of women palming tortillas. Ben wrote, "Always the pit-pit-pat of tortillas. With Contras or without. The grinders are being turned; stone on stone as it has been for so many years and will be for many years to come."

Farmers dragged in from militia duty. Sergio gingerly picked his way down the slope to the coop kitchen for a cup of coffee. A lanky fourteen-year-old kid carrying an AK-47 trooped along beside him. Sergio told Ben that the kid had run off with the Contras the previous year, but after two trips from Honduras loaded down by seventy-five-pound packs of ammunition, he had turned himself in to the Sandinistas and asked for amnesty. When he returned to his family's farm in the countryside, they were gone, perhaps to Honduras or a village in Nicaragua. No one knew. A family in the cooperative had taken him in.

Farmers returned to their shacks to eat before heading out to the fields. A militia squad patrolled the road, sweeping a metal detector to look for land mines. Another militia squad combed the hills.

Ben wrote, "I reach into my change pocket on my Levi's and pull out an AK bullet. I get tired." He was taking up a challenge, trying to prove himself. He wrote in his journal:

> I think I walked into the wrong set. I remember a cartoon about a baby that gets drafted. There he is with oversized clothes marching. But he tries to make them believe that he is a baby. I'm trying to make them believe I'm a man. Once more I'm testing myself. Calculus, math camp, University of Washington, engineering, here I go again. When will it end? Do I want it to?

On May Day in El Cuá, Captain Miguelito, Don, and government officials inaugurated the plant's twenty-four-hour-a-day operation. They baptized the plant

"Denis Sommarriba" after an INE employee who had been electrocuted, and named the electric system "Cien Años de la Lucha Proletaria," (100 Years of Proletariat Struggle) in honor of the hundredth anniversary of May Day.

On the same day, Ben and Oscar finished building the weir in El Cedro and hitchhiked south in an army caravan, following a jeep full of soldiers holding rifles. Ben wrote, "The exploration goes in front. In the back seat is a skinny fifteen-year-old. He survived an ambush 500 meters ahead of where we are now."

When Ben and Oscar arrived in El Cuá, Ben was upset to find the plant had been inaugurated without him. He angrily confronted Don, who shrugged his shoulders, saying that it had been a political mistake not to turn the plant on full-time earlier. Ben knew what Don said was true, but he still felt crushed.

To make matters worse, Oscar found a pile of rusty wire lying on the floor of the brick bungalow with a note from INE instructing the plant operator to make his own bed frame. Oscar scowled, baseball cap pulled low over his eyes. He was insulted that INE officials believed engineers and INE directors had a right to sleep in beds, but that a plant operator, a peasant of El Cuá, had to sleep on the floor, or on rusty tangled wire. Ben calmed him, bundled up the rusty wire, and sent it back to INE, along with a note requesting two beds for the plant operator.

When Ben returned to Managua, he took the bus over to Barrio Linda Vista to talk with Maria de Zuniga. He described the danger working in El Cedro and asked her, in case he was ever killed, to handle the funeral arrangements, as well as the political aspect of his death with the Sandinistas and the United States. Maria, surprised, didn't know how to respond except to agree.

Ben wrote his parents, "Family. Part of my not writing earlier is because of a lot of soul-searching and feeling very distant from the States. I'm sorry. It became a self-defeating circle of cutting myself off and then feeling cut off. I'm trying to get out of it."

"As for my work, and safety: I really don't know what to say. What I am doing is very important to me." He wrote them about El Cedro, how dedicated the farmers were, and also evoked the danger of working there. He explained that for him, it was worthwhile. He wrote:

> Why? Why do we do it? Because they deserve it. They sacrifice and continue sacrificing. They deserve a better life. I have the honor of helping them. Risk is accepted or rejected and I've chosen to accept it. I know its meaningless to say "don't worry." I want you to know what I'm doing and why

I do it. Rest assured that I don't take "undue" risks but "undue" is very relative.

So that is work. 9:00 to 5:00 at Boeing it isn't.

He then wrote his parents that if there ever was an emergency, and they couldn't reach him, they should contact Maria de Zuniga in Managua.

In El Cuá, Don learned not only that no map of the town existed, but that no one even knew the town's population. Every day, war refugees continued to arrive, erecting black plastic shanties on the outskirts of town.

Don drew up a rough map of the houses, light posts, and lines, then estimated the materials needed to connect all the houses to the plant. He found some wire, connectors, switches, and a few lightbulbs in the bunkhouse, but not enough to wire the town.

Mayor Adolfo Zeledon promised supplies, but when Don surveyed the desk, single chair, and one battered typewriter with broken keys in the mayor's office, he doubted that there were any to share. When Don asked his boss Mario Acevedo for supplies, Mario said they would be difficult to find.

Realizing he was on his own, Don swapped with INE, using wire cutters and pliers in exchange for steel-spiked shoes, leather belts, and other climbing gear. "I got materials from anywhere I could beg, borrow, or steal them," said Don. Charlie in Matagalpa persuaded UNICEF to supply some mechanic's tools.

One early morning, Don climbed the plaza's light pole, roped himself onto it, and dropped a cable into El Cuá's schoolhouse, a tin-roofed shed divided into three rooms by plywood walls. When Oscar, Don, and a visiting Canadian internationalist unrolled wire into the classrooms, children stopped their lessons to stare at them. The crew hoisted each other into the rafters, stretched the wire, nailed it down, put in connectors, and screwed in lightbulbs. When light filled the room, the children squealed.

Since Don hated eating in the dark, he next wired the diner, hanging a bare bulb from the center of the tin roof. Don kept his tools in his cubicle, next to his bed, fearing that they would be borrowed and never returned. His cubicle resembled a junkyard, but he tried to make it more livable by stringing a hammock for visitors and buying a kerosene stove. He also got a pet monkey named Sario. "It was like a German shepherd, but on a chain," said Don. He tied her to the door, from which she would climb onto the bunkhouse railing, scramble up to the roof with her chain in her hand, and bare her teeth at passersby.

When Don arrived home, Sario scrambled inside to follow him. If he ignored her, she crawled onto his table, flinging books, pencils, screwdrivers, and other tools out the door. She put her dirty hands around him and hung from his neck, or climbed into his lap. He patted her, even though she was covered with fleas and ticks, but when she snuggled up next to him in his cot, he tossed her to the floor. She chattered at him, then tried to bite him. After a few nights of fighting with her, Don left her tied to a long chain outside a government office, where the employees enjoyed teasing her.

At night, by the light of a kerosene lamp, Don made lists of what had to be done. He knew that both he and Ben had a massive job ahead of them, as they were about to confront underdevelopment head-on.

Underdevelopment, as Don and Ben understood it, meant an existence without reason, a feeling that it was impossible to break out of the misery. Underdevelopment also implied lack of labor discipline, which meant that employees were late if they showed up to work at all. Nepotism was also a serious problem. Jobs were too often viewed in terms of territories or egos, and projects were often derailed by lack of coordination.

Underdevelopment also meant a lack of responsibility. Officials promised materials, resources, and time, without intending to keep their word. Resources were often wasted: machines rusted because of lack of maintenance; spare parts were lost or never ordered; and broken machinery was never repaired. Tractors, graders, and backhoes, donations from developed countries, lay dumped, broken, ruined, and rusting across the countryside because locals hadn't been taught to maintain or repair them. Underdevelopment also implied that authority was unquestionable. Farmers deferred silently to those in leadership positions, never arguing, as they had survived decades of oppression by humbly agreeing. To question authority was to ask for trouble.

Both Don and Ben were unsure whether the Cuá/Bocay project would break the farmers out of the circle of poverty and underdevelopment by teaching them the skills to make a living, but they thought it was worth a try.

In April, the white-hot sun seared Managua. Even people's spirits seemed to droop, and Mira realized that the revolutionary fervor that had gripped Barrio Máximo Jerez was waning. She wrote:

Last night I returned to my barrio for the CDS meeting. They had sent an invitation to each house in the barrio, with a note talking about the lack of vigilance in the barrio and the need to reactivate it during this time. About 200 people were expected; about 30 or 35 showed up. Some said that the meeting was badly timed, because it was scheduled during the soap opera, and all the women were glued to their TVs.

"And the men?" I asked.

"Well, it's Saturday, they're all drinking rum."

I think that they need more than a change of the hour to have a better participation in the revolutionary tasks in our barrio.

At INE, after eight months of work, Mira had finally finished her 40-page report on wood cookstoves. She placed it on her supervisor's desk before he left for Sweden, but back in her windowless office, Mira wondered what to do next. She was interested in working on the El Cuá project, but she lacked the engineering or mechanical skills. She wondered where she could be of most use to the revolution, and considered returning to the U.S. to coordinate and funnel supplies to the Cuá/Bocay project.

As Mira struggled with a decision, she heard a rumor that INE had finally given approval to the Cuá/Bocay project. She wrote:

While I haven't heard any of this from the horse's mouth yet (that the Cuá/Bocay project got the go-ahead by the FSLN), I think it means that Ben will be leaving INE. For personal reasons, I'm sad—I've enjoyed the greater contact I've had with him since he moved to my building. I definitely feel 'left out.' I want very badly to work on this project, but have not yet done anything to pursue it. Don't know exactly why. Big part of it is indecision about coming home.

When Ben learned that INE had finally approved the project, he was jubilant, and planned to return to El Cuá to tell Don the good news. Mira, who wanted to visit El Cuá, suggested she go with him to photograph the plant for the NICAT newsletter, and to practice building a Lorena stove.

Ben agreed, and Mira was overjoyed to be finally going to El Cuá. She explained to a friend in a letter that there was only one remaining obstacle. "If they can get a driver—all of those assigned to this department have refused to go, because it is deemed too fucking dangerous, especially now that they were told by the military command in the area to carry arms on the road in and out."

Chapter 12

Mira Visits El Cuá

On May 22, 1986, Mira bounced along in the back of the INE pickup, clutching the roll bar alongside Ben, Don, and a truckload of welding equipment. Each of them carried guns. The pickup fishtailed around curves, pitching Mira from side to side while she tried to take photos. As she surveyed the thick jungle brush around them, she remembered Ben's instructions in the event of an ambush: "When the vehicle stops, jump out, move away, and space yourselves out every twenty feet."

The rains were late that year, so the mountains were brown and dry. The sun beat down fiercely. Don pulled his leather prospector's hat down over his face. Black storm clouds lay low over the horizon, threatening rain, blotting out the tops of the cordillera, the air clogged with humidity.

The INE pickup zoomed down to a river and then suddenly braked in front of the twisted girders of a bridge, the metal bent in awkward, grotesque shapes. A week earlier, the Contras had blown up two bridges on the road to El Cuá. The driver drove through the river, shallow and sluggish in the dry season. He stopped at every military post along the road, asking if it was safe to continue. "We climb and climb," Mira later wrote in her journal. They passed hills full of shiny-leaved coffee bushes. "We pass the turn off to La Columbina, where I picked coffee." Mira had heard of people referring to traveling into the mountains as going *adentro*. "Now I have some sense of what *adentro*, inside, means," Mira wrote. "We are actually getting closer to the Honduran border, and thus, one would think heading 'up' or 'out.' But what counts is only that we are getting further 'into' isolated areas."

They passed only a few vehicles, as scattered clusters of people waited for rides. "I knew we were finally getting close when we came over a gorgeous ridge and there

171

suddenly were electric lines in the valley below," wrote Mira. "I could feel tension leaving my body, even though I was still bouncing in the back of the little pickup, hanging on with both hands to the roll bar, knees bent, dust getting between my teeth, shoulders sunburned. We'd gotten here."

The pickup drove through the valley, zooming past the main plaza, too fast for Mira to take photos, as she craned her neck, trying to absorb the town of El Cuá. They passed the refugees' black plastic shanties, crossed the El Cuá River, and barreled up to the plant, parking in front of the militia's lean-tos. Teenage militia men poked their heads from the banana-leaf huts, blinking at the sight of three foreigners.

In the afternoon, Ben took Mira into El Cuá and introduced her to the Captain, who liked to keep track of new faces in town. As Ben led Mira down the dusty street, she took photos. At the health clinic Mira met the nurse, Marta Julia, who showed Mira the laboratory, which had been set up after the electricity was turned on. Ben and Mira helped her unload boxes for an upcoming polio and measles vaccination campaign. Marta Julia had only a few months left of her one-year assignment to El Cuá, and she told them she was looking forward to returning to the city. Juana Gonzales, the cleaning woman, followed behind visitors, mopping the floor after they tracked red dust inside.

That evening, the three Americans stayed at the plant with Oscar. Surrounded by the high-pitched buzz of crickets, they sat on the porch under a full moon, drinking Flor de Caña rum. Frogs croaked in the streambed. Oscar took his Suzuki guitar from under the bed and strummed it gently, while Mira and he talked about the Contras' recent attack on Miraflores, a potato cooperative near Estelí. Militia men held off the Contras throughout the night but were eventually forced to retreat. At the end of the fighting, seventeen people were wounded and eight killed, including two children of a friend of his. The Contras had attacked and burned the coop three times because there were mountains around the coop, just like here, Oscar explained. Mira looked at the mountains, black humps against a moonlit sky, and wondered how close the Contras were.

The next day, Mira began building a Lorena woodstove near the brick bungalow. To protect it from the sun, Oscar and Federico built a tin roof held up by four bamboo poles. Mira measured out a four-by-four foot space, then leveled it, digging up hard, red dirt. At noon, Hilda showed up at the plant to deliver lunch and cast inquisitive glances at Mira, the first female foreigner that she had ever met.

After lunch, the three Americans followed the Río Esperanza to a wide, sandy spot where the river crossed the main road, and shoveled sand into buckets. Downstream, in a haze of bubbles, women washed clothes, slapping them against rocks, while their naked children, baked by the sun, splashed beside them, slyly edging over to watch the foreigners.

While they worked, "Goliath," the yellow public transport truck, rumbled up the road packed with farmers, women, children, and bulky burlap sacks. As it lurched across the river, one of the truck's side supports broke, and a few farmers tumbled out, laughing and shrieking as they fell into the knee-high water. They ran after the truck, waving straw hats and baseball caps, whistling for the driver to stop. The truck halted, and myriad callused hands reached toward the farmers, pulling them up in one swift motion. Someone lashed the side supports together with a rope, and the truck lurched northward to Bocay. A short while later another public transport truck, a blue one, came from the opposite direction, going to market, jammed with farmers clutching chickens and dressed in their best clothes.

Back at the plant, Mira mixed the sand with clay, patting the mixture into a neat, square base. Hilda swept her long black hair into a bun, then fell to her knees to help, jamming handfuls of the mixture onto the base, as red clay clung to her legs and streaked her polyester dress. The hot May sun beat down on them, and sweat ran down their faces, forearms, and stomachs. Mira, filthy but satisfied, listened to the steady humming of the plant.

When they finished packing the first layer on the stove, Mira decided to let it dry overnight, and suggested to Hilda that they hike to the dam to bathe. "Hilda thought I was crazy, since the canal of the plant [here] is as good a place as any to bathe," Mira wrote. "I wanted to swim. She doesn't know how."

During the hike, Mira asked Hilda about her life. Hilda replied quietly, addressing Mira in the polite form of Spanish, *Usted.* Mira had trouble understanding her country dialect.

Eighteen-year-old Hilda had been raised near Matagalpa. Her education went only as far as the first grade. When she was sixteen, while visiting her relatives on Christmas Eve, she met Oscar, and got pregnant soon afterward, with Aidé, and later with Oscar Daniel. Her mother looked after her children in the evenings while Hilda attended adult education classes. She had just learned to read.

At the dam, Mira dove into the cool water. She wrote:

The water feels incredible by the time I get there. I swim in underpants and my shirt. I can never figure out what's cool, modesty wise. Hilda bathed in shorts and her bra, first changing into the shorts on top of the dam, in full view of the boys watching below, and the slightly older boys in the trenches on the ridge above us. I just don't get it.

When Mira finished swimming, she put on a cotton dress, and they hiked down the hill. The evening air was heavy with impending rain. "The walk back down along the canal was equally hot and sweaty," Mira wrote, "but I was more comfortable in my dress, and the mountains are beautiful. I said so to Hilda. 'Yes, it's beautiful here. It's just that we can't live in peace.'"

Since Oscar had moved to the plant, Hilda and the children stayed with her mother in El Golfo. She wanted to visit the plant more often, but Oscar had forbidden her to, because, Mira wrote, "it's her duty to stay with the kids." Oscar eventually wanted his family to move to the plant with him, but he was waiting for the Captain to post more militiamen. Hilda wanted to be with Oscar, but she was also scared to move to the plant. "People say that the Contras are going to come and take Oscar away," Hilda confided. "Or that they are going to come and take me."

Back at the brick bungalow, Mira thought about Hilda's fears as she watched the militia guards in their banana leaf huts. She wrote:

I look out at our militia guard—boys, 10–13 years old, one older man, and the group's 'responsable,' a Frente member from La Chata, the neighboring coop.... The kids are so little I just can't digest the fact that they are guarding us. They spend their time building little tents out of banana leaves, and digging trenches and dirt emplacements in the mud. Or shrieking and chasing each other around. Looks like the Boy Scouts, right down to the green uniforms. Except for the automatic rifles they all carry. One kid is so short they had to cut off the stock of his rifle so it wouldn't bang on the ground when he walks.

That evening, Ben, Don, Oscar, and the INE driver went into town, leaving Mira and Hilda alone at the plant. The women checked the gauges, took the readings from the machines, recorded them in the plant's log, and went to bed. Sometime later, the men returned, in a raucous mood after spending the evening doing rum shots with Captain Miguelito.

The next day began a one-day vaccination campaign in Bocay. Because El Cuá had electricity, vaccines could be stored there and taken in coolers to the outlying villages. Early Sunday morning Dr. Sergio Chavarría, the town's current doctor,

Ambrosio Mogorrón, a Spanish nurse, and Marta Julia borrowed the Captain's green Toyota pickup truck, loaded polio and measles vaccines into the back, and sped off to Bocay.

That day the weather was overcast. On Sunday afternoon, the clouds opened up, finally unleashing the May rains. Children ran outdoors to get wet so that they would live another year, according to Nicaraguan lore.

Mira watched the rain worriedly. The small base of her stove was getting wet, and she was concerned that the layers of clay and sand would never dry in the humidity of the rainy season.

Inside the brick bungalow, Don and Ben discussed how to weld the compression chamber. They decided to drain the penstock early the next morning in order to do the welding. Don took Oscar to the powerhouse to practice reading the control panel.

Ben sat on one of the cots that had just arrived from INE and wrote in his journal, "El Cuá is done. El Cuá is done. I repeat it to myself as the far off lightning silhouettes an amazing tree." Suddenly, the lights flickered, then went off. Ben froze. A few seconds later, the lights came back on. Ben relaxed, as he realized what had happened. "The lights just went off for a moment. Don was showing Oscar how to read the kilowatt-hour meter. Power out—high voltage—Contra—gun—powerhouse. Why do these reflexes exist? Why do I want to be where I live with this high level of 'anxiety?' The lightning is beautiful. El Cuá is done. The flicker of the lights was done on purpose."

That evening in Bocay, after completing the vaccination campaign, Dr. Chavarría, Ambrosio, Marta Julia, a nurse from Bocay, and two teachers climbed into the green pickup and headed back to El Cuá amid the steady rain. As the truck rounded a curve near El Cedro cooperative, the air exploded. Passengers in the back of the pickup were tossed through the air like rag dolls. The truck was blown off the road. It flipped over and landed several yards away, pinning the driver underneath.

Wounded survivors thrashed in the mud, screaming and groaning. Bloody body parts, clothing, and orange coolers were scattered in the road. Marta Julia lay crying in the mud, shrapnel from the land mine embedded in her body. Dr. Chavarría was also riddled with shrapnel. Barely conscious, he crawled from body to body, trying to save the lives of his travel companions, but there was little he could do. He later wrote:

One of my companions had his right leg amputated from the force of the explosion. There was blood everywhere. His left foot was also gone. I put on a tourniquet but he died. Another person also had his arm blown open and the bones were completely fractured, too many to even count. All the cadavers were bloody and full of mud because they fell into the road.

Another person had a wound in the stomach, and his large intestines were hanging out. The nurse that was working at the [Bocay] medical post died when two pieces of shrapnel ripped open the artery in her neck.

Eight people lay dead in the mud: the nurse from Bocay, two teachers, two farm union organizers, two Sandinista officials, and the Spanish internationalist.

The next day, Mira wrote:

It's about 7:00 A.M. We sit waiting for the penstock to drain to do some welding on the compression chamber. A little while ago a young *compa* [soldier] from town hiked up and asked us a favor—could we lend them our truck and driver? Last night Miguelito's truck hit a mine on the road to Bocay—there are several dead and wounded and we are the only people here with a vehicle.

Ben closed his eyes for a long moment, his face screwed up, then called in the driver. The two of them were out drinking with Miguelito night before last. Captain Miguelito, the historic Frente collaborator, party representative in the zone ... an old guy. Well known. Well liked.

Ben asked me if I wanted to go with them to take photographs. No.

Don started to talk about a new way to monitor the frequency of the currency generated. I go look for my paper and pen, unable to act as if nothing has happened, needing to talk to someone, not wanting to make them talk about it if they'd prefer not to.

Everything is not normal. A bunch of young kids just got blown into little pieces about 25 km. up the road. Real near the refugee settlement we are going to visit in a few days. It's true, a lot of people are dying in Central America, daily, but I refuse to accept this situation as normal.

The eight bodies, including the Spaniard, Ambrosio Mogorrón, were buried in a common grave in San José de Bocay. Marta Julia and Dr. Sergio Chavarría recuperated and returned to the city, and the Cuá/Bocay area now had one less doctor and two fewer nurses.

Throughout the next few days, Mira completed the cookstove with help from Hilda, who had received Oscar's permission to leave their children with her mother during the day. Mira had not thought her first stove would take so long to build, or be such hard work. After several days, her hands and fingers were covered with blisters, and her fingers ached when she held her pen to write.

"The layers build up slowly," she wrote, "the humidity of the rainy season slowing the drying time."

While buying supplies in El Cuá one afternoon, Ben, Mira, and Don ran into the driver of the Captain's pickup. He told them that after he got out from under the truck, he had walked away from the wreckage. He was the only one who escaped unharmed. Even though Captain Miguelito had not been in the truck, most people in the village believed that land mine had been meant for him. Mira wrote:

> Yesterday the public transportation [truck] refused to take two nurses from El Cuá back up to their health center in Bocay. They aren't armed, just being development workers was enough to make them personas non grata. The owner of the truck that travels the route will say it's because the nurses are targets, and he doesn't want to make his vehicle a target. The man's truck gets stopped by the Contras regularly, sometimes his passengers get taken away. But he continues to live, and to do the run.
>
> In Managua, there is a tendency to talk about people who "aren't participating much" or are participating in a way that's seen as obstructive, as "Contra." I know that purposefully dragging one's feet in a Managua office can do a lot of damage to this sinking wartime economy. But I usually feel like people use the label "Contra" too freely in those circumstances.... But the people who passed on the information about when Miguelito was heading for San José de Bocay? Are they responsible for those eight deaths?

One morning Ben invited Mira and Don to lunch at the house of the widows, Julia and Rosa Amelia. Ben told them to leave their guns in the jeep, hidden from the women, because El Golfo was "pure Contra territory," and the widows were Contra supporters, but Ben assured Mira that the widows were his friends.

Over lunch, Julia complained about Sandinista officials, the lack of farmhands, the draft, shortages, and restrictions on her crops. Mira wanted to leave. When Ben took her to the kitchen to see the ancient clay stove that belched smoke, Mira watched piglets wander around the kitchen. She declined Ben's offer to see the water source, and declined Julia's coffee, while Ben took an extra cup. Mira felt uncomfortable, but Ben was at home.

Mira was glad to return to her stove. She snapped photos of Hilda at work beside Ben and Don. Hilda had always been shy around the two men, but after watching how casually Mira interacted with them, she became more relaxed.

After ten days of intensive work, the stove was done. Hilda noted that it gave off much less smoke than the big, earthen stoves that everyone in the valley used. She asked Mira when she'd come back to build another stove, but Mira wasn't sure when she'd be able to return to El Cuá. Before she had visited, she thought she would be too afraid to live there, but she realized that her excitement about the project outweighed her fear. She thought that the Cuá/Bocay project was a promising model, not just for Nicaragua but for the Third World in general: it had the potential to accomplish tremendous change, like a rise in the standard of living, and an eventual long-term peace.

Back in the INE office, Mira was depressed to learn that her boss had left for Sweden without even glancing at her report. She didn't know what her next job would be, but she had decided to stay in Nicaragua.

Ben was in Managua visiting a friend one weekend when he saw Chile, the thin Colombian woman from Bogotá with whom he had danced on his unicycle at the Sandinista election rally. Over a cup of coffee, she told Ben that when she was twenty, she had flown to Panama, where she joined other Latin American fighters in the final offensive against the Nicaraguan dictator, Somoza, in 1979. Chile was not prepared for life as a guerrilla. "It was awful," she said, "we were constantly hungry, always wet, our feet were soaked. We didn't know if we would live or die—I saw many of my friends get blown apart by bombs."

Chile survived the fighting, only to discover that she had a degenerative disease that was slowly causing her esophagus to close. She had trouble eating solid foods, and lived on a diet of liquids, and was so emaciated that her cheekbones poked though her face. Ben said he would ask his father, a doctor, what could be done to help her.

In spite of her illness, Chile was lively and cheerful. Ben admired her unflagging spirit. She invited him to celebrate her birthday.

The next evening, Ben removed his calculator, pens, and pencils from his front pocket and hopped a bus to "La Piñata," a complex of small outdoor restaurants grouped around a cement dance floor for Chile's twenty-seventh birthday party. Young men dressed in T-shirts and jeans and barelegged women wearing tight miniskirts danced to live salsa bands.

Ben found Chile sitting with a group of Latin American internationalists, drinking beer. She squealed when she saw him, kissed him hello on his cheek, grabbed his hand, and introduced him to everyone, including her best friend, Sonia Rodríguez. Short and wiry, Sonia had close-cropped black hair, smooth features, and a flashing smile. Her eyes sparkled with energy. As the band launched into a salsa song, she swayed her body lightly in time to the music. Ben could not take his eyes off her, and he asked her to dance. When the band took a break, Ben bought her a beer and drew his metal chair closer to hers.

Sonia was also from Bogotá, where she had been active in solidarity movements with Nicaragua and El Salvador. After graduating from the university, she moved to Nicaragua in March 1984, taught at the Nicaraguan University, and then got a job reporting and editing at Agencia Nueva Nicaragua, the government wire service. As Ben and Sonia talked, Ben realized he had much more in common with Sonia than with most Nicaraguan women. She was college-educated, from a similar class background, and had long been active in solidarity movements.

When the band played again, Ben took Sonia's hand and led her to the dance floor, while Chile was delighted to see her two friends so engrossed. At the end of the night, Ben asked Sonia how he could get in touch with her.

Sonia wasn't sure she wanted to see Ben again. She was suspicious of Americans. She considered herself a Latin American revolutionary, an antiimperialist, and therefore anti-American. In Bogotá she had participated in protests and marches against U.S. companies and U.S. foreign policy. When she moved to Nicaragua, she was surprised to discover that there were American internationalists who supported the Sandinistas, and even more shocked to see them every Thursday morning carrying placards and waving banners, demonstrating against their country's policy in front of their own embassy. Suspicious, she had decided not to have anything to do with them.

Nevertheless, Sonia asked Chile about Ben. Chile said he was trustworthy, a Sandinista and a revolutionary. She reminded Sonia that they had seen him clowning the year before at a benefit for victims of the Mexican earthquake. Sonia remembered, "I saw him working here in Nicaragua, as an engineer, and as a clown, and I thought his actions showed what he believed in." She decided they could be friends, and gave him her phone number.

Sonia organized political events and dance parties for the Colombian internationalists, and invited Ben. He began visiting Sonia at her home, a cement row house that she shared with other Colombians.

Ben became smitten with Sonia. She was exactly the kind of woman he had been hoping to meet: energetic, smart, pretty, educated, and politically progressive. In short, she was perfect. Although Ben didn't tell her how he felt, he suspected she felt the same way. She affectionately nicknamed him "Benji." He wrote his parents he had met someone special, but "Nothing is certain. Once more I'm looking for daisies to play, 'She loves me, she loves me not....'" But a journal entry was more optimistic: "I need an unconditional relaxing relationship. I hope to find that with Sonia. I think I will."

One evening, after attending a political talk, Ben and Sonia discussed how their commitment to the Nicaraguan revolution had shaped their lives, and how important it was to have friends who shared that commitment. Ben thought about revealing his feelings about her, but just as he mulled over the words, she confided that she was very depressed because she was in love with a Salvadoran guerrilla who was in love with someone else.

Ben was crushed. He never imagined she would tell him something like that. He listened silently, holding her close, hugging her. He was dismayed that she was unaware of his feelings for her. When he left her house, he resolved to find out about the Salvadoran. The next day he hunted down Chile to tell her he was in love with Sonia, and pumped her for information about the Salvadoran. Chile was reluctant to say anything because she didn't want anyone to get hurt. She also warned him that Sonia was emotionally unstable, and in therapy.

Ben resolved to win Sonia's love. He thought he could make her happy, but wondered how he could persuade her to give him a chance. Ben pedaled his unicycle to Barrio El Dorado to seek the advice of Dina Redman, a graphic artist from San Francisco. Long and stately, with flowing, waist-length brown hair, Dina stood almost a foot taller then Ben. When he arrived, downcast and silent, Dina cooked for him, put on her Bob Dylan and Talking Heads tapes, and drew him out. Ben explained that he didn't understand why he was always the "friend" and never the "boyfriend," how he, a caring, sensitive person who treated women decently, always lost out to the macho, the jerk. He complained that he visited Sonia, brought her presents, borrowed a car to run her around on errands, and invited her to dinner, yet she was in love with this Salvadoran who was breaking her heart. It wasn't fair.

When Dina found out that Ben hadn't expressed his feelings to Sonia, she suggested that perhaps she didn't realize he loved her, and maybe Latin American women were not sure how to deal with him because he did not play macho games. "He was shy about making his interests clear," said Dina, and she suggested that he sit next to her on the couch, snuggle closer, hold her hand gently, stroke her arm, let his hand wander over her body. "But Ben was so shy," said Dina. "He said, 'I can't do that.'"

In early June Sonia was rushed to the military hospital, where she was operated on for fibroid tumors. The military hospital was usually off-limits to foreigners, but Ben wangled a pass to enter and brought her scented soap, shampoo, towels, and sanitary napkins. Sonia was overjoyed to see him. He visited her every day, and after she complained about hospital food, he smuggled in milk and yogurt. He stayed for hours, amusing her, forming shadow dolls on the wall with her sheets.

After Sonia was discharged, Ben often borrowed a car from a coworker during lunch and rushed to her house with a plastic plate heaped with *fritanga*—fried cheese, plantains, and meats—he had bought on the street corner. After work, he often took the bus to her house, where he cooked her curry, one of his specialties, or spaghetti. On weekends he stopped by to help her clean house or handwash her dirty laundry (something, he pointed out to her, that few Latin American men would do). When Sonia had a checkup at Monolo Morales hospital at 8:00 A.M., "He moved heaven and earth to get a car to take me there," she said. "He was a man with incredible human qualities. When I suddenly had a screaming crisis, he was by my side and stayed, until I calmed down. He never talked about his problems because he didn't want me to get upset."

As time passed, they discussed previous loves. Ben told Sonia that he wanted a girlfriend, a *compañera*. She told him he was so nice that any girl would love him, but didn't offer anything more.

When Sonia grew stronger, Ben borrowed Rebecca's Fiat and took her out to dinner; the circus; Managua's tiny orchestra, which played in the huge Rubén Darío Theater; and the folk group Peter, Paul, and Mary. Sonia met Rebecca, Lois Wessel, an American translator from New Haven, Connecticut, and Maria de Zuniga. Sonia asked him why he had so many female friends, since Latin American men she knew had girlfriends, but very few female friends. "He laughed and told me, 'I have a lot of female friends and I don't have a girlfriend, but I prefer to keep all these friends that I have and not lose them because of love problems.'"

One evening, when Ben and Sonia returned to her house after dinner, they found a puddle of water from a leaky bathroom faucet. Sonia turned off the water to the house, unscrewed the faucet, and replaced the washer. Ben watched her work. "He told me that's why he liked me," said Sonia, "because I just saw something and did it, without waiting, without asking for help. He said few women he knew were like that."

Ben took her hand in his. "Then he began to tell me his feelings, that he liked me a lot; but he said it with a lot of fear; fear that I would say no, that he would be rejected. He never directly told me his feelings; he never said, 'Look, I love you.' I was afraid to talk to him about it. I didn't want to offend him. I wasn't hard with him, nor cold, but I also couldn't show feelings that didn't exist. This he understood, but I'm sure that it still hurt him." She told him that she just wanted to be friends. Ben said that he understood, but when he left shortly afterward, she watched as his shoulders shook.

Back in El Cuá, Don heard a rumor that the regional government office had wrecked a jeep and dumped it, so he hitchhiked down to Matagalpa to examine it. However, he was disappointed to find only a smashed blue shell, without doors, tires, or a roof. The jeep had suffered four accidents, and in the last one had flipped over, its engine falling out. Don towed it to a repair shop, then spent long days trying to fix it, but it still didn't run.

One morning, Don stopped by the Casa de Gobierno and handed Charlie Whitaker a list of supplies he needed. Charlie politely nodded, yes—of course, no problem. Don knew this meant there was a problem. Charlie, however, did assign the El Cuá project an office space in a large room shared by several foreigners in the Casa de Gobierno, where Don took possession of the desk and chair and tacked a map of the Cuá/Bocay region on the wall. Foreigners wandered in and out, and Don bantered with them about their projects and financing, making mental lists of which materials they had finagled from the government and international organizations. Don became friends with the Swiss internationalist Yvan Leyvraz, with whom he spoke French, discussions often escalating into long, loud arguments about development. Don also met Bernhard Koberstein, "Bernardo," a West German from Freiburg, who had recently arrived in Nicaragua to work on a potable drinking water system in Wiwilí. Bernardo noticed Don studying German, and offered to practice the language with him.

Don finally got the jeep running and set off for El Cuá. Since the jeep had no roof, the sun beat down savagely, and Don frequently stopped at streams, ladling water into the radiator, then dumping water over his face with his leather prospector's hat. He eyed the road to find the remains of several vehicles, including a John Deere land mover riddled with bullet holes. Some of the vehicles had been destroyed since Don's last trip down the road.

The next day, Don drove the jeep back down the road to the John Deere land mover, cut off its yellow cab, and welded it to the jeep's blue body. If he tied a tarp over the cab, Don could keep dry, and even have room to give a ride to a farmer or two.

On a side street of El Cuá, Don spent afternoons disassembling the brakes, clutch, and radiator, while farmers watched him curiously. Soon the jeep was running, and he drove it up and down the town's one dirt road, gunning the engine, as residents ran to their doors, laughing at the strange-looking blue-and-yellow contraption which Don affectionately christened "El Pelón," Old Baldy.

When Don showed the Captain his vehicle, the Captain advised him to drive with an army caravan, or an armed government supply convoy, whenever he left town. Don heartily agreed. If the Contras were to kill him, Don thought, it most likely would be in an ambush on the lonely dirt road outside El Cuá.

In Washington, D.C., President Reagan continued his push for Contra aid. On June 24, 1986, in a nationally broadcast address, President Reagan said that if the House of Representatives didn't approve Contra aid, Americans would ultimately have to face "the reality of a Soviet military beachhead" in Nicaragua. After two days of telephoning lawmakers, President Reagan succeeded in persuading ten members of the House to change their votes. During the acrimonious debate on the House floor, House minority leader Robert H. Michel (R-Ill.) said, "Let's end the vacillation. Systematic delay is not a policy, it's paralysis. Let's have the guts to fight communism and nurture democracy in our hemisphere now, not later."

House majority whip Thomas S. Foley (D-Wash.) disagreed, saying that lawmakers were being asked to support a "proxy war" against another government, and that this would lead to a "tragic and irreversible" course of U.S. troops being sent to Central America. Contra aid opponents also quoted a newly released General Accounting Office report that said as much as $27 million in congressional aid approved to the Contras the year before could not be accounted for. "We are being asked to vote to send $100 million to drug dealers, gunrunners and embezzlers," Rep. David E. Bonior (D-Mich.) said. "The Contra program has been rotten from the start. It is out of control, a waste of taxpayers' dollars, and a shame on our nation's heritage."

Despite such dissents, on June 25 the U.S. House of Representatives reversed its previous position and, by a vote of 221 to 209, approved $100 million in military aid for the Contras. It also lifted a congressional ban on covert activities by U.S. intelligence agencies, including the CIA, against Nicaragua.

In Managua, at the weekly Thursday morning vigil in front of the U.S. embassy, the gringo club angrily condemned the vote as "more tax dollars for war." Reacting to the vote, President Ortega announced that the state of emergency would be strictly enforced, and that the government would no longer tolerate internal groups that supported the Reagan administration's policies. He announced the suspension of the opposition radio station, Radio Católica, and the indefinite closure of the opposition newspaper *La Prensa*, which he called a mouthpiece for the Reagan administration. Ortega accused some opposition political parties, Catholic Church leaders, and business groups of "taking advantage of our respect for political pluralism ... by trying to open an internal front" for the Contras.

The next day, June 27, 1986, after twenty-six months of litigation, the U.N. International Court at the Hague ruled that the United States had violated international law and Nicaraguan sovereignty by mining Nicaraguan harbors and supporting the Contras, and ruled that the United States should pay reparations to Nicaragua. The Reagan administration, which had renounced its recognition of the court's authority when Nicaragua lodged its case in 1984, said it would ignore the verdict. The court had no power to force the United States to comply with the ruling.

That evening in Managua, tens of thousands of Sandinista supporters gathered in a field next to the Roberto Huembes market for the sixth annual *repliegue*, a reenactment of the 35-kilometer all-night march from Managua to Masaya. In June 1979 the *repliegue* had been a turning point in the revolution, as thousands of civilian supporters joined Sandinista guerrillas in the strategic retreat, preparing for the final offensive. That night Somoza's planes bombed the lines of guerrillas and civilians heading south, and six people were killed.

At sunset, wearing his INE militia uniform, Ben, along with Rebecca, Mira, and other pro-Sandinista INE employees, joined the tens of thousands who jammed the field.

As night fell, President Daniel Ortega addressed the crowd. He said that in less than thirty hours the world had been informed of two major decisions: the "unjust, brutal, and criminal" decision of the United States Congress to give $100 million to the Contras, and a decision by the World Court against the U.S. The crowd cheered and chanted "Somos tres millones, derrotando sus millones"(We are three million people, defeating your million dollars). Then, Ortega and Vice President Sergio Ramirez set off for Masaya, leading the crowd, alongside a few tanks and armored personnel carriers. Police sirens pierced the night. Behind the leaders strode mostly young people, carrying knapsacks and canteens, laughing, waving, and calling out to friends. Palm boughs, flowers, posters, and red-and-black flags decorated the streets, while spectators lined the sides, hanging out open windows, banging pots and pans, shouting encouragement. Onlookers scooped water out of rusty oil drums with plastic cups and passed them to the marchers, who took a sip, then passed the cups on. Marchers danced to ragtag brass bands scattered throughout the crowd. Old tires were lit on fire, and thick noxious smoke billowed through the air, while the light of bonfires reflected in the faces of thousands who passed by. Marchers held hands, trying not to lose one another, and many foreigners mixed in with Nicaraguans.

By 10:00 P.M. marchers left the dirt roads of the Managua barrios and trekked across the dark countryside. The pace picked up, and thousands stretched out along the dirt road as the dim outline of the Masaya volcano, growing larger, marked their progress. Ben wrote:

> 50,000 of us walked the 22 miles. It was strange to walk in the darkness down a small country road with people all around. My emotions switched all over the place. At times, it felt like a March of Dimes walk–a–thon, at other times, I would switch off my mind and think of my unicycle trip or of times Alison and I spent together. But then there was also the feeling that ... years ago people were being killed on the road. Bombs were falling and it was dark. People left their homes not knowing if they were going back.

Throughout the march, Ben ran into people that he knew. When Shelley Sherman, the new TecNica coordinator, expressed surprise at seeing him in uniform, he told her it was "just for the occasion."

Songs by Dimensión Costeña and Stevie Wonder beamed from taverns. A soldier passed, putting his hand on a foreigner's shoulders, giving an encouraging word. Alongside the road a candle flickered next to a cross, etched with the name Edyth Alvarez, June 28, 1979, a victim of the original retreat.

At 1:30 A.M. the marchers reached the town of Nindirí, where marchers drank coffee, ate pork and cornmeal *nacatamales*, and collapsed. A burst of fireworks signaled that it was time to move on to Masaya, another hour and a half down the road. Marchers stood up, limp, wet, aching. Everyone moved onward, stumbling into Masaya, past churches with red-tiled roofs. It was still dark as marchers plopped down on the ground to rest. Mira wrote;

> 4:30 a.m. in a park in Masaya. Every little bit of pavement or bench is covered with prone bodies. It is beginning to rain, wetting the ground, wetting the people, making their already dirty uniforms stick to their skin. No one moves. Down the main street toward the park comes a steady stream of people swelling along with the rain. People limping. People smiling. People occasionally chanting with a burst of energy. They plop exhausted onto the pavement, pushing aside bodies to make room, covering their faces, becoming just another pile of damp, dirty olive green in the rain.

The marchers limped into the plaza, plopping onto curbs and doorsteps to hear a soaking wet Ortega as he climbed onto a makeshift stage. "This march has been one more repudiation of the U.S. Congress' approval of $100 million for the mercenaries. The United States will find that there are three million people here who are ready to defend themselves against this one hundred million dollars. ¡Un solo ejército! [One single army!]" The chant ran through the crowd like an electric charge. People sitting on the pavement jumped up. Thousands of supporters chanted, raising hands, pounding fists in the air: "El pueblo, unido, jamás será vencido" (The people, united, will never be defeated).

Chapter 13

Classes Begin

Ever since the electricity was turned on in May, Oscar had been running the plant alone seven days a week. Don and Ben wanted to train another plant operator from the area, but no one could come up with a candidate. Most villagers were unwilling to switch from farming to a salaried job. Finally, Ben and Don remembered Hilda. They asked her to be a plant operator. She was aghast at the idea. She had only passed first grade, and knew nothing about machines. Moreover, she was afraid of them. Hilda had never held a job before and couldn't imagine taking a man's job.

Ben and Don assured her that they would teach her everything. They had confidence in her. Hilda trusted Ben and Don, and it would have been impolite to refuse. She finally agreed. But Hilda was worried that Oscar would forbid her from working. In El Cuá women cooked, looked after the children, and stayed at home. She knew that people in El Cuá would gossip that Oscar had lost control over his wife. That evening, Ben and Don talked to Oscar, who listened silently to their plan. Oscar respected Ben and Don, so he agreed to let Hilda try.

The next day, Hilda left her children with her mother and arrived at the hydroplant at 8:00 A.M., ready for work. Step by step, Ben and Don explained the turbine, governor, and generator while she turned them on and recorded the readings in the logbook. She asked only one question: What would happen if she broke something? They assured her she couldn't harm the machines, and Don joked that soon she'd be giving orders to the gringos and become *La Jefa*, "the Boss."

The next morning, with Ben, Don, and Oscar beside her, Hilda turned on the machines. After watching Hilda check the readings, the three men left her alone at the plant. Hilda sat in the powerhouse, pleased by the steady hum and the needles holding on the gauges. Above her head, two lightbulbs burned brightly.

Hilda went back to the bungalow, returning every hour to check the gauges and take readings. After lunch, as the machines hummed steadily, she walked down to the Río Esperanza and washed Oscar's shirts on the rocks. Hilda balanced the newly cleaned clothes in a plastic tub on her head as she climbed back up the slope. As she neared the brick bungalow, she noticed that the plant was not humming. Startled, she dashed to the powerhouse, dropping the plastic tub into the mud. Inside the powerhouse, the machines were still, the belts hung loosely, the needles pointed to zero, and the lightbulbs on the ceiling were dark. Hilda knew that the electricity was off in town. She trembled and slumped over the machines, devastated, her tears falling onto the steel. She knew she could not do it, she thought; how could they expect her to do a man's job? She fervently prayed that she had not broken the machines.

A few minutes later Don, Ben, and Oscar barreled up the road in the jeep and ran into the powerhouse, where they found Hilda, expecting to be scolded. Don and Ben assured her that everything was fine. Hilda wiped away the tears and, urged on by Don and Ben, slowly turned on the plant again, while Oscar watched.

The next day Hilda moved into the bungalow with Oscar. By the end of the week, she was proficient at the plant, and soon Oscar left her alone while he went to town to run errands. When Ben and Don informed Hilda they were going to put her on the INE payroll, she was at once scared and thrilled. At the INE office in Matagalpa, Ben and Don introduced Hilda to the regional supervisor as the new hydroplant operator. The man was dumbfounded, feeling it was inconceivable that a young, uneducated farmer's wife could fill a man's job. Hilda remained silent while Ben and Don praised her skills, explaining that she had been operating the plant alone for a week. The supervisor said that INE employees were often mobilized to other parts of the country to repair towers or electrical lines blown up by the Contras, and surely *la señora*'s husband would not allow her to leave the children. For the first time Hilda looked up, and in a trembling voice responded that her mother could take care of her children, her husband supported her working at the hydroplant, and that she'd be willing to be mobilized if needed. Don and Ben hid their smiles as the supervisor begrudgingly added her name to the payroll.

Outside the INE office, Ben and Don formally congratulated Hilda on her first job. Don told her she'd already earned her nickname, *La Jefa*. For the first time on the trip, Hilda laughed.

In late spring, Don met with the board of directors representing the four near-est cooperatives, Santa Rosa, El Trebol, La Chata, and Santa Ana. He asked each cooperative to select two members for a six-month-long training program to wire the town for electricity. The only requirements were that the students be literate, energetic, and enthusiastic. In town, Don convinced the Captain that the govern-ment should pay for the students' lunches while they trained.

El Cuá buzzed with rumors that every house would soon be wired for elec-tricity. Everyone was excited. In the evenings, Don planned his course, basing it on a 1930s Works Project Administration (WPA) manual on rural electrification. Don had wired houses and buildings before, both in Nicaragua and in Canada, but he had never wired electric poles. He disliked climbing poles and dangling in the air because he was afraid of heights, but he said, "My fear of heights was less compelling than my fear of not being able to do the job."

In July, Don began teaching classes. In the early mornings Oscar and Hilda checked the hydroplant, locked the powerhouse door, then hiked into El Cuá. There, they joined up with the only other woman in the course, twenty-year-old Gregoria "Goya" Gutierrez, granddaughter of Cosme Castro, the old Sandinista who lived in the red-and-black house on the edge of town. The five other students were farmers who walked into town from their cooperatives, rifles slung over their shoulders. The men gathered at the bunkhouse, set down their rifles, and perched on the porch rail.

Don sat inside at his desk, studying German. Promptly at 8:00 A.M., Don snapped his book shut and invited the students into his classroom, an empty cubi-cle next to his bedroom. They leaned their rifles against the walls, laid their extra ammu-nition within easy reach, and sat down on stumps, gas cans, buckets, and toolboxes.

Don handed out pencils and notebooks and divided the class of eight stu-dents into two groups, to separate Oscar and Hilda. Hilda's class included her girl-friend, Goya, a farmer who served as El Trebol cooperative's vice president, and Jesus Huerta Montenegro, a short kid with pale skin, nicknamed Chelito, "Little Whitey." Chelito was the most advanced student, at third-grade level. Oscar's class included three farmers: Alfonso Perez, Justo Pastor Rivera Tercero, and Teodoro Arauz. Alfonso was a short, dark, withdrawn sixteen-year-old from Santa Rosa cooperative who moved his lips as he read, often stumbling, sounding out words syllable by sylla-ble. Don admired his tenacity. His family and the whole Santa Rosa cooperative were refugees from the village of El Tobacco, an area of continual battles with the

Contras. Alfonso was in the army reserves, studying to become a medic while trying to get his sergeant's stripes.

Burly twenty-five-year-old Justo Pastor limped and had a crippled left arm, the result of an ambush. Tall, dark-skinned, with a round face and prominent features, he was slow to speak but quick to laugh, and loved to play practical jokes. He was smart, enthusiastic, hardworking, and took initiative.

Justo Pastor was from Estelí. In 1983, as a junior lieutenant in the army, he had been posted to El Cuá, where the Contras ambushed him a year later. Four of the eight soldiers in the jeep died, and Justo spent three months in the hospital, recovering from bullet wounds. In 1985, when he was discharged from the army, he joined the El Trebol cooperative. He was proud of having been in the army and often wore his uniform with its red lieutenant's stripes to class.

Oscar's third student was a skinny, tall, good-looking twenty-two-year-old named Teodoro. He had grown up working alongside his father in the mountains outside Bocaycito. Teodoro had never attended school, but learned to read in the 1980 literacy campaign when he was sixteen. Teodoro always carried his rifle with him, even when he went across the street to buy a Coke, because he had been kidnapped by the Contras and forced to fight with them for two years. He didn't want to be kidnapped again.

Almost all of the students read at a first-grade level. "I was amazed at how low their academic levels were," said Don. Realizing that their lack of general education would handicap their progress in his course, Don talked to the local Education Ministry representative, who arranged for them to attend night classes at their cooperatives. There they studied math, reading, writing, history of the revolution, and public health.

In the mornings Don taught basic math skills, including addition, subtraction, division, and multiplication. He explained fractions and percentages by using mangos and bananas, tested students on their times tables with flash cards, and taught them how to measure in meters instead of *varas*, the traditional Nicaraguan method. Progress was slow. The students were often unfocused, and sometimes Don spent a morning reviewing ideas he thought they had grasped the day before. Don knew they weren't accustomed to being confined in a dark room with notebooks, so he emphasized hands-on training in the field during the afternoon session. His students rolled out wire from house to house, measured it, divided it, quadrupled it, and then figured out 10 percent of it.

Don had taught mechanics and machine repair in Nicaragua for several years, and he found the farmers from El Cuá to be his most challenging students. They required more encouragement, reassurance, and feedback than his previous students, and they were ready to quit at any excuse. After a few weeks of classes, two students dropped out. Another student went on a drinking binge.

As classes progressed, Don taught his students how to use pliers, screwdrivers, and voltmeters, and how to measure currents, install lightbulbs, and connect wires to houses. He took his students to the plant for Hilda's demonstration of how to operate the machines.

After the students had learned how to wire houses, Don gave them a pole-climbing lesson. They gathered around the pole in the main plaza, where Don slipped on spiked shoes, a leather belt, leather pants, and gloves. Shopkeepers, farmers, children, and a few emaciated dogs gathered in the plaza around the group. Don dug his spiked shoes into the wood, grasped the pole, slipped the belt upward, and then eased himself up, jabbing the spiked shoes higher, climbing slowly, not looking down. He climbed to the top, flailed his arms, shouted how easy it was, then scrambled down. No one realized he was scared of heights.

Teodoro had been climbing trees to knock down coconuts since he was a boy, and he scampered up and down the pole like a monkey, using the leather belt like a prehensile tail. Not to be outdone, Oscar jammed the spiked shoes into the pole and scrambled up almost as fast as Teodoro. He balanced himself like a cat on top of the pole, lashed himself in, and yelled for Justo Pastor to climb up.

Because of his war wounds, Justo Pastor was reluctant. He smiled gamely, strapped on the climbing gear, and forced himself upward, wincing and groaning as pain shot through his shrapnel-filled body, his useless arm dangling at his side. Three-quarters of the way he felt paralyzed by pain, unable to climb up farther or get down. Oscar cheered him onward. Gritting his teeth, Justo Pastor continued, scaling slowly to the top, roping himself in. Perched on top of the pole, Oscar and Justo Pasto shouted in jest, "We're from the phone company"; the nearest phone was three hours away. When Don invited everyone to the Disamar tavern for a cold beer, Oscar and Justo Pastor quickly slid down the light pole.

Throughout the weeks, Don discovered the strengths of each of his pupils. Oscar quickly learned how to string wires and drop cables, so Don often assigned him the job of working with lines. Even though none of the students knew how to drive, Don taught them how to fix a car.

Don took his students to examine a broken, abandoned Soviet-made Belarus tractor, and they took turns climbing into the driver's seat. In the glove compartment of the Belarus tractor, the students found an unopened box of tools and spare parts. Don demonstrated how to use a multimeter to trace circuits, and the students discovered that the tractor, among other problems, had three bad fuses.

Just as Don began to notice his students' progress, he became sick. The smell of food brought on waves of nausea. A worker at the clinic diagnosed him with malaria. Don forced himself to swallow the huge bitter-tasting pills, quickly throwing them up. He was miserably ill. When his skin turned yellow, Don knew he had hepatitis A, and there was nothing to do but rest. Pale and weak, Don lay on his cot for six days while Oscar hovered over him like a mother, plying him with rice and potatoes prepared by Hilda. Don forced them down and vomited. Oscar suspected Don was sick from the water, so he collected rainwater for him to drink.

Students visited every day. Don lay on his cot, listening, immobile. One day Teodoro came by and told him about his life with the Contras. In 1984, Teodoro and his older brother were clearing their cornfield near Bocaycito when some hundred blue-uniformed Contras surrounded them. The Contra leader, waving his automatic rifle in the air, asked them to "volunteer." Teodoro and his brother fell in line behind a group of frightened peasant farmers.

When some of the Contra sentries fell asleep that night, ten of the new recruits escaped. They were discovered missing and chased by a Contra patrol, which caught five of them and slit their throats. After that incident, Teodoro and his brother resigned themselves to staying with the Contras, living in constant fear of being executed.

As they hiked north through the jungle toward the Contra camps in Honduras, Teodoro and his brother carried 70-pound backpacks loaded with bullets or mortar tubes. When their rubber boots disintegrated, they continued to march through the jungle, their bare feet raw and oozing pus. They slept on beds of wet jungle leaves and were constantly cold and damp.

After weeks of slogging northward, they finally arrived at a Contra base camp

Ben with children in
Barrio Riguero, Managua,
Nicaragua, 1983. COURTESY OF
THE LINDER FAMILY

clowning during a Sandinista demonstration in
nagua, October 1983. OSCAR CANTARERO

Americans from the "Committee of U.S. Citizens Living in Nicaragua" (CUSCLIN) and U visitors during a Thursday morning vigil in front of the U.S. Embassy in Managua, 1986.
LARRY BOYD

CUSCLIN members demonstrating in Managua against U.S. support for the Contras, 198 Left to right: Sister Mary Hartman, Judy Butler, Rebecca Leaf, Ben Linder, Camilo Dufre
JANET MELVIN

picking cotton in Chinandega, Nicaragua, 1984. DAVID BLANKENHORN

clowning during a vaccination campaign in Barrio Riguero, Managua. The announcer
ed women to bring their children to the local health center to get vaccinated, 1984.
MALONE

Ben with Diana Brook[s] 1984. Ben lived with th[e] Brooks family in Managua prior to moving to El Cuá.
DAVID BLANKENHORN

Main Street, El Cuá, 1987. The bunkhouse is the building with the porch on the left.
LARRY BOYD

Sandinista "IFA"
troop transport trucks
after being ambushed
by the Contras.
Chontales Province,
Nicaragua, 1987.
LOU DEMATTEIS

...wnspeople surround dead Contras in La Trinidad,
...aragua, after the Contras attacked the town on
...ust 1, 1985. MARIA MORRISON

Don Macleay welding in the machineshop in
El Cuá, 1987. LARRY BOYD

Oscar and Hilda operating the El
Cuá hydroplant, 1987. LARRY BOYD

The machinehouse of
the hydroplant in El
Cuá, 1987. Water
enters the plant
through the penstock
(the pipe running
down the hill), runs
through the
machines, and exits
through the stream.
JOAN KRUCKEWITT

o women carry a casket containing the remains of a child. July 4, 1986
San José de Bocay, Nicaragua. LOU DEMATTEIS

Villagers pass coffins down into a mass grave on July 4, 1986 in San José de Bocay. Thirty-two civilians were killed when their truck ran over a land mine planted by the Contras. LOU DEMATTEIS

Ben with Mira Brown building a wood-efficient Lorena stove at the
El Cuá hydroplant, 1986. COURTESY OF THE LINDER FAMILY

Clifford Brown, Ben Linder, Oscar Daniel Blandón, and others eating
dinner in the brick bungalow at the hydroplant. El Cuá, 1987.
COURTESY OF DON MACLEAY

Andres de Bocay, Nicaragua, 1987. Soviet-built Mi-24 helicopters
ed the war in favor of the Sandinistas. LOU DEMATTEIS

San Juan Province, Nicaragua. U.S. citizen Eugene Hasenfus being led out of the jungle by
linista soldiers in October, 1986. Two other Americans died after their plane—part of Lt.
Oliver North's secret weapons supply network to the Contras—was shot down by the
linista Army. LOU DEMATTEIS

Ben with Oscar Blandón, measuring a stream outside El Cuá, 1986. MIRA BROWN

fford Brown, Hilda Granados, Oscar Blandón, Don Macleay, Mira Brown, and Ben Linder
Don's farewell party at the hydroplant in El Cuá, March 1987. COURTESY OF DON MACLEAY

n Cosme in front of his house in El Cuá. He painted it red and black (the Sandinista
rs) after the Contras attacked El Cuá in late 1983. LARRY BOYD

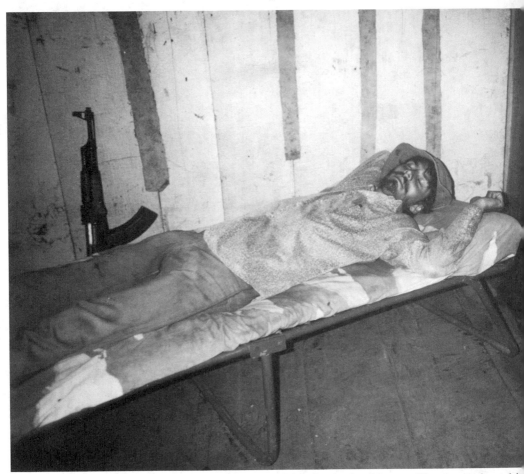

Don Macleay recovering from hepatitis in his cubicle in the bunkhouse. He always kept his AK-47 rifle nearby. El Cuá, 1986. MIRA BROWN

men and children waiting in front of the health center in El Cuá, 1987. JOAN KRUCKEWITT

dren from El Cedro gather around the cooperative's health center shortly after
Contras destroyed it for the third time. March 1987. MARVIN COLLINS

Main Street, El Cuá, 1987, during an army offensive. Sandinista soldiers gather under a banner calling on the Contras to give themselves up under a government-sponsored amnesty plan. The banner reads "Take amnesty, your family is waiting for you at home. Lay down your weapons." LOU DEMATTEIS

Mira and Ben with Old Baldy in Jinotega, Nicaragua, April 1987. TIM TAKARO

's funeral in Matagalpa on April 30, 1987. The funeral procession
seven blocks long. COURTESY OF THE LINDER FAMILY

BENJAMIN ERNEST LINDER
INTERNACIONALISTA

NACIDO 7 JULIO 1959   CAIDO 28 ABRIL 1987
SAN FRANCISCO   SAN JOSE DEL BOCAY
CALIFORNIA   JINOTEGA
U.S.A.   NICARAGUA

LA LUZ QUE ENCENDIO BRILLARA PARA SIEMPRE

The laying of Ben Linder's gravestone in Matagalpa Cemetery, 1987. The gravestone (inset) reads: "La luz que encendió brillará para siempre" (The light he lit will shine forever). JOAN KRUCKEWITT

A mural painted on a wall in Barrio Monseñor Lezcano in Managua pays homage to Ben Linder. LARRY BOYD

in Honduras. Their clothes were in tatters, their feet rotting, their bodies covered with fleabites, chiggers, ticks, and infected ulcers.

At the camp, Teodoro and his brother constructed lean-to shelters of banana leaves and straw. Teodoro learned to aim, shoot, disassemble, and clean automatic rifles, throw grenades, and operate mortars. He did sit-ups, push-ups, and squats, and ran miles along mountain trails, loaded down by daypacks bulging with ammunition. Using machetes, the recruits hacked a runway out of the jungle, where helicopters landed, full of "*chelones grandotes* [big, white people], Americans who did not speak Spanish," Teodoro said.

One day, the recruits assembled to hear a political speech by the Contra leader, Enrique Bermúdez, a former National Guard officer. Short and burly, with a pock-marked face, Bermúdez told the recruits that the Sandinistas wanted to bring communism to Nicaragua, but that the Contras were going to liberate Nicaragua. He said also that the Sandinistas killed civilians and warned the men that if they deserted, the Sandinistas would kill them too.

After four months of training, Teodoro and his brother marched back into Nicaragua alongside a group of two hundred Contras, toward Waslala and the Atlantic coast. "The order was to shoot; to fight with whoever," said Teodoro. They slogged up rivers, hip-deep in mud, moving through the jungle, ambushing vehicles, blowing up bridges, and attacking militia posts and isolated agricultural cooperatives. When they attacked cooperatives, Teodoro was frequently given orders to block the dirt road and burn any vehicle that passed by. He followed the orders.

Sometimes Contra leaders worked with peasant collaborators who informed them about Sandinista army movements, and when collaborators could not be found, Contra leaders strong-armed farmers into scouting for them. The Contras, constantly hungry, ransacked vacant farmhouses. Weakened by bad diets, little sleep, and constant dampness, Teodoro and his brother were often sick with fevers or shaking with malarial chills, but they kept marching. When individual Contras were too weak to continue with the group, they were left behind to recuperate by themselves, or die.

Whenever the Contras arrived at an occupied shack, or a small group of houses, they demanded food. Women furiously ground corn to make tortillas, while unattended toddlers wailed. The Contras ate farmers' stockpiled corn and sugar and killed and ate their chickens, pigs, and cows. They devoured seeds that had been saved for spring planting and dug up cassava, yucca, and other root crops. They stripped the trees of mangos, avocados, plantains, bananas, and grapefruits. In the evening, they hung their hammocks in the yard, while the leaders slept in the families' beds.

Before moving on, the Contras often lectured the civilians, saying they were democrats fighting for God, liberty, and human rights and needed more volunteers to fight the Communists. If the peasants didn't volunteer, Teodoro said, "We took them by force, tied them up with a rope, and pointed a rifle at their backs." Often the leaders also selected a few pretty teenage girls to accompany them. During the day the women followed along, crying, afraid, and ashamed. In the evenings the women cooked the meals, and at night, Contra leaders passed them around.

Occasionally, when the Contras needed supplies, C-47 cargo planes dropped crates of mortars, mines, bullets, boots, and food. Parachutes buffered their fall into the jungle. Teodoro remembered that all the farmers marveled over fruit in cans.

Teodoro and his brother, not recognizing the territory and afraid of getting caught, didn't attempt to flee until May 1986, when the Contra group entered Jinotega province and marched into the mountains where Teodoro and his brother were born. Because the area was familiar, the two brothers edged their way to the perimeter of the encampment where they were assigned guard duty. Then they hid their guns and escaped. The brothers soon recognized the ceiba and *guanacaste* trees, and their neighbors' coffee fields. Around 11:00 P.M. they banged on the door of their mother's wooden shack. She had not heard from them in two years, and worried that they were dead. When she saw them alive, she burst into tears, thanking God for her good fortune. Teodoro and his brother knew that they would be pursued, so they changed into civilian clothes, buried their Contra uniforms, and hid out in the familiar mountains. The Contras scoured the area but soon gave up and moved on.

For three days Teodoro and his brother hid in the mountains. Rumors of their appearance had spread throughout the town. Teodoro and his brother were questioned by army officials, received amnesty, and were released. A few days later Teodoro and his brother moved into El Cuá, afraid that if they stayed in the countryside, one of the Contra units would find out that they had deserted and kill them.

As Don was recovering, Oscar told him that Jesus Huerta Montenegro and Chelito had been mobilized into a militia battalion. Don had now lost four out of eight students, and he didn't want to lose any more.

The next morning, Don, his skin still sallow, slid into a chair and propped himself against a wall. He barked math problems at his students and berated them for forgetting their multiplication tables. He told them to study math that afternoon, then crawled back onto his cot, where he slept for fifteen hours.

Every day, Don grew stronger. He drank the rainwater that Oscar collected for him and ate the mashed potatoes Hilda made. Craving sugar, he sucked on hard candies to alleviate the dryness in his mouth. He began to eat rice and bread, and a week later he began teaching the afternoon field classes, sitting underneath a broad-leafed tree.

In summer 1986 Juan Tercero, a well-educated Sandinista official from the cotton-growing city of Chinandega, was transferred to El Cuá as the FSLN representative, a position second in importance only to that of Captain Miguelito. Juan established a formal, amicable relationship with the Captain, but considered him to be uneducated and crude.

Shortly after arriving in town, Juan met the Americans. He recalled his first meeting with Ben: "He came to my office, wearing, as usual, big boots, glasses, loose, ill-fitting blue jeans, a cotton sport shirt, and that certain smile that he always had—he knew how to warm up people quickly, to make friends."

Juan had visited the town before it had electricity. He noted that, even with only a small part of the town wired, "there had been a radical change. Before, it was a town in darkness, where people went to sleep at 6:00 or 7:00 P.M.," where no one owned radios or tape players, because batteries were expensive and scarce. But now, salsa hits blasted out of shacks, and ice was sold by five family-owned corner stores with refrigerators or freezers. "You could drink a cold soda, or a beer. It was a different dynamic—even the corners were lit up," said Juan. In the evenings, along the main road, families opened doors to catch breezes, while bright lights illuminated women shelling beans and children copying lessons into notebooks.

Juan, who had spent his life in cities, was accustomed to a varied diet and better hygienic conditions, so he found it difficult to adjust to life in El Cuá. Even though he drank boiled water, he suffered from mysterious fevers, recurrent colds, coughs, diarrhea, malaria, and dengue fever. Juan wondered how Ben and Don had acclimated to the countryside.

Shortly after Juan arrived in town, a drunken soldier shot at the main trunk line, piercing the cable and knocking out power to the town. The soldier was jailed, but the line had to be replaced. Don, furious and still weak from hepatitis, left for Matagalpa, knowing he'd have to spend days searching for heavy cable.

While the electricity was out, Dr. Chepe Luis, the new doctor in El Cuá, wanted to fire up the health center's old diesel-powered generator, but couldn't find any fuel; the government caravans had temporarily stopped running due to the Contras. Awakened by the shouts of several farmers, he arose to find that they had brought in an unconscious 16-year-old girl, her face covered in blood. She had been accidentally shot in the face, and farmers had carried her out of the mountains. By the time she arrived at the doctor's doorstep several hours later, she had lost a lot of blood and was in shock. Dr. Chepe Luis operated by the light of a kerosene lamp and a flashlight. The girl died before morning.

Three days later, Don arrived with the cable, and the town's electricity was restored.

In late spring, a Swedish engineer asked Ben to house-sit his modern apartment for the summer. Ben couldn't believe his good luck. The apartment, located in central Managua near the Intercontinental Hotel, had a sunken living room with spotless glass tabletops and white wooden furniture. Stairs led to a loft bedroom. The efficiency kitchen included sparkling white appliances and a full set of Corelle dishware. The kitchen overlooked a small patio with trees, and the apartment was among a mere handful of buildings in Nicaragua to have hot water. "You walked in, and you didn't think you were in Managua anymore," said Shelley Sherman.

As soon as the Swedish engineer left the country, Ben distributed copies of the key to Lois, Rebecca, and Mira so that they could use the apartment as a "crash pad." After settling into his new apartment, Ben invited Sonia out to dinner to celebrate his twenty-seventh birthday. "He told me he wanted it to be 'just you and me,'" said Sonia, who accepted.

Ben meticulously planned the evening. He ironed his least-faded cotton shirt and jeans, borrowed Rebecca's Fiat, picked up Sonia, and took her to Antojitos, an outdoor patio restaurant across from the Hotel Intercontinental where tables were always crowded with delegations of foreigners and Sandinista officials. Two red-plumed macaws screeched from cages at the edge of the restaurant.

Sonia thought that Antojitos was one of the most elegant restaurants in Managua. She ordered grilled steak and fried plantains, while Ben asked for a half bottle of rum and mixed Sonia a Nica Libre—rum with Coke and a lime twist. Sonia confided that she was unhappy where she was living and needed a quiet place to recuperate. She didn't have any money, but she was still looking for another place to live.

Ben paused. He had the modern apartment to himself, and he could easily share it with another person. There was only one bedroom, but Ben hoped that wouldn't be a problem, as he was sure he could make Sonia fall in love with him. He asked her to share his apartment. Sonia hesitantly accepted. "He was my moral support, my spiritual support, he was the only support that I had at that moment," she said.

Ben, ecstatic, had received the best birthday present he could imagine. Everything was set. The apartment was cozy and private, the perfect place to have a relationship. The next day Ben moved Sonia's old suitcases, books, bags, and mattress into his apartment. Sonia put her mattress on the floor of the loft, sleeping separately from Ben. He was disappointed, but didn't suggest anything different.

Since Ben wanted Sonia to recover, he told her he would cook, clean, and take care of her. In the mornings, he often bought sticky pastries at the bakery across the street, warmed up milk with cinnamon, and brought breakfast to her bedside. In the evenings, after work, he often arrived home carrying a large banana leaf piled high with *fritanga*. While she ate, he entertained her. When she was depressed, he consoled her.

On weekends, they slept late, Ben in the bed, Sonia on her mattress. He cooked a brunch of scrambled eggs with onions, tomatoes, and green peppers. Sonia taught him to make coffee Colombian-style, using a plunger. They discussed their families, their countries, and the revolution.

Ben told her how he enjoyed working in El Cuá but revealed how frightening it was to work there. They talked about what would happen if an American were killed in Nicaragua. "He said that the American could be converted into a hero, but he was joking, only joking," said Sonia. "He didn't talk about Marxism or Leninism—he wasn't even a member of any political party—but he was the most revolutionary man I knew. A good man, warm, sensible, human, in solidarity."

Ben had always been one of the first engineers to arrive at work, but after Sonia moved in, he was consistently late. When Sonia's health improved, Ben made quick trips to El Cuá. Before creeping out of the apartment before dawn, he would leave a short note on the glass-topped table. "Sometimes I'm afraid, I'm afraid of the war," he wrote, or, "My friend, sometimes I feel afraid when I go out into the countryside, but your friendship helps and supports me." When he returned from El Cuá, he frequently brought back sacks of new beans, plantains, or *cuajada*, fresh salty white cheese tied up in a banana leaf. They cooked dinner together in the tiny kitchen, bumping into each other, laughing and joking as they talked about the future.

At first Mira, Lois, and Rebecca frequently dropped by the apartment, using their keys to let themselves in when Ben wasn't home, but after Sonia moved in, their visits decreased. They observed how cranky and demanding Sonia was, and how Ben catered to her desires. They thought that she was monopolizing Ben's time, energy, and attention, and wondered if she was taking advantage of him. She had no money or place of her own, but Ben had both, and was willing to share them with her. They resented Sonia, referring to her as *una chica plastica*, a fake person. They knew that Sonia was in a very bad emotional state, and although they didn't think that she was leading him on, they were concerned that Ben was misreading her. They subsequently felt protective of him.

Ben was oblivious to his friends' concerns. Since she had moved in, Sonia's health and mood had improved. She frequently touched him, stroked his hair, held his hand. One afternoon, while washing laundry on the patio, Ben decided it was time to take Dina's advice.

Sonia was washing her jeans in the cement basin when she asked Ben to grab the pant legs to help her wring them out. Ben twisted the ends round and round, tighter, sprinkling droplets over her, when he suddenly dropped the jeans, leaned over, took one of her hands in his, and told her he wanted to get closer to her, to have a serious relationship, to be her *compañero*.

Sonia drew back. "But I told him I couldn't. I could only offer him my friendship," she said. "Then he made a face, and out came the sound, 'pipipipipi,' the sound of a crying clown, a sad clown, a clown that has his feelings hurt." Ben turned away from her and said he understood. Then he left the house without telling her where he was going, or when he'd be back.

Chapter 14

The War Closes in on El Cuá

The weekend of July 4, 1986, was declared "Liberty Weekend" in New York to commemorate the Statue of Liberty's centennial. The festivities included four days of shows by drill teams, marching bands, and choirs, along with fireworks and a laser display over the newly restored statue. In Managua, the U.S. embassy invited journalists and dignitaries from other embassies to celebrate the Fourth of July.

The preceding Wednesday, the public transport truck bound for San José de Bocay left the Jinotega market at 6:00 A.M., loaded with some three dozen passengers, sacks of seeds, and two drums of diesel fuel. The truck lurched up the muddy road during a downpour of rain, straining up the steep Cuesta de los Muertos (Hill of the Dead), pulled into El Cuá in the early afternoon, then continued northward.

Around 3:30 P.M. the truck began climbing Cuesta de La Camaleona, a steep hill where the Contras often crossed the road. The passengers huddled in the truck bed, except for a Protestant pastor named Nicolas Castilblanco, who perched on the back running board. As the truck rounded a bend in a banana tree grove, it switched into low gear to climb the hill. The next thing he knew, Castilblanco lay crumpled on the grass, moaning, surrounded by burning bodies. Small fires crawled along the grassy slope. Castilblanco could only hear his own cries.

The steel carriage of the truck lay flipped over in the banana grove, a twisted mass of steel. Eight men, twelve women, and twelve children were dead. Castilblanco was the lone survivor.

Late the next day in Managua, word got out to foreign journalists that a public transport truck had run over a Contra land mine, and a mass burial would be held in San José de Bocay. Before dawn on July 4, a fourteen-vehicle caravan of for-

199

eign journalists left Managua for the burial. Ministry of Defense spokeswoman June Mulligan rode in the lead jeep, followed by camera crews from ABC, CBS, and NBC and photographers and journalists from major U.S. newspapers. Hoping to avoid more land mines, journalists nervously instructed drivers to follow the tire tracks of the vehicle in front. The caravan wound between mountains obscured by low, black clouds. Rain fell in sheets, cascading down hillsides, turning the dirt road into a quagmire. The caravan frequently stopped to pull vehicles out of the mud, and finally snaked into the squat muddy plaza of San José de Bocay.

The journalists climbed a muddy hill to a long wooden building, where the charred bodies were laid out under black plastic tarps. The smell of burned flesh filled the air. Small bundles of charred infants were laid out next to the blackened, unrecognizable skeletons of their parents. Villagers encircled the bodies, slumping against each other, sobbing, trembling, awash with resignation. Everyone in the village had lost a relative or a friend.

"I was stunned," Reuters photographer Lou Dematteis said. "It was the first time in five years of covering the war that I was so shocked that I could not take pictures."

Men rolled the bodies in the black plastic tarps, laid them in wooden caskets, closed the lids, then shouldered the larger caskets and carried them outside along the main road. The rain beat down incessantly. Women followed behind, carrying the tiny coffins of children. Townspeople followed the two dozen coffins to the cemetery on a hill overlooking the Bocay River. A few hundred wet and shivering people were gathered on the slope while a half-dozen men, stripped to the waist, shoveled out a deep pit, a ten-by-thirty-foot mass grave. Women wailed as the caskets were lowered, side by side, into the red earth. The rain pelted down. Farmers in ragged shirts and rubber boots, baseball caps in hands, stood silently, staring at the mass grave, only a few yards from another mass grave, where eight other mine victims, including Ambrosio Mogorrón, were buried.

As darkness fell, the townspeople stumbled home, drained of energy. Clouds blotted out the stars. The town's shacks were dark, as if enveloped in gloom. The journalists had to spend the night in Bocay, as it was too dangerous to leave. The NBC camera crew slipped out of town, unnoticed in the heavy rain.

That night in New York, red, white, and blue fireworks burst over the Statue of Liberty while tens of thousands of celebrants waved sparklers in the air. In Managua, at the U.S. Embassy's party, waiters in long-sleeved white shirts poured whiskey at the bar. Men in *guayaberas* (formal white shirts) and women in exquisite cotton dresses tinkled ice cubes in the soft, warm, tropical night. Guests from other embassies arrived, and the patio filled with the murmur of laughter. U.S. officials noted that few journalists attended the party.

In Bocay, the two dozen muddy and exhausted journalists huddled on the cement floor of the town's coffee warehouse. No one was prepared to spend the night, and there was nothing on which to sleep.

A few journalists gathered in front of the warehouse, discussing their shock at the carnage they had seen. Someone found some rum in a shack nearby and persuaded an old woman to mash up pineapples for a mixer. NBC radio reporter Maureen Meehan brought out her battery-run tape deck, *Newsweek* photographer Bill Gentile found a Rolling Stones tape, and another person cranked up the volume. "Brown Sugar" blasted into the night, overpowering the sound of the pouring rain, as the journalists drank and danced by the flickering candlelight, trying to erase the ghastly images from their minds.

The next morning dawned overcast but dry. The plaza was a sea of red mud, but the rivers had receded, and army officials passed the word that the caravan could leave. Within minutes, the journalists were headed out of town. The jeeps crawled in single file across the Bocay River. At the second river crossing, the journalists found the NBC cameraman and soundman, disheveled and dirty, sitting on the riverbank next to their Toyota Landcruiser, clutching their TV camera and tapes. The vehicle was filled with mud, its hood buckled, its windshield cracked, and its windows broken. The night before, their Landcruiser had stalled halfway across the river. Uprooted trees smashed the windows, water poured inside, and the vehicle rocked and pitched. The crew, fearing the truck would overturn, had grabbed their TV equipment and crawled out an open window onto the roof, where they were rescued by a farmer who dragged the Landcruiser out of the river with his team of oxen. When the journalists' caravan arrived, the NBC crew abandoned their ruined vehicle and crowded into another jeep.

A few miles south of Bocay, army officials suddenly halted the caravan. A rumor spread that the Contras had been spotted nearby, and an army patrol had been sent to scout ahead. Journalists waited nervously. A half hour later, when no

Contras were detected, the caravan continued to Managua, but by the time the journalists edited their footage and sent film, photos, and stories to the United States, most of the deadlines had been missed, and footage of the funeral was never aired.

In Managua, Mira was riding her bike to work when she spotted the headline of *Barricada*: "32 Civilians Assassinated." Mira pulled over and bought the paper. She wrote:

> I am reeling, trying to absorb it. 32 civilians assassinated on the collective transport, the transport that doesn't allow anyone with guns on, that won't take out wounded soldiers, that, in May, after the mining of Captain Miguelito's truck with all the health workers on it, refused to take the nurses back to Bocay. The collective transport about which everyone makes snide comments about their "good relations" with the Contras.
>
> Almost all the bodies were in pieces in the mud on the highway. I can't really imagine this—little pieces of bodies in the mud. What I see when I close my eyes are the trucks full of people—as they passed by in El Cuá, a month ago. Was it that yellow one, with *"Goliath"* painted on its nose that went by so jammed packed with people hanging on the sides, that one of the side supports broke as it lurched through the River Esperanza, and people came tumbling out, into the river, laughing and shrieking, and went running off after the truck?
>
> Or was it the blue truck, the one that passed us that morning on its way down from Bocay to El Cuá? We were digging sand out of the river for the Lorena stove, and it comes splashing through, also jammed packed, full of campesinos [peasants], all looking like they have on their best sombreros, carrying chickens, heading into town ... all looking at us like we are an odd sight—three gringos shoveling sand.
>
> Was it the blue truck?

When she read about the mine explosion, Mira worried about Don and Ben, who had been in Matagalpa looking for parts to replace a bad transformer. She tried to get El Cuá on the INE radio, but the radio in El Cuá had been out for more than a week. She called the Casa de Gobierno in Matagalpa, and was relieved to find out that Don and Ben were still there, waiting for authorization to travel.

When Don and Ben heard about the land-mine explosion, they strengthened their safety rules, including contacting each other by radio before driving to or leaving from El Cuá. They devised a code about Contra activity, rating it from one to five. "Five was stay put, don't move," Don said.

While waiting in Matagalpa, Ben and Don discussed ways to expedite the project. Ben was tied to INE in Managua until his contract expired in December. Initially, they had thought it would be better for him to stay in the capital to pressure INE to provide personnel and materials for the project. Eventually they began to think the project would move faster if he moved to El Cuá. The local government of El Cuá, as well as the regional government in Matagalpa, had been very encouraging, although Don's supervisor had just been transferred to Wiwilí, and neither the local nor the regional government had produced financing for the project.

Ben and Don met with Noel Escobar, a high government official, and suggested that the regional Matagalpa office assign Ben full-time to the Cuá/Bocay project if money could be raised to cover materials and salaries for the team. In that way, the project would be freed from the INE bureaucracy, yet remain connected to the government. After meeting with Charlie Whitaker and other government officials, the group proposed that Don and his students start building the mechanic's shop while Ben worked on the hydroplants farther north. Don's students would then wire the area and train new students.

Noel had often seen the Americans in the Casa de Gobierno in Matagalpa hunched over topographical maps, doing calculations. He knew they were serious, dedicated workers, and reasoned that if they found their own financing, it would be one less burden for the cash-strapped Sandinista government. He agreed to their proposal.

That night, Don and Ben celebrated the revised plan over beers and discussed how to raise the money. They knew that Mira had raised thousands of dollars for NICAT by giving slide shows to progressive groups in the United States, and Ben suggested that he could do the same. A few days later in Managua, Mira suggested a "Ben-and-Mira Road Show," a speaking tour to raise money through the Northwest, where she and Ben had contacts with solidarity groups.

They threw themselves into planning the trip. In the evenings, Mira pedaled her bike over to Ben's modern apartment, her daypack heavy with notebooks and slides. Mira spread out maps of California, Oregon, and Washington and measured driving distances. They sorted slides, wrote a script for the slide show, and mailed letters to solidarity groups, asking them to arrange and publicize presentations according to their schedule.

"Ben and I did a speaking tour because we felt that the project served as a great example; not only in educating Americans about the effects of the war, but also in communicating an understanding of the revolution," said Mira. "The project was possible because we were in a country with a revolutionary government, a country with an agrarian reform, a country where people not only have the freedom to organize themselves—which isn't true in most of Latin America—but are encouraged to organize themselves by their government, to resolve their own community's problems. And we were living in a country that had a commitment to literacy, had an institutional structure to support self-run adult educational collectives for people in the countryside. The Cuá/Bocay project couldn't have existed without the institutional backing that had been developed over the [previous] seven years of the revolution."

After confirming the dates of the tour, Ben wrote Alison, saying that he'd be in the United States and would like to see her. It had been so long since he had received a letter from her that he no longer had her current address, so he sent the letter to her parents' house. He didn't know how she would respond.

For a long time, Ben had been looking for someone to survey El Cuá. He picked the résumé of Joel Schmidt from the TecNica applicants. Joel, bearded and heavily built, moved into a cubicle in the bunkhouse next to Don. Joel had just flown in from Washington, D.C., and was bewildered by the primitiveness of the place where, sight unseen, he had agreed to spend the summer.

Don listed sites for Joel to survey, including the waterfall at El Golfo and the stream at El Cedro, but the Captain ordered Joel to stay in town, since the countryside was too dangerous. Joel's first assignment was to make a topographic map of the town so that Don and Ben could decide if the plant's altitude was high enough to build a gravity-flow water system, where water that powered the plant could be used for drinking.

El Cuá was small but scattered. The surveying crew would usually catch rides to the edge of town, packing their theodolite, tripod, level, and stadia into any vehicle that came along. They often scrambled up next to young recruits in green army trucks, perched on tractor sideboards alongside farmers, and crammed into pickups alongside government workers. Most days, though, they walked in the pouring rain, or the hot sun.

In the evenings, Joel sat with Don on the front porch of the bunkhouse, watching as farmers carrying rifles hurried to their militia posts. Joel and Dr. Chepe Luis often drank rum and Cokes and talked idly while Don studied German grammar.

"In the evening, I really felt the isolation of the place," said Joel. A week before the seventh anniversary of the Sandinista revolution, El Cuá ran out of beer. Army officials had stopped running the government supply caravans to the town for fear of a Contra ambush.

On July 19, a national holiday, Don and Joel dragged stools out into the shade of the bunkhouse porch to watch the festivities. Captain Miguelito ordered government employees to drape red-and-black flags near the plaza. Sandinista supporters hand-lettered placards in Juan Tercero's office, misspelling words. Families on muleback streamed out of the mountains, children well scrubbed and smelling of soap, dressed in Sunday clothes.

Around 10:00 A.M., Don and Joel ambled to the stage in the plaza, where they joined a crowd of townspeople. A small brass band tooted out revolutionary songs, while officials led the crowd in revolutionary slogans, "Siempre será el 19 de Julio" (It will always be the 19th of July). Captain Miguelito gave a short speech, and the polite clapping turned to cheering as he called for the games to begin.

Farmers strung a rope across the road some eight feet off the ground and tied ribbons with rings onto it. In the crowd, townspeople passed around jugs of *cususa*, a homemade corn brew. At one end of the town men on horseback gathered, galloping under the rope one by one as they stood on their saddles, attempting to grab a ring off the rope. The crowd cheered at those who grabbed rings and presented them to the girls of their choice. At the end of the game, the pretty, dark-eyed farming girl with the most rings was crowned the princess of El Cuá.

After a few weeks, Joel became sick with parasites and spent several days clutching his twisting stomach, drinking boiled water, and dashing to the outhouse. Dr. Chepe Luis prescribed medicine, but Joel's condition worsened, and Don took Joel to Managua, where he deposited him in Ben's modern apartment before flying him home to Washington, D.C. When Ben saw Joel and Don, both rail-thin and sallow, he joked about the "El Cuá diet": Anybody who went to El Cuá returned twenty pounds lighter.

The map was still unfinished, but Ben persuaded Ingrid Bauer, an American surveyor working at the State Mechanization School in Chagüitillo, to go to El Cuá to complete the project. When Ingrid arrived in El Cuá with her seventeen-year-old daughter, she was apprehensive about the village, which looked much worse than she expected.

Don wanted to introduce Ingrid and her daughter, Bridget, to the Captain, as he always did whenever visitors came to town, but the Captain was meeting with the officers' corps from another war zone: Wiwilí. Ingrid and Bridget huddled over Joel's map, listing areas that still needed to be surveyed. Bridget wandered outside and bought a Coke at the corner store, idly watching as a caravan of trucks lined up along the main road, waiting for the all-clear signal to leave town.

In the late afternoon the Captain finished his meeting with the officers' corps from Wiwilí. They piled into their jeep, cocked their rifles, and roared out of town. A few seconds later, an explosion rocked the village. "I heard a big roar, so power-ful that the tin rooftops trembled. It was a sound from another world; no one imag-ined that it could be a land mine," said Dr. Chepe Luis.

Townspeople ran to their doors, peering out onto the road. Militia men grabbed rifles. Dr. Chepe Luis ran out of the clinic, commandeered a truck, and sped to the site of the explosion. There was nothing he could do. "Everyone was dead," said Dr. Chepe Luis. "Parts of their bodies hung from the trees. The vehicle was completely destroyed, the tires were some twenty yards away, and the bodies were unrecog-nizable."

Dr. Chepe Luis trudged back to town. In his cubicle, he opened a bottle of rum, drained the bottle, and opened a new one. He continued drinking for the next two weeks.

After the explosion, Don and Ben took Ingrid and Bridget to the plant, think-ing it would be safer for them to sleep there, rather than in town. That evening, under the bare lightbulbs on the bungalow porch, Oscar strummed his guitar as bursts of machine-gun fire sounded in the distance. He mentioned to Ingrid that she shouldn't worry if the Contras attacked that night, because he and the militia would defend her. Oscar further suggested that she and Bridget follow Hilda into the coffee bushes. Ingrid watched the militiamen, teenagers in green uniforms, swing-ing back and forth in hammocks. "It was unsettling to be protected by militia younger than my children," she said.

When everyone went to bed, Ingrid lay awake, worrying about herself and her daughter, and the young men with guns just a few yards away. Everything seemed too vulnerable, she thought. The next morning, she told Don that she and her daugh-ter were moving into town.

In the afternoon Ben visited the widows in El Golfo, informing them of a coffee shortage in Managua. He explained that he couldn't find any Nicaraguan coffee to take to his friends in the United States. The widows, delighted to help him, gave him five pounds of their homegrown coffee beans.

When Ben returned to El Cuá, Don directed him to drive to the jeep that had hit the land mine. When they got there, Don pried off the headlights while Ben stood petrified, overwhelmed by the putrid smell and sickened by the shredded clothes still hanging from the branches above him. Don yelled at him to help drag the jeep's winch back to El Cuá.

Late that afternoon the Captain sent an order to Ben and Don that Ingrid and Bridget had to leave immediately because it was too dangerous. Don and Ben were reluctant to drive out of town so late in the day, but they had no choice and left. An hour out of El Cuá, Old Baldy suddenly lost power in the rain. Don jumped out and yanked the hood open while Ben climbed out of the jeep, rifle in hand, and hiked to the top of a hill to stand guard. Ingrid and Bridget stayed in the jeep, watching Ben, a lone figure on the hill. Don, having fixed the jeep, gunned the motor as Ben ran down the hill and jumped in. They dropped off Ingrid and her daughter in Matagalpa.

Back in Managua, Ben was eager for his friends to get to know Sonia, so he convinced Lois to host a dinner party. Ben arrived early to help Lois cook. Everyone talked and drank as they waited for Sonia. But after several beers, Sonia had not yet arrived. Worried, they went to look for her, slowly driving down the roads, Ben peering at the crowded bus stops. He couldn't find her, and she never arrived at the house. "Sonia was jerking him around, and it was unrequited attraction," said George Moore, one of the dinner guests. "The fact that he was let down was not a big surprise to anybody."

At dinner, everyone was subdued. Afterward, Lois gave Ben a ride home. As they turned the corner, Ben spied Sonia's doctor's car in the driveway. He ran up the steps and flung open the door to see Sonia and the doctor lying on the couch, embracing. Ben pivoted, ran out the door on the verge of tears, and flagged down Lois, telling her what he had seen.

"He asked what he should do," said Lois, "and I told him, 'Throw him out.'" Ben's face dropped; he couldn't do that, he told her. Lois parked her Fiat, and they took a walk around the block. They walked past the ABC office, three houses where

U.S. journalists lived, George and Alice's house, and the neatly clipped lawn of the *New York Times* correspondent's house. Lois consoled Ben, but realized he was not listening to her. When they turned the corner to return to Ben's house, the doctor's car was still parked in the driveway.

It was late, and Lois had to leave. As she drove off, she saw him sitting on the curb, his knees pulled under his chin, hands over his face. After waiting for some time, Ben marched up to the door, knocked loudly, and announced to Sonia that he wouldn't enter the apartment until the doctor left. He turned on his heels and stormed off. Sonia ran out onto the porch, calling his name. He didn't turn around. Instead he stomped around the block again. This time, when he returned, the doctor's car was gone. When Ben walked in, Sonia put her arms around him, telling him he had no reason to be jealous. She loved Ben as a friend. He was very upset, but he also knew that everything she said was true. She had never claimed to be his girlfriend. Gradually, he calmed down. "He told me," Sonia said, "the most important thing is that we stay friends, during the good times and the bad times."

Shortly after that incident, Ben visited Dina, in whom he confided that he was upset with Sonia because his caretaking was not being reciprocated. As much as he hated to admit it, his hoped-for romance with Sonia was not working out. He was beginning to feel used. Dina told him to let her go, advising that he would continue getting hurt until he broke off whatever kind of relationship he had with her. Ben looked as if he was going to cry. "It was painful for him," Dina said, "as he felt rejected and insecure."

In the late morning of July 28, 1986, two pickup trucks departed from Wiwilí. Yvan Leyvraz drove the second truck, a double-cab pickup, with Bernhard Koberstein, Joel Fieux, a twenty-eight-year-old French printer and graphics artist whose Nicaraguan wife had just given birth, and Mario Acevedo, Don's former boss.

As the first truck rounded a turn near Zompopera, a fusillade of gunfire hit, blowing out the windshield and popping the tires. The truck careened off the road. Carlos Lazo, one of the passengers, hurled himself out of the cab, diving into the jungle as his rifle clattered out behind him. Carlos scrambled up a hill and saw the second truck carrying the *internacionalistas* round the bend. The Contras immediately aimed gunfire at them. A rocket-propelled grenade slammed into the driver's side, hitting Yvan point-blank. The truck exploded in a ball of fire. Somehow, Bernhard was able to jump out. Wounded and bleeding, he ran seventy yards, until the Contras emptied their rifles into him. "They could easily see that he was unarmed, and a European," said Carlos.

Later that day, the news bulletin on Radio La Voz de Nicaragua echoed through the halls of the INE office. Engineers clustered around the radio to hear that the Contras had ambushed two vehicles in the northern mountains. Five civilians had been killed, and another three were wounded. The dead included Nicaraguans Mario Acevedo and William Blandón, and three foreigners, Bernhard, Joel, and Yvan.

Ben appeared at Mira's door. She wrote:

> He came into my office, just *hecho huevo*—like he was about to collapse. He took off his glasses and pushed his face and squeezed the skin on his forehead—which he did every time he heard that somebody had gotten killed. He looked at me, and told me that it was just a matter of time. I said, "until what?" And he said, "until you or me goes down in combat." But what he really meant, although he couldn't bring himself to say it, was, "until one of us dies." Then he composed himself, and repeated to me a slogan we always heard at Sandinista demonstrations: "Por estos muertos, nuestros muertos, juramos defender la victoria [For these deaths, our deaths, we vow to defend the Revolution]." Then he went home, and took the next day off, because he couldn't concentrate on anything but the deaths.

Don heard the news in Matagalpa. "It was a shock," he said. "We all knew we could be killed in an incident like that—driving along in a government caravan, and the Contras hit it, open fire. They don't know who is in it or not." Don vowed to tighten his security.

The next day, nearly 2,000 foreigners protested in front of the U.S. embassy in Managua, where they burned an American flag. All of the victims of the attack were buried in Matagalpa, their caskets covered with Sandinista flags and blue-and-white Nicaraguan flags. Hundreds of mourners attended the funeral, but Don resisted, believing it ridiculous to make so much of foreigners' deaths when thousands of Nicaraguans had also been killed in the war.

That summer, El Cuá had two doctors for the first time. Dr. Maria Felisa de Solán, a short, husky Argentine woman, moved into one of the cubicles in the bunkhouse, leaving behind her French husband and two children in Matagalpa. A close friend of Ambrosio Mogorrón, she had vowed to move to El Cuá after he was killed to carry on his legacy.

In early August, Captain Miguelito declared a town holiday to celebrate the release of a group of *desalzados*, forcibly recruited Contras who had taken amnesty and were returning to civilian life. The Captain ordered all government employees to attend the public ceremony in the plaza. Don and Dr. Maria Felisa wandered down together, listening to Captain Miguelito's long political speech, while the ex-Contras stood in the sun, staring at the ground, baseball caps in hands.

Suddenly, an explosion pierced the quiet. Dr. Maria Felisa winced; the public transport truck was due to arrive in town any minute. Dr. Maria Felisa ordered Don to run to the health center and prepare the stretchers. Half an hour later, the wounded arrived in El Cuá, covered in blood. Dr. Maria Felisa patched up seventeen wounded civilians. Because all of the passengers had been sitting on top of corn sacks, which absorbed the mine fragments, no one was killed.

Sometime that summer, Don began to develop nervous tics. His hands began twitching and stopped only when his fingers grasped something tightly, like a grenade. When the tics began, Don knew he needed time off from El Cuá. The strain and isolation of being in the war zone was taking a psychological toll on him. He had lost so much weight that he looked skeletal. His golden eyes darted around the room like the eyes of a cornered animal. Friends noticed that he could not sit still. Don knew others living in the war zone had similar problems. The town's ambulance driver had a hand grenade and a bottle of rum under his seat for courage.

Part of the problem, Don thought, was that the enemy was sensed, rather than seen. The Contras seemed to be everywhere, and nowhere. Gunshots and mortars were often heard in the distance, and farmers whispered that the Contras passed by, but few people saw them.

As Don's nightmares and twitches worsened, he imagined that it was only a matter of time until the Contras attacked El Cuá, overran the town, and executed the Captain, Juan, Sandinista supporters, and him. He envisioned a scene in which they went house to house, pulling civilians into the plaza and executing them, the rotting bodies piling up in the sun. To combat his fears, Don joined the El Cuá militia.

El Cuá was defended by the civilian militia, along with a small army battalion composed of two companies. The army guarded the most strategic hills around town, including the hill where the rocket launchers were located. Whenever the army detected a group of Contras, they chased them into the mountains to isolate and surround them, while the militia stayed behind to guard the town.

The town was surrounded by seven hills that had guard posts on them. The militia was made up of four squads who rotated guard duties so that each squad was on duty every fourth night, but when the Contras were spotted nearby, the army often ordered two, three, or all four of the militia groups onto the hills.

Don was assigned to Maximilian Merlo's militia squad, which covered the southern edge of town. On his first night of militia duty, Don stuffed his rain poncho, hammock, and jacket into a daypack and took his rifle and ammunition clips as he hiked up the hill. Maximo, a short, stocky man with a mustache, showed him the firing hole and told him to string his hammock from the bamboo frame with a tin roof near the crest of the hill. Don was assigned a two-hour shift. That night, he didn't sleep at all.

In mid-August, Mira made another trip to El Cuá to take photos for the slide-show. While there, a government order arrived, summoning all foreigners who worked in the war zones to a mandatory meeting in Matagalpa. Mira was worried. On May 17, 1986, the Contras had kidnapped eight West German volunteers who were building homes for war refugees near the remote town of Nueva Guinea. The Germans were released after twenty-four days, frightened and thin but unharmed. After their kidnapping, Contra spokesman Frank Arana stated that, "any foreigner who voluntarily aids in development and reconstruction projects is considered an enemy," and that such "collaborators" would be treated accordingly. In July 1986, a Belgian development worker was kidnapped, held for a day, and warned by Contras to tell other foreigners not to work with the Sandinistas. After that warning, a leader of the gringo club, Reverend Jim Goff, met with U.S. Ambassador Harry Bergold to discuss threats against internationalists. In late July the three European internationalists were killed. Like many foreigners, Mira believed that, through intimidation and killings, the Contras thought killing a foreigner was worth a few days of bad publicity if it meant having fewer foreigners work in Nicaragua.

Mira asked Don about the meeting, but he dismissed the summons with a wave of his hand. He explained that in 1983, after the Contras killed a French doctor in a mortar attack, officials had called a mandatory meeting of foreigners. It had been a big show of solidarity, he said, where foreigners announced they would continue working. The meeting was a waste of time, Don claimed. And the road to Matagalpa was especially dangerous to travel.

Mira disagreed. She thought it was important to respect government rules, and she planned to attend. On the day of the meeting, however, she couldn't get a ride out of El Cuá. Two days later she caught a ride to Jinotega and was dropped off at the edge of the highway during a heavy rainstorm. She stuck her thumb out to hitchhike, wearing a bright banana-yellow rain slicker and carrying a toolbox in one hand, a gun in the other. Soon a vehicle took her to the Casa de Gobierno in Matagalpa, where she discovered that she was just in time for the meeting, which had been postponed.

Almost 200 foreigners were packed into the room. Mira squeezed into a place along the wall as Carlos Zamora, the regional governor of Matagalpa, spoke. He told the assembled Europeans, Latin Americans, and Americans that after the Contras had razed two state-supported farm cooperatives in May that had been financed and built by Swiss volunteers, the Swiss government had demanded an explanation from Washington. Washington told them to direct their complaints to the Contras. On August 7, 1986, both the Swiss and West German governments officially urged their nationals not to continue working in Nicaragua. After two Swiss nationals were killed in less than six months, the Swiss government warned the Nicaraguan government that it would suspend its commitment for a $20 million aid program if any more Swiss nationals were killed. The French and West German governments had sent the same message. The room buzzed with complaints in a dozen languages. "Everyone agreed that the European governments were just looking for a pretext," said Mira. "It was a way to give in to U.S. pressure to stop aid to Nicaragua."

To everyone's shock, Zamora announced that the Sandinistas were immediately pulling all foreigners out of the war zone. Remembering Don's words, Mira protested. "I stood up and said, 'Wait a minute, this is the time when we are all supposed to stand up and say we won't be intimidated and let ourselves be chased out of the war zone by the Contras!'" The foreigners cheered.

Zamora was adamant. The government had made its decision, and it must be respected. The crowd became quiet as Zamora read a list of foreigners' names, ordering them to move to Matagalpa immediately. Zamora never called Mira's name, nor those of Ben or Don. He hadn't even mentioned their village. As the meeting noisily adjourned, Mira was certain that Ben and Don would be furious when they heard the news that they might have to leave El Cuá.

The August 15 relocation order immediately affected some 430 foreign volunteers. Teachers, doctors, nurses, day-care organizers, sanitation engineers, and architects were pulled out of villages throughout the war zone. Many were not even allowed to return to their villages to collect their belongings. Swiss and Basque construction brigades left houses half-built, without doors or roofs. A Belgian veterinarian abandoned a herd-improvement program, and a French doctor had to leave his patients in Río Blanco. Twelve French citizens who had collected $20,000 in France to build a school in San Juan del Río Coco had to abandon the construction before raising the walls. It felt as if the Sandinistas were admitting that control in the countryside was eroding, and the Contras were winning the war.

Don, Ben, and Mira met in Matagalpa to contemplate the order. They wondered if the project would be moved, or halted, when they found out that the restrictions only applied to projects sponsored by foreign governments. Because the Cuá/Bocay project was independent, largely initiated by Nicaraguans, it was exempt from the edict.

In spite of the increasing attacks against foreigners, the Americans presumed they were safer than most foreigners because the Contras didn't want to jeopardize their congressional funding. Don, Ben, and Mira decided to go ahead with the fund-raising tour in the United States.

As Ben was packing for the United States, Rebecca dropped off a list of items she wanted from the States and told him that she was wrapping up negotiations for the house with the vines on the window, and wanted him to move in when he returned. The night before Ben left, Sonia folded his clothes, packing them into his suitcase. She rolled up Sandinista posters that Ben had agreed to carry back for Anil Gupta, a coworker at INE. Sonia then cut Ben's hair, gently clipping the edges and trimming his scraggly beard. As she leaned over him, Ben asked her if she would live with him in the new house as his girlfriend. Sonia set down the scissors and looked at Ben. "I said, How am I going to share a house with you if I only have fraternal feelings for you? I love you as a friend." Ben looked as if he were going to cry. That night, Sonia felt that they were closer than they had been in a long time.

The next morning, before dawn, Sonia accompanied Ben to the airport, where she cried as she bid him good-bye. After Ben checked in, he sat in the departure lounge and began writing a letter to her, pouring out his feelings, telling her how unfair it was that she was using him. He continued writing the letter on the plane, from the Mexico City airport to Oregon.

Chapter 15

Ben Goes to the United States on a Fundraising Tour

Twenty-four hours after leaving Managua, Ben, disheveled and groggy, was met at the Portland airport by his parents. They had not seen him in more than a year and a half, and barely recognized the scruffy, thin, bearded man in faded jeans and work shirt who confidently strode toward them. As they drove home, Ben chatted incessantly about El Cuá and Mira. Ben had written about Mira in letters and spoke of her over the phone, but he had never defined their relationship to Elisabeth. She was hopeful that Mira had come to replace Alison in Ben's affections.

When Mira arrived, she strode into the Linders' house, dumped her bags on the floor, shook David and Elisabeth's hands, and spread her new slides on the table. Elisabeth looked at the bags in the entryway. She hadn't told Ben where Mira should sleep, but when Ben put Mira's bags in the guest room, she was disappointed to realize they were not a couple.

The next day, Ben and Mira gave their fundraising talk in Portland. The Linders and the local solidarity group had promoted the slide show for weeks, and political activists, neighbors, and family friends overflowed the church meeting room. Elisabeth, David, and Ben's sister Miriam sat near the front.

While explaining the project, Ben and Mira flashed slides of El Cuá's main dirt road, Ben and Rigo climbing through coffee trees in the rain, Oscar repairing a grinder, Don adjusting the turbine, Mira building a stove, Hilda and her two toddlers, Dr. Chepe Luis inside a bullet-scarred ambulance, Julia, the widow, stirring a cauldron of beans, and Alfonso puzzling over the Belarus tractor manual.

After the slide show, the audience felt as if they had visited El Cuá. Miriam, who had never understood Ben's fascination with Nicaragua, finally appreciated his work there. David was proud of his son and realized that, in Nicaragua, Ben had grown up. "He was a man," David said. "The baby fuzz had worn off. He had his own style. He no longer lived under the shadow of John, or Miriam, or anybody else."

Mira and Ben answered questions, each in their own style. Mira was enthusiastic, energetic, defiant, and self-possessed, and had a ready answer for every question. Ben was soft-spoken, casual, and thoughtful. After they passed the hat and saw that they had raised more than $1,500, they were jubilant.

The next day Ben borrowed his parents' car, and he and Mira set off on a tour across the state of Washington, speaking at churches, schools, and solidarity groups. In Seattle Ben looked up his old friend Jim Levitt. "When he got out of the car, I just started laughing because he looked so Nicaraguan! He was scrawny, all edges, even thinner than he had been. He looked like he hadn't been eating for a long time. He had his high-water pants on, and instead of the white shirts he used to wear, with pens in the pockets—the semi-engineer look—he had this cheap, plaid shirt on; it was real Nicaraguan."

Over lunch, Ben told Jim that he felt weird returning to the United States, where everything was readily accessible. He didn't plan on staying in Nicaragua forever, but, as he told Jim, he wanted to continue working in the Third World. He talked about the shortages, and his frequent loneliness. "Yet, in spite of all the difficulties, he seemed happy," said Jim, "because he was doing what he really wanted to do."

Ben spent an afternoon with his old friend Peter Stricker, who had finished his master's degree in engineering. During college, Peter and his girlfriend and Ben and Alison had spent a lot of time together. However, during this visit, Ben never mentioned Alison. When Peter hesitantly asked, Ben, who had never received a reply from Alison, curtly responded that their relationship was over.

When Peter had last seen Ben, he thought that Ben seemed unsettled, with one foot in Nicaragua and one foot in the United States. A year and a half later, Ben seemed to have found a community and a support system. Peter was impressed with his commitment to the El Cuá project and his courage in giving up a mainstream engineering career in the States.

Ben looked up a few old college friends whom he had not seen for three years. They were shocked at how he had changed. "I felt he'd been hardened," said Brian Toal. "He'd lost some of the sense of humor he'd had. We used to be able to call him a Communist, and he'd laugh. Now he didn't laugh."

Ben and Mira traveled throughout the Northwest. After every talk, the project's bank account increased. Suddenly, Ben became overwhelmed with exhaustion. His bones ached, he felt lightheaded, he had no appetite, and the smell of food nauseated him. Driving back to his parent's house, he was so weak that he pulled off the freeway into a rest stop, curled up in the back seat, and slept for hours. Ben had hepatitis A.

When he arrived at his parents' house, Ben stumbled upstairs to his childhood bed and slept continually. His skin and eyes turned yellow. Elisabeth tried to coax food down him, but he turned away, face to the wall.

In El Cuá, Don's students spent the summer wiring 140 houses, about half the town. Soon they ran out of the materials that NICAT had given them. Don hoped that Ben and Mira's tour was successful, so they'd return with more supplies.

In order not to lose momentum, Don switched his students to the mechanic's shop. The road-building crew cleared a piece of land behind the main street, flattened it, and dug a pit for the foundation. Then Don's students surveyed it with pieces of string, mixed concrete, poured a cement floor, and erected a tin roof over a bay to work on vehicles. The nearby cooperatives and local government agencies shared whatever material resources they had and donated manpower to make the project successful.

Don taught his students how to work with tools they had never seen. In the mechanic's shop, they repositioned bearings on worn axles, filed and drilled out sheared-off bolts, and put new threads in holes. They visited cooperatives, examining the wiring, piping, and machinery, then disassembled, cleaned, and reassembled water pumps, insecticide sprayers, and diesel generators. At El Trebol, they fixed the waterwheel that powered the coffee-processing plant.

Every third or fourth evening Don did militia duty, which was an excellent place to learn town gossip. He found out that the whole town was convulsed over an incident at a party at El Trebol, where a nurse had refused to dance with a man from the road construction crew, who in turn called her a "whore." Since then, there had been bad blood between the health ministry employees and the road construction crew. Rumors were circulating that health workers had refused to treat a member of the road construction crew, and that the health workers (MINSA) and the road construction crew (MICONS) had divided El Cuá.

One night, as Don was preparing to go to bed, he heard shouting on the porch outside his door. "Someone was yelling, 'I'll kill them!'" Clad only in boxer shorts, Don pulled on a pair of rubber boots and flung open the door to see Dr. Chepe Luis, swaying in his rubber thongs, clutching the porch railing, and waving a rifle above his head. The intern, the ambulance driver, and a teenage soldier, wearing ammunition belts with hand grenades, also leaned against the porch railing, all cradling rifles, passing around a bottle of rum. Two nurses who lived in another cubicle peeked out their door.

When Don asked Dr. Chepe Luis where he was going with his rifle, the doctor stumbled, jammed a bullet in the chamber, and cocked the gun. "He said, 'I'm going to kill those sons of bitches from MICONS,'" Don recalled. "He said, 'MICONS can't get away with this—they call our nurses whores, they drive the roads like fools, and then, when they get blown apart by land mines, they expect us to patch their bodies back together again. Watch out, MICONS. Here we come.'" The two nurses whose honor Dr. Chepe Luis wished to defend opened their door wider.

The doctor stumbled off the porch, followed by the other three drunken men, and staggered down the road toward the two-story house where MICONS lived. Don ran after Dr. Chepe Luis and grabbed his rifle. "He yelled, 'Give me my gun,' and he went for the rifle, but I swung it out of his hands. I told him, 'No man, let's talk.' And then I turned to the soldier, and told him that he should give me his gun now or else he'd go to jail."

The soldier surrendered his rifle, ammunition belt, and the grenades. Don darted into his cubicle and stacked the weapons in a corner. "Then I heard, 'Pssst, Pssst,' and looked up to see the two nurses leaning in through my open back window, each clutching a rifle. They had disarmed the other two men." Dr. Chepe Luis and his friends disappeared in the other direction, "no doubt to have a drink."

Don slung the four guns around his shoulders, tied the ammunition belts around his waist, clutched the grenades, then clumped down the street, toward the Captain's office, when he noticed three children hiding in a ditch on the side of the road. "I couldn't believe it," said Don. "The kids saw me armed to the teeth, dressed only in my shorts and rubber boots, with four guns. One kid raised his head and said, 'No somos de MICONS: We're not from MICONS.'"

Don gave the Captain the guns, then went to bed, forgetting the incident. But the next morning, when Don entered the diner to eat breakfast, he saw Dr.

Chepe Luis sharpening a bayonet, muttering threats, saying the diner was the health ministry's turf. Don suddenly realized why the MICONS crew regularly ate at a diner on the other side of town. Later that day, the Captain called Don into his office to identify the rifles and ammunition that he had turned in, while the Captain lectured Dr. Chepe Luis.

That evening, as dusk fell, Don was meeting with the adult education teacher in an office near the plaza, when "I heard the sound of bullets, and saw the red glare of tracer bullets whiz down the main street." The teacher and Don hit the floor as a fusillade of bullets rang through the air, coming from opposite directions. Don, who usually carried his rifle with him, cursed himself for leaving it in the bunkhouse, twenty yards away. "I was thinking of running to get my gun when I heard more shots, and I thought, funny, the shots seem to be coming from the front porch of my house. How could the Contras have entered the town so quickly?"

Don looked up the road toward the other end of town, and his eyes widened. At the top of the dirt road, a half-dozen men from the road construction crew marched alongside a slow-moving dump truck, clutching rifles, crowbars, shovels, and chains, moving forward like a Panzer tank division, intent on attacking the health workers.

On the porch of the bunkhouse, health clinic employees prepared to fight back. The intern leveled his gun at the construction crew, while the ambulance driver crouched on one knee, rifle resting on the porch rail, finger on the trigger. Hand grenades hung from his ammunition belt. "It was war," said Don, "between the government employees."

In the fast-falling dark, "I saw some movements, then a swarming of soldiers around the dump truck, as the Captain moved the army in to stop the attack. At the same time, a half-dozen policemen surrounded the bunkhouse, ran onto the porch, and grabbed the weapons of the health workers." The intern, who had fired the shots, sprang out the back door of the bunkhouse and ran into the hills to hide at a militia post.

The Captain, waving his pistol in the air, strode down the main street, roaring at soldiers and police to detain everyone. Suddenly Dr. Chepe Luis appeared, wearing white cotton pajamas and his rubber thongs, wandering out of the bar, a beer in his hand, and two nurses at his side. "He was 'Señor Inocente,' and he told the Captain he had no idea what was going on," recalled Don. The next day the

Captain issued a statement blaming the incident on the Contras, and threw Dr. Chepe Luis and the road construction crew out of El Cuá. Don wandered over to the far side of town to watch the MICONS crew pack up and leave. As they carried mattresses and tools out of their large second-story room, Don realized he could move into the newly vacant spot. He did, and set up his kerosene stove and espresso maker, draped mosquito netting from the ceiling over a double bed, and stowed his rifle under the bed.

Don loved his new home. Sun streamed in through four windows, and the room commanded a view of the road into town. The owner's noisy parrot perched in the bougainvillea, its incessant chattering keeping him company. In the backyard, the house had a private latrine, one of only four in the town. Don was later dismayed to discover that the trench from the latrine emptied into the El Cuá River.

After about a week, Ben was rapidly recovering from hepatitis in Oregon. As he regained his strength, he sat up in bed, read, watched TV, and received visitors. He called Sonia in Managua, pleased to hear that she missed him. She said she felt lonely in his apartment, and was moving back to her old house in Batahola Norte, but that she'd meet him at the airport when he returned.

Ben wandered around the house, ate soup and toast for lunch, and joined his parents for dinner in the evenings. Elisabeth was relieved to see him recovering, but as he chattered on about Hilda, Oscar, Don, and his students, she often found she couldn't follow his conversations. Nicaragua seemed so far away, so different from her reality. "He mentioned people in his letters, and I forgot I'd heard of them," said Elisabeth. She felt that she didn't know him anymore. He seemed more intent on his own purposes, more anxious, more uncomfortable, almost a stranger. She told him stories about the neighbors and his childhood friends, but he seemed preoccupied. "He seemed less interested in other people's stories," said Elisabeth. "We had to continue with our daily lives; you can't just stop and drop it and suddenly be into Nicaragua for three weeks when the kid is home."

All the time he'd been away, Elisabeth had worried whether he was happy, well fed, and safe. She knew El Cuá was dangerous, but she never asked him about the danger because she was afraid of finding out. Instead, she asked him if he was still considering graduate school. Ben said no. She asked him about finding a job in the United States, and he responded that he would probably stay in El Cuá for several years, and perhaps move to another Third World country thereafter. "This trip," David said, "when he said he was 'going home,' he meant Nicaragua."

When Ben recovered, he went shopping for repair parts, tools, and personal items like shampoo, soap, tampons, batteries, and cassettes for his friends. While shopping with his father, Ben began confiding his fears about working in El Cuá. "He told me he worried about three things; that he wouldn't be knowledgeable enough to do the work, that he wouldn't be able to fit into such a small town, and finally, the war—the danger, that was the third thing he was worried about. It was way down on the list," said David.

The most dangerous part about working in El Cuá, Ben said, was traveling the mountainous dirt roads. Everyone took precautions, but they all knew that an ambush could happen at any time. Don had developed security precautions, but there were some dangers that could not be controlled. Ben tried to reassure his father by telling him he was planning to learn to ride a horse, because horses walk on the side of the road, and the Contras usually planted land mines in the middle.

He decided to tell his father that he carried a rifle when he worked in El Cuá. David was stunned. "I knew it was wrong, morally, in a way, because I was a company aid man in World War II, and I told him I carried a shovel, and I'll take a shovel anytime before having a gun." David found it hard to believe that his youngest son, who had been a pacifist and vegetarian, could be telling him he was armed. He questioned Ben sharply, asking him if he had been pressured into it. Ben assured him that the careful decision was his. "He said if he did not carry one, people would be sent along with him to protect him, and he didn't want Nicaraguans endangering their lives for him."

"I told him what General Patton said about World War II; that he didn't want his men to give his life for their country, he wanted the other guy's men to give theirs. I told him people might seduce him, or cajole him, or encourage him to put himself in a position of danger. I told him I can't tell you not to, but just remember, as they cheer you on, it's your ass, not theirs, that might get hurt."

David couldn't imagine Ben pulling the trigger of a gun. "I told him that he'd never hit anything with a gun anyway, and he agreed with me. He said he hoped he didn't hit anyone. But if the Contras heard a lot of noise, they'd stay away."

As Ben continued talking matter-of-factly about land mines, ambushes, and funerals, David asked him to stop talking about it. David had always supported his work in Nicaragua and had become involved himself, writing letters against Contra aid and becoming the treasurer of the Portland/Corinto Sister City Project. But when Ben began working in El Cuá, David had distanced himself because he didn't want to know about the danger. He and Elisabeth had raised their children to be independent, and although David didn't approve of Ben's decision to carry a gun, he did respect it. If Ben had made such a serious decision, David felt there must be good reasons for it, even if he couldn't understand them. Ben was an adult, after all.

David said, "He told us about dangers, but every young person censors what they tell their parents, so I really do not know what he didn't tell us about. I think he was passing through that wonderful moment when a person finds a meaning in his life. But I think as regards the danger, he also made a pact with destiny." He knew that Ben had not told his mother he was carrying a gun, and David decided not to tell her, either. If she knew, she'd worry about him constantly.

Ben had spoken with Reed Brody, a lawyer working with the New York-based Center for Constitutional Rights, who had been interviewing Americans in Nicaragua. Brody was looking for plaintiffs who could say that the $100 million in Contra aid would put their lives in jeopardy. Ben drew him a map of El Cuá and Bocay, marking x's where the Contras had attacked in the past few months. The map was crowded with x's. "The lawsuit included four other Americans, Susan Norwood, Mark Cook, Carol Bowman, and Sandra Price, but of all the people that I could identify, Ben was the furthest out and the least protected," said Reed. When Ben was in Portland, he visited a notary to sign an affidavit for the lawsuit, which sought an injunction against further U.S. government support to the Contras. The lawsuit was based on the June 1986 ruling by the United Nation's International Court of Justice that aiding the Contras was illegal.

Ben's three-page deposition said that U.S. funding for the Contras placed his life in danger because of the Contras' policy of attacking civilians and civilian targets. "I plan to remain in Nicaragua for the foreseeable future. If the U.S. continues to train, support, finance and aid the FDN [the Contras] in violation of international law and the June 1986 decision of the World Court, I will be subject to personal danger to life and limb as I carry out my work." Back at his parent's house, Ben attempted to show the affidavit to his father, but David turned away.

On behalf of the five Americans, CUSCLIN (the gringo club), several aid and solidarity organizations, the Center for Constitutional Rights filed the lawsuit in September 1986 in federal court in Washington, D.C. "I didn't think we would win," said lawyer Reed Brody, "but I thought we were right."

Through mutual friends, Ben learned that Alison was visiting friends in Seattle. He was apprehensive about calling her because she had not written him since their breakup a year earlier, but he was eager to talk. When she heard his voice and his funny, wry jokes, she realized how much she missed him. At the end of a long conversation, she agreed to fly down to see him.

As soon as they saw each other, they immediately slipped back into their easygoing intimacy. They had so many stories to tell each other, so much news to share, so many questions. Ben borrowed his parents' car, and they drove to a cozy hotel on the Oregon coast for two days. "It was hard to change the relationship the way we thought we could," said Alison. Neither of them had found someone else, and the bitterness that each had harbored since the breakup had melted. They each still recognized those qualities that had attracted them to one another, and decided to remain friends.

Alison asked Ben about returning to the United States. Ben said that he had decided there was no place for him in his native country. Alison was disappointed but told him she would always support his work. She reminded him of his unopened letter to her, written in late 1983, with the words, "Not to be opened unless there is an emergency" on the back of the envelope. He told her, "Everything in it still stands."

They promised to write regularly before they parted. Neither of them knew what would happen, but they hoped that their lives might intersect again. Back at his parents' house, Ben often reflected on his time with Alison. After she returned to New York, he received a letter from her, to which he responded:

I've read and reread your letter many times. I love you my dear friend. I love you much deeper than I expressed when we were together. I'm sorry that we couldn't have talked more. I was so confused about being back in the U.S. that all I could do was go through the motions of being here without really being here. The time with you seemed more like a dream than reality. One day we were together and the next day apart. It struck me but didn't sink in. I'm sorry about that. Sorry to you, sorry to me.

Next year we will spend time together. I was scared to plan on seeing you this year. I'm not sure what I was scared of. What I realized was how much we still love each other, how much it means to know that the other is there. I now know that that will never change. That feels very good. I've often wondered if we should be together, either up here or in Nicaragua. I've asked myself a thousand times if that would make us happier. But deep in my heart I don't think it would. It is very exciting to hear of your world. I'm truly pleased to think of the work you are doing and will do. The joy, even among the problems, comes through. But I can't do it. I look around me and I see a world that while I like I can't share. Our joy in living—yours and mine—comes through from our strength in what we are doing. It is a shame, I often regret it, but can't deny it. Our love comes from what keeps us apart. It is also what makes being together so very, very special.

Before Ben left for Nicaragua, he attended a Permaculture workshop on the use of renewable resources. There he met Niko Kozobolidis, a Canadian who volunteered to survey San José de Bocay the following spring. Having fully recovered from hepatitis, Ben went on a short backpacking trip with his brother, and he sent a postcard of the snow-covered Cascades to Oscar and Hilda.

Back in Portland, Ben asked David to start a Portland support committee for the Cuá/Bocay project. Portland had a large activist community, and David knew most of the progressive people in town. David refused. "I actively did not involve myself in the Cuá/Bocay project because I did not want to be a participant to his being in danger." Ben understood.

A few days later, toting suitcases and boxes, Ben hugged his parents good-bye, then flew to his last fundraising stop in Berkeley, California. David Creighton, a director of TecNica, met Ben for lunch in the cozy Homemade Cafe. David spotted him immediately, because Ben was "dressed head to toe like a nerd," wearing a faded cotton shirt and rolled-up jeans with white socks. David was one of the TecNica staffers in charge of sending materials and information to Americans living in Nicaragua. But doing this work for Ben was different. "Every month," said David, "little parcels appeared on my doorstep at the TecNica office in Berkeley, addressed to Ben. As the years went by, the boxes started getting larger and larger—not one, but several seventy-pound boxes. Over time, we understood that he had an important project that stood out from the others in terms of what he was trying to do, its ambitiousness, and the danger of where it was located. So we broke the rules in his case."

During lunch, Ben tried to persuade David to assign more TecNica volunteers to El Cuá. David, concerned about safety, was reluctant to do so. Ben argued that El Cuá itself was relatively safe. "He told me sometimes the roads were 'clean,' and other times, 'You should wait, it's not so good.'" He compared the Contra attacks to a weather report. When it was good weather, you travel, and when there is bad weather, you don't travel, you wait. "He was so matter-of-fact," said David. "A meat and potatoes, unaffected, practical guy." David said he "tried to get a global statement from him that day. Why was he there? Why was he taking these risks? And he resisted it. 'Gee, I was in college, and I was looking for some place to put my talents to work, and I looked around down in Nicaragua and it seemed like a good place.' I was expecting theory to come rolling out, but he was one of the most unideological people I'd ever met. He never made political statements like the importance of the sacrifice for the revolution. He was a humanely motivated revolutionary. His revolution had everything to do with people, and nothing to do with theory."

David said he would discuss the idea of sending TecNica volunteers to El Cuá, but he couldn't promise anything. While he was in the Bay Area, Ben visited a hydroplant library to research turbine designs that could be fabricated from materials in Nicaragua, and he secured a $4,500 grant from the San Carlos Foundation, a group that sponsors Americans working in the Third World. The $4,500 would be divided to pay salaries to Ben, Don, and Mira.

Ben gave his last slide show at the University of California, Berkeley, where more than one hundred students, political activists, and former TecNica volunteers attended, donating a total of $1,000.

After about six weeks, Ben and Mira had raised enough money to cover salaries for the entire team and buy equipment. Before flying to Nicaragua, Ben wrote, "The trip was very good both work-wise and personally. Playing Portland was a high. I felt like I had come back a somebody."

Chapter 16

An American Contra is Captured in Nicaragua

On October 5, 1986, a lumbering C-123 transport plane took off from Ilopango Air Force Base in El Salvador and headed for Nicaragua as part of the secret gun-running operation organized by Lieutenant Colonel Oliver North. It carried a Nicaraguan radio operator and three Americans, including Eugene Hasenfus, a thirty-eight-year-old former U.S. Marine from Mariette, Wisconsin. Tall, broad-shouldered, and sandy-haired, Hasenfus was a prudent man who always flew with a parachute strapped to his back. The plane flew south over the Pacific Ocean, paralleling the Nicaragua coastline forty miles offshore, turned east into Costa Rica, and swung north over the border into Nicaragua, flying over a roadless stretch of triple-canopy jungle at 9,000 feet. It descended into the drop zone—3,000 feet, as always.

The pilot scanned the jungle, looking for the Contra troops awaiting them. Hasenfus readied the parachutes attached to the crates that contained 10,000 pounds of jungle boots, rifles, ammunition, and hand grenades. About four minutes from the drop zone, he opened the cargo hatch door, and the dark jungle swirled by. On the ground, underneath layers of tree canopies, a Sandinista army patrol heard the drone of a low-flying plane.

Nineteen-year-old José Fernando Canales, a dark-skinned draftee with a page-boy haircut and a plastic rosary around his neck, dashed to the nearest clearing, shouldered a SAM-7 heat-seeking missile, took aim, and fired. The missile sped toward the target, leaving a trail of smoke, and smashed into the right wing of the plane.

The plane rocked wildly, and Hasenfus grabbed onto the webbing. The right wing burst into flames, and the plane lost an engine and part of the wing. Hasenfus, deciding he didn't have time to grab his survival kit, flung himself out the cargo door into space.

The plane spiraled downward with the pilot, the copilot, and the Nicaraguan radio operator still strapped into their seats. Meanwhile, Hasenfus pulled the cord to unleash his parachute. Below him, the plane crashed.

Hasenfus landed among the trees, disentangled himself from the parachute, and stared into the brush. He knew the Sandinista army was nearby. He bolted into the bushes, following a trail that was soon swallowed by the jungle. He kept wandering through the jungle, uncertain if he were heading south toward Costa Rica, north toward Honduras, or west toward Managua. In the morning he stumbled upon an abandoned hut and lay down in a hammock hanging from the rafters.

When the Sandinista army patrol arrived at the crash site, they found three charred bodies, rifles, bullets, boots, broken crates, and the pilot's briefcase, intact. Patrols fanned out through the jungle, searching for the parachutist, and finally spotted him lying in the hammock, eating a mango. On the table beside him lay an unsheathed pocketknife. Hasenfus slowly put his hands up in the air.

The next day, October 7, 1986, photographs of Eugene Hasenfus being led from the Nicaraguan jungle by a Sandinista soldier—the first proof of direct U.S. involvement in the Contra war—appeared on the front pages of newspapers across the United States. Two days before the Hasenfus capture, Mira had just returned to Nicaragua with seven boxes of electrical and laboratory equipment.

Rebecca was waiting for Mira at the Managua airport. "It was the fourth time I had flown into the Managua airport, and the first time that anyone had met me," said Mira. In the parking lot, Mira handed Rebecca a pair of windshield wipers. Rebecca had been driving without windshield wipers for five months, since the rains had begun in May, and she gratefully slid them onto her car. As they drove into town, Rebecca told Mira that shortages had worsened, and that if a shipment of oil didn't arrive from the Soviet Union by the end of the week, INE was going to lengthen the daily four-hour electricity cuts in the capital.

Mira shipped the supplies up to El Cuá and Don surmised that there were enough supplies to connect the rest of the town.

A short while later, Ben returned to Nicaragua. His plane flew in over gray-blue Lake Managua, but instead of making the usual low, languid turn, it circled high, then descended rapidly like a dive bomber. As a security precaution, all commercial planes had changed their landing patterns after the Contras had acquired surface-to-air missiles.

Ben brought back presents for everyone: a kitchen knife and bicycle tires for Rebecca; diapers, pins, and cough medicine for Diana Brooks's new baby; a blouse for Hilda; a new baseball cap for Oscar; toys for Oscarito and Aidé; sheets and towels for the widows of El Golfo; and a bottle of brandy for Sonia. Rebecca and Mira were waiting for him at the airport, but Sonia wasn't there.

The next day Ben went to the INE office and met Barbara Francis, a newly hired expert on solar power from Albuquerque, New Mexico. She wrote, "I met him the first day he returned to the office.... People's reactions to Ben were unmistakable. When they spotted him their eyes lit up. They grabbed his hand. They patted him. The meaning was clear; where had he been? When had he gotten back? How long was he staying this time?"

Ben advised Barbara that the work pace in Nicaragua was much slower than in the United States. After lunch, he took her to his office. She thought it resembled a junkyard, crowded with greasy machine parts and tools. Barbara watched Ben at work, and wrote:

> Ben, in his tool hoard, represented organization in the face of entropy and hope in the face of demoralization. Anyone could sidle into his domain and start chatting casually about maybe borrowing the big wrench. Ben would chat back—he was one of the least threatening souls on the planet. By the time the borrower left, maybe with the big wrench, maybe with something entirely different, he knew exactly what task he was hoping to do, exactly how to use the tool to do the task, how to avoid breaking the tool, and how to judge correctly when to give up. He went away confident and brought the tool back. It was technology transfer at its height.

That evening, after work, Ben took the bus to Sonia's cramped cement house in Batahola Norte, but she was off organizing her good-bye party, as she was leaving for Colombia to visit her family. Ben left her a note telling her he was back and asked her to call him.

By Friday, the night of Sonia's good-bye party, Ben still had not heard from her. He stuffed the bottle of brandy in a daypack and persuaded Rebecca to go to the party with him. They parked Rebecca's car in a dark street, then followed the loud, pulsating beat of a salsa song snaking down the dirt alleyway to a house, packed with people.

Ben and Rebecca hesitantly entered the house. When Sonia saw Ben, she flashed him a smile, welcomed him with a kiss on the cheek, and rushed away to greet someone else. Jostled by dancing couples, Ben fled to a corner, arms crossed, lips pursed, not saying a word, while Rebecca shifted from foot to foot. She didn't know anyone and wanted to leave. Ben found a piece of paper and scribbled a curt note to Sonia, telling her it wasn't fair that he had just returned from the United States, and she couldn't even welcome him properly. As Sonia flirted with a Salvadoran, Ben thrust the note into her hand and stormed off with Rebecca, the bottle of brandy still in his daypack.

Sonia read the note. "I ran after him," said Sonia. "I called out to him, 'Benji, don't be that way, we're still friends.'" But he didn't stop. She stood in the doorway, tore up the note, and dropped it into the muddy alleyway. Someone put on a new salsa song, and she returned to the party.

The next evening, Sonia showed up unexpectedly at Ben's apartment. She walked in, flashed her magnetic smile, and apologized for not getting in touch with him. Ben's anger slowly dissolved, as he thought she was making an effort. He presented her with the bottle of brandy, opened it, and poured each of them a drink. He told her about his successful trip, and that he was going to resign from INE soon to move to El Cuá. But he also revealed that he was disappointed in her. He had always looked after her during hard times, but she didn't reciprocate. Sonia promised to write him from Colombia, and she asked for a ride to the airport. When she boarded her plane, he felt as if a burden was lifted.

Now that he was back in Nicaragua, Ben did not want to lose Alison's friendship again, and he resolved to write her more often. He wrote:

My dearest friend. It's dinner alone. Today has been a crummy day. A lot of administrative bullshit getting in the way of work. I was going to resign from INE today but I couldn't even do that as my boss was in a meeting all day. Then I went to visit my friend, Chile, in the hospital. She has a degenerative disease and will be in and out of the hospital forever. Now I'm home eating dinner. The running around of life has stopped for the evening, a rarity, and I have a chance to think about me and my world. In some ways I have a very nice life. A good group of friends that are like a family, for now a nice house, and I'm looking forward to a new job.

And I miss you. I miss looking at you, talking, holding your hand and being with you. I miss not having lived with you. I think it would have been very nice. I'd like to say maybe, someday. I wish it could happen, I don't think it will. It is nice to dream. Halloween is in two days. 1978. It was eight years ago that we met. We've known each other for a long time. Also a very important time for both of us. A fateful unicycle ride, another downtown.... When we set out we never really know where we end up although we may know exactly in what direction we are going. Perhaps someday we will be together again. I still like the idea of riding up to a New York awards affair on a donkey.

For now I am in Nicaragua.... Soon I move to El Cuá to be head of hydroelectric development on the last 25 miles of road going into the interior. Who would have thought? But here I am. I'm going way over my head and who knows where I'll end up. But I know it is right. So here goes nothing. Off into the great unknown.

A few days later, Ben rode the public transport truck up to El Cuá. He was fleshed out and rested, dressed in new jeans and stiff new work boots. The truck rumbled into town in the early afternoon. The driver handed Juan Tercero a stack of *Barricadas*. Juan greeted Ben, clasped his hand, slapped him on the back, and gestured to the papers under his arm, informing Ben that he had become a paperboy. With half the houses in the village wired for electricity, townspeople were staying up later, reading the paper at night.

The next day, Don and Ben drove to El Trebol to measure how much wire they needed to connect the cooperative. Seven miles from the plant, El Trebol was the most distant place they would reach with electricity. The cooperative was built around a concrete coffee-drying patio and a two-story pink house, La Casa Grande (The Big House), back when El Trebol was a private farm. Now the Big House was used for meetings and Saturday-night fiestas, while two small rooms next door were used as classrooms.

Don measured the kitchen, while Ben measured the cavernous Big House and one of the small classrooms, deciding where to place lightbulbs. In the other room, Silvia, the lively popular health educator from El Cuá, was giving a workshop on tuberculosis and potable water to a dozen thin men and women, crammed into children's desks, copying from the blackboard into notebooks.

Silvia explained to Ben that none of her students—reserved farmers—had volunteered to participate in the sociodrama she had planned. "'No one wants to play the role of diarrhea,' I told him, but then he said, 'You have me.'"

A few minutes later, Ben burst through the door of the classroom, his hair combed back and a blanket stuffed under his shirt like the inflated belly of a malnourished child. "He yelled 'I am diarrhea, where are the children? I want to be with them,'" remembered Silvia. Playing the role of a mother with many children, she swept the floor with a broom. "He said, 'I ride on the back of a fly, sticking to your food, giving you diarrhea.'" Ben buzzed around the room, his arms outstretched, his big belly jiggling as he dive-bombed the grinning farmers and swooped past the desks of tittering women. "I hit him with the broom, and batted him on the head, and on his fat stomach. I yelled, 'Get away, you nasty diarrhea, you won't get my children,'" recalled Silvia

Ben buzzed weakly, circling, then crumpled onto the floor. The farmers shrieked with delight. "I told the farmers," said Silvia, "'This is what you must do, you must fight diarrhea, and protect your children.'" Ben stood up, laughing, glanced at his watch, quickly measured the room, and then dashed across the coffee-drying patio to meet Don, who was waiting impatiently. A few days later, Mira, Don, and a few of his students wired El Trebol. Mira wrote:

Justo, a student in the class who lives at El Trebol, and I got assigned the task of wiring in the "Big House"—the immense building that was the home of the hacienda owner. Justo has a couple of days of wiring experience now—he and the others put lights into some of their coworkers' houses here already. But this was a different story. This building actually has ceilings and walls with interior paneling and the wires can theoretically run behind them, out of sight. We ended up crawling around on the rafters, through dust and mouse turds, the tin roof baking the space. Below us are two rooms which are now the schoolrooms. It is Saturday, no classes, but the two young teachers are there preparing a test for Monday. Sweat runs into my eyes.

Donald sticks his head up through a hole in the floor and inspects our work. "This is a shabby job. Two wires, parallel and tight, got it?" Justo grunts and begins to pull out the staples and straighten the wires. I realize that he is afraid of heights, and realize that I am surprised. No reason to be. Just because I know he was in these mountains with the guerrillas eight years ago, fighting the [Somoza] National Guard, just because I have seen the remains of a tank full of Guardia that he and Oscar and a small group of combatants disabled, this is no reason to expect him not be human, not to be afraid of heights or anything else. I crawl over and take the staples out of the wire running nearer the edge. More sweat drips in my eyes. "Justo, does it make a difference which side of the bulb goes to the live wire?" He doesn't think so—there are no switches here.

Shouting down to the teachers over the noise of the radio we pound on the ceiling and locate the center of the room and drill the holes. I wipe a grimy hand across my forehead, smearing in the dust. Justo's sleeve moves, revealing a huge scar on his arm, a big chunk gone out of it.

The radio show is interrupted to bring us a special broadcast. I go back and staple down the wires, tight and parallel, like the boss said. The teachers' voices stop and the radio comes clearly up from below. Daniel Ortega is giving a special press conference because Reagan has just signed into law the bill authorizing the financing of the Contras and the overt CIA direction of the war. "Más minas [more mines]," says Justo, wiping the sweat out of his eyes, and gingerly moving himself over to the edge of the wall—here the ceiling ends and the room opens out into a barn-like space, now used for cooperative meetings. We stick a light bulb out there as well. Daniel's voice continues, detailing the U.S.'s flagrant violation of international law, and the sacrifices this will mean for the Nicaraguan people. "More work, more discipline, more participation in the Defense, more firmness." Donald comes back and looks over our work, approves, and informs us his crew has finished the kitchen. "Hey, I've never done this before!" He smiles. And goes out to the pole and thrills to pieces all the kids on the farm by climbing up it with his linesman's equipment and turning on the lights on the farm.

In the meantime, the congressional ban on CIA aid to the Contras had expired. The $100 million began to flow, and the CIA resumed day-to-day management of the war, stockpiling weapons and dispatching supply planes from a secret air base on Swan Island, off the Caribbean coast of Honduras. From El Salvador, Honduras, and U.S. ships cruising the Nicaraguan coast, the CIA directed Contra attacks deep into Nicaragua. In Washington, D.C., the Reagan administration considered direct air strikes and a naval blockade.

Top Contra commanders were sent to U.S. army bases in North Carolina and Florida, where Spanish-speaking American instructors taught two-month courses in map theory, navigation, and patrolling and instructed them how to use new weapons, including artillery and explosives.

When the Contra leaders returned to their bases in Honduras, the CIA supplied them with intelligence data, including blueprints of Nicaraguan government installations and aerial reconnaissance maps that showed Sandinista army bases in such detail that every outhouse was noted. The CIA supplied the Contras with Datotek minicomputers to encode and decode messages, portable solar panels to recharge field radios, and 200-channel scanners to eavesdrop on the Sandinistas. Contra troops received new FAL and Kalishnakov AK-47 automatic rifles and heavier machine guns. Each group was assigned a surface-to-air shoulder-fired missile, either a Soviet-made SAM-7 or a sleek U.S.-made Redeye, worth $30,000 each.

Thousands of Contras left the Honduran base camps and moved into Nicaragua through the Bocay River valley to the hills of Jinotega, dispersing into smaller units. CIA-operated flights parachuted sapper squads into Nicaragua on sabotage missions and airdropped supplies to the Contras three or four times a week. Deep in the jungle, clashes between the Sandinista army and the Contras increased to more than a dozen a day. The Contra leaders planned to boost the Contra army to 30,000 combatants. From there, they wanted to seize and hold territory and declare a provisional government.

On October 21, 1986, the Sandinista government put Eugene Hasenfus on trial, charging him with terrorism, conspiracy to commit illicit acts, and violation of public security laws. The trial was held at the Tribunal Popular Anti-Somocista (People's Anti-Somocista Tribunal), a low-slung one-room building on the Southern Highway near the U.S. embassy.

During the month-long trial, solemn-faced guards from the Ministry of the Interior surrounded Hasenfus, who sat impassively in jeans and tennis shoes, blue eyes glazed over, large frame crammed into a small wooden chair. The tattoo on his upper arm, "Fly-Boy," peeked out from under a tight T-shirt. The concrete courtroom was sweltering, packed with journalists, internationalists, and curious passersby. One lone fan sputtered near the prosecutor.

Spectators gathered outside, peering through glass slats into the room, while ice-cream vendors with pushcarts congregated in front of the courtroom, clanging their bells. Big rig trucks rumbled down the highway, drowning out the words of witnesses.

The Reagan administration enlisted former U.S. attorney general Griffin Bell to defend Hasenfus. Hasenfus revealed what he knew about the CIA arms-delivery operation to the Contras, saying that top-ranking Honduran and Salvadoran officers were complicit, and weapons and ammunition from the United States were stored at a warehouse at Ilopango Air Force Base. The operation, he said, was coordinated by a man known as Max Gomez, whose real name was Felix Rodríguez, a right-wing Cuban who had cooperated in the murder of Cuban hero Che Guevara. Hasenfus explained that he and his buddies, many of whom he had worked with in Vietnam with Air America, had been hired by Corporate Air Services to ferry arms and supplies between San Salvador and Aguacate Air Force Base in Honduras. He had participated in at least nine airdrops over Nicaragua, receiving $3,000 a month plus expenses, and a $750 bonus every time he flew into Nicaragua.

Throughout Managua, new graffiti appeared on buildings:

Señor Imperialista,
en la tierra Sandinista,
les hacen ... fus.

Mr. Imperialist,

in Sandino's land,
your plans ... fall apart.

On October 31, at the CISAS office less than a mile away from Hasenfus's trial, Maria de Zuniga threw a Halloween party. Ben and Lois dressed as Eugene Hasenfus and the Sandinista soldier who caught him. Ben wore a black "Soldier of Fortune" T-shirt, jeans, army boots, and a U.S. army cap, with "I Love Ronny" penned onto his upper arm, and ensnared himself in a red-and-black typewriter ribbon. The ribbon was yanked by Lois, who carried a toy AK-47 rifle and wore camouflage army pants, a Sandinista T-shirt, and an army jacket sprinkled with political buttons: RADIO HAVANA and SANDINO SIEMPRE (Sandino forever).

People flowed in and out of the house, dancing to salsa songs, eating enchiladas and *indio viejo*, shredded meat in sauce. Ben told Ana Quirós, a Costa Rican woman, about the El Cuá hydroplant, and she said, "I told him that a mini-plant was an ideal project for him, because he was so small, a *gringuito chiquito*, a mini-gringo. I teased him—telling him that he shouldn't worry about the plant because the Contras were going to blow it up soon. But he just shrugged his shoulders, and said, '*No me importa* [I'm not worried]. I'll build another one.'"

Ben also ran into Ani Wihbey, a vibrant 50-year-old U.S. nun and nurse from the gringo club. Ani frequently worked in the countryside and offered to give a workshop on safe drinking water in El Cuá. In the midst of the party, Ben suddenly became serious and pulled Ani aside. He asked her about God. He described his religious beliefs, which, to Ani, sounded like a mixture of Jewish tradition and revolutionary liberation theology. "He made jokes about being a Jew and going to church," said Ani, "and he told me that at one time he believed in God but now, he wasn't sure, because he couldn't understand that if a God was supposed to be good, then how could so much evil exist? Because he saw all the Nicaraguans, almost all Catholics, almost all deeply religious, who continued to believe in God—in spite of all the atrocities. And so he was confused."

Ani didn't have an answer for him.

In Managua, foreign journalists sifted through the business cards, memos, flight logs, and other documents found on Hasenfus's plane. Included in the briefcase was a list of thirty-four Americans in El Salvador who worked on the arms-supply operation. *Washington Post* reporter Julia Preston tracked down the phone bill of one of the safe houses where Hasenfus stayed in El Salvador, and traced some of the calls to Vice President George Bush in Washington, D.C.

About the same time, the Lebanese weekly *Al-Shiraa* reported on the secret trip made by Lieutenant Colonel Oliver North and former national security advisor Robert McFarlane to Teheran, Iran, in May 1986, uncovering their attempt to exchange weapons for American hostages held in Iran. The Iran-Contra scandal had begun.

Chapter 17

First Anniversary of the Plant

In Managua, Mira resigned from INE to move to El Cuá. In her windowless office, Mira untacked her revolutionary posters, newspaper clippings, and photos, leaving the room as barren and ugly as the day she moved in.

Mira packed her belongings and took the bus to Jinotega. Before dawn, on November 17, she trudged alongside a caravan of parked trucks wrapped like a snake around the muddy Jinotega market, searching for the truck driver with whom the regional government had arranged to take her to El Cuá. She found him asleep on the floor of his truck's cabin. He awoke with a grunt and stashed his bedroll under the seat, next to his gun, which was discreetly stowed out of sight but within easy reach. Two clean bullet holes punctured the windshield. When Mira asked about them, he told her he had survived three Contra ambushes while hauling coffee out of the Jinotega Mountains.

The truck driver told Mira the caravan wouldn't be leaving for a while, so she wandered impatiently through the market, sipping sugary black coffee from a plastic cup, eating strips of roast pork wrapped in tortillas. Throughout the morning, trucks pulled into the muddy field while strong-shouldered men loaded sacks of sugar and rice, soap, cooking oil, and barrels of diesel fuel destined for the settlements along the road to San José de Bocay. The truck driver ordered the men to load Mira's rolled-up mattress and supplies on top of the sacks. "Forty trucks, a crane and a mobile shop. And a good sprinkling of *compas* [soldiers] on top of all the sacks. Everyone says this is not a convoy that the Contras are likely to attack. That is why I am being sent up to El Cuá in it," wrote Mira, trying to convince herself that she was safe.

The day heated up, as women bustled through the market stalls. Mira waited close to the truck, but midday came and went and the caravan still had not moved. Throughout the afternoon, Mira swung back and forth in the hammock. No one knew when the caravan would leave.

The caravan finally left the next day, with Mira in the cab next to the driver. The trucks whipped around hairpin turns, never slowing, and barreled across swollen rivers. It was the fastest trip Mira had ever taken to El Cuá. When the caravan snorted into town, the driver safely deposited Mira and her belongings on Don's front porch.

After living alone in El Cuá for seven months, Don was glad to see Mira. He dragged her mattress up the stairs into his second-story room. Mira claimed a corner, organizing boxes, tools, files, and books, and setting her alfalfa sprout canisters on the windowsill. As soon as Mira settled, she visited the Captain to ask for a gun. Before moving to El Cuá, Mira had made the decision to go armed.

A few days after Mira arrived, Don decided to throw a huge party on the first anniversary of El Cuá's electrification. He visited government officials in town, personally inviting them to the party, as he wanted it to build social and political support for the project. Two days before the party, just after midnight, Hilda spied thick plumes of smoke curling out of one of the bearings on the turbine shaft. She called for Oscar, who dumped water on the bearing, turned off the plant, and disassembled it. Shortly after dawn, Oscar banged on the door at Don's house, clutching a plastic bag with a broken bearing.

Don shook his head in disbelief. The party was the next day, and the nearest bearing was in Managua, a twelve-hour round trip. Mira suggested that since it was a temporary problem, they should hold the party and fix the plant afterward. Don, feeling it was imperative that the plant be on-line, decided to drive to Managua.

After consulting with the Captain, Don headed for the "shortcut," a narrow one-lane road to Matagalpa that had been closed to government vehicles for more than two years because of Contra ambushes but had recently reopened since the main road had become so dangerous. Outside El Golfo, Don spied Federico, the former hydroplant operator, and jokingly invited him to Managua, "just for the day." Federico, who had only been to Managua once, joined them.

Don and Mira cocked their rifles. The few houses that they passed were abandoned. They skirted cloud-shrouded mountains and passed the ragged crags of Peñas Blancas. Mira was sure that the area was infested with Contras and wondered where they were hiding. She was relieved Federico was with them. "It was good to have him," she wrote. "We'd gotten clearance for this road, but I looked at the green mountains straight above us and thought that if we had been ambushed and survived long enough to get out of the car and into the bush, he could have gotten us to safety on foot."

They arrived in Managua at night and drove directly to Ben's apartment, but no one was at home. Mira tacked a note to the door, telling him that they had just come from El Cuá. When they returned to the house after dinner, "we found Ben going crazy thinking that someone had been hurt at the plant," said Mira. "He told me never to leave him a note like that again. I felt bad because we only meant to surprise him with our presence."

They slept on mattresses strewn across the floor, and at 8:00 A.M. they began scouring machine shops and hardware stores throughout Managua, pleading with clerks to sell them a bearing, even the floor model from the display window. In the late afternoon they finally found one and headed for the mountains. By the time they reached Matagalpa, dusk was falling and traffic stopping as travelers settled in for the night. Don zoomed through Matagalpa, heading for the shortcut. They passed wooden huts, lit by kerosene lanterns, but there was no other traffic on the road.

The jeep was speeding through the tiny village of Empalme La Dalia when a rope suddenly loomed across the road before them. Don braked as a half-dozen camouflaged soldiers emerged out of the dark. They surrounded the jeep, asking everyone for identification, but Don told them that they had to get to El Cuá for an emergency. The soldiers ordered him to park the jeep. Don objected.

Don suggested to Ben and Mira that they jump the rope, but they protested so vehemently that Don jerked the key out of the ignition, and the jeep died. He hopped out, saying that he was going to find someone who had just traveled down the road who could tell him if it was safe. Ben followed him to the small army office, where Don sat down with a state security officer, offered him a cigarette, chatted with him about the rain and the coffee harvest, then shook his hand and walked out of the office without asking anything about the road to El Cuá.

Ben was furious. He asked Don why he hadn't even asked about the road, and Don retorted that some of the officers never got out from behind their desks. "I told him I didn't ask because then the officer might get himself involved, and get us hurt." Don said he was going to ask a driver from a supply caravan. "Ben just couldn't understand that the people in the supply trains knew more about the day-to-day situation than a state security officer."

Don found someone who had arrived from El Cuá a few hours earlier, and said the road was safe. Ben spoke to another officer, who advised that the road was dangerous. They met back at Old Baldy and yelled at each other in English, while soldiers at the roadblock watched them, amused. "Don was so annoyed that he wouldn't get out of Old Baldy," said Mira. "We didn't talk our way out of it," said Don. "I was miserably upset because we were only one and a half hours from El Cuá."

The others wandered around town, searching for a place to spend the night, but there were no pensions or hotels. Finally, in desperation, they asked some Ministry of Interior officers who were locking their office if they could sleep there, and the officers agreed. Don sat in Old Baldy, refusing to join the others. Federico strung up the hammock in the office, while Ben and Mira lay down on some boards and wrapped themselves in plastic sheeting.

During the night, rainclouds burst, unleashing sheets of water that drummed on the office's tin roof. Ben and Mira awoke with a start, and thought of Don. They ran through the rain to Old Baldy, where Don huddled in the driver's seat, his rain poncho drenched, his gun resting across his lap. He refused to come in.

The next morning, the crew waited in Old Baldy. Don smoked one cigarette after another as the sun rose, burning off the mist. At ten to nine, Don started the jeep, floored it, and drove over the rope, yanking it loose from its posts, while Ben and Mira clutched the sides of the jeep, not saying a word. Don lit another cigarette, and drove the hour and a half to El Cuá in stony silence.

At the plant, Oscar quickly installed the new bearing, and that afternoon Captain Miguelito, Juan, Dr. Maria Felisa, Silvia, Casilda, and other nurses, teachers, and Sandinista leaders arrived at the plant for the party. No one from INE in Managua showed up.

When everyone had gathered, Oscar and Hilda turned on the electricity, Don passed around bottles of Victoria beer, and Hilda dished out pork and cornmeal tamales made from one of the two pigs she had been fattening. As everyone ate and drank, Ben gave a formal speech, saying that a cooperative effort had brought electricity to El Cuá and thanking everyone for their hard work in making the plant a reality.

Then Don spoke up. "Don wasn't supposed to speak, but he did because he didn't think Ben's speech was adequate," said Mira. He explained that the plant was only a first step, and that over the next year the team would finish wiring the town and the four cooperatives, and then build other hydroplants throughout the valley. All of the officials pledged their support. Ben was impressed by Don's performance. "Don orchestrated the show," wrote Ben. "In fact, he really is damn good at running things."

That evening, the crew held a public party in the whitewashed barn of La Chata cooperative. Celebrations were rare occurrences, so families rode for miles out of the mountains on horseback to attend. More than 150 people crammed into the barn, and home-brewed *cusuza* flowed freely. The band, Frente Norte, comprised of Oscar and two farmers from La Chata, played guitar, *bandoneón*, and *guitarron*, while farmers shuffled to the music in their black rubber boots, dancing with their wives beneath the lightbulbs that Don's students had recently installed.

Mira stood at the edge of the dance floor, drinking a beer. Men invited her to dance, shyly holding out their hands toward her, but she shook them off, refusing to dance, because she knew that in such a small town, even accepting a dance with someone was seen as significant. If she danced with a man, people would gossip that she was chasing him.

Ben and Don, however, didn't care what people thought, and danced both fast and slow, romantic dances. Ben danced with each of the teachers, then invited Dr. Maria Felisa to a slow dance. Although they were about the same height, Ben could not clasp his hands around her 250 pound bulk, and Oscar, strumming his guitar, slowed the music, feasting his eyes on the sight of Ben and Dr. Maria Felisa lumbering around the barn. After the dance, Oscar sidled up to Ben. "I told him, 'Mucha mujer para tí, Benjamín' [That's a lot of woman for you, Ben], and he just laughed."

When the band took a break, Ben wheeled his unicycle to the center of the barn, and the crowd hushed, falling back. He jumped onto the unicycle, balanced, pedaled it forward, then backward. Children's mouths fell open. He circled, then pirouetted around the children, who stood numb, unsure how to react. The farmers were spellbound. "Look at the one-wheeled bicycle!" they said. Ben tooted a whistle, circling the room, motioning, inviting children to follow him, and they began shrieking and chasing him around the barn. Women covered their mouths and giggled.

Don tossed Ben three oranges, and he pedaled back and forth, juggling them from atop his unicycle. The farmers stood hypnotized. Ben pretended to drop an orange, then, at the last minute, snatched it back, tossing it high enough to graze the rafters. Don threw him a fourth orange, and they team-juggled, as Ben balanced atop his unicycle. One farmer whispered in Oscar's ear, asking him if all gringos could do that.

Don put the oranges aside and tossed his Aerolite juggling pins to Ben, who nudged the unicycle backward and forward, dipping slightly as he learned forward to catch the pins, then hurled them quickly back at Don, the pins becoming a blur. Ben waved a few children into line between them and tossed the pins over their heads, while the children froze, afraid but delighted. Scores of children jumped in, pushing themselves between the two jugglers, and when Ben caught all the pins to end the show, the children chorused, "¡Otra! ¡Otra!" (Again! Again!). He dismounted, holding the unicycle for some farmers who mounted it, but they immediately fell off, to the drunken, raucous laughter of their friends.

"Ben rode his unicycle, but he thought it was too much to put on his costume and face paint," said Mira. "He hadn't done any clowning in El Cuá before, because he wanted to be known as the engineer and be taken seriously, so riding his unicycle was an indication that he was feeling more comfortable."

When Frente Norte resumed playing *ranchera* songs, Ben left the party to relieve Hilda, who was minding the hydroplant. Mira went with him as they hoisted AK-47 rifles to their shoulders and hiked down the dirt road to the hydroplant. Ben and Mira turned off the road, glanced nervously into the hills, and climbed a muddy trail, where the hydroplant hummed steadily. They slung their guns around their chests and shimmied across a wet, slippery log over the Esperanza River, when the log shifted, throwing them off balance. They both slid off. Mira grabbed some branches, steadied herself, swung her body back onto the log, then looked down to see Ben, facedown in the knee-deep river, soaking wet, clothes and gun caked with mud. "He was so upset," said Mira. He scrambled up the path to the plant, where Hilda gave him a set of Oscar's clothes. Ben insisted that Hilda and Mira go to the party. When they disappeared down the trail, he hung his wet clothes over the generator to dry and cleaned his gun. Before he fell asleep, he wrote his parents:

It's hard to describe how I feel about life and work. While in Managua my social life is very good, although my love life is nonexistent. My work has been made hard by company policy and bureaucratic inertia mixed with generally inept people.

Here in El Cuá I'm faced with very challenging work, a dismal social life, unforeseen as well as foreseen problems, and more responsibility than I ever imagined I'd have. Also, and most important, I have the good fortune to start one of the most exciting hydroelectric projects perhaps in the world. The technical excitement is part of it but really only a part. The concept of social development on a revolutionary context, especially in the outback, is an amazing idea. Key in all plans for Cuá-Bocay is where the electricity is. Key in that is me.

Chapter 18

El Cuá Graduates Four Local Electricians

Three years after signing his first contract, Ben resigned from INE to move to El Cuá. He threw his own good-bye party, then stopped by the Brooks house to pick up some belongings. Ana jokingly suggest that he make out a will. Ben asked what she wanted, and she responded, "Your books, of course."

The night before leaving, he wrote a short letter to Sonia in Colombia and sent her two books by Nicaraguan author Guillermo Cortéz Domínguez, *Una de Arena y Dos de Cal* and *Un Nicaragüense en Miami.*

The first week of December, Ben moved into Don's house in El Cuá, along with his red suitcase, a battered briefcase, a burlap sack full of juggling pins, and his unicycle. Don considered Ben, like Mira, his guest, and insisted that Ben use his bed with the mosquito netting, while Don moved onto an air mattress on the floor.

With Mira and Ben around, Don realized that during the seven months he'd lived alone in El Cuá, he missed speaking English and being with people from his culture. "Culturally, in El Cuá, a person felt isolated, unless you like *ranchera* music, rice and beans, and getting shit-faced drunk every Saturday night," Don said.

The three Americans joked about the town, dubbing a greasy diner where breakfasts consisted of beans, rice, fried bananas, and noodles "the Frijol Feo" (the Ugly Bean). They shared news about townspeople: Doña Casilda was in love with handsome, swarthy Juan Tercero; Dr. Maria Felisa's French husband was moving to El Cuá; Silvia, the health worker, had not shown up for work again. They told jokes, poking fun at the Nicaraguan diet: "What are the four food groups in Nicaragua? Grease, fat, alcohol, and sugar."

After dinner, the three usually returned to Don's room. Like soldiers in boot camp, they grew closer, and whenever anyone brought back letters from Managua, they read them aloud so the others felt as if they had received mail, too. Don and Mira talked about their love lives, but Ben rarely added to the conversation, and whenever he received a letter from Alison, he read it in private.

The Americans also complained to each other about the lack of productivity and motivation of certain townspeople. They discussed how these problems were directly related to colonialism and underdevelopment. As they worked more closely together, it also became clear that Don was the boss. "It was a relief to have Don in charge," said Mira. Don was self-assured, unruffled, and radiated authority. He established priorities, set the rules, knew how to give orders, and expected others to carry them out. Working with Don, Mira and Ben felt confident that the project would be successful, because they knew that Don would not settle for anything less.

"Don moved up to El Cuá to create space where they could work," said Tom Kruse, who lived in Matagalpa. "Don established credibility. Don's a working-class dude who knows how to deal straight with other working-class people; work with them, establish credibility, gain their trust, move ahead. And when given the opportunity, and the conditions, he's a genius."

At the same time, Don intimidated Ben. Don was so self-assured, while Ben was afraid of failing. "I like working with Don but he is so intense in his way of thinking, living and acting. In a lot of ways it is similar to being with [my older brother] John. Not the intensity, as much as I keep feeling that I don't live up to his expectations. And that bothers me. I do want to."

Not only was Don qualified technically, but by the time Ben and Mira moved up to El Cuá, he had established solid, trusting relations with town officials and residents. Don understood the social and hierarchical structure, and explained it to Ben and Mira. While Ben had understood the hierarchy at INE, he didn't understand the more subtle structure in the countryside.

Don also understood the dangers of working in the countryside and established security rules: avoid routines, check with the army before working outside the town, and always carry rifles, even if only walking a short distance. "Not that I expected any trouble," said Don, "but if anything went wrong, I wanted the gun with me, and not in my house, two miles away."

He instructed them to check with the army, or with supply caravan drivers, to see if the road was safe before leaving town, and gave them the names of trustworthy officers. If they drove Old Baldy to Jinotega, they should attach themselves to a caravan but shouldn't ask the officers' permission. Don said, "I told them if you can figure out when the caravan's going, and just join them, as soon as they drive out of town, you just follow right behind, and they make their first stop, and you're part of the caravan. It was little security things like that that are important that just took a while to figure out."

However, Don and Ben disagreed on one safety measure. Don was suspicious of people he didn't know, and rarely talked to strangers, while Ben thought it was safer to talk to everyone, especially strangers. He thought that if town gossip spread into the countryside and the Contras heard that the foreigners in town were Americans, then maybe the Contras would leave them alone. While Don only made friends with officials, Ben made friends with everyone.

In Managua, Ben's closest friends—Lois, Maria, Rebecca, and Dina—had listened to his problems, advised him, and given him emotional support. Ben worried that he'd never make similar friendships in El Cuá. Don had told him he'd find friends among the *estatales*, government employees from cities posted to El Cuá. They had a political consciousness, and might have studied a year or two at the university. But after moving to El Cuá, Ben found he disliked them, for they exclusively hung out with one another, drinking, gossiping, and making fun of the locals. Ben thought they were arrogant and ignorant, and preferred to spend time with the villagers.

Although most villagers didn't know the foreigners' names, they knew they were Americans, and, as they walked down the street, townspeople warmly remarked, "Ay—ya vienen los gringos" (Here come the gringos). Don was dubbed *el gringo malcriado*, "the bad boy," because he never used *Usted*, the formal form of "you," and didn't allow others to refer to him as *Usted*. Unlike Nicaraguans, he was very direct. They called Mira *la chelita*, "the white-skinned one," and because Ben had brought light to the village, he was dubbed *el hombre májico*, "the magic man."

Now that he was a village resident, Ben wanted to be included in local activities. He stopped by the clinic to meet with Silvia, the health educator, a dynamic, intelligent twenty-one-year-old from a family of eleven children. Silvia had grown up on a cattle farm in La Pita del Carmen, where her father was active in UNAG, the Sandinista-affiliated National Union of Farmers Association. One day the Contras had appeared at Silvia's house looking for her father; since he wasn't home, they kidnapped Silvia's twenty-eight-year-old sister instead. She didn't return, and fearing the Contras would kidnap others, Silvia's father moved the family to El Cuá.

Silvia had completed the first year of high school, making her one of the most educated people in town. She had held some of the most important jobs in El Cuá: school administrator, bank cashier, and her current job. Being a health educator, Silvia would do home visits, where she encouraged women to keep pigs and chickens out of the house, bathe children, sweep the floor, use latrines, wash hands, clean fingernails, and boil the drinking water they got from the Cuá River.

In the mornings Don rose before dawn, made coffee, and left the house before 8:00 A.M. to teach classes. Ben usually left for the plant about the same time, awkwardly hoisting his gun to his shoulder. "He'd pick up his briefcase, calculator, and gun, and say, 'I'm off to work, dear,'" said Mira. "He didn't like it, but there was also a macho part of Ben that enjoyed it."

After they left, Mira often lingered in bed, postponing the day, because she didn't know how to organize her work. She had two projects: building Lorena woodstoves, and improving the area's ceramic work. She wondered how she could persuade local women to spend two weeks shoveling and compacting sand to build a Lorena stove when their huge clay stoves worked well for them. How could she prove that the stove would be better than their present one, when there wasn't even a stove in town to show them?

She eventually got out of bed and forced herself to visit different sites in town in search of soil samples. Villagers often stopped to ask questions, but Mira could only smile back because she didn't understand their dialect. "I ask the peasants to repeat themselves, and they just smile and look down at the ground," she wrote.

To Mira, everything in El Cuá seemed difficult, even walking on the clay soil. She worried that she was falling behind on her schedule. Frustrated by her own ineptitude, she turned to Ben and Don for advice. Ben suggested that she hang out with the locals, talk to people, observe their customs, their ways of speaking, their hand motions, their way of doing things, and try to do the same. Don advised her to slow down. He said she was having trouble because she was too eager, too frenetic, too demanding, too *gringa*.

Mira followed their advice, slowing down, spending afternoons hanging around the hydroplant. She helped Hilda weed the garden, feed the pig, and gather newly laid eggs. Mira fried eggs and topped them with alfalfa sprouts from her plants. Whenever Hilda cooked on the plant's Lorena stove, Mira felt reassured about her own work. In the evenings she often watched Oscar and Hilda do their homework, constructing circuits with lightbulbs, sockets, switches, outlets, and wires.

Mira improved her Spanish by talking to Hilda, who knew that Mira often couldn't understand her. She taught her expressions and gestures only used in the countryside. As Mira hung out at the plant, she realized she was receiving a lesson about traditional and acceptable relationships between men and women in El Cuá. She wrote:

> Oscar seems to be Hilda's owner. Both are paid the same, and theoretically split the 24-hour shifts. But he, as her husband, can tell her to stay here, and he goes off and does as he pleases, including hanging out with his girlfriend in town. They don't divide household tasks. So Hilda cooks. Watches the kids. And watches the plant. His behavior toward Hilda disgusts me, although Oscar is a good friend and one of the more conscientious and respectful men around.

When Mira complained to Ben about Oscar's behavior toward Hilda, he advised her to be less judgmental about people. Mira wrote, "An important lesson Ben gave me was when he pointed out that my vision of people is basically static (once a sexist pig always a sexist pig, once a Contra always a Contra), and that I must remember that people can change, and are changing, every minute. And with each change we become more revolutionary."

As the coffee harvest began in November, word got out that small Contra groups with new weapons had begun infiltrating the zone. Sandinista military intelligence reported that the Contras were targeting the Cuá/Bocay area. Shortly after the news, Ben and Mira heard gunshots. If the town was ever attacked, Don had instructed them to join the militia up the hill, so Mira and Ben grabbed their guns, ran to the guard post, and became integrated into El Cuá's militia. They were assigned to Don's group, joining twenty-five other people who were responsible for covering two hills, one that overlooked the southern entrance of town, the other in the town's cemetery.

Maximo, the militia leader, assigned the three Americans to the hill in the cemetery. Every third night at dusk, Ben, Mira, and Don joined some half-dozen men on the cemetery hill, including Wilfredo Montes, an evangelical pastor, and

Manual Nicaragua, the owner of El Cuá's only pool table. There they strung hammocks from a structure of four posts and a tin roof and stood guard duty, staring above the crosses and blue-and-white tombstones across the valley to the silhouetted mountains. Nicaraguans believed that during full moons the blue-colored ghosts of the newly dead rose out of their graves to walk the streets of El Cuá. Don airily dismissed such stories, explaining that newly buried bodies created gas, which reflected the moonlight, emitting a blue glow.

During the first hour of guard duty, when everyone was awake, militia members often told stories. One of their favorites included the "heroic defense" of El Cuá, when villagers held off some 600 Contras. Before dawn, on December 20, 1983, a large group of Contras surrounded and attacked the town. The rattle of machine-gun fire punctured the morning, and mortars exploded on the streets of El Cuá. "It was like hell," said one farmer, "like 100 tractors racing their motors." In 1983, the El Cuá militia was poorly organized and poorly armed. Some fifty villagers had World War II–vintage guns in their houses, while the small army post had only a few automatic rifles. Villagers grabbed their single-shot guns, took cover behind houses, and fired into the dark cornfields and banana palms that surrounded the town. Women barricaded doors, then huddled with whimpering children on the floor, protected by the huge earthen stoves. On one hill, the militia sprayed the Contras with an M-60 machine gun that they had captured from the Contras only a few weeks earlier.

In the house on the edge of town, Cosme Castro grabbed the rifle next to his cot, slammed a round into the chamber, stuck the barrel out the window, and fired across his pasture into the darkness. Two villagers joined him, but, as the machine-gun fire got closer, Cosme and the two men abandoned the house, running low to the ground. Other men joined them, retreating to the center of town.

The Contras were advancing. The seven militiamen guarding El Trebol fled, and the Contras overran it but didn't burn it. Townspeople say it was spared because the farm was still privately owned. Justo Pastor was stationed on a hill between El Trebol and El Cuá, where he was in charge of a squadron of militia volunteers, none of whom had combat experience. He divided 900 bullets between them, and they dug in, resolving to hold the hill.

By midmorning, the Contras had overrun the southern edge of town and ransacked several houses. Shouting, "¡Viva el FDN!"(Long live the Democratic Forces!)

and "¡Somos hijos de Reagan!" (We're the sons of Reagan!), the Contras advanced, house by house, down the main street.

At the plaza, militia volunteers regrouped. They knew they had to make a stand to defend their town. Officials distributed the army's few automatic rifles to the militia, and several dozen villagers ran down the road toward the southern edge of town. They confronted the Contras in the cemetery, where for half an hour they fought hand to hand, a confusing, bloody battle of bayonets and knives, until finally the Contras retreated. Bodies from both sides, a tangled mess of blood and camouflage, were strewn among the wooden crosses.

When the attack began, army headquarters in El Cuá had radioed for help. The army dispatched reinforcement troops by helicopter, but the troops landed in Bocaycito, an hour's drive north. Since there were no vehicles, the troops had to travel on foot, arriving in El Cuá as twilight fell, hours after the Contras had slipped back into the mountains. In El Cuá, two civilians, twenty-nine Contras, and twelve militia volunteers had been killed.

It was after this attack that Cosme painted his shack *rojinegro*, red and black.

One rainy night, Don, Ben, and Mira were asleep when an insistent knock on the door summoned all militia volunteers to report to duty immediately. The Contras were near El Trebol, less than a mile away. A round of gunshots pierced the dark. Ben and Mira threw on their uniforms, Don dressed in dark clothes, and they ran to the cemetery, where they jumped into the muddy trenches.

As the gunshots moved closer, Ben and Mira huddled side by side, clutching their guns. Don hunkered down in the dark, rain beating on his poncho, listening to Ben and Mira jabbering in English. Throughout the night, they constantly asked if he was awake, if he thought the Contras were getting closer. Don grunted at them to shut up.

As the sun rose, everyone emerged from the trenches. Ben and Mira animatedly chatted about their work plans for the day, while Don lagged behind, silent and angry that they had talked all night. He thought of them as "tagalongs" and resented their fear.

That morning, Don told Ben and Mira that he thought they should be in separate squads so that they wouldn't all get killed at once. Don had himself transferred to another militia group on the far side of town.

As the alert continued, Ben and Mira's militia group was ordered to stand guard every other night. One morning, Maximo ordered his group to extend the trenches. He sent Ben and Mira to fetch pickaxes and shovels from army headquarters. As they walked through town in their uniforms, Ben noted that residents looked at them cautiously. "We both felt odd, like we were masquerading," said Mira, "because we weren't military people." Ben and Mira returned with the tools, then hacked at the trenches, carefully avoiding crosses and tombstones. The early morning was hot and humid, and sweat dribbled down their arms and necks. When Juan Tercero strolled by, Ben called him over. "He told me, 'Stop supervising, and start working,' so I put down my notebook, grabbed a pick, and worked with him and the other militia men for three hours," Juan recalled.

In the afternoon, Maximo assembled his militia group in Cosme's pasture to practice shooting at a cardboard target. When Ben lifted the gun to his shoulder and shot wildly out of control, Maximo assigned him to the early watch, the least dangerous one.

Ben often shared his duty with Wilfredo Montes, "Don Wil," who was good company during the long nights on the hills, when he wasn't on a drinking binge. He had grown up in the mountains near El Cedro, and was very religious. "When the revolution occurred," he said, "it wasn't hard for me to accept it. I read the Bible, I knew that the Bible said that love is shown in practice, and, like Jesus, one should help the poor." After the revolution, Wil became a UNAG organizer.

On December 9, 1982, Wil and his thirteen-year-old son were working in the family fields when a group of Contras surrounded them and accused Wil of spreading communism through his work with UNAG. They beat him with their gun butts, leaving his hands and arms inflamed, his face battered, and one eye swollen shut. The Contras tied Wil's and his son's hands behind their backs and marched them through the mountains. At dusk, they ordered them to lay facedown in a corral. Wil asked the Contra guarding him to loosen his hands so he could urinate, but "the Contra told me, 'If I untie you, it won't be you who'll be dead, but me.'"

The corral was surrounded by barbed wire. Thirty-five Contras armed with FAL and M-79 rifles, rocket-propelled grenades, mortars, and hand grenades had set up camp nearby. A light rain was falling, and clouds covered the moon, so the night was dark. Wil whispered to his son, "If we get over the barbed wire, and they don't shoot, we'll escape alive, because on the other side is jungle, and we can lose them there."

Wil's son managed to free his hands but, while untying his father, bumped into the barbed wire, which clanged against a metal post. The Contra sentry heard the noise and walked back to check, but an orange tree obscured his view. Seeing nothing amiss, he continued talking with another guard. Wil whispered to his son to follow him the instant he made a move. A few seconds later Wil sprinted toward the barbed wire fence, leaped over it, ran into the jungle, and disappeared toward a pond. "My son was terrified, and didn't follow me," said Wil, "and the Contras grabbed him." Wil submerged himself in the pond. The Contras combed the area but couldn't find him. "They probably thought I was still tied up and drowned," said Wil.

Four days later, the decomposed, decapitated body of Wil's thirteen-year-old son was found in the mountains. Wil sold his farm, moved his family to El Cuá, and became the manager of the state-run Farmer's Store.

When Wil went on drinking binges, Ben stood watch alone. Ben and Mira thought the militia was crucial in defending El Cuá, but Don was less reverent. He saw them as a bunch of ragtag, hung-over, exhausted corn farmers. In theory, a half-dozen men were assigned militia duty each night, but often only a couple showed up. After joining the militia, Don joked that he was more worried than ever about a Contra attack on El Cuá.

In early December, after most of the houses in town were wired, the team decided it was time to start charging residents for electricity. Up until then, residents had been receiving it free. The team wanted to make the hydroplant financially self-sufficient, and hoped eventually to make it independent of INE.

In class, Don's students formulated a billing system, and Don hired an ex-Contra to collect the bills. One afternoon, Don's students walked throughout the town, nailing notices about the forthcoming charges on lightposts while residents worriedly watched them. Soon rumors ran through the town that electricity would be more expensive than in Jinotega or Managua, and only storeowners would be able to afford it.

To quell the rumors, Don called a town meeting. One afternoon, over sixty people overflowed the porch of Wil's wooden house. The meeting started an hour late. Ben asked the townspeople to unhook their radio antennas from electric lines and warned parents to prohibit children from sticking fingers or metal objects into light sockets. He had wanted to demonstrate how dangerous electricity could be by electrocuting a pig, but Oscar could not find anyone with one to spare.

Since electricity had been installed, townspeople had been buying appliances. Ben said that radios, tape players, and refrigerators were allowed, but other appliances, such as percolators, electric stoves, and irons, used up too much electricity. Irons, he said, were especially prohibited, because they used eight times the amount of energy of one lightbulb.

A murmur of discontent ran through the crowd. Villagers were upset because well-ironed clothes gave residents a sense of dignity. In the mountains, even the poorest farmers owned a thick metal iron, which they heated over the coals to iron their patched and tattered clothes.

At the meeting, Don announced that each family would be charged a flat rate of 500 córdobas per lightbulb per month, while storeowners would be charged a commercial rate of 1,000 córdobas.

When Don finished talking, there was silence. Residents shifted uncomfortably. Finally, one farmer spoke up; he didn't want to connect his house because it was too expensive. Don explained that they were trying to keep the charges as low as possible. Families would only be charged per lightbulb used. Most residents seemed satisfied.

The next day, Ben and Don held a separate meeting with storeowners, who suggested they pay a metered price, so that they could be charged by the kilowatt, as they were sure it would be cheaper. Don and Ben told them if they acquired the meters, it would be more expensive. One storeowner demanded that his store be disconnected: he had never needed light in Somoza's time, and he didn't need light now. Don was so angry that he sent Oscar to unhook the man's store before the meeting finished. "Later, I went to his store to buy cigarettes," said Don, "and the guy started complaining about how expensive the electricity was. And I said, 'Well, look, you have batteries for watches and look how much you charge for them—30,000 córdobas; five times their price in Managua.'" The storeowner argued that transportation to El Cuá was expensive, so he had to charge more.

As Don's students continued wiring the town, and more houses were connected to the grid, the system became plagued by an increasing number of blackouts. Don and Ben worried that they had overestimated the capacity of the plant.

Unbeknownst to the Americans, however, the blackouts were being caused by clandestine ironing. Whenever someone plugged in an iron, lights in nearby houses dimmed. Villagers believed that ironing made even the oldest clothes more elegant. Schoolgirls attended classes in faded cotton skirts with firm, straight pleats. Farmers gathered in front of stores, guzzling beer in threadbare but crisply ironed shirts. Militia men trotted off to their posts in spotless green uniforms with clean lines and crisp folds.

One afternoon, while walking past a house, Ben glanced inside the open door to see Doña Chica, an elderly woman, ironing a shirt. He rushed up onto her porch to scold her. She was so shaken by the incident that she avoided Ben in the street, and eventually she sold her iron. Ben, finally realizing that the blackouts were caused by ironing, threatened a house-to-house search to ferret out irons. The town buzzed with ugly rumors.

Finally, Mayor Adolfo Zeledon stepped in, speaking to Ben and Don. He said that ironing was part of the social changes that electricity had brought. Ben and Don reluctantly changed the rules, allowing ironing only during the day, when demand for electricity was low.

Don's classes ended in December. Of the original eight students, only Justo Pastor, Teodoro, Oscar, and Hilda had completed the classes. They had two days of finals. On the first day, Anibal, the adult education teacher, gave a comprehensive exam that included division and multiplication, with word problems. All of the students, who had begun the course at the first-grade level, graduated to the third grade.

On the second day, Don tested the student's technical skills. At 8:00 A.M., "everyone got their box of materials, wire, and tools," and Don instructed each of them, alone, to wire a house. "I walked through four houses," said Don, "and told the students, put a bulb there, a switch there, a bulb over there. Then I left to drink beer."

Don assigned Teodoro a small wooden house across the street from Cosme's shack. Teodoro worked quickly and confidently, in two hours installing lightbulbs in the living room, the bedroom, and on the porch.

Since Oscar was the most advanced student, Don gave him the hardest assignment. Oscar strapped on the linesman's gear, shimmied up the main post, dropped a heavy cable from the lightpost to his assigned house, connected it, and installed three lightbulbs. He finished in the early afternoon.

Hilda was assigned to wire a house that belonged to a widow who, along with her six children, plopped down on a bench to watch her work. She coiled her long hair into a bun, got out her screwdrivers and pliers, and measured the house. She then measured and clipped the wire and peeled back the insulation, the whole time chatting with the widow and trying to appear confident. Don glided in and out wordlessly, checking her work, grunting occasionally. After a few hours, Hilda had three lightbulbs glowing.

Justo Pastor was assigned to connect three bulbs and three switches in a wooden house behind the Protestant church. "I told them, 'I'm going to see if I can put in these lights.' I didn't tell them I was going to do it—I said I'd try," he said.

Justo measured the house and then measured and peeled the wire. He lowered the cable from the lightpost, but it wrapped itself around the house, and he lost an hour untangling it. Then he became confused while working with the fuses, and took the covers off. Don wandered by to tell him that he was doing something wrong. "But he didn't tell me how to fix it!" said Justo. "Oh, *chocho*, I thought, I'm really doing badly and he didn't say a thing, what am I going to do?"

A few minutes later, Oscar came by and peered over Justo's shoulders. "Oscar told me, 'Man, you're going to kill yourself! You shouldn't have taken the tops off of these because they'll throw up sparks. If you stick your hand in there you're really in trouble.'"

Justo reviewed each step. He unrolled the wire, nailed it to the ceiling, and attached the wire to the switches and the plugs. When Justo flicked the switch, sparks flew out of the socket—a short circuit! Justo slammed off the switch.

Don wandered by again, looked at the wires, and shook his head, then walked away. Justo still didn't know what was wrong. He disassembled his work, laying the wire, switches, and lightbulbs on the floor, and rewired the house, using new wires and fuses with more amperage. When he flicked the switches a second time, the bulbs remained unlit. He recalled a class discussion in which they explored this issue, but he couldn't remember the solution. Perhaps if he switched the wires?

Outside, the shadows were lengthening, and Justo knew that it was after 4:00 P.M. He had to hurry; if he didn't get the lights on, Don would fail him. His cooperative, El Trebol, was counting on him. Even the coop's vice president had dropped out, claiming he didn't have enough time.

Justo hooked up the wires again, reconnecting them in a different combination, then, saying a silent prayer, flicked the switches. The three lightbulbs burned brightly, spreading light in every corner, enlarging the tiny shack. Don told Justo he had confidence in him and bought him a beer.

A few days later, Captain Miguelito announced a public ceremony in the town plaza. Don told his students that the Captain had ordered all of them to attend. Villagers were confused because it was not a government, religious, or town holiday.

Captain Miguelito urged everyone to join the militia, and announced that another achievement had been attained by the Sandinista revolution: El Cuá now had its own electricians, including the area's only female electrician. As Captain Miguelito called the four electricians' names, they hesitantly walked across the stage to accept their third-grade diploma and a domestic electrician certificate. As the villagers clapped, Don boasted to everyone within earshot how the four electricians from El Cuá were better than all the INE electricians from Managua combined.

Chapter 19

Three Americans in One Small Room

After Don finished teaching his class, he began spending more time at home. He soon realized how comfortable his "temporary guests" had made themselves in his room. Their files, notebooks, water bottles, paperbacks, and laundry were strewn around the room. Mira's alfalfa sprouts clogged the windowsills, and Ben was still sleeping in Don's bed. Don's large room seemed to have shrunk significantly, and he began to feel under siege. During the months he had lived alone in El Cuá, he had established a relaxed work schedule, which had been disrupted by Ben and Mira's eager enthusiasm.

"It became suffocating, partly because of the physical space, but partly because of their attitudes, which was anytime was work time to them, 24 hours a day. I couldn't take it, I got real mad. With them there I couldn't sit down and study," said Don.

Before dawn one morning, Don was awakened by the murmur of their voices. When they saw that his eyes were open, Mira leaned over his air mattress, "and she asked me 'Why does a generator not hold a frequency at the higher end of the mode?'" Don told her to leave him alone: work didn't begin until 8:00 A.M. Mira continued the technical discussion with Ben. "Ben and Mira were constantly turning to me because I had much more knowledge of what was going on in the town, and the area, and the war," said Don. "They were also resentful of me for not giving extra time to them, because they thought of me as a resource, and that I was punishing them if I did not want to explain things for them."

Don established a firm work schedule: an eight-hour day during weekdays, 8:00 A.M. to noon on Saturdays, and Sunday a day of rest. There was to be no talking about work during off hours. "Ben and Mira resisted that extremely," said Don.

"Why? It was their 'camping trip' attitude. They were out there to do their job and were not seeing that it was going to take years. It's been a problem with every foreigner who came up there. They're out-of-phase with the situation, all excited about getting everything done and they lose sight of what the job really is; because the job is development, it's changing people and it's a social thing more than it's a technical thing. Machinery has been dumped all over the countryside, but people can't maintain it, let alone build or innovate anything."

Even after Don established the new work schedule, Ben and Mira continued holding what Don called "touchy-feely" discussions, analyzing their relationships with the townspeople. Don refused to participate. "I had spent half a year working with Nicaraguans and I was not used to having everything hauled out and talked about, or used to going to 'clearing sessions,'" said Don.

The situation worsened. Don increasingly resented his guests. Don's father had been in the Marines, so Don had been shunted from place to place, never establishing a sense of home. In contrast, Ben and Mira came from settled, upper-middle-class families where, Don felt, "things are easy." Ben's father was a doctor, his mother was a college graduate, and Mira's parents were both Ph.D.s. After Don's parents divorced, he had been dispatched to a military high school, which he hated. He ran away to Canada, where he supported himself by learning a trade. In contrast, Ben and Mira both had university degrees, paid for by their parents.

Don was a natural linguist and spoke Spanish, French, and Italian. But he was often inarticulate in English, confusing syntax, peppering his sentences with "you knows" and "right?" Ben innocently corrected his grammar, a habit that enraged Don. "He was a goody two-shoes," said Don. "Didn't drink, didn't smoke pot, didn't go out with too many girls. Been to college, always writing his mom."

To add to the problems, Don felt that his housemates did not take security issues seriously enough. Don instructed Ben to wear his uniform whenever he worked in the countryside so he'd blend in with the surroundings, but Ben refused. On the other hand, when Don asked to borrow it, Ben said no. Ben and Mira respected Don's experience in the war zone, but they began to wonder if he hadn't become paranoid, and felt he was thinking too much about security and too little about work.

Before leaving town in Old Baldy, Don and Ben frequently argued over whether the road was safe to travel. Don always assumed it dangerous, and drove like a fiend until he reached Jinotega. If the army told Ben the road was safe, he would drive at a leisurely pace, frequently making stops to examine streams or visit with farmers. "Ben was always thinking about how to get the best information, and which officers he could trust," said Don. "He tried to use logic to figure out what the Contras might do, whereas I just assumed myself to be a target, twenty-four hours a day, and that way I didn't have to think about it anymore."

"I was a person who could get pretty mad," admitted Don. "It was unacceptable for me to die up there. I was not accepting that as an option, and I wasn't taking it lightly. There were some things that were not discussible with me. I wasn't going to go for any stops when I was going through certain areas, whatsoever. Yeah, I'd stop for five minutes, and that was it, and if you weren't in the car in five minutes, you were staying. Not because I didn't trust the place so much, but because that allows the communication to get out. I'd constantly change plans, because Ben and Mira would say, 'Can't we stop at some farmer's house that we are friends with?' 'Oh, we'll see you Thursday on our way back down.' I'd say, 'Thanks,' and then I'd change our travel plans, right then and there. The last fucking time I was going to turn up was the time they said so. They'd say, 'Oh well, I don't think Doña Licha would talk to anybody,' and I'd say, 'Come on. You know how Nicaraguans gossip.' It could be totally innocent gossip, and your friends could die; it would still get you killed."

Whenever Don worked in the countryside, he spent a long time gaining the trust of farmers before he told them when he'd return. In El Golfo, he assumed that everyone supported the Contras, so he never revealed his plans.

Don especially disliked working in the countryside with Mira. "A farmer you might trust wouldn't like to have Mira Brown standing right next to him and interrupting your conversation and asking you really delicate questions in a clumsy manner. She always wanted to speak in Spanish," said Don. "She'd come up and ask me some ... delicate question, in Spanish, in public. I got mad at her. I'd answer her in English. That was a constant problem."

Don told her that gaining trust was more important than doing a particular job on a given day. "Mira couldn't deal with that," said Don. "Mira was a very insistent person. She doesn't leave people much space."

At first, Ben and Mira were oblivious to Don's frustration. He never explicitly asked them to move out of his room. As time passed, though, Mira noticed that Don was becoming increasingly laconic and short-tempered. She realized he needed his own space. One morning, Mira accompanied Don into the countryside. Mira noted, "[Don] gives silent, grudging answers, as usual. Being with me twenty-four hours a day is wearing on him. I have *got* to find a place to live."

Mira and Ben planned their day together in the mornings, while Don strode out of the room wordlessly, not telling them what he was doing or where he was working. He only spoke to them during work hours. In the evenings, when one of them entered the room, he stomped out. He stopped eating with them at the Frijol Feo, and shot them threatening looks that did not invite small talk.

"Don hated us being in his house," said Mira. "All the negative things that he hadn't thought about happened. It was pretty miserable there."

By mid-December, Don was so irritated with their presence that he feared he might get violent. "They just wouldn't shut up. To my credit, I never hit either one of them. I felt like it." Afraid of his own reaction, Don packed up Old Baldy and left to scout sites for the Bocay hydroplant. He didn't know when he'd be back.

When Don left, Mira suggested that the two of them better start looking for a new place to live. Until then, Ben hadn't realized how bad the situation had become. "Ben didn't really appreciate the fact that we were guests in Don's room," said Mira. She pointed out that they were accustomed to not having privacy. Don's years in Nicaragua were spent living alone, and he valued his privacy.

Ben wrote to a friend, "I've been sharing a room with the two other North Americans that I'm working with. It gets too intense. Cabin fever is an occupational hazard. Did you ever see Charlie Chaplin in *The Gold Rush*? If you haven't, there is a great scene where he is locked up with a *big* miner as they are starving in a little cabin. Someday you'll see it and understand." He wrote in another letter:

> Here I am in El Cuá. When I was here before it was always a quick trip to get something done. Now I'm "living" here. I write living like that because it really is a strange sort of life. I'm sharing a room with Don and Mira. That is strange, as both are sensitive about space. Living with the Brooks I've become much less concerned. I need to get out. The problem being that there really aren't many places to go.

There was no excess housing in town. The bunkhouse cubicles were full of government employees, and most families in El Cuá lived in two- or three-room plank houses, a whole family sleeping in one bed. Mira suggested that they pool their money, buy a dirt-floor shanty for $50, then lay a cement floor and build an outhouse, but they soon realized it was socially unacceptable for a man and a woman to live together in El Cuá if they weren't a couple.

Stymied by the housing situation, and not wanting to be around when Don returned, Ben hiked up to El Golfo to look for a place to build a weir, a small wooden dam. There, he stayed with the widows. Although Ben trusted them, he knew that the Contras frequently passed by El Golfo. As darkness fell, he pulled a table underneath an open window, set the cot next to it, and readied his boots. He laid his gun and ammunition belt within arm's reach, "the table just so, so that I can get out the back window," he wrote. "I wish the war was over."

The night passed peacefully, however, and the next morning, carrying his rifle, Ben descended with Federico into the valley of gray clouds, past the twenty-yard-high waterfall, and followed the river upstream. "Corn, beans, coffee, bananas, undergrowth and muddy paths, muddy boots, muddy pants, mud everywhere," wrote Ben to Alison. "And here I am in the middle of it all. Ben the engineer. What's a nice boy like me ...?"

Federico knew all the valley's residents and told Ben about the different clans that "lived on each side of the holler." They followed muddy paths to the tin-roofed plank houses, tucked around bends, "getting some feeling for the land, getting some feeling for the people."

When night fell, Federico offered to let Ben sleep at his house. It was prudent to stay in a different place every night in El Golfo. The next morning, Ben met Federico's uncle and described the weir to him. He immediately grasped what they were looking for, and led them to a perfect spot, where the river was neither too deep nor too wide. Together, they measured the site and gathered wood for the project.

While Don and Ben were gone, Mira worked alone in El Cuá, testing soil samples for her cookstoves. After a few days of digging clay, she hiked to La Chata cooperative, where she loaded wood for Ben onto an oxcart and climbed aboard, rifle slung over her shoulder. Antonio, the driver of the oxcart, goaded the oxen's thin flanks with a pole as the wooden-wheeled cart creaked down the road to El Golfo.

Under a hot sun, rifle banging against her hip, Mira hiked back to El Cuá, where she talked to the mayor about December's electric bills. She stopped at the health center to volunteer for the People's Health Brigadista Training Commission. Mira took a bucket bath in the cement enclosure next to the house. As she sat on the mattress, lacing up her heavy work boots, she wished she could take a nap. The temperature in the room was about ninety degrees. Even the parrot that lived outside in the bougainvillea was silent. As Mira braided her hair, Old Baldy's unmuf-fled tailpipe roared outside the window, announcing Don's arrival. Dusty, hot, and sweaty, Don returned in a surprisingly talkative mood. Mira was relieved. Don had located a possible site for the hydroplant in Bocay, a steep mountain ridge called La Camaleona. As he spoke, Mira heard the roar of another truck in front of the house but didn't recognize it as either of the Toyotas in El Cuá.

She stuck her head out the window and greeted the familiar people. After eight months of waiting, INE had finally arrived to, according to Mira, "write out a work plan and a budget for the repair job in the hill that is falling out from under-neath the canal that feeds water to the hydroelectric plant." Don took the INE offi-cials to the hydroplant, where they hiked along the cement canal, examined the erosion, and measured the slippage. They left the next morning, promising to send equipment and technicians to fix the collapsing canal. Don knew that he'd proba-bly never see either the equipment or the technicians.

By December 19, 1986, Ben had finished building a wooden weir, so he felt free to hike back to El Cuá. For the first time in weeks, Don stayed in the room, huddling over a map with his housemates, pointing out possible sites for the Bocay hydroplant.

Sometime around 5:00 A.M. the next morning, a blast of automatic gunfire catapulted the Americans out of their beds. Shouting erupted toward the center of town, "¡Muerte a los piricuacos!" (Death to the rabid dogs!), "¡Muerte a los San-dinistas!" "¡Viva Reagan!" Bursts of gunfire echoed down the road, punctuated by the explosions of hand grenades. From another direction, others yelled, "¡Patria Libre o Morir!" and "¡Muerte a Reagan!"

Then someone giggled. Townspeople, celebrating the anniversary of the bat-tle of El Cuá, were re-creating it with live ammunition. The "Contras," dressed in camouflage, ran through the street, shouting, "¡Viva los luchadores de la libertad!" (Long live the freedom fighters!), "¡Muerte a los comunistas!" (Kill the Commu-nists!), and "¡Somos los hijos de Reagan!" (We're the sons of Reagan!). The "San-dinistas," also in camouflage, with red-and-black kerchiefs around their necks, dashed from house to house, ducking into doorways, threatening to drive the "Contras" into the hills. Both groups waved rifles wildly, firing bullets toward the sky. Com-batants tossed hand grenades into fields, shrieking with joy as dirt and shrapnel flew though the air. Women peeked out of doorways as wailing children hugged their legs. The three Americans stayed in their room. Don and Ben both thought the attack sounded genuine.

Outside on the main street, the battle continued. Some townspeople pretended to be hit, screaming, writhing, and laughing. "Wounded men" were flailing on the ground, grabbing the legs of giggling women, demanding a last kiss before dying.

A few hours later, the Captain appeared, dressed in full battle gear, rifle crossing his back, chest harness stuffed with ammunition, pistol in his side holster, grenades bouncing from his belt. He hauled himself up onto the stage in the plaza, where he was flanked by Juan Tercero. The two officials congratulated the villagers on the successful defense of their town.

As Christmas approached, the temperature in Managua steadied at eighty degrees. Radio Sandino played "Jingle Bells" in English, interspersed with salsa, cumbia, and reggae songs. In Managua's outdoor markets, vendors sold locally-made toys like ceramic whistles, rag dolls, wooden trains, airplanes made out of plastic bleach bottles, and wooden airplanes decorated with MiG-24 insignia.

In upper-class Managua neighborhoods, families decorated houses with blinking lights and plastic trees. In poor neighborhoods, they strung multicolored paper cutouts inside their shanties. Everyone celebrated Christmas with mass at dawn, piñata parties, and fireworks.

Throughout the month of December, Rebecca had spent long hours at INE, and she was delighted when Ben invited her to celebrate Christmas with him in El Cuá. For almost a year Rebecca had been an unofficial coordinator for the Cuá/Bocay project in Managua, passing on Ben's requests to solidarity groups in the United States. But she had never been to the town.

On Christmas Eve, Ben and Rebecca left Matagalpa, hitching a ride in the back of a Toyota pickup with several militiamen and Circles Robinson, from Los Angeles, who worked for UNAG. During the drive, Ben and Circles discussed the ambushes with a nonchalance that disturbed Rebecca. She reasoned that their matter-of-fact tone was just a way of releasing tension.

As the pickup drove northward, the whir of helicopter blades cut through the air, and two MiG-24 helicopter gunships appeared on the horizon, flying low, metal bellies almost skimming the treetops, pods heavy with rockets. They were providing cover for an army convoy. The pickup driver pulled to the side as the convoy of high-wheeled trucks bristling with soldiers gained on him. Some two dozen troop trucks carrying the Socrates Sandino battalion, almost 1,200 strong, roared north toward Bocay.

Rebecca knew El Cuá was dangerous, but peering at the disappearing convoy, she wondered about the prospects of a peaceful Christmas. When they arrived in El Cuá, Don and Mira took the visitors to a Christmas Eve party at El Trebol cooperative, where the vice president often organized festivities which often turned into drunken brawls where gunshots were exchanged.

When the four Americans walked into the Casa Grande, a soldier asked them to check their weapons at the door. Rebecca was shocked to see so many guns stacked near the entrance. Ben, Don, and Mira added their rifles to the pile and walked into the room. Rebecca couldn't get over the room full of men in camouflage; "It was the first time I had seen so many people in green uniforms."

Frente Norte strummed love ballads and *rancheras* while soldiers led women onto the dance floor and clutched them closely. As soon as Mira and Rebecca entered the room, men besieged them with offers to dance. Mira brusquely refused the multitude of worn, callused hands extended to her. Rebecca followed her example.

Ben politely invited a farmer's wife to dance. She followed him to the center of the room, where he respectfully put his arms around her. Ben noted,

> La gran fiesta. The party scene is grim and depressing. A group plucks out ranchero [songs]. Most men get disgustingly drunk. Six men standing around a girl with their hands stretched out, sticking them in her face. She accepts without a smile, they dance without smiling, then, at the last beat of the song—not a note earlier, or a pause later—she walks quickly back to the bench. The cycle goes on. A very strange frontier isolated life. I no longer expect more from these dances so I don't find them personally saddening, but rather a sad reflection on an isolated, and, especially for the women, limited life.

After a short time at the party they drove to the hydroplant, while the distant sound of machine-gun fire and mortars echoed in the dark. Somewhere, a battle raged on Christmas Eve.

At the plant, Hilda and the widows from El Golfo, who were making their first visit to the site, were cooking five stuffed chickens on the Lorena stove. Rebecca was exhausted and overwhelmed by the ride to El Cuá, the dance at El Trebol, and the intensity of the few hours she had spent in the countryside. She told Ben she wanted to spend a few minutes alone, and walked away from the arc of lights. The cicadas chirped, and the hydroplant hummed steadily. Rebecca wandered down the hill, sat on a grassy spot, and contemplated the stars.

An hour later, the widows set the chickens on the table and fried the rice on the woodstove. The men opened another bottle of rum, but Rebecca still had not returned. Oscar and Don were concerned and distributed flashlights, instructing everyone to look for her, but not to call out. They didn't want anyone to know she was missing. The searchers silently combed the area. Mira finally found Rebecca slumped on the grass near the planthouse, sound asleep. When Rebecca realized how worried they had been, she apologized profusely. Don was quietly furious.

After dinner, Ben and Don drove the widows back to El Golfo, headlights off for security, and spent the night at the plant. The sound of gunfire opened Christmas morning. Ben gave Rebecca a tour of the plant, followed by a hike up to El Golfo. As the gunfire drew closer, they quickly returned to town, where most of the small stores and diners were closed for the day. To Ben, "Christmas '86 comes and goes without much feeling. Rebecca came up and made it special."

Don had decided to take the month of January to "cool out." He spent the afternoon packing and giving instructions to Ben and Mira. He warned them to "get some other place to live. My room is not where everyone hangs out." The next day, Don left for Managua with Rebecca.

That night, the Sandinistas and the Contras clashed three miles outside El Cuá. The next day, a farmer headed for El Golfo was hurled into the air when his mule stepped on a land mine. The farmer lost his foot. On the same day, a truck delivering lunch to coffee pickers at the state-owned La Sorpresa farm hit another land mine, and two people were killed.

As 1986 ended, the radio station La Voz de Nicaragua played a New Year's song:

> *Yo no olvido el año viejo,*
> *me dejó una chiva,*
> *un burro negro,*
> *una yegua blanca,*
> *y una buena suegra.*

> I won't forget the old year,
> The old year gave me a goat,
> a black donkey,

a white mare,
and a good mother-in-law.

Soldiers posted on the hilltop at the entrance to El Cuá gathered rocks and whitewashed them to spell out the government's new slogan for the year, "1987: Aquí, No Se Rinde Nadie" (1987; Here, No One Surrenders).

Mira, assigned to militia duty on New Year's Eve, threaded her way around the crosses and graves, taking her post at the top of the cemetery. Few people showed up for militia duty that night. Militia leader Wil assigned single shifts and woke everyone at 4:00 A.M., the most likely hour for an attack. Mira and the militiamen peered into the dark, awaiting the first shot, the first mortar, the first grenade blast. "But the light grows slowly," Mira noted, "the first day of the New Year goes from gray to green and soft and rose around the edges, and there are no Contras. Wilfredo says, 'Maybe it will be peaceful like this until April [the start of the electoral campaign in the United States] and then there will be peace.'"

But the first four months of 1987 were not peaceful in El Cuá.

Mira was desperate to move out of Don's room but could only find a windowless storeroom downstairs, which was pegged onto the main room of the house. Ben helped her carry some of her belongings, but the room was so small she had to leave her boxes and files in Don's room. In her new room, there was not even a windowsill for her alfalfa sprouts. Sitting on the cot to write, she had to open the door to avoid scraping her knees against the wall. When she threw an armload of blankets on the cot, a huge rat scurried out the door into the backyard. The smell of urine from the nearby latrine permeated the air. The room was like a cage:

> Taking one last load of stuff downstairs, I say goodnight to Ben, who was already in bed on Don's cot. He says, "You know what it feels like? Like you're going to camp out in the backyard." ... I sit on my cot in the room below, practically able to hear his breathing upstairs. Yup. In the backyard. This is not far enough. Not independent enough. I need to start having a life here aside from my work and my workmates.

The next time she reported to militia duty, Mira complained about her new room and Wilfredo invited her to move into his house. He had a large family, but what was one more? Wil suggested that she buy some wood and close in the back porch to make her own room. Mira loved the idea. She bought the wood, built the room, and even hung the door.

Wil's large family made Mira feel welcome, though sometimes Mira would not see Wil for days because of his drinking binges. He worked at the UNAG store, and every so often was found sprawled under a tree, sleeping off a hangover. On those days, his wife ran the store without him.

Alone in Don's room, Ben missed living with Mira. At dinnertime he picked lemons from Maximo Merlo's tree next door and cooked his dinner alone on a kerosene stove, boiling noodles, mixing in cabbage, onions, sardines, and a generous sprinkling of pepper. After eating alone, he topped off his meal with a cup of tea. "Not a bad meal," Ben wrote to his parents. "I'm much more involved with life here than I ever was before. I kind of like it. That isn't to say that I've developed 'close' friendships here in town, but then again in my first year in Managua, I didn't either."

Ben envied Mira's success in finding a family to live with, and he asked Casilda, the principal, who knew everyone in town, if she could find a family for him. Casilda doubted she could find a place, and thought it might be easier to find a family for a woman than a single man.

After careful consideration, Casilda thought of a possibility: seventy-one-year-old Cosme Castro. She knew Cosme was unpredictable and hard to get along with. When she approached the old man, he pointedly told her he didn't want to share his house with a stranger. Casilda persisted, "I told him that Ben was a nice person, a good person, but he told me, 'He's probably a drunk.'" After convincing him that Ben was an enthusiastic foreigner, a Sandinista supporter like himself, Cosme agreed to meet him.

When Casilda told Ben about Cosme, he was ecstatic. Cosme was a hero to him, almost a mythical figure, because he had fought with the original Sandinistas. Oscar and Wilfredo warned Ben that Cosme was an incessant talker and a drunk with a violent temper. Undaunted, Ben visited Cosme at his house. Cosme launched into a story about the Sandinista guerrilla training camp that he ran for two years in the 1970s. Running the camp was incredibly risky. Somoza's soldiers once found a piece of soiled tenting in the isolated mountains, and in retaliation attacked the closest village, Varilla. They shot, bayoneted, and strangled forty-four residents, including twenty-nine children.

Most of Cosme's students came from the cities, including Sandinista leaders Claudia Chamorro and Carlos Agüero Echavarría. Day after day they dragged their mud-caked bodies through the thick jungle underbrush, learning to handle old, cast-off weapons like .22-caliber guns, carbines, pistols, hunting rifles, M-1 rifles, and Garands. Since ammunition was scarce, they practiced firing empty guns. Most had never fired live rounds until they confronted the dictator Somoza's National Guard in the streets of Managua or Leon.

Cosme showed the young guerrillas, mostly students from upper- or middle-class urban families, how to survive in the countryside. "I taught them how the jungle could be your friend, and not your enemy," said Cosme. "We ate everything we could find." The guerrillas learned to start fires in the rain, cover their tracks, and read bent twigs or smashed grass to discern when someone had passed by. When they left the camp to carry out training missions, the guerrillas avoided populated areas and stayed deep in the jungle.

Life in the camp was difficult. During the wet season, when some 200 inches of rain drenched the jungle, blankets and clothes never dried, rifles rusted, and leather rotted. During the night, mosquitoes, horseflies, and black stinging ants often made sleep impossible. Bites, scratches, and sores became infected, and guerrillas suffered crippling skin diseases. Undernourished, they often fell ill with malaria, pneumonia, typhoid, dysentery, and dengue fever.

After a few months, some of the Sandinista leaders returned to the cities to launch their first assault. "They told me that I should stay in the camp and be very careful," said Cosme. "So I stayed behind, and they were killed in their first attack."

Afterward the National Guard suspected a guerrilla camp to be in the area and dispatched patrols on search-and-destroy missions. They combed the mountains, interrogating farmers, jailing and torturing them. When Cosme and the guerrillas heard about the sweep, they knew it was only a matter of time before the camp was discovered, so they smashed their tree-branch shelters and fled into the mountains.

For years Cosme was a fugitive. During most of the 1970s, as the National Guard scoured the mountains, rooting out tiny bands of guerrillas, Cosme lived among the crags of Peñas Blancas. He slept under a different tree every night, living off the jungle. He was caught twice by Somoza's soldiers, who arrested him. They tied him to the avocado tree in front of La Chiquita jail and beat him. Both times, he was released and disappeared into the mountains. When the Sandinistas took over the country in 1979, they rewarded Cosme with a small plot of land in El Cuá.

Ben was enraptured by Cosme's story and intrigued by the old man who he thought resembled Sandino. In turn, Cosme took a liking to Ben, deciding that he could move in. He even suggested that they partition the front part of the house for privacy. Ben was excited:

> I'm going to build a room at Don Cosme's house. Everyone, except Casilda, warns against it. The guy is crotchety, cantankerous and at times gets violent when drunk, which happens more than just at times. But I like the guy. He also likes me. I'll see what happens....
>
> He stands my height with my build except he is made out of steel. If you were to take a reinforcing bar that is used for construction, make a life-size model of me out of it, hand an army uniform to it, and top it off with a turquoise hat you would have Don Cosme. He fought with Sandino, he fought with the FSLN, and he keeps on fighting.

Cosme's house was one long, bare room, made out of cement and plank walls, with four open windows, a dirt floor, and a tin roof. Sunlight and rain streamed in through bullet holes in his roof, and his small kitchen, tacked onto the back of the house, had a hard-packed dirt floor and a huge, earthen wood-burning stove. Plates, cups, and pots hung from nails on the walls, and chickens wandered in and out of the house, pecking at insects.

Together, Cosme and Ben erected the plywood partition. Ben moved in, pushing a narrow cot against the wall, away from the holes in the roof. He hooked up a single-burner kerosene stove and hung plastic bags of spices from a crossbeam. He thumb-tacked FSLN posters to cover gaps in the planks, arranged his juggling pins on a ledge, and stacked his American Juggler's Association magazines on a shelf next to his paperback library.

Cosme arose every day around 4:00 A.M., boiled coffee, then greeted farmers from the mountains who paid him a few córdobas to pasture their horses in his corral. Ben quickly acclimated to his new surroundings:

> I rolled over and listened to the morning sounds. It still takes a while to identify sounds. Last night there was one that had me puzzled for a while. It was a chomp, chew, clump that sounded like it was next to my bed. I knew it wasn't a rat; the other lodgers in the house are an assortment of rats and mice that grow to ten times their size when they scurry around at night. After five minutes, I figured it was a cow. Cows and horses are the next-door neighbors. On the morning a cow is killed I eat well. Fresh meat shish-kebobs with a lot of onion, a hot tortilla and coffee.

Up by 6:00 A.M., Ben reheated the boiled coffee and took his coffee and saltine crackers outside, where he sat on the bench. Cosme often joined Ben. "There is peace at certain times," Ben noted. "My favorite is the morning coffee with Don Cosme. Sitting out in front of the house, looking across the pasture to the cornfield and beyond, sipping coffee as the sun comes up and burns off the early morning mist. It is a very special time that I miss when I'm not there." Ben often slipped a cassette into his tape recorder:

> It's 7:30 A.M. I'm sitting on a bench of Cosme's listening to the Brandenburg concerto, drinking a cup of coffee and looking out over mist and around rolling hills. Cosme is walking down the field with his turquoise hat. Chatting for a bit he pulls out two ears of corn, I move the water over on the grill and toast an ear up for breakfast.

Cosme began calling Ben *mi hijo*, "my son," while Ben, in turn, referred to Cosme as *el roca*, "the rock," an affectionate nickname typically used for fathers.

Ben often left the plant around 4:00 P.M. to talk with Cosme and cook dinner before night fell. Cosme's house had yet to be wired for electricity. After the older man went to bed, Ben wrote accounts of Cosme by the flickering light of a rag stuffed in a bottle of kerosene. "For some reason, we get along. Maybe because I'll listen to him. I hope it works out and I don't go crazy. But even if I do, some good stories will come out of it."

On the other side of the plywood partition, Cosme coughed and hacked through the night. He suffered from respiratory infections and tuberculosis, and was weak from decades of bad nutrition. His eyes were blue with age, his vision clouded by cataracts, and his brown skin toughened and blotched from years in the sun. During the day, a neighbor cooked him greasy rice and beans, but she never prepared vegetables or varied the menu. Ben began to worry about Cosme's health.

Chapter 20

Working in Bocay

The Cuá/Bocay project was taking shape, at least in theory. Clifford Brown, a Nicaraguan mechanic, joined the team, which included El Cuá mayor Adolfo, Ministry of Education representative Anibal Gonzalez, Don, Mira, and Ben. Over time, they developed "Fiscal '87," a timeline, plan, and budget for the project. During a meeting of Sandinista party officials, the plan was read, debated in small groups, and, in a large plenary, amended and approved. It was then submitted to the regional government in Matagalpa. Ben, Don, and Mira were proud of the participatory nature of the process, which distinguished the Cuá/Bocay project from most projects in Nicaragua.

Mira was in charge of building cookstoves, Don was to run the mechanic's shop, and Ben was in charge of hydroplant studies. They proposed to build a mechanic's shop and carpentry shop in the town and scheduled construction of a concrete weir in San José de Bocay before the next rainy season.

However, Bocay would be much more challenging to work in than El Cuá. Sixteen rocky river crossings separated the towns. During the dry season, Bocay was a two-hour trip in a four-wheel-drive vehicle; in the rainy season, the trip took twice that.

In early January Ben and Oscar drove Old Baldy to check out sites for the next hydroplant. Ben dodged the puddles, passed El Cedro, and rumbled past the black carcass of the transport truck destroyed by a land mine six months earlier near La Camaleona. They zoomed through a green valley along the river, pivoted around a hairpin corner, passed a waterfall, and entered Bocay. Since the war began, the community had grown from 500 to some 2,500 inhabitants. Bocay was safer than the countryside. Refugees constructed shelters from materials provided by the government, including two-by-four planks, black plastic sheeting for walls, and a few pieces of tin roofing. Camouflage militia uniforms flapped in the wind, drying on strands of barbed wire in backyards.

Bocay was the jumping-off point to the northern mountains for the Sandinista army since the Honduran border was about twenty-five miles north. The military headquarters dominated the bluff above town. Long-range artillery squatted in emplacements dug into the hills, and a military base and dirt airstrip was located two miles north of the town.

Oscar and Ben dropped their bags at the only diner in town, a ramshackle building overlooking the plaza where the owner, Alejandra Altimirano, offered her storehouse for the night. Alejandra told them about the town, which boasted a brick bank, a primary school with four teachers, and a new health center with a doctor and three nurses. A basic field hospital, housed in a large green tent and staffed by two military doctors, was located at the army base. Ben noted this information in his workbook.

Bocay was the hub of twenty-five smaller communities, roadless jungle villages to the north. After the revolution, doctors and teachers had flooded Bocay, setting up clinics and schools in the tiny settlements. Bocay was the only place in the region where farmers could buy supplies they could not produce themselves, like salt, oil, sugar, flour, machetes, hand mirrors, combs, boots, and plastic sandals. But when the war intensified, farmers feared the hike into town, and families learned to subsist on beans and corn tortillas. Their coffee had no sugar, their soap was made from pig fat, they went barefoot, and they used parachutes from the Contras' supply drops to patch tattered clothes.

The townfolk were predominantly women, many of whom lived in plastic-tarp shacks with their numerous barefoot, swollen-bellied children. Their husbands were either fighting with the Contras, or with the Sandinistas. Some of those men left behind often drank. Many of them guzzled *cusuza* or Ron Plata, the cheapest liquor available, and could be found passed out along the road. Some soldiers drank, looking for solace from the war. They stumbled down the dirt road, dragging rifles, grenades jiggling from their chest harnesses. Although uniformed soldiers were forbidden to drink, laws were rarely enforced. In Bocay, drinking was a way of escaping misery, anxiety, and fright, even if the escape only lasted as long as the bottle was full.

Bocay radiated fear. Residents braced themselves for the inevitable Contra attack. In El Cuá, children played on the rusty swings in the plaza, but in Bocay they were often kept indoors.

That evening Ben and Oscar strung their hammocks in the storeroom next to a woodpile. Alejandra warned them to sleep with their boots on and to keep quiet. With the sunset, Bocay sank into darkness. Fear and silence paralyzed the town. Sometimes, before dawn, the roar of motors and yell of soldiers would shatter the silence, as a flurry of troop transport trucks careened into the plaza. Some mornings, shortly after first light, a bevy of Mi-24 helicopters would swoop overhead.

The next morning Ben and Oscar drove to La Camaleona to inspect the spot for the next hydroplant. Ben mapped the river, occasionally stopping at one of the widely scattered shacks to talk to farmers about their property lines and religious beliefs, trying to discern their political leanings and determine if it would be safe to work there.

Because La Camaleona was along a major Contra infiltration route, Ben and Oscar were reluctant to work there. If the hydroplant were built in La Camaleona, the Contras could easily blow up any of the posts along the five miles of wire to Bocay and cut off the town's electricity. They inspected several other streams outside Bocay, but each was lacking in some way. The water flow was not constant, or the dropoff was not steep enough to support a hydroplant. The two reluctantly returned to La Camaleona and began measuring it for a weir.

Back in El Cuá, Mira worked alone. She continued experimenting with soils for the Lorena stove, with little luck. Frustrated with her results, Mira turned to chimneys. Instruction books on Lorena stoves recommended using six-inch cement pipes, but none existed in El Cuá, and Mira knew she had to use local materials. She fashioned a chimney out of bamboo, which burned, and made another out of bamboo and clay. It fell apart. Puzzled, she tried wood. She confided to her journal:

> Working completely alone is for the birds. Today I almost finished the wood form for the stoves. I had to figure out how to make it come apart to be reusable. No big mistakes—I think this design will work. I feel good with the work. . . . I'm worried about the slowness of the progress. I need to work with community participation and support, but lack the confidence to start initiating it without having built at least one successful stove with the new technique.

Using her new mold, Mira built a prototype. While she was working, one of Don's dropouts stopped by to tell her that another student from Don's class, Jesus, had been killed by the Contras in an ambush. Mira wrote about him in her journal:

> He died over by Kilambé.
> They say ten Contras died in the same battle.
> It doesn't seem like a victory. Ten other young kids, maybe kidnapped, or confused, fighting without desire to do so. The only good thing about these deaths is that they are ten more the U.S. will have to replace. And they can't. New recruits to the Contras are few and far, far between.

On January 24, 1987, Mira was instructed to report to the plaza for a special meeting of the militia. Irritated, she arrived late to the plaza. Wilfredo, Maximo, and other militia men were lined up in front of the Sandinista headquarters. Wil threw out his arms, gesturing "What happened to you?" and waved her into line.

Juan Tercero paced in front of the militia, congratulating them on their persistence, courage, and revolutionary spirit in defending the town. He said he had awards to announce.

Mira felt extremely uncomfortable as the only woman and the only foreigner in the group. She blushed as Juan called out her name, handed her a little package, and asked everyone to give her extra applause. She was the only woman who had decided to carry a gun and help guard the town. Mira squirmed inside. She had taken the gun for self-defense, after all. Mira opened the package to find three slim books by revolutionary heroes Augusto César Sandino, Carlos Fonseca, and José Benito Escobar.

Juan then asked the *compañeras* from Asociación de Mujeres Nicaragüense Luisa Amanda Espinosa (AMNLAE), the Association of Nicaraguan Women, for a revolutionary slogan about women. One lone voice shouted, "¡Sin mujeres ... no hay revolución" (Without women ... there's no revolution!).

It was important to get more women involved, but Mira didn't like Juan's approach. "He was ignoring a very real problem that women have if they join vigilance. People are going to ... call them whores and speculate about what they are doing up there all night long with those men. And it is a small town. It matters a lot what people say about you."

Ben and Oscar returned to El Cuá, and shortly thereafter Don returned from his vacation, refreshed, talkative, and thrilled that Ben and Mira had moved out of his room. Don had visited the beaches of the Atlantic coast and San Juan del Sur, where he'd met his new girlfriend.

Ben and Mira gave Don progress reports. They discussed "Fiscal '87." Concerned over the project's lack of long-term financing, they wrote up several grant requests and dispatched them to nongovernmental organizations and solidarity groups in the United States and Europe. Adolfo assigned the project a corner office in the mayor's small building. As of January, the project had become the responsibility of the local government. When Mira told Don about his student's death, the crew named the El Cuá electric company "Jesus Huerta Montenegro" for him.

Don immediately threw himself into organizing the mechanic's shop, which would be the only welding and machining facility in the zone. As word spread about the new facility, farmers traveled miles by mule, foot, or oxcart, bringing tools to be repaired. Don worked with Clifford Brown, a mechanic, refrigeration technician, and sawmill operator. Together they repaired trucks, oxcarts, coffee processing equipment, irrigation pumps, corn grinders, sugar cane presses, plows, radios, and anything else farmers brought them.

One day, Ben showed up unannounced at Juan's office, demanding to see him. Ben asked for soldiers instead of militia volunteers to guard the El Cuá hydroplant. Juan and the Captain replaced them with eight regular soldiers, but soon afterward, Ben asked Juan Tercero for two dozen soldiers with heavy weapons.

"Ben was really like a mule about his work," said Juan. "He never stopped!" Juan admired Ben's tenacity, but he also thought he involved himself in issues that were not his concern. When the town had a corn shortage, and local officials sold corn above the controlled price, Ben appeared again in Juan's office, demanding to know why it was priced so high. Juan set aside his work to give Ben a lengthy explanation and finally calmed Ben down. Juan had little time or patience to spare for Ben, and he thought that unlike Don, Ben did not know his place.

On January 20, seventy young soldiers from the area were discharged from service after completing two years in the army. To celebrate the first demobilization of local draftees, Juan and the Captain declared the day a holiday and organized a public presentation on the small stage in El Cuá.

The nineteen- and twenty-year-old veterans assembled on the cement coffee-drying patio in El Trebol cooperative and marched in formation a mile down the dirt road into El Cuá. They had fought in more than a hundred battles. They wore frayed camouflage uniforms and ragged red-and-black bandannas, and as they marched in step through El Cuá, they stared straight ahead. Children flocked to porches, and women who seldom left their houses peeked outside to glimpse the military parade.

Juan watched as the soldiers marched toward the plaza. "When we least expected it—because it wasn't on the program—[Ben] appeared, wearing his clown's nose, his multicolored costume, his makeup, on his unicycle that he drove with much daring, and about 100 kids chased him, and he led the kids in front, and he made a parade with all the townspeople, and he appeared like a touch of happiness." Ben dodged into the rows of marching soldiers, a flash of reds and yellows among a wave of camouflage. He darted between the solid, straight rows of green and tan, a broad grin on his face, his red nose shining like a beacon. Children spilled onto the dusty road, stretching hands toward the clown, tangling themselves among the soldiers. The soldiers stumbled, regrouped into columns, and continued marching, while Ben, followed by a gaggle of children, dove into their lines again. The soldiers broke ranks, their discipline dissolving into confusion and cacophony. Juan, standing on the stage next to the Captain, couldn't help but smile.

Next to the plaza, a group of sixteen- and seventeen-year-old recruits stood stiffly at attention. After the Captain restored order, the veterans fell into formation, then marched up to the stage in single file, handing over their well-used rifles to the young recruits.

Eight days later a truck pulled up in front of the Health Center, carrying a body covered by a camouflage tarpaulin. A few townspeople, including Mira, gathered to identify the corpse:

> Today I had my first real-life, close-up, face-to-face look at a dead person, a kid from Bocaycito, who joined up eight days ago.... He was one of those in the ceremony who received a gun from those who were leaving.... His camouflage uniform [was] already worn and dusty, with a red and black scarf around his neck. He was killed in a battle at La Pita.
>
> All I can see is his boots and one dusty pant leg—a faded camouflage uniform. The blood is running out down by his legs.... I look at the spot where his head is, wonder if his face has been blown away, and go over and lift up the tarpaulin. Just like that. Like I've been looking at dead bodies all my life. His face is intact. And unknown. Good. I'm glad I didn't know him. I don't want anyone I know to die.... There is a little blood, dried,

coming out of his nose, mouth, even his eyes, shut, are rimmed with it. I let the tarp drop again. An old man steps up and lifts it, and then an old woman—sons in the army? Probably.

That month, Don established another rule: after four weeks in El Cuá, all team members not from the area had to leave the war zone for one week to "cool off." Clifford, Ben, and Mira agreed with him.

Ben headed for Matagalpa during his time off, where he stayed with architect Tom Kruse. "He stayed at my place because it was free, he had someone to talk to, and he also dumped things on me to do," said Tom. Ben usually showed up by dusk, exhausted, yet eager for conversation. "When he came down from the mountains, I'd ask how it was going," said Tom, "and he'd say, 'Well, the canal is sliding down the hill, my two operators want to leave, Mira and Don are not getting along, we don't know if there's any money for the project, but otherwise things are pretty good, we'll take care of it.' He talked about people, not turbines or generators. I don't think he ever saw people as 'the Nicas,' but as Oscar, Hilda, Federico—as people."

In the evenings, Tom and Ben roamed the streets of Matagalpa, eating *fritanga*, visiting internationalists, occasionally seeing movies or attending the cultural events—circuses, dance performances, plays. Late nights, they drank beer at Tom's house, discussing how their respective projects suffered from lack of money, skilled personnel, and materials.

Conversation often turned to their love lives. Ben confided in Tom about how he lost his relationship with Alison, and how he had given Sonia love and attention, but in the end she didn't love him, and he subsequently felt sad and bitter. Tom told Ben he feared losing his long-time girlfriend, Pamela, who was studying in the United States.

In the mornings, Ben and Tom often ate breakfast in the Morales cafe, located near several government offices. Ben always sat at the table facing the window, watching for officials he wanted to talk to. One morning, Chico Javier, the head of UNAG, walked by, and Ben shot out the door. When he returned a few minutes later, he announced that he had just acquired materials for the hydroplant. Tom admired Ben's connections and his persistence.

Not all internationalists admired Ben, or the Cuá/Bocay project. Some joked that the project was nothing more than three Americans and a rusty jeep. Ben struck some internationalists as being self-absorbed and self-righteous. Some Americans thought the El Cuá team was cliquish. They acted as if their work was so much more important than the work of others, and as if they were braver because they carried guns and worked in the war zone.

While in Matagalpa, Ben looked up Lillian Hall, a U.S. agronomist from Tucson, Arizona, who worked at La Cumplida, a state-owned dairy farm outside Matagalpa. He told her he wanted to buy a horse because he thought it would be easier to avoid land mines riding a horse than driving a jeep. He quipped that he needed a horse big enough to carry him and his briefcase. "Ben didn't know a thing about horses," said Lillian. "I told him how to buy it, the things to look out for, how to take care of it." Ben took notes, stashing them in his battered briefcase.

After a few days in Matagalpa, Ben headed to Managua for the rest of the week. After six years of war, Managua was dirtier, uglier, and more destitute than ever before. At red traffic lights, children and adults swarmed cars, brandishing toilet paper, lightbulbs, and other scarce goods in drivers' faces. Children in the street approached foreigners, begging for food.

The economy was in hyperinflation. Córdobas were openly traded on the black market, but foreigners and Nicaraguans alike preferred dollars. People with many córdobas were poor, while those with a few dollars were considered rich.

The $100 million in U.S. aid was being pumped to the Contras. Fighting in the northern mountains turned fearsome, and the consequences could be felt in the capital. Managua streets were often clogged with funeral processions. Pickup trucks holding recruits' coffins drove slowly over the paving stones toward the cemetery, weeping relatives dressed in black following behind. A few weak voices shouted "Patria libre o morir," but by 1987 revolutionary slogans were no longer chanted with the fervor of earlier years.

When Ben visited his modern Managua apartment after four weeks in El Cuá, he felt confused:

> Being here in Managua is a change from El Cuá in every way.... My clothes are different, my friends are different, and in general I feel as if I've come to another country. The cup of coffee at Cosme's isn't the same out of a Corelle-ware cup on a glass-topped table. I get confused as to 'who' I am and which is my world. I guess the answer is that it all is, including the States.

During trips to Managua, Ben always dropped into the INE office. While examining INE's twenty-year-old topography maps one day, he spied a stream near Bocay he had never seen before, and made a note to scout it.

Ben usually ended his visits to INE in Rebecca's office, providing her with the latest news from El Cuá. That day, he mentioned that a Contra radio program considered the El Cuá plant as "the type of project that should be destroyed," according to Rebecca. "He was really upset about that."

Another of Ben's usual stops was the TecNica office, where he would sift through new résumés. He often addressed the group if a delegation was in town. Whenever he ran into his American friends in Managua, he tried to recruit them to El Cuá, regardless of their skills. When he ran into an American radio reporter at a restaurant one evening, he described the characters living in El Cuá and suggested she produce a *Prairie Home Companion*–type series about the village.

Ben, terribly lonely in the modern apartment's loft bedroom, ran around so much in Managua, that he literally exhausted himself. Sonia had left for Colombia and never answered his letter. He was eager to have a girlfriend.

When Rebecca advised Ben that the contract to buy the house with the vines was ready to be signed, the reality of establishing roots in Nicaragua hit him, making him want a permanent relationship with a local woman even more. While waiting for his friend Lois at the CISAS office, Ben met one of her coworkers, Marta Hernández, a pretty, petite Nicaraguan with straight black hair. Over lunch, he quizzed Lois about her. She said that Marta was intelligent, a good worker, and newly single. Ben wanted to get to know her, but didn't know what to do. Lois suggested he visit the office whenever he was in Managua. As Ben prepared to return to El Cuá, Lois promised to think of ways to get the two together.

Chapter 21

Attack on the Hydroplant

Ben and Oscar returned to Bocay in mid-February 1987 to scout the stream Ben discovered at the INE office. Accompanied by a few militiamen, they climbed a trail to Los Angeles, where they spotted a stream with a strong, steady flow. The Contras often passed by that area, so Ben and Oscar quickly returned to Bocay without measuring the stream. The next day they drove to La Camaleona to examined the flat, narrow site they had first chosen for the weir. Since they had already measured La Camaleona, they decided to build the weir there, and returned to El Cuá to consult with Don.

Later that month Susan Cookson and Tim Takaro, two American doctors who ran a tuberculosis clinic in Jinotega, drove into El Cuá, looking for Ben. "He wasn't difficult to spot," said Tim, "as he was the only one in town with a briefcase." After lunching with Ben, Susan and Tim drove to the hamlets outside El Cuá, searching for tuberculosis patients who had stopped showing up for their weekly treatments in Jinotega. The doctors picked up the local health promoter, who knew which farmers were taking prescribed drugs. After stuffing medicines into their daypacks, they continued into the jungle on foot to reach their patients. As the doctors hiked along, gunfire and mortars echoed over the next ridge.

When Tim and Susan arrived at the farmhouses, they learned that some of their patients had died, so they just tested the remaining family members for the disease. While the doctors were in the countryside, Ben crawled into one of El Cuá's water sources and scrubbed the bottom of the cement holding tank with a toothbrush. He scraped off a paint sample and asked the doctors to check it for lead and other toxins. He also asked them about setting up a potable water system. According to their calculations, 40 houses could be hooked up to one of the existing tanks, and 120 to the other. Ben wanted to survey ten families and record how often the children got diarrhea or fevers, then examine the difference after the town got potable water.

One afternoon, after the doctors finished their work, Ben and Mira took the doctors to see the waterfall in El Golfo, stopping at several farmhouses where Ben chatted with families. At one house Ben drained a fruit drink, while the others politely declined. "We later chided him about accepting the fruit drink the family offered him," said Tim, because the water source was probably contaminated. "But he replied that that was part of his job ... to include local people in the project, and for him that meant drinking their fruit drinks and eating whatever was offered."

Sitting atop the roaring waterfall in an isolated gully, they decided to fire their rifles. Tim shouldered Ben's heavy weapon, released the safety, aimed at a tree, and squeezed the trigger. The bullet veered off to one side, disappearing into the hills. The sound echoed throughout the valley. Susan, Ben, and Mira each aimed at the tree, and each time the bullets strayed wildly.

"I was amazed at what poor shots both Ben and Mira were," said Tim. "The sights were off on the rifles, so there was no way you could hit something by using the sights. It became clear to us as we went around with them that they were certainly targets. The places where they worked were dangerous. And when we shot off the rifles I had to revise my view about exactly what protection these rifles offered—I suppose they served as deterrents."

After finishing their work, Tim and Susan invited Ben to stay at their house any time he was passing through Jinotega.

El Cuá's slow rhythm ground to a halt on the weekends. Women sat on porches, fanning themselves in the sweltering heat, watching children play on the rusty teeter-totter in the plaza. Men played baseball on Sunday mornings and spent the afternoon in the shade, drinking rum with neighbors.

Don rigidly enforced his rule of no-work weekends, but it was difficult to find ways to pass the time. Don studied German and occasionally drank rum with the men. Mira made detailed entries in her journal and wrote letters to parents and friends. Ben wandered from house to house, visiting neighbors and picking lemons to juggle for Maximo's nine children. He performed magic tricks, told Nicaraguan history stories, and quizzed the kids about revolutionary heroes. Frequently he visited Casilda for coffee or hiked to whitewashed La Chata, where he visited Cosme's son, the president of the cooperative.

Ben confided to Mira that he was lonely. He knew he would probably live in El Cuá for many years, and having a relationship was part of staying there. He longed to have a family. When he was hiking the mountain streams with Oscar, he would jokingly ask farmers if they knew women for him to marry—he was looking for a widow with a waterfall.

When Ben became depressed, he often thought of Alison. One night, in the quiet of Cosme's house, he wrote her a letter about their anniversary, February 29:

> I'm sitting here writing by the flickering light of a rag stuck in a bottle of kerosene. After putting light into El Cuá I still don't have it in the house where I live. I'm drinking a cup of coffee that was made in the morning and reheated throughout the day. Nicaraguan animal crackers go well with it.
>
> I think back to the night seven years ago when two very young people admitted their love for each other. A nervous embrace that we didn't know where it would lead. A kiss that we didn't know where it would stop. Seven years ago we said we loved each other. Now I can still say it with all of the feeling of before and even more certainty. It doesn't have the urgency of seven years ago but rather a calm quietness, the knowledge that we don't grow apart as we travel.

In late February, Ben and Don visited El Trebol for a health workshop run by two American nurses, Mary Risacher and Annie Souter. After they left that night, the El Trebol militia received word that Contras were nearby. The Nicaraguan health workers were assigned militia shifts and took up guard posts in the hills surrounding the coop. Machine-gun fire echoed across the valley throughout the night. Annie and Mary lay awake in their clothes, tensing whenever they heard gunfire, dreading the next burst, wondering if it would be closer, and fearing the Contras' advance. At dawn, health workers gathered in the kitchen, bleary-eyed and exhausted. A soldier arrived with news that a nearby cooperative had been attacked, and the house of one of the health workers had been burned, leaving his father wounded. Even though the Contras were still around, the health workers hiked back to their own villages.

Due to the danger, the army closed the road from El Cuá to Jinotega, trapping Annie and Mary in El Trebol. The Captain put the town on alert and called out the militia groups for a rotation of every other night. When Mira joined her militia group in the cemetery, Wilfredo showed up with Luis, a friend visiting from

El Cedro cooperative. Mira joked, "What a way to treat a house guest!" Luis said he was in the El Cedro militia, and was used to sleeping in the hills.

Everyone took turns doing watch until dawn broke. Military intelligence reported that the Contras had moved up into the mountains. The road reopened, and Annie and Mary finally returned to Matagalpa.

In town, Mira and a farmer contracted to work with her looked for a household that would allow them to build a Lorena stove. Mira convinced Cristino and Chaya, a couple who lived near the plaza, to let her build a Lorena stove in their kitchen. Mira, the farmer, and Cristino dug up soil in Cosme's pasture and began their work.

As Mira and the farmer were hammering the stove base, they heard an echo and suddenly realized that gunshots were coming from Cosme's house. They froze. A barrage of rapid-fire gunshots sounded, followed by an explosion and more gunfire. One of Cosme's sons ran down the street, clutching his gun. Wilfredo, rifle in hand, raced after him. Mira dashed out the door with her rifle and sprinted after them, wondering what was going on.

As they neared Cosme's house, Mira slowed down to spy a group of men carrying a wounded Contra.

> They brought the guy into the Health Center, on a stretcher. Everyone went out to see. I hung back, embarrassed by everyone's frank desire to see the body, not anxious to see it myself. But curiosity won out. Four men from the militia carried the stretcher, sweat pouring down them. I thought he was dead—feet first, naked except for bloody underwear, an abdominal wound bandaged, another on his shoulder, eyes closed, blood on his face.
>
> Turns out he was alive, and up eating soup two hours later. People said he closed his eyes coming through town because he was ashamed.

Mira heard rumors throughout the day, but was eager to hear what happened. It wasn't until that night, during militia duty, that she got the full story. Apparently Fermín, an old toothless farmer, was picking corn outside town when he glimpsed a stranger in his cornfield, a gaunt teenager wearing civilian clothes and carrying a military daypack. When the teenager saw Fermín, he asked him where the road to El Cuá was but ran off before he got an answer.

Suspicious that he was a Contra scouting El Cuá for an attack, Fermín alerted Maximo, who got four militiamen to comb the area. They surrounded the teenager in an abandoned hut and ordered him to surrender. Instead of emerging, the teenager tossed a hand grenade out the window. The grenade bounced off the branch of a tangerine tree and sailed back toward the house, where it exploded, knocking him to the ground. Afraid the youth might throw another grenade, Maximo ordered the militiamen to fire, "only to wound him, not to kill him."

That night, no one slept during guard duty, as the militia members discussed whether the captured Contra should have been killed. Mira, Wilfredo, and Maximo agreed that the Sandinistas should rehabilitate and release every captured Contra.

Before dawn on March 7, 1987, Oscar and Hilda were awakened by the sound of gunfire near the hydroplant. Oscar and the militiamen spread out through the coffee bushes, but they didn't spot any Contras. Later, Oscar heard that three militiamen from La Chata had been patrolling the hills half a mile from the plant when twenty Contras ambushed them. One person was wounded. Wilfredo's uncle died.

Three days later, a group of Contras launched a predawn attack on March 10 on the Francisco Estrada cooperative, eight miles from El Cuá. The Contras had a mule train waiting nearby to carry off the supplies of beans, rice, sugar, and cooking oil.

During the first minutes of the attack, a farmer from the coop panicked, jumped out of the trench, and was killed. However, seventeen militiamen, armed with automatic rifles, returned fire from the trenches, and the Contras were unable to overrun the coop. They retreated, leaving the mule train tied up in the jungle. Coop members slung the dead Contras across the mules and brought the bodies into El Cuá.

Ben wrote to his parents:

> I was talking with a friend afterwards about the Estrada coop attack, and he said, "You know, Benjamin, we're winning this war." I was a bit confused, after waking up that morning to mortars going off and the exchange of machine-gun fire. The end of the war seemed very far away. [Then] he told me that one-half of the [Estrada] coop used to be with the Contras. The farmer that led the defense of the coop used to be a Contra military leader. They had all, one by one, turned themselves in to the government. They are now organized into the coop. Now they fought to defend their land and they won.

By March 1987, the Cuá/Bocay team had undergone several personnel changes. Don had fired the bill collector after he used electric-bill money for drinking binges, and the crew hired several good workers, including another mechanic to work with Don in the shop.

One day, walking past the army post, Mira spied a long, cylindrical, used mortar tube lying in the dirt. She picked it up and examined it, noting that it was heavy, made of metal, and not combustible. It was perfect for a chimney for a Lorena stove. Used mortar tubes, although not manufactured locally, were abundant around army posts. She wrote her parents about her discovery for the chimney, adding, "There is nothing romantic at all about this war, and the way it affects life here in El Cuá. There is a lot that is depressing and dulling to the senses. And, there are some things, some people, that are inspiring. Sometimes the mountains are romantic, the poverty intense, the work itself most important, and the war fading to background status."

In mid-March Ben and Oscar worked in La Camaleona for a week. They followed the river and mapped out where to build the dam, penstock, canal, pipeline, and powerhouse. Ben described the work for his parents:

> Greetings from Bocay. I've been here for the last three days. I'm at the last part of the most relaxed part of the job—walking around streams. I've spent the days climbing up and around a stream. . . . Climbing through pasture and cornfields. The sun beats down at midday. The sugar cane is sweet. The beans are being harvested. I took shelter from the midday sun in a little pool formed at the base of a two-meter fall.
> It was good to be out among the waterfalls. I almost have the basic pipeline layout done. With a bit of basic surveying and a weir I'll be able to define the basics of the project.
> But now it is time to start to put my ideas into action. I started to figure out a little dam to measure how much water there is in the stream. This is a scary part for me. Bit by bit I get the experience I need. But I'm always nervous before I start to build anything.

When Don had returned from Europe, he said he'd give the Cuá/Bocay project one year of his life. He reminded the others that his one-year commitment was coming to an end; he was sad to leave, but he felt that it was time for him to move on.

Ben and Mira dreaded Don's departure. He was the expert in mechanics, machining, running crews, security, even small-town relations. They wondered how successful they would be without him. "Don was a tough act to follow," said Tom Kruse. "Don had a tremendous understanding of people: why they do the things they do, what motivates them, what their relationships are with other people, why they treat other people the way they do. Ben was getting into Don's shoes. Ben said that it would be hard to build a pillar."

Ben was worried: "Don will leave and I'm slated to take his place as field director. I'm scared. I really don't want it. I want to work *under* someone for a while still."

Don devised a long-term work plan for the project. Clifford, Don's assistant in the mechanic's shop, was named to head the team. With the support of officials and well-trained local electricians, Ben and Mira felt confident, but they were still nervous.

March 19 marked the first day of the new school year in El Cedro cooperative. The evening before, the new teacher swept the cement floor of the one-room schoolhouse and washed the chalkboard, ready to begin classes the next day.

The Contras attacked El Cedro at 4:00 A.M. Militiamen radioed the nearest army garrison in Bocay, and asked them to send army troops. The army immediately dispatched troop transport carriers brimming with soldiers, but the Contras had already positioned themselves along the only road to the coop from Bocay. When the first army carrier passed them, the Contras opened fire. Rocket-propelled grenades smashed into the vehicle, killing many of the soldiers. The truck ignited in flames. Recruits stumbled over their dying buddies to jump out of the truck, but the Contras strafed them. The Contras moved out of the hills and swarmed over the bodies, stripping them of guns, ammunition, and boots. As the sun rose, the dirt road was covered with bodies.

At dawn the army dispatched another troop carrier, but the driver, seeing the billowing smoke down the road, returned to Bocay. Army officials realized they could not break the Contras' hold on the road.

In El Cedro, twenty-five militiamen held off the Contras. After four hours of fighting, coop members desperately radioed the Bocay base that their ammunition was gone and they were retreating. Women strapped babies on their backs, grabbed hands of toddlers, and ran into the hills. Two children and a fourteenth-month-old who had become separated from their family took refuge inside a house, where they crawled under a metal-frame bed.

The Contras, noting the decreasing fire, advanced. A Contra lobbed a hand grenade into one of the militia's trenches, where it exploded in a burst of mud, shrapnel, and flesh. The Contras jumped to their feet, sprayed the trenches with gunfire, then ran into the deserted coop. Moving from house to house, they smashed flimsy wooden doors with gun butts, yelling, "Sandinistas, hijos de puta piricuacos, rindense" (Sandinistas, you fucking rabid dogs, surrender). When they burst into the shack where the children were hiding, the toddler cried out from under the bed and was killed by machine gun shots. The Contras set fire to several buildings and looted the general store.

When the army realized that Bocay residents had abandoned the El Cedro coop, they swung the long-range heavy artillery around, trained it on El Cedro, and fired. The shells roared through the air like freight trains in the sky, and nine miles south, chunks of steel exploded, a direct hit on the cooperative. One shell fell near the general store, instantly killing ten Contras, and the rest of the terrified rebels fled into the mountains. Within minutes, El Cedro was deserted. More shells rained down, splintering buildings.

By the time the army troops from Bocay arrived at El Cedro, they found the coop destroyed—the schoolhouse in ruins, the carefully swept cement floor fractured, and the clean blackboard in pieces. Houses had disintegrated into planks, concrete chunks, and twisted pieces of metal sheeting. The health center was reduced to a broken cement floor, strewn with oral rehydration salts and shattered medicine bottles. Charred clothing, mangled pots, melted plastic bowls, and bloody body parts littered the coop.

The coops' residents streamed out of the mountains. Trembling mothers, surrounded by howling children, besieged army officers, begging to go with them to find a safe place.

Ben was stunned:

> The attack on El Cedro hit me particularly hard. Last year I worked there putting in a weir, and at night I sat around talking with people getting to know them, becoming friends. When I heard about the attack those moments flashed through my mind. Who? Which of those people died? It was a victory. We only lost four and the Contras between 25 and 40. Luis had been killed. A farmer defending his land. They had been outnumbered at least eight to one. The coop had to be abandoned. Four men gave their lives to cover the retreat. Luis was one of them.
>
> The Contras came in and sacked the houses but selected several buildings to destroy. Not all, just several—the health center, the house of the coop's president, the store which sells the basic goods at fair prices and the coffee-buying center. Certainly not military targets.
>
> But the war is much deeper and the victory much more than just the end of the gunfire. The attack was on the first day of classes in the zone. The day before, I was struck by the farmers coming into town and to the schools in the coops for the school books and pencils for their children. Wrapped

in a plastic bag they carried them carefully away, some walking, others on horse, or the kids with them just thrown into a bag running down the dusty street of El Cuá. That is the war that is also being won. A war against poverty, illiteracy, and disease.

After the attack on El Cedro, Don and Ben asked the Captain to increase the number of soldiers guarding the plant. Miguelito said it was impossible, as 130 men from the region were being mobilized for the road construction project to Ayapal, and no soldier could be spared.

One hot Sunday afternoon, Ben gathered his straw hat, towel, calculator, and a book Alison sent him, *Durov's Pig: Clowns, Politics and the Theater* by Joel Schechter, and wandered down to the creek in Cosme's pasture. He sat on a rock, kicked off his plastic sandals, and stuck his feet in the cool stream. As he watched the water rush by, he plugged an equation into the calculator, figuring out how much energy the water passing in front of him could produce. Farther down, a woman carrying a tub of dirty clothes on her head arrived at the river, surrounded by her naked, pot-bellied toddlers.

Clifford joined Ben at the stream. As he watched the toddlers splashing in the stream, Ben wondered if they would grow up to be engineers or hydroplant operators. He said he had once counted eighty mules and horses tied up in front of the bank, as their owners were inside, asking for loans to finance coffee plantings. "He said that someday these people would arrive at the bank in jeeps, instead of on horses," said Clifford.

Ben imagined El Cuá in fifty years, when surrounding mountains would become national parks filled with hiking trails. "When I have grandchildren," he told Clifford, "I'll tell them that when I first came to this place, people rode on horseback, and drove cattle down the main street." When the fighting was over, Ben wanted to kayak the Bocay River and climb the crags of Peñas Blancas. He dreamt of buying a farm on the slopes of Mount Kilambé, which he considered one of the most beautiful places in the world.

On weekend evenings, Ben often wandered up to the hydroplant to join Oscar on the porch, where Oscar tuned the shortwave radio to a Contra frequency, Radio 15 de Septiembre or Radio Liberación, whose broadcasts originated from Honduras or Costa Rica. "Fight for a free Nicaragua, for democracy and freedom," the announcer shrilled. "We're on our way to Managua." The station called agricultural cooperatives "armed garrisons," and urged Contra supporters to sabotage equipment, destroy crops, steal rifles, and join the *luchadores de la libertad* (freedom fighters). The station punctuated its announcements with the rapid staccato of machine-gun fire.

To Oscar, the broadcast always said the same thing. After a while, he clicked off the radio and strummed his Suzuki guitar. Sometimes Silvia, the health educator, brought her guitar to the plant and sang duets with Oscar. "Ben told me that I sang like an angel," she said. One of their favorite songs, "Flor de Piño," was about Sandino and his sweetheart, Blanca Arauz, the telegraph operator of San Rafael del Norte.

In late March, Don packed his German books and a stuffed parrot head that Oscar had given him into his daypack. Leaving behind his ripped shirts and grease-stained jeans, he set his daypack at the door, ready to go. He strolled through town, saying formal good-byes to important officials, shaking hands with Juan Tercero and the Captain. Then he drove Old Baldy to the plant to find Hilda. He knew he was one of the few men she trusted, and he felt bad that she would now have to fend for herself. He gave her a radio-cassette player and tapes by Luis Enrique Mejía Godoy and the Nicaraguan group Mancotal. "Para la jefe" (For the boss), he said.

Don gave various reasons to different people for his departure. Jenny Broome, his ex-girlfriend, had the most accurate explanation: "When Don left for good, he was getting upset and freaking out about the military situation. He felt his name was on a list, and it was only a matter of time; and he hadn't figured out yet if he was willing to die for what he was doing."

On March 23, Oscar and Hilda held a *despedida*, a farewell party, for their friend at the hydroplant. Hilda selected her fattest chickens and prepared them on the Lorena woodstove. Oscar mixed rum and Cokes and served them to Don, Ben, Mira, Clifford, and Hilda. As they drank, the few remaining chickens clucked about in front of the brick bungalow, scratching in the dust. Hilda tied the pig to the bungalow to keep it away from both the dinner table and the garden she had just planted. Don opened a second bottle of rum, and when the Coca-Cola ran out, they drank straight shots. Oscar played his guitar and sang, jumbling the lyrics and slurring his words, until the Suzuki slipped from his hands. Hilda stowed it under the bed and turned on the radio-cassette player. "It was happy and sad at the same time," said Hilda. Don, Ben, Oscar, Mira, and Clifford, flushed with rum, slumped over the table and pledged eternal friendship.

The next day, everyone except Hilda suffered from ferocious hangovers. Don stowed his daypack in Old Baldy, jumped into the driver's seat, checked his AK-47, and laid it across his lap. Ben and Mira climbed in as Don gunned the motor, waved good-bye to Oscar and Hilda, then disappeared down the dirt track, heading to Managua.

After Don left, Hilda listlessly did the household chores, stuffing wood in the stove, reheating the beans, washing clothes in the river, looking after her children. When her friend Goya stopped by to visit, Hilda burst into tears. She was afraid she would never see Don again. Goya had rarely seen her friend so upset, and offered to stay the night.

In the evening, Oscar dragged stools out onto the porch. Sitting beside Hilda and Goya, he watched the children chase each other and tease the pig. When the sun set, the soldiers guarding the hydroplant crawled into their banana-leaf huts, while Oscar stared into space, too depressed to play his guitar or radio. When the children tired, Goya crawled into bed with them, while Oscar and Hilda took late-night readings on the plant before going to bed.

Shortly after midnight, Oscar, Hilda, and Goya awoke to the dry rattle of automatic rifles. As Oscar struggled into his clothes, a mortar exploded in the coffee bushes on the far side of the brick bungalow. Militiamen scrambled out of their huts and fired into the dark. Oscar heard the Contras' gunfire coming from a grove of banana trees, two hundred yards from the house. He grabbed his rifle, charged to the powerhouse, and turned off the plant. The hum of the generators fell silent.

Hilda pulled her two whimpering children out of bed. She and Goya shielded them with their bodies as mortars, hand grenades, and bullets rained down around them. Oscar joined the militiamen behind a ridge in the garden, trampling the tiny radish plants Hilda had planted just days before. Seeing that the Contras were firing at the house, he realized he had to get his family out of there. He ordered Hilda to run into the coffee bushes with the children, and recovered his post behind a ridge. Oscar emptied a clip at the Contras, hoping to draw their gunfire away from the house. A mortar thudded over the roof, landed down the slope, and exploded. The pig screamed.

At last Hilda rolled the children up in blankets like little sausages and told Goya to follow her. Goya scooped up Oscar Daniel. Hilda pressed Aidé to her breast and dashed out of the house amid the confusion and noise. Mortars thudded, grenades exploded, and bullets whizzed around her. She fled into the coffee bushes.

Six militiamen on the ridge moved down and opened fire on the Contras. Oscar and the militia crawled into trenches near the bungalow and increased their fire. Every few minutes, Oscar changed positions so the Contras wouldn't know how few men were guarding the plant. He saw a black object flying over his head and instinctively flattened himself to the ground. Some twenty yards away, the hand grenade exploded, pelting his backside with dirt and rocks. He had narrowly escaped injury.

Head low, he dashed across the yard and rolled along the ground, then fired from behind a rock. Suddenly, he sensed a tremendous rush of air and heard a *thwack*. The ground shook. A rocket-propelled grenade slammed into the brick bungalow. As it penetrated the house, Oscar saw a part of the tin roof fly through the air. The enemy was advancing.

Oscar wondered where the army troops were; he and the militiamen were quickly running out of ammunition. They decided they had no choice but to retreat. Clutching their rifles, they dove into the coffee bushes and ran up the mountain to the other militiamen, who gave them forty-five bullets each. Oscar couldn't wait for the El Cuá reinforcements; instead, he ordered the ten militiamen to follow him. He slammed his weapon into rapid-fire, and then, from a different direction, ran back toward the bungalow, yelling, "¡Rindanse, hijos de la granputa guardia, aquí viene la refuerza de El Cuá!" (Give up, you sons of bitches, here come the reinforcements from El Cuá!). The ten militiamen followed, screaming and firing in the direction of the tiny brick house.

The Contras' gunfire weakened. Oscar and the militia advanced, running down the mountain slope, firing off bursts of bullets, rifle muzzles flashing in the dark. The Contras stopped shooting. They were retreating.

A few minutes later, the actual El Cuá reinforcements appeared. Juan Tercero, uniformed and in full battle gear—bullets crisscrossing him, bandolier-style, grenades hanging from his chest harness—jumped out of the jeep, a score of well-armed soldiers behind him. It was almost an hour after the attack had begun, and Oscar told him the battle was over. Juan strolled down to the powerhouse, which was intact, with its door shut. Juan, thinking the Contras may have booby-trapped the plant, ordered Oscar to open the door. Oscar hesitantly pushed it and jumped back. The door swung open freely. The powerhouse, tucked away in the ravine, was untouched; the Contras had mistaken the bungalow for the hydroplant.

Oscar wanted to inspect the transformers, but Juan ordered him to restore the electricity immediately. They couldn't allow the Contras a psychological victory. Reluctantly, Oscar turned the machines on. By 2:00 A.M. the lights were back on in El Cuá.

While working in the powerhouse, Oscar expected Hilda and the children to arrive. When they didn't appear, he began to worry. He retraced the route Hilda would have taken, but couldn't find her. Beginning to fear the worst, he stared at each rock, stump, and small coffee bush, afraid to see her body or those of his children. Militiamen joined him in the search. Oscar worried that she was wounded, or worse, that the Contras had kidnapped her. After combing the hills around the plant, Oscar hiked to La Chata, but no one had seen her. Oscar was frantic.

The sun rose: a bright, hot, March morning. Oscar hiked along the road to El Cuá, but no one had seen his family. Oscar cursed himself for making his family run off into the night, allowing the Contras to get so close, and letting Hilda and the children live at the hydroplant.

As he began turning back to the plant, he heard a cry. Four-year-old Aidé ran down the road, throwing herself at him. Behind her was Hilda, clutching Oscar Daniel, and Goya. They embraced and cried. Hilda told Oscar that she had fled into the gully and crouched under the overgrown coffee bushes, staying hidden long after the shooting stopped. Afraid of running into the Contras, they hiked to a neighbor's house hidden in a banana grove and stayed there until morning.

The couple went to the hydroplant to inspect their house. "It was horrible," Hilda said. "Everything was burned, and broken bricks were everywhere." The living room wall had a gaping hole from the rocket-propelled grenade, which luckily had not exploded. Sun streamed in through the roof where the tin sheets were blown off. The planks that divided the rooms were riddled with grenade fragments and bullet holes, and the tail of the unspent rocket lay in the living room.

The Contras had ripped the sink off the wall, pulled the electric wiring out of the ceiling, shattered the mirror, smashed the beds, ripped the sheets, and pulled the stuffing out of the mattresses. They had stolen boots, tennis shoes, vegetable seeds, diapers, bottles, baby clothes, the children's only pair of shoes, and Hilda's radio-cassette player and cassettes. They also took photos of Don, Ben, and Oscar from the walls, smashed the picture frames, and tore up Ben's postcards from Oregon. And they stole Oscar's guitar.

The yard was strewn with jagged pieces of tin, broken bricks, and the remains of the pig. The woodstove was destroyed, cracked and filled with shrapnel. Oscar found grenades, daypacks, rifles, and a bottle of gasoline in the banana grove. The Contras had planned to burn down the hydroplant.

Later that day, Oscar visited the Captain to give a report on the attack. Hilda took the children to stay with her mother and returned to the plant alone to sort through the debris. She collapsed on top of the rubble, sobbing.

In the evening, as the shadows lengthened, Hilda jumped at every sound; the snap of a branch, the roar of a holler monkey, the call of birds as they settled into trees for the night. When Oscar returned, Hilda told him she didn't want to spend the night there. They turned off the plant and hiked into El Cuá. The village seemed more dangerous without lights. Oscar dropped Hilda off at a relative's house, not telling her where he was going. Hilda tried to sleep.

Around 10:00 P.M., Hilda was awakened by banging on the door. The lieutenant in charge of the Ministry of Interior stormed inside with several soldiers and began screaming at Hilda, accusing her of sabotage. Hilda remained quiet. The officer claimed she and her husband were Contras because they had turned off the electricity. The lights had to be turned on immediately. Hilda didn't know where Oscar was. Furious, the lieutenant ordered her to return to the plant, but she quietly explained that she didn't want to operate it at night because she was afraid the Contras might return. The officer insisted that the army would defend it, but Hilda remembered how long it took for the soldiers from El Cuá to arrive the previous night. When the lieutenant left, she slumped down on the bed. She wanted to quit, but she knew how disappointed Ben and Don would be.

On the night of March 28, Ben gave a good-bye party for Don in Managua. Oscar planned to attend the party, so he left El Cuá at dawn, arriving in Managua at sundown, exhausted, filthy, and worried. As soon as Oscar appeared on Ben's doorstep, he suspected something terrible had happened.

Oscar told him the plant had been attacked. "Ben didn't believe me," said Oscar. "He said, '*No jodas*' [You're kidding]." Oscar told him the whole story while Ben listened in silence, shaking his head. "Ben asked me, 'Brother, what are you going to do? Are you leaving the plant?' and I said, 'No,' and he said, 'Look man, be careful, if the Contras attack, get Hilda and the kids out of there, and if you want to stay, well then, stay, but be careful.'"

When Rebecca, Mira, Tom, and Lois arrived, Oscar told them about the attack; they were all relieved that everyone had survived. When Don finally showed up, Oscar told him what had happened, and Don congratulated Oscar for successfully defending the plant. He noticed that the party was out of liquor, and left to drink beers at the Comedor Sara a few blocks away.

As Ben climbed into Tom's blue pickup to go to the market the next day, Tom noticed that Ben was pale, shaking, and strangely silent. He followed Tom through the Roberto Huembes market. Finally, Tom paused to ask what was wrong. Ben's eyes welled up with tears. "He was thinking about Hilda," said Tom. He was angry that she had to go through the attack, and upset that the town officials had treated her so badly when she refused to return to the plant. "She was having basic maternal instincts about protecting her children's lives, about protecting her life so her children would have a mother. And the response of some of the officials in El Cuá was, 'What are you talking about?' 'Aquí, no se rinde nadie [Here, no one gives up]. 'Sandinistas don't give up, no one quits.' 'Of course you're going back to work.'

"Ben said that's what pissed him off—that the officials were so insensitive; that they didn't understand how far she had come as a human being, and as a woman, to get to the point where she was now. All they saw is how far she had to go to become some sort of fucking super-Sandinista.

"When Ben got her the job at the plant, he knew precisely what he was getting her into," Tom added. "He created the support network that she needed, so that she could do something—be somebody—that she could never have conceived of. It was a little revolution in and of itself. And in one little ten-minute rap on her, the officials had destroyed a whole year's work of building up her self-confidence."

Tom and Ben returned to his apartment, saddened and depressed.

At dawn on Monday, March 30, 1987, Ben, Mira, and Oscar drove Don to the airport for his return to Europe. After the plane lifted off, Ben assumed Don's place, climbing into the driver's seat of Old Baldy.

Chapter 22

Ben and Mira Build in Bocay

March and April are Nicaragua's hottest, most unbearable months. The searing sun beats down relentlessly, drying up rivers, turning dirt roads to dust beds. People naturally migrate to the shade, while clothes became saturated with sweat and dust. In early mornings, farmers prepare fields for planting, waiting impatiently for the May rains.

Late in March 1987, Sister Ani Wihbey arrived in El Cuá to give a workshop on safe drinking water. Ben had planned to meet her, but found himself stuck in Managua. While there, Ani was asked to help bury twenty-four bodies, militiamen and members of the construction crew building the road to Ayapal.

On March 25, 130 men, including 30 from El Cuá, had gone north with a score of backhoes, bulldozers, graders, dump trucks, and other road construction equipment. They set up camp several hours north of Bocay and organized guard duty.

On the second night, before the militia had explored the territory, dug trenches, or fortified their positions, the Contras attacked with heavy machine guns, mortars, and grenades. The rebels pinned down the militia and construction crew and, during a six-hour battle, slowly picked them off. When the gunshots waned, the Contras overran the site, shot and bayoneted the wounded, poured diesel on the bodies and the construction equipment, and set everything afire. Among the dead were Miguel, Cosme Castro's oldest son, and Alfonso, one of Don's former students. They were brought into town in the back of an army truck, covered by a tarpaulin.

Ani lifted the tarp and stared at the bodies in horror. The corpses were naked, burned, and fused together, limbs askew. Blood oozed from mouths, eyes, and ears.

Several bodies were burnt head to toe. Two were charred from the chest down and had swollen to twice their normal size. Not one person was identifiable.

Dr. Maria Felisa ordered the bodies to be sent to El Trebol cooperative, where they could be laid out on the cement coffee-drying patio to be prepared for burial. Nicaraguan custom dictated that the bodies were to be washed in soap and water, then dressed in new clothes for the wake. These were so bloated they would not fit into clothes. "We couldn't do much to prepare the bodies," said Ani. "It was awful— the bodies were blown into pieces. Their skins rolled off like cellophane." Ani and Dr. Maria Felisa cut the only material available, orange T-shirt fabric, into makeshift shrouds. The coffins would not close over two swollen bodies, so the lids had to be hammered shut.

In the early morning, the coffins were buried in a shallow, hastily dug mass grave. Physically and emotionally drained, Ani caught a ride out of El Cuá. The drinking-water workshop would have to wait for another time.

Ben learned of the Contra's ambush of El Cuá while he was in Matagalpa. He wrote:

> Miguel dead. Miguel is the oldest son of Cosme Castro, and the father of Gregoria [Goya], who sometimes helps us at the plant. Cosme started to fight for a just world when he was in his teens with Sandino. He has fought ever since. Many of his friends have died fighting. This was his oldest son. Two days later, the helicopter brought in his nephew—also dead.
> The town suffered. All of the coops around El Cuá lost several members. Everyone lost a friend. Who were these 13? Men, members of coops, farmers who form the local militia. They went to defend the road construction crew. The crew was attacked. The construction workers alongside the militia did what they could. Twenty-four died.
> This is probably the final offensive of the Contras. Losing soldiers daily as they desert, the Contras are desperate. Like any desperate animal backed into a corner they are fighting with all they have. The people of Cuá/Bocay know 1987 will be a very hard year. But they also know they are winning the war. Next week for the first time, high school classes will be taught in El Cuá.

When Ben and Mira returned to El Cuá, they drove directly to the plant to survey the damage. Since the attack, Oscar and Hilda had been sleeping at her mother's house in El Golfo. They hiked to the plant every day to check the machines, but Oscar planned to move his family back to the plant as soon as a mason fixed the hole in the living room.

Since the Contras hadn't destroyed the plant, Ben feared they would attack again. For security measures, he decided the facility would be turned off at nine every night. That evening, as Oscar was turning off the plant, an officer from the Ministry of Interior zoomed up the hill and harangued him, ordering him to turn the electricity back on. After the officer left, Oscar went to El Golfo without turning on the electricity.

After the bungalow was repaired, Oscar and Hilda moved back. Hilda refused to bring the children. She packed her few remaining belongings in a burlap sack and stashed it by the door, ready to run if the Contras attacked again. Oscar wouldn't let her leave the plant. Mira wrote, "Truly, she'd like to leave now, but doesn't know where else to go."

On April 1, Ben and Mira held a meeting of the "Technical Team," which on that day consisted of only one other member: Clifford. They drew up a timetable for April, which included building the cement weir in Bocay and collecting dry-season readings before the rainy season began in May. Ben asked local officials to send cement and iron rebar for the weir to Bocay.

For many months Silvia, the health promoter, had been neglecting her job. She failed to organize workshops, stopped making house-to-house visits, and rarely showed up at the health center. After Dr. Maria Felisa lectured her on responsibilities, she quit, and the doctor immediately regretted it. Even though Silvia was lazy, she was one of the best-educated people in town and would be hard to replace. The health care system was based on empowerment. Local residents were taught skills and given the self-confidence and support to carry out preventive health care on a village level. Their training eased the doctor's workload, as health promoters dealt with dehydration, poor nutrition, and inoculations, allowing the doctor to deal with complicated childbirths, broken bones, and gunshot wounds.

When Silvia quit, Dr. Maria Felisa scoured the town in vain. No one in the village had the training, the education, the confidence, or the initiative to do the job. Early one morning before the clinic opened, the doctor eyed twenty-five-year-old Juana, the cleaning woman. Juana had only finished third grade, and could barely read and write, but the doctor knew she was always willing to help. She pressured Juana into accepting the position, promising she'd help her, and suggested that she start by planning the upcoming vaccination campaign against polio and measles. Juana agreed to it, but the days passed, and Dr. Maria Felisa never found time to train her. Disorganized and scattered, physically and mentally exhausted, Dr. Maria Felisa jumped from one emergency to another. Juana was overwhelmed, too. She had never organized anything before, and she didn't know where to begin.

Ben heard about the vaccination campaign and stopped by the health clinic to find Juana sitting at a bare desk, empty notebook in hand. When he asked her about the campaign, she began to cry. Ben soothed her, trying to build her confidence, and offered to help her. They spent the afternoon organizing.

On Saturday, April 4, town officials held a public celebration to kick off the vaccination campaign. Dressed in a ripped shirt, hair combed back into a rat's nest, Silvia limped onto the stage. She was Polio. Ben followed her, dressed in pajamas with ugly, red spots drawn over his body. "I am the Measles Monster," he shouted, as the children booed.

In the play, a mother took her children to the clinic to be vaccinated. As they left, smiling and happy, a frustrated Polio and a puzzled Measles circled around the children, unable to attack. However, another mother refused to have her children vaccinated, and Silvia attacked one of them. Chasing him around the stage, she tackled him. When she released the child, he collapsed, flailing his useless limbs, unable to walk. Ben attacked another, throwing him onto the stage floor. While he writhed and struggled, the disease covered him with red spots. Horrified, the other women onstage ran to the clinic to get their children vaccinated. When they emerged, they grabbed brooms and chased Polio and Measles offstage.

Ben ran down the steps and hopped onto his unicycle. He zipped through the crowd, a blur of red spots and white pajamas. The crowd parted while children tugged on their parents' hands, begging to be released. Ben zoomed up the dusty road, followed by scores of shrieking children who reached out to finger his red spots. He pedaled from house to house, stopping at the front doors, rocking back and forth as he called to mothers inside. Women peeked out, hesitantly emerging onto porches. In a serious voice, Ben reminded them to get their children vaccinated the next day.

Ben cycled up the road, past the plaza, followed by a pack of children, until he reached Cosme's house on the edge of town. He quickly pivoted, and the children scattered, running down to the plaza ahead of him. He chased them, yelling, "¿Dónde están los niños? ¡Aquí viene sarampión, si no se le vacunan, yo voy a agarrarle! ¡Muerte al sarampión!" (Where are the kids? Here comes Measles, and if you don't get vaccinated, I'll get you! Death to Measles!)

As Ben approached the plaza again, the pack of children boxed him in. He jerked the unicycle back, then forward. His foot slipped on the pedal, and the unicycle's cotter pin pierced his ankle. He teetered off balance and fell under the unicycle. Blood seeped from his ankle. The children suddenly fell quiet, and stepped back, afraid. Ben laughed, raised himself off the ground, dabbed at the blood with his pajama sleeve, and got back on his unicycle. He told Mira, "The show must go on!"

His wound continued bleeding, so Ben washed his ankle in the river, bandaged it with a rag, and continued clowning, up and down the dirt road.

The next day, Ben told Mira he'd return in four or five days so they could start building the Bocay weir. He hitchhiked to Managua and met Dr. Anne Lifflander, his old gringo club friend, who was visiting Nicaragua as the leader of a delegation of American health workers. He told her about the attack on the plant over cold beers that night and admitted that he felt isolated from his culture, asking countless questions about friends in the United States, the work in stopping Contra aid by solidarity groups, and the latest jokes from the *Doonesbury* comic strip.

Anne, who hadn't seen Ben in almost two years, remembered him as light-hearted and crazy, but during this visit, he was serious, even somber. She wondered if the war was what had changed him.

The following Monday, Ben dropped by the CISAS office to visit Lois and her Nicaraguan colleague Marta. Ben knew Marta's birthday was approaching, and he wanted to ask her out but feared she would say no. Lois helped him out by inviting them both to a dinner she was arranging. Ben ran to the market, bought a book and flowers, borrowed a car, and took Marta to Restaurante Tiscapa. The band struck up a salsa song, and everyone filed out to dance. Marta danced rhythmically, in perfect time to the music, while Ben danced spasmodically, jumping all over the dance floor, a wide grin on his face. At the end of the evening, Ben took Marta to her house, walked her to the door, and said good night.

A few days later Ben met Lois for breakfast at El Eskimo, a dark, over-air-conditioned restaurant. While eating eggs, rice, and beans, he asked her what Marta had said about that night. Lois twisted uncomfortably in her seat, and finally told him Marta liked him as a friend. She said she wanted a boyfriend in Managua, not in the countryside. Ben looked down at the table. As they were talking about Ben's love interests, Lois mentioned that she had heard Sonia was back from Colombia. "He got defensive," said Lois. He had no interest in seeing her, or talking to her, and as he stabbed his eggs, he wryly told Lois, "Don't give her my address."

Then Ben abruptly changed the subject to the plant in El Cuá. Lois asked him if he regretted not being there during the attack. He said, "Hell, no." When she asked how he felt about going up there again, he answered with a Sandinista slogan: "Por estos muertos … juramos que defender la victoria" (For these deaths, we swear to defend the revolution).

Ben also sought advice about how to handle an interview with John Lantigua from the *Washington Post* about Americans working in war zones. "'Should I tell the reporter I was carrying a gun?'" he inquired. She felt he shouldn't. Ben disagreed. He felt that Americans in Nicaragua were always too "wimpy" with the press. "He told me that we're always saying what we think they want to hear—but that it is important for American people to know that in Nicaragua the engineers, the doctors, the coffee pickers, and the farmers have to be armed." It was a fact of life that both Nicaraguans and foreigners were targets, and he felt the American people should know that. Lois argued that Americans would not understand he was carrying it in self-defense, and right-wingers would use the information against him, and all American internationalists. Eventually, Ben was convinced.

The next day, in the interview, Ben told the reporter about growing up in the 1960s in San Francisco, and knowing that he always wanted to be an engineer and use his skills to help humanity, but he never mentioned the gun.

While in Managua, Ben's injured ankle became red and swollen. He cleaned it with soap and water, but soon it became so inflamed that he couldn't wear his work boots. He switched to tennis shoes.

Before returning to El Cuá, Ben wrote Alison a long letter, telling her that he was going to be at a hydropower conference in Portland, Oregon, on August 19, 1987. He suggested that they spend a week together afterward.

Ben had stayed away from El Cuá longer than planned. He knew Mira was waiting for him, but he still needed to get the design for the Bocay weir from Juliet Thompson, a civil engineer from Colorado who worked in Matagalpa. He caught Juliet just as she arrived at the Casa de Gobierno with a hangover.

"I was filthy dirty, and feeling really raw," she remembered, "and Ben comes in and says, 'I need that design right now.' And I just sat down and started working on it." Ben gave Juliet the information—how wide the opening should be, La Camaleona's flow rate—and together they computed how thick the cement wall needed to be.

"For a mechanical engineer, Ben knew a lot about water," said Juliet. "He had a good feel for pipe sizing and flow. He had the mentality, the curiosity, and the preciseness that lead you to investigate thoroughly what you're trying to do. It was a bit intimidating; it made me more conscientious." She worked alone for four hours. When Ben returned, they reviewed the calculations, and Juliet sketched the project.

They finished in the late evening, then set off for a party at Charlie Whitaker's. As they walked along a narrow street, Ben spied Chumbalú, a caravan driver who regularly hauled supplies up to Bocay, and one of the best informants on the road.

At the sight of Ben, Chumbalú broke into smiles. He had just returned from Bocay, and reported that the situation was really bad. "It's super-dangerous up there; there are Contras all over the place, and you shouldn't go up there," Juliet recalled him saying. "When Ben asked about La Camaleona, Chumbalú said it was especially hot right now." Then, "Ben suddenly turned to me and said, 'Listen, I'm changing where I'm going to work.'" In that instant, Ben changed the project site from La Camaleona to Los Angeles, the river he had seen on the INE map.

While Ben was away, Mira worked alone in El Cuá. Some days she felt useful and optimistic, believing that both her work and the revolution were progressing. At El Trebol, Mira began building that coop's first Lorena woodstove with a single mother named Carmenza. Throughout the long, hot afternoon, Mira and Carmenza shoveled and compacted the dirt. Layer upon layer, the stove took shape. Women frequently stopped to watch, shyly asking Mira questions, but when she invited them to lend a hand, they always declined.

At sundown, Mira drove Old Baldy to the river to take a bath, where she noticed three other women stripped naked from the waist up washing themselves. Even after several months in El Cuá, Mira still hadn't figured out the acceptable bathing protocol. She approached one of the bathers, and asked her. "When there are others here undressed, you can undress yourself," she was told. Nevertheless, Mira bathed in her bra and shorts and scooped cupfuls of water over her hair, washing her long, thin braid.

At Wilfredo's house she puffed on the wood fire to reheat the early morning's rice and beans. At 6:00 P.M., she taught an English class to seven students, mostly government employees, who ranged from a Miskito Indian with a sixth-grade education to a college graduate, an official from the city. "I love being part of the 'studying scene,'" admitted Mira. "Most people seem to be studying something. Even the busiest Sandinista representatives, the busiest housewives, the people with the most time-consuming, thankless jobs—everyone is studying. For most, it is just completing their primary education!"

After class, Mira returned to her room, perched on the cot in her room, turned on a Talking Heads tape, and took out her last sheet of blank paper to write to her parents before "lights out" at 9:00 P.M.:

> We've been turning the plant off at night since the attack—locking the barn door after the horse is stolen. Actually it's part of an effort to pressure the army to beef up security out there. They have already stationed more soldiers, which is good, but Oscar and Hilda are still holding out for a mortar or a heavier machine gun ... odd demands for a work stoppage, no?

As the days crept along, Mira kept busy. She drove Clifford and the others in the "coffee-machinery repair brigade" to La Chata, but then had to drive them back because they couldn't find repair parts. Another day, in El Trebol, she worked on the woodstove alone. That evening she held a slow, late meeting with Clifford. She looked for someone to work at the hydroplant during Holy Week, so that Oscar and Hilda could take a vacation, but no one was willing to stay there. After the attack, few people even visited the plant anymore.

Mira tried not to get depressed over the sluggish pace or the frequent solitude, but sometimes she felt she was falling further behind on her timetable. "Yesterday," she wrote, "I felt shitty, physically and emotionally, and I got nothing done." Some days she felt overcome by "the smell of shit that pervades the town, the little kids with swollen bellies, the drunken fights, the tiredness in people's eyes, the endless meetings, waiting for people who never show up, waiting and having meetings and not getting anything done."

She was anxious for Ben's return. When he failed to show up by the date they set to start building the weir, she became worried. It was unlike Ben to stay away when they had a deadline. Two mornings in a row Mira went to the FSLN office to send a radio message to Matagalpa, in search of Ben, without any luck. She wondered if something had happened to him.

Ben arrived in Jinotega during the beginning of Semana Santa, Holy Week, and hobbled down the deserted streets to the American doctors' house. Tim opened the door to find Ben standing on one foot, "looking sheepish." As he limped into the doctor's living room, he confessed he had injured his ankle and cleaned it in the El Cuá River. "The reason he looked sheepish was because we knew that his father was a physician, and had taught him better than to stick a wound in a filthy river," said Tim.

Tim and Susan examined the wound and were dismayed to find that the infection had gone to the knee. A spreading inflammation of the connective tissue called cellulitis had set in. His entire leg was swollen. They were amazed that he could even walk. They soaked the wound, bled and cleaned it, confined Ben to their extra bed, and put him on an intravenous antibiotic drip. They also discovered that Ben had amoebas.

Ben spent the next day sleeping. After twenty-four hours, the infection still resisted the treatment, and the doctors worried he would develop gangrene. They suggested he return to the United States to recover. "At first he was very resistant to the idea, but then he came around, and began planning things he could do there in connection with the project," said Tim.

After another twenty-four hours passed, Ben's condition improved considerably, and the doctors relaxed. He was out of danger. Ben rested with the IV drip in his arm, and gradually was able to limp from room to room, IV in tow. His appetite improved, so they cooked him quiche with snow peas and tomatoes from their garden. Since he wanted to be useful, they let him clean rice. He sat at the table for hours picking pebbles out of the grains. When he regained his energy, he cooked them a curry dinner.

The cool summer climate and thick fogs of Jinotega reminded Ben of Portland. He told the doctors about his childhood, and described his parents' disastrous visit to Nicaragua. Reflecting on his family, Ben thought about Miriam. They had never been close, but after his last trip to Portland, they had developed a bond. He did not want to lose that closeness, so he wrote her a long letter, describing life in the war zone:

Perhaps [war] is the hardest part of Cuá-Bocay to describe. When we think of war all sorts of images come to mind, everything from *M*A*S*H*, *Hogan's Heroes*, shots of Vietnam, *War and Peace*, *All Quiet on the Western Front*, to our own imaginations. What I'm finding out is that there is really no one image to describe war. I can't find one, and I hope I never have the experiences to try to.

Here in Nicaragua it changes from region to region.... In Cuá/Bocay it changes every mile, literally. In Managua the war is felt through the economic problems—which get worse daily—through the draft, and through workers such as myself who work closer to the actual fighting. But if you have a lot of money and close your eyes you can ignore it. In Matagalpa you are much closer to the fighting although still not in danger. The military trucks are much more present, more soldiers standing around, the news of skirmishes is more frequent and realistic and there are more people who work closer to the fighting. Jinotega is similar. Then there is the 55 miles from Jinotega to El Cuá.

On the road the situation is very different. The "war" in general terms doesn't change, but the possibility of fighting nearby changes every three miles, that is to say the danger becomes more or less depending on where you are. It depends also on time, that is it depends on where the Contras are ...

Peace. If peace were just the end to the guns of war, it would be simple. If there were no peace amongst the guns of war and the starvation of poverty, life would be miserable.

But there is peace at certain times. My favorite is the morning coffee with Cosme ... or when I'm walking along a stream, looking at the stream for its own sheer beauty, looking at it for generating electricity, or just walking along a stream, scrambling over rocks, taking a quick bath in a little pool formed in the rock.

The other day I found a lovely white orchid with a white and mustard center part. Tucked among the rocks, it clung on. I stopped and looked at it. Further up there were more. Beautiful flowers.

These are my personal peace-moments when I feel good, sometimes calm, sometimes excited, but with that deep-down feeling of contentment.

But my feeling of peace also comes from what is happening around me.

On April 17, Good Friday, Jinotega was silent and solemn. All offices and stores were closed, and women in black with young children in tow walked silently to mass under a strong, hot sun.

Gary and Ches Campbell, American Protestant missionaries living in Managua, visited Tim and Susan, and together with Ben they went on a picnic in a pine forest near the Selva Negra Hotel. Ben hobbled alongside the others, carrying his IV bag on a stick, holding it above his heart.

They spread a blanket under shady trees and enjoyed gazpacho, pasta salad, bread, and wine, while trading stories about their favorite restaurants in North Carolina and Oregon. Later the conversation turned to the war, and Ben told them about the latest attacks in El Cuá. They discussed how they could make Americans more aware of what was happening in Nicaragua. "We were convinced that if we could make them feel the horror and terror that people in the war zone felt, then the war would end—because, if Americans really felt that horror, they would not be able to support it," said Tim. But they realized they didn't know what to do.

In El Cuá, Mira's concern for Ben grew. On April 12, Palm Sunday, Mira moved to the hydroplant to give Oscar a vacation. Hilda stayed with Mira, and they spent the week building a new woodstove and speculating that Ben had fallen in love and forgotten about them. Late that week Mira stopped by the FSLN office and finally heard that Ben was in Jinotega with a seriously injured foot, and wouldn't be able to return to El Cuá for three or four weeks.

Mira was relieved that Ben was safe, but disappointed about losing time on their schedule. She calculated that, if she quickly got another engineer to work with her, they still could build the weir in Bocay before the May rains began. She fired off several radio messages to the official at the Casa de Gobierno in Matagalpa to send a civil engineer. After not receiving a response, she radioed the FSLN office in Jinotega, asking them to contact Ben at the doctors' house with the message that she'd like him to come back to work, and would drive down to pick him up. Ben agreed to return.

On Good Friday, April 17, Mira drove Old Baldy out of El Cuá with two armed passengers. It was the first time she had ever driven to Jinotega. She remembered what Don had taught her about traveling in the war zone; drive fast, don't pause on hilltops, don't follow other vehicles too closely, check the depth of rivers before crossing them. Mira frequently stopped at streams, quickly scooping water into the radiator while glancing furtively at the surrounding dry, brown hills. Somewhere along the bumpy road, the jeep's windshield supports collapsed, but Mira didn't stop again until she arrived in Jinotega.

Ben was ecstatic to see her, and felt bad for falling behind schedule. Although his foot was still swollen, Tim and Susan took him off the intravenous drip.

Over the weekend, Ben and Mira examined the design of the weir and decided the two of them could share the work. Ben would direct the construction, and Mira would run errands. She wrote:

> Ben and I spent yesterday getting the jeep repaired, a small miracle considering it was Saturday of Holy Week. We had to find someone to make two new supports for the windshield, the old ones having ripped out when I drove down this time. Now we've done away with welding directly to the canopy and have a system with bolts and rubber washers. Much better. I can hit potholes with relative impunity. And potholes abound.
> Ben is much better, though very tired still. I will go with him to build the weir, basically being his feet. I look forward to it, I should learn a lot about weirs and water measurements, and a bit about concrete form work. I love this job—where else would I get called off of Lorena stoves to build a weir for a small hydroelectric plant?

On Easter morning, Ben and Mira decided to find a machinist to work with them. They drove to the agricultural mechanization school at Chagüitillo, but it was deserted because of Easter vacation. Back in Matagalpa, they passed women wearing high heels and red lipstick and girls in frilly dresses walking home from Easter mass. Ben and Mira wanted to take the shortcut from Matagalpa to El Cuá, but a rope was stretched across the road. Contras had been spotted, and the road was closed. Returning to Jinotega in late afternoon, they spent the night at Tim and Susan's house and drove to El Cuá on Monday. They reached Bocay on Tuesday, picking up three hitchhiking soldiers along the way.

Mira had been to Bocay eight months earlier, but with the influx of refugees the town looked different. As they drove along the main road, lined with refugees' shacks of black plastic sheeting, Ben pointed out the main buildings: the coffee warehouse, the army headquarters, and farther out, the army base. Barricades of sandbags surrounded the FSLN office, and soldiers in camouflage lounged in the plaza.

Ben and Mira met with Pablo Araus, the Sandinista coordinator in charge of Bocay, who reported that only four bags of cement had arrived for their weir. From the bank office, Ben sent a radio message to Juan Tercero in El Cuá, asking him to send up the rebar and the rest of the cement as soon as possible.

On Wednesday, Ben wore one high-top work boot and a tennis shoe on his swollen foot. Ben and Mira asked soldiers to accompany them to the stream at Los Angeles. The officer in charge informed them that he was shorthanded. Unbeknownst to Ben and Mira, the Sandinista army was preparing to launch one of the biggest operations of the war, a massive counteroffensive against the Contras to sweep them out of northern Nicaragua.

After much wrangling, the officer finally assigned them two soldiers. The four of them climbed a steep trail out of town, passing through groves of wild plantains and thick jungle brush. Ben leaned on a stick for support and stopped frequently, taking notes on the terrain. He pointed out possible routes for the pipe that would carry water from the dam to the town. They slowly crossed small streams and a ridge, followed the trail downhill into the Valle de los Angeles (Valley of the Angels).

They stopped beside the fast-running river, where a small pool led into a waterfall. Large rock outcroppings jutted into the water, creating a narrow section about five feet wide, a perfect place to build a weir. The narrow waterway was flanked by steep banks, a cornfield on one side, and overgrown jungle on the other. The crew measured the river, then followed a side path through a banana grove. After a five-minute walk, they emerged at a mud-and-wood farmhouse tucked around a bend, hidden from view. The gaunt farmer, Fidel Molinaris, gave Ben permission to build the weir on his land. Ben also arranged to buy boards from him, and commissioned his wife to prepare lunch for the work crew, who would be working daily at the site for more than a week.

As they descended the trail into town, Ben and Mira discussed Don's advice about working in the war zone; only work with an armed escort, never give people information on your movements beforehand, and—his cardinal rule—never work in the same place for a long time. They knew they were already breaking several rules, but they agreed this was a special case. The weir had to be built before the rainy season began, only a week away. They needed the dry-season flow measurement in order to design a turbine. Without the data, they'd have to wait until the next dry season began in May, leaving the residents of Bocay to spend another year in darkness, without running water. Another dozen children would likely die of waterborne diseases.

Back in Bocay, the army advised them they could not continue to provide an armed escort, so they decided to ask the militia. Ben and Mira walked through the refugee settlement, where Enrique Morales, the settlement's coordinator, motioned them inside his black-plastic home. In one corner stood an altar, decorated with tree branches, white candles, and a rough-hewn cross and flowers. He had posted a list of names of his relatives who were killed by the Contras. Beside it sat a bench and empty ammunition crates with Cyrillic writing on the sides, which served as chairs.

Enrique was in charge of the sixty-seven refugee families living in the settlement, whom he described as "broken people who had barely begun to rebuild their lives." Most had fled their land quickly, leaving behind houses, crops, animals, and possessions. Often the only clothes the men owned were uniforms given to them by the militia.

After talking with Ben and Mira, Enrique agreed to send militia from the coop to help them, and drew up a list of thirty-two men to rotate duty on the weir. As they were leaving, Ben spied Sergio Hernández, a thirty-three-year-old mason with whom he had worked previously. Sergio had moved to El Cedro to Bocay two months earlier because he thought Bocay would be safer for his wife, Bertilda, and their seven young children. He agreed to work with them for a small amount of córdobas per day. But they could not build the weir without materials, and the cement and rebar still had not arrived. Mira tried to radio El Cuá, with no luck. Ben's foot had improved, and he insisted he could work with the militia. They decided to start construction, while Mira took Old Baldy into El Cuá to get the materials.

At the diner that evening, Ben modified the weir design according to his new measurements. Half-listening to a conversation about the Bible on one side, and the price of firewood on the other, Mira wrote to her solidarity group back home, "If we build this week, and get a few weeks water flow readings before the end of the dry season, Ben will have the data he needs to design the plant. Eighteen months from now, I may be writing you all under an electric light."

On April 23 at 7:00 A.M., Ben met with Sergio, the mason, and several volunteers from the refugee settlement, some dressed in fatigues and carrying AK-47s. The group climbed the trail, arriving by 8:00 A.M. at Los Angeles, where they began sawing boards.

In Bocay, Mira asked Pablo, the FSLN coordinator, to assign some militia to ride with her to El Cuá. He claimed the road was so dangerous that not even the public-transport truck was leaving town, but promised that if an army convoy left, she could caravan with it. Mira parked Old Baldy at the gates of the base, waiting impatiently, but no such caravan materialized.

The town buzzed with military activity. Mi-24 attack helicopters lifted off from the landing pad, loaded with rockets. They circled the town, heading north into the jungle. IFA troop transport trucks and army jeeps shuttled between army headquarters and the dirt runway a few miles north of town. Young soldiers crowded the area.

When Ben returned to Bocay late in the afternoon, he went directly to Pablo's office to discuss his concern about security in Los Angeles. The militiamen were jumpy, startled by the buzz of helicopters and the shots in the hills. Ben asked for regular soldiers, but Pablo refused. All troops were being mobilized.

On Friday, April 24, Mira was still waiting for a vehicle to head out. She was surprised to spot Ben in town at 9:00 A.M. He was having trouble getting a mule to haul cement to Los Angeles and enough militiamen to accompany him. Eventually, he left for the site.

Mira radioed El Cuá the next day, angry and frustrated after two days of waiting. She had a terse, uncoded conversation with Juan Tercero, demanding that he immediately send the cement and rebar. Juan confirmed that the construction materials were in El Cuá, but the road was closed. There was nothing he could do. After the exchange, Mira returned to the army base, demanding to get to El Cuá. The officer in charge urged her to wait for an IFA truck, which was leaving for El Cuá later that day.

The green, high-wheeled troop transport dwarfed Old Baldy when it pulled alongside the back of the truck, which held several young soldiers armed with rifles, chest harnesses bulging with ammunition. Mira insisted she wouldn't leave until three soldiers jumped into her jeep. It took several minutes of cajoling before they climbed into Old Baldy. The driver of the truck swung out of Bocay, barreling down the dirt road, making turns at full speed, plunging into rivers without slowing. Mira drove Old Baldy as fast as she could, hands gripping the steering wheel, rifle clattering on the seat beside her. The militiamen clutched the sides of the jeep. She bounced down the rutted road, trying to keep the army truck in sight. Steam hissed out of Old Baldy's radiator, and the jeep subsequently fell behind and stalled while crossing a river. The soldiers jumped into the water, pushing the jeep out, push-starting it on the road. Old Baldy's battery was dead.

The foursome arrived in El Cuá by 2:00 P.M. Normally deserted at that time of day, the main road was filled with clusters of villagers silently waiting in the searing heat. Twenty minutes earlier, the Contras had ambushed two vehicles five miles south of El Cuá.

Mira's stomach lurched. She tried to calm herself by concentrating on her work as an army vehicle rumbled around the corner and pulled into the plaza. Four bodies lay in the truck bed in a pool of blood. The dead included the head of state security for the region, the head of state security for Bocay, one soldier, and one civilian who had been hitching a ride. The head of the Bocay army battalion, Lieutenant Tulún, was the lone survivor.

Clifford told Mira not to return to Bocay. Ben was able to walk again, and the military truck would be taking the cement and rebar back to Bocay.

On Monday evening, April 27, Enrique, the refugee settlement coordinator, checked his rotating list. He informed forty-year-old Cecilio Rosales that he was slated to work on the weir with his cousin, Pablo Hernández, the next day. Cecilio was glad they would be working together, as they had grown up on nearby farms only a few miles apart, and even escaped from the Contras together.

In 1982 Cecilio had been kidnapped by the Contras, and he fought with them for two years. He escaped and returned to the Bocay area. In July 1986 six Contras abducted him again, this time forcing him to take them to Pablo's house. They tied his cousin up and beat him, accusing Pablo of passing information on Contra movements to the Sandinistas.

At gunpoint, Cecilio and Pablo were forced to hike through the jungle. When the Contras hung their hammocks that night, they placed the captives securely in the middle. But the rebel guarding them fell asleep. The cousins crept away and fled to Bocay, where they knew the Contras could not follow. Pablo brought his wife and four children into town, erecting a house of plastic sheeting in the refugee settlement. Three days later, Cecilio also moved his family there. Both men disliked town life and longed to return to their farms, but knew that was impossible. If the Contras found them, they would surely be killed.

Chapter 23

Ambush

Early Tuesday morning on April 28, 1987, Laurie McQuaig and Gary Hicks boarded the public transport truck in the Jinotega market. Laurie had only been in Nicaragua a few weeks, but Gary, fluent in Spanish, had lived in Costa Rica for ten years. They came with the U.S. ecumenical group Witness for Peace whose volunteers lived in villages scattered throughout the war zones, and their role was "to stand with the people" in times of hardship, and document the war. Many volunteers took strength from a Biblical verse:

> If you cease to pervert justice,
> to point the accusing finger and lay false charges,
> if you feed the hungry from your own plenty
> and satisfy the needs of the wretched,
> then your light will rise like dawn out of darkness
> and your dusk will be like noonday ...
> you will be like a well-watered garden,
> like a spring whose waters never fail.
> Isaiah 58:9–11 (NEB)

Laurie and Gary had just received their new assignment; they would visit and document the war in San José de Bocay.

Before the first rays of sun streaked the sky of Jinotega province, a dozen Contras marched south through the jungle, carrying automatic rifles and wearing camouflage. Only Chico, their guide, wore civilian clothes. He led the men around massive ceiba trunks, underneath banana fronds, through groves of hanging vines, and past occasional shacks. A gaunt farmer eyed the Contras, stooped under heavy, bulging backpacks, as they passed.

Chico had informed the Contras that a group of armed Sandinistas, including a foreigner, had been working for six days in an isolated ravine, building a dam for a hydroplant to bring electricity to the village. "It is a zone of combat," Alcide, one of the guerrillas, later said. "He who moves with the military and with a gun is an enemy of ours."

A thirty-year-old Contra leader known as "Tiro al Blanco" (Bulls-Eye), who commanded 1,200 troops, ordered Mapuchin, the head of a special unit, "to destroy that dam, or whatever, no matter who is there." Tiro al Blanco had just completed two months of training at a U.S. military base in North Carolina. His troops were newly armed with automatic rifles, land mines, surface-to-air missiles, and C-4 plastic explosives.

Mapuchin led the eleven-man Contra unit. Half of his squad was illiterate. The other half wrote with the uncertain penmanship of first-graders. The youngest guerrilla, sixteen-year-old William, became a Contra when he was eleven, following his two older brothers, who had joined the rebels to avoid the Sandinista draft. As a teenager, William was already a sharpshooter with five years of combat experience.

Mapuchin was also an expert marksman, having fought with the Contras for five years. He, too, was illiterate, but he knew how to follow orders, and this next order would be easy: a hidden ravine, a smooth ambush, a quick kill, a fast getaway.

The guerrillas arrived at Los Angeles sometime around dawn. The trail from town, from where the Sandinistas would arrive, dropped thirty feet into the gorge and crossed a log bridge to a small, flat work area. Boards partially dammed the stream, and piles of sand, stone, wooden beams, bags of cement, and tools were scattered around the area. The only escape route was down the ravine, among rock outcroppings and boulders. It was a perfect ambush site.

Mapuchin selected three men, Estrella, Avestruz, and Wamblán, as lookouts, posting them some sixty meters away from the ravine. He distributed hand grenades to the other men. Each man had one hundred bullets for his automatic rifle.

As the sun rose, the Contras lay low in the jungle grasses, waiting.

Shortly after dawn, in Alejandra's Bocay storeroom, Ben crawled out of his hammock. Light filtered through the cracks of the plank walls as Ben put on his wire-rimmed glasses. He pulled on a blue cotton shirt and a pair of brown pants, still caked with mud from working on the weir the day before. It was the first day he could fit his high-top work boots over his injured foot. Ben tucked his notebook, wallet, and a small camera into a bag and tied it to his waist. He crammed ammunition, a calculator, and tools into two pouches and walked out onto the porch.

Alejandra greeted him with a cup of boiling coffee. On the porch, a green parrot strutted along a stick. The mayor, Pablo Arauz, waved at Ben while passing through the plaza. On his way to work, Ben stopped by the health clinic, greeted the nurse, and then dropped in at the house of his newest volunteer, Antonio Chaw. Antonio told him he couldn't work on the weir that day because he had to repair a clock, but promised he'd work the next day and gave the engineer a watermelon and a stalk of green plantains. Ben dropped them off in the storeroom, picked up his AK-47, and headed toward the plaza to meet his crew.

By 7:00 A.M. Sergio, the mason, dressed in camouflage and carrying an automatic rifle, was waiting for him, along with five other farmers from the refugee settlement. Three of the other crew members were outfitted in uniforms, rubber boots, and rifles. The other two wore civilian clothes and were unarmed.

When Ben arrived, Sergio roped two hundred-pound bags of cement onto a mule and handed the tether to José Luis Torres. The group climbed a path out of town, crested a ridge, and descended into a high mountain valley. They climbed over a second hill, with Sergio in the lead and Ben third in line, before dropping some thirty feet to the work site. One by one, the men crossed the fallen log, balancing themselves over the shallow creek, while the clear, fast-flowing stream bubbled down the gorge below them, forming pools and tiny waterfalls. Boards and bags of cement littered the area.

Ben set his rifle down and walked over to a rock overlooking the river. Sergio stood downstream, waiting for instructions, while Pablo stood near his cousin Cecilio. The rest of the crew milled around the work site, waiting for the mule to arrive so they could unload the cement. Ben sat down on a log, opened his small bag, took out a pen and notebook, and began writing.

The Contras, hidden in the tall jungle grasses above, took aim. Mapuchin gave the order to fire. Each of the Contras emptied an entire clip of ammunition—thirty bullets—into the clearing.

At the first sound of gunfire, Cecilio, standing behind Ben, jumped into the river. He ducked behind boulders, fleeing downstream. After firing the rounds, the Contras pitched grenades toward their targets. The explosions hurled dirt, sand, and water into the air. Shrapnel shot through Cecilio's hand. He glanced back to find Ben slumped on the ground. Cecilio crashed through the jungle, down the path, heading to town.

While leading the mule, José Luis Torres heard the shots from the path below the stream. He dropped the tether and raced down the path, stumbling and falling, twisting his leg. He scrambled into the thick brush, and crawled into a banana grove.

A mile away in the village of Bocay, Antonio Chaw sat at the wooden table, repairing a clock. As the minute hand marked 8:43, he heard the short, staccato bursts of machine-gun fire, followed by the low, echoing rumble of grenade explosions. Ambush. So close to town, he thought. There could only be one target.

When the dust from the attack settled, one man lay slumped in the clearing, with two others sprawled nearby. Mapuchin and his men slammed fresh clips into their rifles, cautiously emerging from the grass. They scrambled down to the clearing, weapons leveled at the three motionless figures. The Contras knew that the shots would have been heard in Bocay. Sandinista troops would soon arrive, so they quickly finished the men off. They bayoneted one man in the heart, then stripped the bodies of cartridge belts, loaders, ammunition, and identification. They took Ben's wallet, camera, and watch, and removed the glasses from his face.

Within fifteen minutes after the attack, Cecilio arrived in Bocay, bruised and trembling, his hand bleeding. He told the townspeople gathered at the foot of the trail that the Contras had ambushed the crew.

Ministry of Interior troops departed immediately, arriving at the clearing less than half an hour after the ambush. They skirted the clearing and "secured the heights," spreading out along the ridge in an attempt to flush the Contras into the open.

The mayor, two nurses from the military hospital, and a few townspeople arrived at the site, spying the three bodies. Pablo ran toward the first and stopped short, sickened and overwhelmed. Ben lay facedown in a shallow hole, a few feet away from a log, the back of his skull open and hollow. His left forearm had taken a bullet. His face was covered with tiny pockmarks.

Sergio and Pablo lay dead in the river. The mason was hit below the ear. Pablo was riddled by grenade fragments, shot in the legs, and stabbed in the chest.

Afraid the Contras had mined the bodies, Pablo gingerly tied a cord to Ben's belt and tugged at it, dragging the body along the ground for a few feet. Some of the townspeople surrounded Ben, gazing sadly at him. "Pobre gringo, pobrecito gringuito" (poor gringo, poor little gringo), they said, lifting his body onto a stretcher. Sergio and Pablo were placed in hammocks dangling from long poles. The men shouldered the hammocks and cautiously descended the mountain.

In Bocay, the small crowd at the foot of the trail had grown. When the bodies arrived, two sallow peasant women collapsed in hysterical sobs when they glimpsed the faces of their dead husbands. The villagers carried the three to the field hospital. The only medic there, twenty-four-year-old Dr. Miguel Garcia, had just graduated, with only one week of forensic training. He had been in Bocay only a few weeks. After examining Ben's body, he reported that he died as a result of the bullet wound to the head.

Unsure of how to prepare bodies for burial, the doctor bathed and redressed the two Nicaraguans in uniforms. He removed Ben's clothes, washed his body, redressed him in a pair of blue pants and a blue shirt, then sewed the back of his head together.

Later that morning, the mule arrived in Bocay by itself, still loaded with cement.

The daily public transport truck from Jinotega rumbled into the Bocay plaza at 3:00 P.M. Gary and Laurie were hot, tired, and thirsty. Gary quickly learned from a woman sitting on a porch stoop that a foreigner had just been killed by the Contras, and his body was at the military hospital. His mind reeled, realizing the political impact the death of a foreigner had in Nicaragua. Gary knew that the killing had to be carefully documented. He grabbed his camera, tape recorder, and notebook and, with Laurie, ran to the military hospital to see Ben's body. A group of townspeople surrounded the army troop transport truck that held three corpses. Next to the two Nicaraguans lay Ben Linder, the engineer Gary had met once in El Cuá. His bare white feet protruded out of his pants at an odd angle. His body was clean, but bruiselike marks covered his face. An Ace bandage swathed his head. His body had been prepared for burial Nicaraguan-style, with cotton stuffed in the nostrils and ears.

As Gary stared, aghast, the truck driver turned on the ignition, so he jumped into the truck bed next to the bodies, pulling Laurie up beside him as the truck drove off. As the bodies of the two Nicaraguans were delivered to a black-plastic house at the refugee settlement, someone turned Gary's attention to Cecilio, a survivor of the attack. Gary convinced Cecilio to jump into the truck bed with them, to interview him. The vehicle zoomed to a clearing where a Hind helicopter vibrated like a giant trembling wasp, rotor blades whirling, sending up clouds of dust, tall jungle grasses bowing before it in rhythmic waves. Gary shouted questions at Cecilio over the noise.

In the meantime, soldiers loaded Ben's body onto the aircraft. A nervous young recruit begged Gary and Laurie to get into the helicopter. Gary looked in vain for officials at the airstrip but quickly realized that no one from the Sandinista government or army wanted to be seen arriving with an American body in their possession.

Gary and Laurie found themselves inside, seated on a bench facing a line of porthole windows. They sat across from Ben's body, which lay on a homemade stretcher, pitching, rolling, and shifting as the helicopter lifted. They rose vertically over the village, shuddering violently, flying southward over jungles and mountains. The tail gunner swiveled his machine gun, pointing the muzzle out an open porthole.

In Bocay, the mayor radioed Captain Miguelito in El Cuá, informing him of Ben's death, and told him that the army was sending the body back in a helicopter. He asked if Mira could accompany her colleague's body. Miguelito agreed, and sent Juan Tercero to find Mira.

When the aircraft landed in El Cuá, Gary watched Mira climb into the helicopter. She was dressed in camouflage and carried a military backpack, gunbelt, chest harness bulging with ammunition, and an AK-47. "She was unemotional—holding it all in," said Gary. Mira quickly glanced at her friend's body, then looked away without acknowledging Gary and Laurie. She clutched her rifle and stared out the door as the landscape beneath them whirled by at dizzying speed.

Witness for Peace volunteers were forbidden to ride in military transportation. Gary didn't know where the helicopter was headed. He pictured it landing in Managua, in front of the country's main hotel, the Intercontinental. He imagined the American journalists, flashbulbs popping, network cameras rolling, as Ben's body was unloaded, followed by Mira in fatigues with her gun, and the two Witness for Peace volunteers. That would be a nightmare, thought Gary. Perhaps, when they landed, it would be better if Mira left her rifle and military gear inside the aircraft. But being male, Gary didn't think it was his position to ask her, so above the noise of the rotor blades, Gary asked Laurie to say something. She asked Mira to leave her military gear inside the helicopter because of the journalists.

"Mira snarled at us," said Gary. "She said, 'Hey, look, I'm wearing this stuff because this is a revolution. People are out to kill me, and I have to protect myself. There's nothing to lie about. This is what I'm doing, and I'm fighting for what I believe in.'"

Gary thought, she's right.

The helicopter, however, did not land in Managua. It touched down in Apanas, a military hospital outside Jinotega. There, Dr. Francisco Balladares, a forensic specialist with three years' experience in war zones, performed an autopsy.

At the hospital, Mira telephoned the Casa de Gobierno in Matagalpa to relate the death as she heard it from Gary. A government official asked her to deny that Ben was carrying a gun when he was killed. Mira didn't want to lie, but she also didn't want to violate specific instructions from the Sandinista government. She decided to avoid the question when asked.

Back at the Casa de Gobierno, Charlie could not locate Ben's parents' phone number. He called Rebecca in Managua. When she heard the news, Rebecca listened to the words, but the reality didn't sink in until she hung up. She burst into tears as she stumbled out of INE. Rebecca drove to TELCOR, where she got in line for the long distance phones, tears running down her face as Nicaraguans glanced at her sympathetically. When she finally called the Linders, no one was home. Rebecca called her mother to have friends at TecNica inform the Linders. When she returned to her office, she called the gringo club members and in a quivering voice told them what she knew.

In El Cuá, Casilda was cooking a late lunch when a teenager from Bocay poked his head through the doorway to announce that her American friend had been killed. Casilda wasn't sure if she believed the boy. She bolted out of the house to the Sandinista Front office, where she found Juan Tercero sitting alone. He raised his head, his red-rimmed eyes meeting hers, and confirmed Ben's death. Casilda staggered outside, to lean against the avocado tree in front of the health center. "I cried because I felt like he was my brother, because he came to my house, because we shared so many things, so many difficulties, so many hardships, so much sadness—the sadness of all our friends who died in this struggle for Nicaragua."

At the hydroplant, Hilda spent that day alone, tending the machines. Late that night, Oscar returned home from picking plantains, more silent than usual. He first told Hilda that Ben had suddenly gone to the United States. Later that night, he told her that Ben was killed. "I felt so sad," said Hilda. "I thought it was a dream that he had died. I hoped that maybe it was a lie."

In Managua, around 4:00 P.M., a Nicaraguan press official, told U.S. journalist Jan Howard Melendez that the Contras had killed an American internationalist in Jinotega province. Jan phoned government offices, the Red Cross, and the military hospital outside Jinotega, but she couldn't get any more information.

At 5:00 P.M. the government radio station, La Voz de Nicaragua, interrupted its programming with a government communiqué read by announcer Luis Cabrera, stating that the Contras had killed an American for the first time. International journalists in Managua scrambled to file the story to the United States.

Ana Brooks was listening to La Voz when she heard the announcement. She collapsed into a chair on the patio, buried her head in her hands, and sobbed. Rodolfo, just back from work, shook his head, poured himself a tumbler of rum, and laid his hand softly on Ana's shoulder. "My heart is heavy for Benjamin," she told her husband, "but surely his death is a great example."

On the other side of Managua, Sonia was unpacking a suitcase in the bedroom of her new house when she thought she heard Ben's name on TV. She walked into the living room and asked her friends what happened. They told her the Contras had just assassinated an American. "'No, no, no, that can't be,' I said. But then I called the Nicaraguan news agency and they confirmed it, and I threw myself on the bed and cried and cried."

Rebecca drove to the CISAS office, where shocked Americans began gathering, aghast at the news, uncertain about the consequences. Not knowing what else to do, they started planning a demonstration in front of the U.S. Embassy.

Back in Oregon, David and Elisabeth Linder were vacationing in a small town when Miriam was able to track them down. They braced themselves for bad news, but they never expected to hear that Ben was dead. Miriam told them to stay where they were, and a friend would pick them up. But David and Elisabeth went to a gas station, filled up the tank, called their daughter from a pay phone, and drove home to make arrangements to fly to Nicaragua.

In Italy, one of Don's friends spotted the story of Ben's death at a newspaper stand. Plastered on every front page was the story that U.S.-backed Contras had killed an American. He told Don the news. "I was ... stunned, just stunned ... not surprised," said Don. "After I left El Cuá, I found myself thinking a lot about the people on the project, and worrying about them. And I already knew that if anything happened to Ben or Mira, it would be on the front page of the newspaper. So when the guy brought the newspaper in, all I wanted to know was ... which one was it? I knew the rest of the story."

Alison received a phone call from Miriam, asking her to fly down to Nicaragua with the family. She sat on the couch, paralyzed by shock. When she turned on the TV, Ben's death was the lead news story. She got out the shoebox where she had saved the stacks of Ben's letters, handwritten in his cramped, childish scrawl on typing paper, lined notebook paper, government letterhead with Sandinista slogans, torn, wrinkled scraps that he must have carried in his pocket while exploring streams in the Nicaraguan mountains.

She fingered the one letter that she had never opened, the letter he wrote after the United States invaded Grenada, when he feared that Washington was going to attack Nicaragua. Four years earlier, Ben had written, "Not to be opened unless there is an emergency." Now it was time.

Dearest Alison,

I write this letter hoping that it will never be read. Please read it only when you have heard that there are major military attacks in Nicaragua.

As my life stands, I'm planning to stay if there is an invasion. That was a hard sentence to write and I know it is a hard sentence to read. It is almost impossible to comprehend. But you must try to understand it. Dear Alison, as you know, I can't and won't leave something that is dear to me when I think/hope that I can help. In the history of my life I think that has been a good quality of my existence. I can only hope that in the future I'll look back at my time in Nicaragua and still think the same.

I often wonder why I think the way I do. Some ideas have their roots clearly marked in my environment. Knowing you has left clear, and cherished, imprints in my mind. My parents have also left their marks which I also hold dear. Although my life has gone smoothly I relate to my near history, Elisabeth and David, as well as my far past as a Jew.

When my mother was ten, in 1938, she was forced to leave her parents as ... the Nazi invasion of Czechoslovakia was imminent. She went to Switzerland, then to England, then to Mexico, and finally to the U.S. Her parents only got out because the German soldier that was stationed near their house let them escape. My mother was fortunate; many of her friends were not.

At 18 my father was drafted. Without any notion of what he was doing he ended up as a medic in the winter campaign in Europe. Two weeks later a bullet tore up his left arm.

He always talked of Passover as a time to celebrate. The liberation from the oppressor is a truly wonderful thing. But it is getting near to Hanukkah. In the stores here in Nicaragua people are buying candles, not because they are Jewish, but because they are preparing themselves for a siege on their revolution. I don't think we can count on miracles this time.

And so I plan on staying.

There is a possibility I'll be hurt, even killed. That is our reality that we must recognize. But we must not dwell on that. I have no plans ... [to be] a martyr. I know that isn't my place on this earth.

If I don't come back, don't remember me by this letter, don't remember us by our last kiss in a strange city, don't remember me by photos from a newspaper in a strange country. Remember the first time we saw each other at the University of Washington.... Remember that first blissful, long, wonderful kiss on the 29 of February, 1980. Remember waking up to a kiss.... Remember what we have built together.

Remember, but keep moving forward.

In a letter I wrote we started a walk through the streets of Seattle. That walk will never end. We may feel that at times we are walking alone, without each other, but that is only an illusion. Always I'll be by your side, as you'll be by mine. Whatever happens to either of us, keep walking. Keep your eyes looking forward. Keep your head up; stand tall. Live a wonderful, energetic, exciting life.

I love you dear Alison. I love talking with you. I love reading your letters and I love writing you letters. I love thinking about you. I love lying next to you and feeling your body pressed next to mine, breathing the same air as we just lie there. I love hearing about your day and telling you about mine. I love taking care of you and being taken care of by you.

And most of all I love to think that—come what may—these parts of our lives will continue forever more.

Love, Ben

Alison packed a small bag, and boarded a plane for her second trip to Nicaragua.

In Washington, D.C., White House spokesman Marlin Fitzwater issued a statement saying that the U.S. government "regretted Mr. Linder's death," but that Americans who went to Nicaragua "certainly understood that they put themselves in harm's way whenever they're involved in any internal strife in another country."

The night of April 29, over a thousand people held a candlelight vigil in Portland, Oregon. Flags in front of the federal building slumped at half-staff. Across the country, radio talk shows were swamped with callers opposing aid to the Contras. At the University of Washington in Seattle, students protested Reagan's support of the rebels by carrying a mock coffin to the administration building.

In Managua, on the morning of April 30, some 300 demonstrators—foreigners and Nicaraguans—rallied in front of the U.S. embassy to protest Ben's death. Some sobbed and embraced, clutching each other, while others chanted angrily. They displayed posters of juggling clowns and banners calling for peace. Engineer John Kellogg waved a handmade placard:

> Ben Linder: humanitarian, engineer, clowned during children's vaccination campaigns.
> Oliver North: traded weapons with terrorists, used profits from deal to give weapons to other terrorists, destroyed evidence, and a 'national hero.'
> Now, you tell me: who is the hero, and who is the clown?

A spokesperson for the gringo club read the following statement: "Americans would not be intimidated by Ben's death, they would keep working in the country, and they would continue demanding a stop to the war."

Another American, Jean Carroll, led the gathering in a revised version of a Holly Near song:

> One day in Nicaragua
> Benjamin Linder died,
> because he had some dreams
> Reagan's Contras wanted to hide.
> There's talk of National Security,
> they say he wasn't on the right side.
>
> And it could have been me,
> but instead it was you,
> so I'll keep doing the work you were doing

Six members of the gringo club met with U.S. ambassador Harry Bergold to tell him they believed Ben had been targeted for assassination. Bergold said he felt this allegation was "counterintuitive," believing that the Contras would lose Washington's support if they murdered Americans.

In Matagalpa, Ben's casket was carried to the Casa de Gobierno for a wake. The open casket revealed Ben's body from the waist up, his pallid features facing skyward, one arm stuck at an awkward angle. Friends, acquaintances, and even Nicaraguans who had never met Ben attended the wake. Government ministries, officials, and solidarity groups sent huge freestanding wreaths. The room was so crowded with flowers that mourners had to squeeze in a few at a time.

The plane carrying David, Elisabeth, Miriam, John, and Alison Quam landed in Managua in the late afternoon. David, who usually stood so tall, arrived with his wide shoulders stooped, a sad, blank expression on his face. He shuffled down the staircase onto the runway. Elisabeth, her face contorted in pain, followed behind in a daze, while Miriam choked back tears. President Daniel Ortega and his wife, Rosario Murillo, along with Lois Wessel, Maria de Zuniga, and Ana Brooks met them at the airport. As the Linders entered the lobby of Las Mercedes Hotel, they were quickly surrounded by two dozen journalists. One reporter asked why Ben had come to Nicaragua. David explained, "He felt he belonged here. He wanted to help people. He wanted to make a better place for people to live in, and Nicaragua is the place he decided to do that." When the ABC radio reporter asked who killed his son, David said, "Someone who paid someone who paid someone, and so on down the line to the president of the United States." His voice broke, and he wept. The Linder family disappeared to their rooms.

Alberto Fernandez, the U.S. embassy press attaché, appeared moments later. Impatiently brushing aside journalists' questions, he said the embassy was not going to investigate the death because there was so much fighting in the area. When asked why embassy personnel had not even identified the dead man, he said, "The body is being moved around. It's unclear whether it's coming down from Matagalpa, whether it's going to stay there—those kinds of things." Journalists corrected him; the body had been laid out in Matagalpa for the past twenty-four hours. "That's right," he snapped. "Well, this embassy was not informed of the death of Ben Linder by the Sandinista government until yesterday night at around 6:30 P.M. That's all the information I can give you right now, I have other duties I have to do." He pushed through the journalists and scurried off.

At 2:45 P.M., Alison and the Linders arrived in Matagalpa to spend a few minutes alone with Ben's body. Ben's friends lifted the casket and carried it through the streets toward the cemetery. President Ortega and his wife followed, walking arm in arm with David and Elisabeth, who were dazed by the heat, limp with grief. Tom Kruse, his face a pasty white, shouldered the casket for a few blocks. Then President Ortega and his bodyguards stepped in as pallbearers. Oscar walked alone, head down, the brim of his baseball cap covering his face. Performers from the National Circus, sad-faced clowns, their large painted mouths pointing downward, joined the somber march. Sonia, gripping the hand of a Colombian friend, quietly kept in step.

Along the streets of Matagalpa, thousands of Nicaraguans followed the casket. The funeral procession stretched for more than seven blocks. A local woman displayed a handwritten placard: "The American people are not the people of Reagan; They are the people of Benjamín Linder." An elderly, white-haired mourner carried another sign: "Benjamín, your death was not in vain." Kathy McBride, an American religious volunteer, held up a sign in English; "Ben, they can cut all the flowers but they will never stop the spring." Schoolgirls in white blouses and blue skirts chanted Sandinista slogans as the funeral cortege wound its way to the cemetery. Thousands more Nicaraguans lined the narrow streets of paving stones, while others watched from rooftops and balconies.

A group of Nicaraguan women dressed in black handed Elisabeth a long-stemmed agapanthus, a flower of remembrance, the symbol of mothers who have lost sons in the war. A stout matron embraced her, while Elisabeth clasped the large purple blossom, almost half her size, and cried.

The cemetery in Matagalpa spilled down a hillside. At the entrance, the funeral cortege paused. Father Miguel d'Escoto, the Nicaraguan foreign minister, spoke: "In the book of Isaiah—we've come from our mother's womb to be a servant to people, but not just a servant of one people, but alike to all the nations, all the people." Father John Spain, an American priest, addressed the crowd. A group of American Jews from the gringo club read the Mourner's Kaddish in Hebrew.

Ben's father, white hair downy in the wind, face creased with age, solemnity, and pain, spoke in English haltingly: "It is clear that many people here love him, and appreciate what he's done, and for that I'm grateful. My family and I are proud to have him come to rest in your city." Elisabeth stood next to him, trying not to cry, struggling to translate her husband's words into Spanish.

Composed and lucid, John said, "He came here because Nicaragua represents hope. It represents hope for the people of the world. He knew that the suffering of a person knows no boundaries. And that, for him, to give all he had in a country where he was not born, was just the same as giving it to his people. It is because of the hope, because of the example that Nicaragua is to the world, that the government of my country is carrying out a war against you. But this hope is too deep to die with one person, or to die with all of you who have died. This hope lies within all of us. Today all of us take a part of my brother, take a part of his hope, take a part of your hope, to do what we have to until Nicaragua can live in peace."

Alison spoke in a tearful whisper. "Because of the beauty of his life, his commitment to the country of Nicaragua, and to freedom all over the world, his death will not be forgotten."

President Ortega pinned the medal of the Order of Commander José Benito Escobar, the country's highest civilian honor, onto Elisabeth's dress. The decoration had never before been awarded to a foreigner. Ortega turned to face the silent mourners:

"For whom the bells toll," Hemingway wrote, in the midst of the fire that incinerated the Spanish people, and then fascism was imposed on the ashes. But out of the ashes and the fascism, the song and the hopes of the people of Garcia Lorca rose up.

Today we are gathered before Benjamin Linder, a North American citizen who, full of love and happiness, gave his life for the peasants of Nicaragua. He knew the risks of working in Nicaragua, of the danger of going into the mountains, to the communities—to contribute through his knowledge, his dedication, and his example—to improve the living conditions of rural people.

He did not arrive in a flight full of weapons, or with millions of dollars. He arrived in a flight full of dreams, which were born, in his belief that the ethical values of the American people were much greater than the illegal policy of the United States government.

He demonstrated that the North American people are noble, that the North American people are enemies of those who assassinate Nicaraguan children, women, teenagers, and farmers. He demonstrated that the people of Lincoln are enemies of slavery, of terrorism, and are firm defenders of peace among peoples.

He lived and died for the American people and for the Nicaraguan people ... The song of Benjamin Linder—filled with love, peace, and hope—is multiplied by his sacrifice.

What is more powerful than war, than one hundred million dollars, than the threat of invasion? Even more powerful is the strength and love of the people, the example and sacrifice of men like Ben Linder, the smile of children who saw him dressed in his clown's outfit, illuminating the future that together we are building in the new Nicaragua.

What salary did he earn? None, other than the satisfaction of serving and sharing with others like himself. Because he did not live on the CIA payroll, they killed him, along with two Nicaraguan farmers while they were working in the countryside.

For whom do the bells toll here in Nicaragua? For Ambrosio Mogorrón, a 34-year-old Spanish nurse; for Pierre Grujean, a 33-year-old French doctor; for Albert Pflaum, a 32-year-old West German doctor; for Maurice Demierre, a 29-year-old Swiss agronomist; for Paul Dessers, a 39-year-old Belgian civil engineer; for Joel Fieux, a 28-year-old French radio technician; for Bernhard Erick Koberstein, a 30-year-old West German potable water technician; for Yvan Claude Leyvraz, a 32-year-old Swiss construction engineer; and for Benjamin Linder, a 27-year-old American engineer.

For whom do the bells toll here in Nicaragua? For more than a dozen Cuban teachers, technicians, and volunteers murdered over these years.

For whom do the bells toll here in Nicaragua? For the 40,000 victims that six years of United States aggression have produced among the Nicaraguan population.

May the blood of the innocents move the conscience of those who govern the United States, so the bells no longer toll, so the aggression ceases, so that the military maneuvers end, so that dialogue with Nicaragua will be accepted.

No to war! Yes to peace. Benjamin Linder's blood cries out, so that the bells no longer toll in Nicaragua.

The funeral procession climbed the hillside cemetery, then stopped in front of a freshly dug grave, where the coffin was lowered into the ground. David sprinkled a handful of Oregon soil over the casket.

In the Matagalpa cemetery lies a tombstone inscribed with a unicycle, and "Internationalista Benjamin Ernest Linder." Above the unicycle is a circle of juggling balls, a dove taking off in flight, and the words, "La luz que encendió brillará para siempre" (The light he lit will shine forever).

Chapter 24

Finishing Ben's Work

In the days following the funeral, Mira spent a lot of time with Rebecca, talking about Ben's murder. Mira was determined to finish building the weir. Together with Rebecca, they drew up lists of tasks that remained to be done. "My way of keeping myself together was to focus on the work, and be sure that ... specifically, the work that he was doing at the moment would be immediately finished," she said. "It seemed to me that letting the project falter because of the assassinations would be giving the Contras a victory."

Six days after Ben's death, Mira caught a ride to El Cuá. She made the trip to Bocay in a military caravan on May 5, and from there, went directly to the Sandinista army headquarters to request an armed escort for her trip to Los Angeles. "I didn't want to wait until the next day, when word had got around town that I was back. I figured an ambush was more likely once people knew that I was in town," she reasoned.

Accompanied by fifteen soldiers, Mira climbed the hill, wary, nervous, fingering her rifle, while her escort urged her to hike faster. She had a fever, and became winded and faint. Mira was having trouble breathing, the air thick with smoke as farmers burned their fields in preparation for the May planting.

At the ridge crest, the troops fanned out before entering into the gorge, combing the cornfield and the jungle. They hid in the grasses and took firing positions.

Mira and a few of the soldiers cautiously approached the site. "At first glance, it looked like it had been any other construction site; the wooden forms, the half-poured concrete dam, some materials lying around. Then, I started noticing the bullet marks on the rocks, and then one of the soldiers there showed me the place where Ben had died—some of his brains were still lying there."

Mira looked away, trying to focus on what had to get done. She worked fast, measuring the unfinished structure, estimating the amount of cement still needed, marking the water level on rocks upstream so she'd know if the river was rising. She finished quickly, packed up her tools, and headed down the trail as soldiers emerged from the brush, falling in line around her. Mira hiked rapidly downhill, alert, clutching her rifle with the safety released. Her eyes constantly swept the hillside above and the trail below.

She wanted to build the weir quickly but doubted that villagers would be willing to help after the killings. She was wrong. "I tried to find people to go back to work, being very skeptical about it," she said. "Right away I found a young guy who is a mason and several people from the same coop who were willing to go back up with me the next day. This was just incredible for me."

The next day Mira returned to Los Angeles with Enrique, the head of the refugee settlement, along with his ten-year-old son, and a few others from the refugee camp. Before long, Mira's fever worsened. When they returned to Bocay, she was diagnosed with malaria.

Despite this, she returned to the site the next day with Transito, a mason, Enrique, and Oscar. Work progressed rapidly, and in two days they were finished. Enrique scratched a message into the wet cement: "Aquí murió Benjamín Linder, su obra seguirá. Sergio Hernandez, Pablo Rosales, Presente, Presente, Presente" (Here died Benjamin Linder, his work will continue. Sergio Hernández, Pablo Rosales; they are with us).

On the concrete base supporting the water-level meter for readings, Mira added her own message: "Benjamín, te amo" (Ben, I love you).

The next day, they hiked back up to the site to take the first flow readings. Mira was pensive:

> The conflict between my feeling of victory and my sadness was tearing at me. I was swimming around in the pool, trying to swim underwater, carrying great rocks to block the water flow under the weir, laughing at myself as I tried to throw the rocks forward and went moving backwards through the water myself, imagining a conversation with Ben about our trajectories (mine and the rocks), and the forces involved, knowing that I would never have the conversation, knowing that I keep some part of Ben with me, that

they cannot take from me the smile and the knowledge of the appreciation he would have had for the ideas.

The cold water washed my tears away before the others noticed. Oscar and Transito, a young mason who took Sergio's place, crowed with excitement as the rising water reached the O level on the scale at the same moment as the O level on the weir—the method Transito had worked out for measuring had worked. I grinned and splashed with my rocks, anxious and triumphant, feeling incredibly vulnerable there, half-clothed in the pool, barefoot, with my gun out of reach on the dry rocks.

Mira dried off and noted the flow readings in Ben's workbook. She gazed at the weir, knowing that Ben would have been proud of their work.

There it sat, a cubic meter of cement Ben had died for, electricity and drinking water for Bocay, the sheet of water falling through it, glittering in the sun.... No one had known if it would work, no one had made a weir like this before. "Oscar, it works! Oscar, Ben wanted to build a weir like this so much, he wanted to see this...." My words failed, but it didn't matter, Oscar felt the same, understood better than any words ... written all over him, in his brief grasp on my shoulder, in the reflection in his eyes of that sun on the sheet of water, the set of his hips against the weight of his cartridge belt as he turns and goes on up the trail in front of me.

Mira spoke to Fidel Molinaris, a farmer who agreed to take measurements every day. They would have data on the rest of the dry season. Leaving the site, they hiked out of the gorge, turning to look at the dam, its notched wooden panel in place, the spout of water spilling over it and down the rock face. "We've done it," she said to Oscar. But he answered, "No, not yet, we haven't gotten out alive."

Later that night, under the light of a smoky kerosene lantern, Mira sat in the Bocay diner and wrote to the Linder family:

There is a profound change in me and my attitude about my work since Ben was murdered. My greatest weakness here has been my lack of self-confidence, and my unwillingness to make errors. Ben was always delighted upon discovering an error he'd made, because this meant he was learning how to do things better. I agreed intellectually with his philosophy, but never could put it in practice. I continued to feel basically incompetent.

But then suddenly Ben was murdered, gone, taken away from us, and I had to take over his hydro studies. I know little about building weirs or coordinating surveying teams, or arranging military precautions or running construction crews. But I had to do these things and so I have just been doing them. Not well. With many mistakes, socially and technically. Learning as I go along. For the first time in years I am not on my own case about being incompetent. And for the first time since I got to El Cuá, I have a clear vision of the steps in front of us.

Throughout May, June, and July the farmer took daily readings from the weir, carefully recording them in the log book Mira had given him. The rainy season began late that year.

Don flew back from Italy in June and returned to El Cuá, moving into Ben's old room in Cosme's house. Oscar wrote in the plant's logbook, "Hoy vino Don-aldo, nuestro amigo" (Today Donald, our friend, arrived). The machinist would stay until Mira and Clifford felt comfortable taking over the project.

In July Rebecca's supervisor at INE agreed to allow her to work on the Bocay plant part-time. She caught a ride to the town and hiked to Los Angeles with Mira and Clifford. Mira pointed out the places Ben had marked as possible routes for the penstock. Thumbing through Ben's workbook, they realized how much importance he had placed on the local people. "He spent time getting to know the community," Mira recognized. "I have spent time here working … always saying to myself that I'll spend the time hanging out once this work pressure eases off. But Ben knew that the hanging out was as much a part of work as anything else (to say nothing of good for one emotionally). He wasn't tempted to make my technician's error of putting short-term results over making the project truly belong to the community."

After weeks of collecting data, Rebecca analyzed the water flow and realized that there were more than 150 meters of headflow, which was too strong for a cross-flow turbine, and further saw that the project was more complicated than she had initially thought. She decided to leave Managua, move up to El Cuá, and work full-time on the Bocay facility.

On July 7, 1987, what would have been Ben's twenty-eighth birthday, Mira climbed up to Los Angeles with Rebecca and Clifford to take readings from the weir. Every time she returned to the site where Ben was killed, she was filled with outrage.

She wrote her parents:

Standing in the spot, seeing the mountains the Contras had to climb … all to kill Ben, a technician who dared think about San José de Bocay, nestled into the hills here at night, electric lights glowing in the surrounding darkness—standing there I boil with anger. The fuckers, the fuckers. We stand in Fidel Molinaris' corn and beans, planted on the steep slope above the stream (the slope that should never have been cleared, that we'll have to convince him to put trees back on), the morning's rains boiling and frothing in the pool behind the weir, passing through it and on into the muddy rapids below. Fidel Molinaris' log book shows that we finished the weir exactly four days before the waters rose with the first hard rains of the wet season. Four days before we would have lost all dry-season data, four days before the construction would have become impossible, delaying the project a year. Four days before the hurry Ben had, the time pressure he worked under, which led in part to his death, four days before this would have all been for nothing. The water has risen so much, it has washed the rocks around the pool, taking away the blood stains, and the last of his brains, I imagine. The thought of the bits of gray gush and the flies buzzing around on them makes me faint. And outraged. And amazed that I didn't feel faint the day I saw them.

Perhaps it was needing to finish the weir that kept me from feeling faint that day. It kept me going. I am glad. Looking back now, I am happy with my decision to stay here working. I couldn't really have done anything else.

I said something to Donald about his having chosen to come back. 'It wasn't really a choice,' he said. 'What else could I have done?' Being him? Nothing. Nothing at all. There have been no choices for us in this, but I say this to myself and know at the same time that this is not something imposed from outside, either. We have no choice. And we are making our own decisions, as free individuals. Both things are true, completely contradictory, and completely true.

And so Rebecca, Clifford, and I stood in the mud and the beans and the corn, wet with the rain that was being measured below us as it flowed through Ben's weir, having made our decisions, and having no choice at all, angry, sad and elated.

Epilogue

In Managua on May 5, 1987, the Linders held a news conference, announcing the results of Dr. Francisco Balladares's autopsy. According to Ben's father, the findings showed that the Contras executed Ben while he lay on the ground, injured. "Someone, I believe, came up to him, saw him, and instead of taking him prisoner or leaving him alone, killed him."

The autopsy found powder burns around the entry wound to the head. "The powder burns suggest that he was shot at very close range, possibly two feet away or less." David's voice trembled. "What I'm telling you is that they blew his brains out at point-blank range as he lay wounded. Ben and other workers had been there long enough for the Contras to know who they were and what they were doing. This was not a chance encounter. This was murder."

John stood up and spoke firmly: "This is murder. For every crime there is a criminal. In this case, the criminal is the government of the United States. It is the U.S. government that brings Contra leaders to Washington and shows them off while Reagan declares 'I'm a Contra too,' calls them 'freedom fighters' and vows to make the Nicaraguan government 'say "uncle."'"

"The U.S. government is guilty of murder. The Contras who killed Ben were hired guns. The real killers are in Washington, enjoying a pleasant lunch, or perhaps a game of golf, while my brother lies dead at age twenty-seven."

In the northern Nicaraguan mountains, Mapuchin, the leader of the Contra squad that carried out the ambush, turned over the guns, cartridges, and Ben's wallet and camera to his commander, Ráfaga. He received orders to march to Yamales, the Contra base camp in Honduras. There they were first debriefed by an "unnamed source," then interviewed separately by U.S. embassy officials. A few days later, representatives from the Contras' human rights organization and journalists from ABC-TV, the *New York Times*, and the *Los Angeles Times* interviewed the squad.

There were numerous discrepancies between the Contras' version of events and that given by survivors.

Mapuchin and his unit claimed that a local resident, an *oreja* (collaborator), told them a crew of Sandinistas, including a Cuban and another foreigner of undetermined nationality, probably a Spaniard, were building a dam for a power plant to bring light to Bocay. They further declared that they ambushed a ten-man work crew, all uniformed and carrying rifles. In some interviews they denied knowing a foreigner was among the crew. In others, they stated that the foreigner was third in line. They asserted that they called out, "Halt! Surrender!" but the Sandinistas shouted back, "A free land or death" and opened fire first. The Contras said they returned fire, killing five soldiers and wounding four others. After throwing grenades, they checked the bodies, where they picked up two guns, "still hot from firing." They said the other three guns fell in the river.

At the Contra camp, there was a meeting between Contra head commander Enrique Bermúdez, Mapuchin, and English-speaking foreigners whom the Contra unit were led to believe were members of the Linder family.

In Managua, the U.S. embassy never conducted an investigation into the death of Ben Linder. U.S. officials never publicly reported on the ambush, nor did they interview survivors, but several U.S. journalists did, among them Richard Boudreaux from the *Los Angeles Times* and Chris Hedges from the *Dallas Morning News*. When the Linder family carried out a private investigation aided by the Center for Constitutional Rights, the U.S. embassy in Honduras refused to cooperate and obstructed the effort. Embassy officials in Tegucigalpa refused to help the Center's investigators arrange interviews with the Contras responsible for the attack, denied their requests to interview the embassy personnel who had debriefed the Contra squad, and further refused to provide notes from the interviews. When the Linders made a formal request for these materials, the State Department claimed they had been destroyed.

The U.S. Congress held hearings on Ben's death. Representative Connie Mack, a Florida Republican, attacked David and Elisabeth Linder. "I can't understand how you can use the grief I know you feel to politicize this situation, or be used to politicize the situation.... I don't want to be tough on you, but I really believe you're asking for it."

Some observers in the audience gasped and hissed.

Elisabeth Linder said, "That was the most cruel thing you could have said."

Mack continued, "Your son chose to go into an area he knew was dangerous; he was carrying a gun."

Elisabeth responded, "He had a commitment, and that is why he was there—not because it was dangerous. That is unfair."

At the hearings Elliot Abrams, assistant secretary of state for Inter-American affairs, blamed the Nicaraguan government for Ben's death, calling it "a tragedy which need not have occurred," except for the Sandinistas' "practice of permitting and even encouraging Americans ... to travel in combat zones."

"The U.S. government cannot protect U.S. citizens traveling in Nicaragua," Abrams said, and Ben appeared to be "a legitimate target." He refused to explain the guidelines Contras used in choosing targets. Such things, he said, are classified. "They have their own guidelines—an elaborate system and a code of behavior."

For weeks, newspapers across the country analyzed Ben's murder. Right-wing columnist William F. Buckley Jr. demanded to know whether Ben was a Communist, while columnist Richard Cohen called the engineer "a man whose intent was to make life better for Nicaraguan peasants ... a dreamer out to bring a little light to a dark corner of the world." *Washington Post* columnist Mary McGrory commented, "We really cannot spare many more Americans like Ben Linder." *New York Times* columnist Anthony Lewis said support for the Contras was jeopardizing the very soul of America. Representative Peter Kostmeyer, a Democrat from Pennsylvania, called Ben "a national hero, the kind of person of whom our country can be very, very proud."

Former Contra leader Edgar Chamorro, who had been asked to resign from the Contra Directorate by the CIA in 1984 after he criticized the publication of the Contra's "Assassination Manual," issued a statement from Washington: "The Central Intelligence Agency is very much in control of the Contras. The CIA is sending a message to those in the international community who provide political support for Nicaragua that they no longer are safe there. The CIA and the Contras are killing the best, the people who want the best for Nicaragua."

In Washington, D.C., on the sidewalk outside the Contras' main office, someone wrote in paint, *Ben Linder, Presente.*

That summer the Linder family, along with Lois, Tom, Ani, and Rebecca, organized the Ben Linder Peace Tour, which traveled to 220 cities in forty-three states throughout the United States and Canada, raising $250,000 to continue the Cuá/Bocay project. The Linders received thousands of letters of support and sympathy. The number of American internationalists working in Nicaragua increased. In El Cedro cooperative, the Veterans Peace Action Team, a U.S. solidarity group, rebuilt the health clinic.

In Bocay, before dawn on July 16, 1987, the Contras attacked the town. Contra spokesmen in Miami called the attack "a major military victory." They claimed that their troops overran the town and destroyed its military installations, including the dirt airstrip. During eight hours of fighting, the Contras never actually entered Bocay, nor did they destroy the military installations. They killed nine militiamen, three children, and a pregnant eighteen-year-old woman, and injured thirty people, most with shrapnel wounds. Twenty-one Contras died in the attack. On the edge of town, the rebels ransacked the plastic houses in the refugee settlement, looting clothes and household items. They stole 120 head of cattle, the town's milk supply, and twenty mules. Resettlement head Enrique Morales reported that Contras destroyed eleven refugee houses, including his own, and wounded four refugees, including his two youngest children.

On August 7, 1987, the presidents of Costa Rica, El Salvador, Guatemala, Honduras, and Nicaragua signed a regional peace plan in Guatemala City. The agreement, known as Esquipulas II or the Arias Peace Plan (after Costa Rican president Oscar Arias, who designed it), established: a cease-fire timetable for the region's guerrilla wars, an international verification commission for the cease-fires, negotiations with unarmed guerrilla groups, free elections, freedom of the press, and a lifting of the states of emergency in all countries in the region.

On September 10, just a month after the signing of the Arias Peace Plan, President Reagan announced his intention to ask the legislature for an additional $270 million in U.S. aid to the Contras. Some members of Congress, along with the foreign ministers of Costa Rica and El Salvador, sharply criticized Reagan's request, charging that the Contra aid would contradict the letter and spirit of the peace plan. In late September, Congress approved only $3.5 million in "humanitarian" aid for the rebels.

On October 13, Costa Rican president Oscar Arias was awarded the Nobel Peace Prize for his efforts. The following February, in the wake of the Iran-Contra scandal and the Arias Peace Plan, the House defeated Reagan's request for $3.6 million in military aid to the Contras. The vote was seen as the death knell for the Contra war. October 1, 1988, marked the last time Reagan would sign a bill on Contra aid, granting them $27 million in "humanitarian" assistance.

On April 20, 1988, the Linders filed suit in federal district court in Miami against the Contra organizations and their leaders, Enrique Bermúdez, Adolfo Calero, Aristides Sánchez, and Indalecio Rodríguez, charging that the Contras ordered Ben's killing. They maintained that the rebels condoned the practice of killing civilians and executing the wounded. The case sought $50 million in damages for the "wrongful death, battery, torture, and cruel and inhuman treatment of Ben Linder." The Linder family announced that any monies awarded would be used to build schools, hospitals, and hydroelectric plants in Nicaragua. In 1990 the Miami district court dismissed the case on political question grounds, a discretionary doctrine that precludes federal courts from deciding cases that could interfere with foreign policy. But in 1992 the appeals court reversed the ruling, setting a precedent.

The new ruling signified that, for the first time, a U.S. court found that tort suits could be based upon violations of the customary laws of war. According to the circuit court, "Even though a civil war was in progress ... does this immunize the defendants from tort liability for the torture and murder of Linder? We think not." The court case continues.

On February 25, 1990, Sandinista presidential candidate Daniel Ortega lost to Violeta Chamorro. Two days later, the U.S. government lifted the five-year-old economic trade embargo and granted $21 million in emergency aid to the incoming Chamorro administration.

On April 25, 1990, after more than a decade of Sandinista rule, Ortega peacefully turned power over to Chamorro. In the village of San Pedro de Lóvago, Contra leaders relinquished their guns to the new government on June 27, 1990. After more than 40,000 deaths, the eight-year-old war was finally over.

Following Ben's murder, Rebecca moved to San José de Bocay and directed construction of the plant. On April 28, 1994, the seventh anniversary of Ben's death, the hydroplant was completed and provided electricity for the entire community. David and Elisabeth Linder, John, Miriam, and other family members and friends attended the inauguration ceremony.

When the war ended, many ex-Contras settled around Bocay, and the hydroelectric plant became part of the efforts to reconcile the polarized population. The plant's turbine, produced at the shop in El Cuá, was made by two machinists—one a former member of the Contras, the other a former member of the Sandinista army.

Oscar and Hilda still live in the village. The hydroplant is still running. And the lights still shine in El Cuá.

Notes

Prologue

11   funeral procession: Author's notes.

11   "national hero": Peter Kostmeyer (D-PA), House Committee on Foreign Affairs Hearings, Subcommittee on Western Hemisphere Affairs, reported in *Washington Post,* May 14, 1987.

11   martyr of the left: Colman McCarthy, "Politics Versus Peacemakers," *Washington Post,* May 17, 1987.

11   "legitimate target": Elliott Abrams, *Testimony of Elliott Abrams, Assistant Secretary of State for Inter-American Affairs,* House Committee on Foreign Affairs, Subcommittee on Western Hemisphere Affairs, May 13, 1987.

11   "Was he a Communist?": William F. Buckley Jr., *Washington Post,* May 21, 1987.

11   "I'm a Contra too": Speech by President Ronald Reagan given March 14, 1986, as reported in the *San Diego Union,* March 15, 1986.

11   "on the other side": Vice-President George Bush, quoted in *New York Times,* August 1, 1987.

11   "Benjamin Linder was no revolutionary": Comment by Dan Rather, CBS Radio Network, April 30, 1987.

12   "I see the kids": Ben's journal, November 14, 1984.

Chapter 1: Ben Moves to Managua

13   Information on 1983 commencement ceremonies: interviews by author with Beverly Gessel, Director of Office of Public Exercises, University of Washington, Seattle; interviews with Alison Quam, Elisabeth Linder, David Linder, Jim Pittman.

13   "It was the high point": Alison Quam, interview by Larry Boyd, New York, August 20, 1988.

15   "I learned that politics": Ben Linder, interview by *Washington Post* journalist John Lantigua, Managua, March 1987.

15   Trojan nuclear power plant: Protest occurred on August 8, 1977.

15   "I didn't spend five years at the University of Washington": Ben Linder, interview by Scott Harris, WPKN Radio, University of Bridgeport, Conn., December 20, 1984.

15   "You read in the paper about repression in Nicaragua": Ibid.

16   Ben's plane landed . . . in Managua: Author's notes

16   "richness-gone-to-pot": Ben's journal, August 20, 1993.

17   "symbolic act of permanence": Ben's journal, August 15, 1983; Ben's letter to parents, August 16, 1983.

17   no political posters: Ben's journal, August 17, 1983.

18   "People are very friendly": Ben's letter to Alison, September 26, 1983.

18   "So why am I here?" Ben's letter to Alison, August 15, 1983.

18   "Quizás mañana": Ben's letter to Jain Rutherford November 22, 1983.

19   "I've started to eat some meat": Ben's letter to Alison, August 21, 1983.

19   Nicaragua seemed cut off: Author's notes.

20   "Somoza left the country": Ben's "Dear Gang" letter, September 24, 1983.

20   the Contras' first air attack: Registration documents in the plane linked it to U.S. compa-
      nies working with the CIA, which had approved the bombing and supplied the planes.
      Sandinista officials showed Senators William Cohen (R-Maine) and Gary Hart (D-Col-
      orado), who arrived at the Managua airport that day, the pilot's U.S. identification cards,
      and CIA documents which the senators recognized as authentic. Later, Hart admonished
      the Managua CIA station chief for attacking a civilian target and for the incompetent
      manner in which the operation was carried out. Bob Woodward, *Veil: The Secret Wars of
      the CIA 1981–1987*, 271-275. Agustin Fuentes, "Managua Airbase Bombed; Nicaragua
      Protests to the United States," Reuters, September 8, 1983; UPI, September 8, 1983;
      declassified cable from Ambassador Anthony Quainton to Secretary of State George
      Shultz, September 8, 1983. From *Nicaragua: The Making of U.S. Policy, 1978-1990*, National
      Security Archives microfiche collection, edited by Peter Kornbluh.

20   "All of this is very bad": Ben's journal, September 8, 1983.

21   "I've just begun to fight": Ben's journal, September 2, 1983.

21   "This seemed so much more interesting": Quam, interview.

22   Ben fell into a depression: Ben's journal, October 14, 1983.

22   "Sometimes I just feel great going with the flow": Ben's letter to John Linder, September
      7, 1983.

22   "stateside with the folks": Ben's journal, October 13, 1983.

Chapter 2: Clowning in Nicaragua

23   he spotted a patched circus tent: Ben's journal, September 6, 1983.

23   "We thought he was a tourist": Douglas Mejía González, interview by Larry Boyd, Man-
      agua, December 4, 1987.

24   "It was such a Don Quixote": Dave Finnigan, interview by Larry Boyd, Seattle, August
      13, 1988.

24   "Well, if I can't stay as an engineer": Ben's journal, September 4, 1983.

24   Ben headed for Circo Libertad: "We joked he was the number one cause of traffic acci-
      dents in Managua," said Curt Wands in an interview by Bob Malone in Washington,
      D.C., October 1987.

24   "We realized here was a circus artist": Mejía, interview.

24   "Off with the wheel": Ben's journal, September 9, 1983.

25   "Logged too many miles": Ben's journal, September 16, 1983.

25   characterizations of Contras, Sandinistas, bourgeoisie: Ibid.

25   "I accused them of typecasting": Ben's journal, September 21, 1983.

25   "It was a great feeling": Ben's letter to parents, September 24, 1983.

25   "After the show": Salvador Rodríguez, interview by Larry Boyd, December 1, 1987, Man-
      agua.

25   "When Ben showed up": Mejía, interview.

26   "The teachers are these hot Cuban performers": Ben's "Dear Gang" letter, Sept. 24, 1983.

26   "As of tomorrow": Ben's journal, October 21, 1983.

26   Contras increased attacks across the country: After President Reagan signed a CIA covert finding on September 19, 1983, paramilitary actions against Nicaraguan increased.

According to CIA documents, Unilaterally Controlled Latino Assets (UCLAs), specially trained CIA operatives of Hispanic origin, carried out attacks on Puerto Sandino from speedboats launched from a "mothership" anchored in international waters. The operatives were covered by American fighter pilots who fired directly on Nicaraguan positions (*Wall Street Journal*, March 6, 1985; UPI, March 6, 1985).

UCLAs attacked the oil storage facilities at Port Benjamín Zeledón on the Atlantic Coast (*New York Times*, October 13, 1983). Acting on CIA director William Casey's orders to increase economic warfare, two CIA planes attempted to bomb the oil infrastructure at Corinto ("Contras Bomb Corinto," Reuters, September 9, 1983; cable from Quainton to Shultz, October 14, 1983).

27   Contras destroyed customs posts: The Contras destroyed two major border posts on the Pan-American Highway: El Espino in the north with Honduras, and Peñas Blancas in the south with Costa Rica (Jane Bussey, "Anti-Sandinista Rebels Attack Border Post," UPI, September 28, 1983; Stephen Kinzer, "Nicaraguan Rebels Do Damage but Are Halted," *New York Times*, September 28, 1983; Robert McCartney, "Nicaraguans Regain Post near Honduras after 2-Day Battle," *Washington Post*, September 28, 1983).

27   Three thousand guns: *Support for Nicaraguan Democratic Opposition*, November 4, 1983. Declassified cable from Nicaragua: *The Making of U.S. Policy, 1978-1990*, National Security Archives microfiche collection, edited by Peter Kornbluh. "Since the beginning of September, the military struggle inside Nicaragua has entered a new phase. The tempo of the fighting has stepped up following the relative lull during the summer. But of even greater significance, the Contras have clearly reworked their strategy. They have begun targeting in earnest the economic infrastructure, hitting petroleum facilities, power lines, bridges, etc. While they continue to conduct small unit operations and occasionally major assaults along the northern border, they concurrently have been moving units deeper into the interior.

"... The Contras are engaged in a political battle for the hearts and minds of the Nicaraguan people, and for them to succeed, they need to build an infrastructure, particularly in the population centers. It remains to be seen if the new strategy initiated in September will generate the popular support needed to build that infrastructure" (cable from Quainton to Shultz, October 14, 1983). Ibid.

27   Daniel Ortega addressed the nation: "Nicaragua Evacuates Port Raided by Rebels," *New York Times*, October 13, 1983.

27   Americans who supported the Sandinistas: William Branigin, "Americans in Nicaragua Undeterred by Killing," *Washington Post*, May 3, 1987; Joanne Omang, "U.S. Groups Counter Contra Aid with Private 'Quest for Peace,'" *Washington Post*, April 19, 1987. Author's notes.

27   "stronger liberal than radical bent": Ben's journal, August 23, 1983.

28   "He'd say to me, 'Which restaurant'": Dr. Anne Lifflander, interview by Larry Boyd, Managua, 1988.

28   blew up five huge fuel storage tanks: For many years, the Contras were accused of carrying out the attacks, but much later it was revealed that the sabotage team consisted of UCLAs (Unilaterally Controlled Latino Assets, specially trained CIA operatives of His-

panic origin) who were part of an operation directed by CIA director Casey to escalate the level and visibility of paramilitary operations inside Nicaragua. Woodward, Bob. *Veil: The Secret Wars of the CIA 1981-1987*, 281; *Wall Street Journal*, March 6, 1985; *New York Times*, October 13, 1983; Agustin Fuentes, "Firefighters Control Blaze Started by Rebel Attack," Reuters, October 13, 1983; John Lantigua, UPI, October 14, 1983; Robert McCartney, "Exxon Bars Oil Ships to Managua," *Washington Post*, October 15, 1983.

29   Henry Kissinger, leading a commission: Reagan's Bipartisan Commission on Central America's visit to Nicaragua is described by John Lantigua, UPI, October 15, 1983; Reuters, October 15, 1983.

29   "The march was wonderful": Ben's journal, October 21, 1983.

29   Contras swooped down on . . . Pantasma: Robert McCartney, "Guerrillas Devastate Nicaraguan Town," *Washington Post*, October 21, 1983; John Lantigua, "War Becomes Reality to Baseball-Loving Nicaraguans," UPI, October 23, 1983. Author's notes.

30   "He always had little gifts for the kids": Mejía, interview.

30   "There are 23 circuses": Ben Linder, interview by Wally Priestly, Portland Public Cable TV, January 5, 1985.

30   Ben asked him if his clown . . . could perform: Ben made his debut on October 16, 1983.

31   "The kid smiled": Ben's journal, October 17, 1983.

31   "Ben hugged me and said": Mejía, interview.

32   "No hay divisas para narices": Jim Levitt, interview by Larry Boyd, Seattle, August 16, 1988.

32   "I go to school for five years": Ben's letter to parents, October 16, 1983.

Chapter 3: Ben Finds a Place for Himself

33   Invasion set off shock waves: Richard Meislin, "Regional Neighbors Predict Broad Effects from Action," *New York Times*, October 26, 1983; John Lantigua, "Nicaragua Fears Possible Attack," UPI, October 26, 1983; Tim Coone, "Nicaraguans Fear Attack," *Financial Times*, October 27, 1983; "Nicaraguan Rebels Step Up Attacks," Reuters, October 28, 1983; cable from Quainton to Shultz, October 28, 1983; Michael Drudge, "Nicaragua Digs In for Possible U.S. Invasion," UPI, November 15, 1983; "Fearful Nicaraguans Dig Air-Raid Trenches," Reuters, November 17, 1983; Stephen Kinzer, "Nicaraguans Are Drilling to Fight the 'Yankees,'" *New York Times*, November 19, 1983; Agustin Fuentes, "Nicaragua Mobilises Militia Fearing U.S. Invasion Imminent," Reuters, November 20, 1983; "Nicaragua: That Next-in-Line Feeling," *Economist*, November 26, 1983; Anthony Harrup, "Thousands Rehearse Evacuation in Managua Refinery Area," UPI, November 28, 1983.

33   "People don't talk about 'if'": Ben's letter to Jean Myers, November 22, 1983.

33   Overnight, Managua became militarized: Author's notes.

33   "For Ben and me": Lifflander, interview, Managua.

34   joint military maneuvers with . . . Honduras: Reuters, November 17, 1983.

34   Victor Tirado warned: Speech reported by Reuters, November 10, 1983; cable from Quainton to Shultz, November 9, 1983.

34   Miguel d'Escoto addressed the U.N. General Assembly: UPI, November 10, 1983; cable from Quainton to Shultz, November 9, 1983.

34   "To be armed or not armed?": Lifflander, interview, Managua.

34   "INE goes on and on": Ben's journal, November 2, 1983.

34   "Tourist, beach": Ben's letter to parents, September 7, 1983.

34   "The worsening aggression": Ben's letter to parents, October 16, 1983.

35   Ben returned to dig: Ben's journal of late November 1983 deals with digging trenches in detail.

35   "They are all there working": Ben's journal, November 26, 1983.

35   "My hands are blistered": Ben's journal, November 19, 1983.

35   "Guess it pays": Ben's journal, November 23, 1983

36   U.S. embassy in Managua: Author's notes. For years, the embassy had been separated from the Southern Highway by widely spaced iron bars. After the October 1983 suicide car-bombing of the U.S. embassy in Beirut, in which 271 marines died, Washington tightened security at embassies around the world. In Managua, workers erected a ten-foot cement wall, installed concertina wire above the iron bars, constructed a bomb-proof guardhouse at the embassy's main entrance, and erected an obstruction course to prevent car-bombing.

36   letters frequently disappeared: Author's notes.

36   "I almost started to cry": Ben's journal, November 20, 1983.

36   "I talked with Alison at night": Ben's journal, October 31, 1983.

37   he had been given a job: Ben's journal, November 24, 1983.

37   "It's incredible what connections": Ben's journal, August 26, 1983.

37   tacked up postcards: Ben's "Dear Gang" letter, August 14, 1987.

37   "one to the States": Ibid.

37   "This will put me in contact": Ben's "Dear Gang" letter, December 27, 1983.

38   "Larisa and I dreamed of apples": Ben's journal, November 29, 1983.

38   "No church-state separation law": Ben's journal, December 7, 1983.

38   stray bullet: Jaime Merizalde, interview by author, Managua, September 6, 1987.

38   "The circus is a very warm community": Ben's journal, December 8, 1983.

38   "Evening at Circo Infantil": Ben's journal, November 1, 1983.

39   "All I have left . . . is my bell": Ben's "Dear Gang" letter, September 24, 1983.

39   "I thought, who is this professional juggler": Elisabeth Linder, interview by author, Managua, February 15, 1989.

39   "I was numbed by the poverty": David Linder, interview by author, Managua, February 15, 1989.

40   "It was gruesome": Elisabeth Linder, interview, Managua.

40   "Spooky emergency room": Ben's journal, December 23, 1983.

40   "I'm glad the folks are here": Ben's journal, December 25, 1983.

40   "In the States we talk": Ben's "Dear Gang" letter, December 27, 1984.

40   "I think Ben was relieved": Elisabeth Linder, interview, Managua.

41   Ben visited Diana Brooks: Ana Brooks, interview by author, Managua, November 11, 1987.

42   Sandinistas launched their final offensive: Bernard Diederich, *Somoza and the Legacy of U.S. Involvement in Central America*; Ana Brooks, interview by author.

43   "Their house is an amazing jumble of revolutionaries": Ben's journal, October 25, 1983.

43   "It should be interesting": Ben's journal, December 17, 1983.

Chapter 4: Life with the Brooks Family

45   "a strange, rodent-type animal": Ben's "Dear Gang" letter, August 14, 1984.

45   "My New House": Ben's journal, January 2, 1984.

46   "I had just learned the expression": George Moore, interview by author, Managua, October 28, 1987.

46   "He didn't just want to speak Spanish": John Kellogg, interview by author, Managua, September 4, 1987.

46   Ben frequently used body language: Tom Kruse, interview by author, Managua, April 27, 1988; Jeff Hart, interview by author, Managua, August 27, 1987; Barbara Wigginton, interview by author, Managua, August 27, 1987.

46   "He had lots of energy": Ana Brooks, interview by author, November 11, 1987.

46   a small corner park . . . dedicated to Bill Stewart: Author's notes.

47   "I almost got squashed": Fred Bruning, "One American Life: The Killing of Benjamin Ernest Linder," *Newsday Magazine*, December 6, 1987.

47   "Every several weeks": Ben's postcard to Jain Rutherford, March 1984.

47   Ben hopped onto his unicycle: Ben's "Dear Gang" letter, August 14, 1984; Ben's journal, February 14, 1984, February 17, 1984.

48   "Hundreds of kids were chasing him": Dina Redman, interview by author, Managua, September 9, 1987.

48   "Driving around lost": Ben's journal, February 17, 1984.

48   "they don't even have tennis balls": Nancy Levidow, interview by author, San Francisco, March 29, 1988.

49   he had scheduled performances: Ibid.; Celia Contreras, interview by author, Managua, November 4, 1987.

49   "It was a huge cake": Levidow, interview.

49   the Contras escalated attacks: On January 6, 1984, President Reagan authorized the "stepped up intensity" of covert operations in Nicaragua. The decision ratified already ongoing CIA sabotage operations against major Nicaraguan economic installations, including ports, oil pipelines, and fuel storage tanks. Following this decision, CIA attacks on communications towers, arms depots and transmission lines escalated. National Security Archive: *The Iran Contra Affair: The Making of a Scandal, 1983-1988.* The Reagan administration also authorized new options to undermine Nicaragua economically, and isolate it diplomatically. Peter Kornbluh, *The Price of Intervention: Reagan's War Against the Sandinistas,* 95.

49   Mines soon began exploding: In late November 1983, President Reagan approved the mining of Nicaragua's ports. The mines were manufactured in the U.S. and contained up to 300 lbs. of explosives. Bob Woodward, *Veil: The Secret Wars of the CIA.* According to international law, this was an act of war.
      In January 1984 the CIA launched a U.S. helicopter and armed speedboats from a mothership in international waters. Latin American assets (UCLAs) raided and machine-gunned coastal cities, accompanied by American pilots who fired on Nicaraguan positions from armed helicopters. A CIA plane provided reconnaissance guidance for nighttime attacks. The CIA contract agents in "Q" boats mined the shipping channels at El Bluff, a port on the Atlantic coast, and the ports of Corinto and Puerto Sandino, on the Pacific coast. Between January and April, the CIA carried out 19 direct covert operations with agency personnel. *Wall Street Journal,* March 6, 1985; "American Pilots Fired on Nicaragua, Report Says," UPI, March 6, 1985.
      Ex-Contra leader Edgar Chamorro, a former Jesuit priest and a university dean, later

testified before the United Nation's International Court of Justice at the Hague as to how he was first informed of the mining on January 5, 1984. "At 2:00 a.m., the CIA deputy station chief of Tegucigalpa [Honduras], the agent I knew as 'George,' woke me up at my house in Tegucigalpa and handed me a press release in excellent Spanish. I was surprised to read that we—the FDN—[the Contras] were taking credit for having mined several Nicaraguan harbors. 'George' [John Mallett] told me to rush to our clandestine radio station and read this announcement before the Sandinistas broke the news. The truth is that we played no role in the mining of the harbors. But we did as instructed and broadcast the communiqué. . . . Ironically, approx. two months later, after a Soviet ship struck one of the mines, the same agent instructed us to deny that one of 'our' mines had damaged the ship to avoid an international incident."; Reuters, March 29, 1984; "Nicaragua: U.S. Navy Ships Back Rebel Attacks," UPI, January 9, 1984; Reuters, January 10, 1984.

Mining continued throughout February, when Lt. Col. Oliver North developed a plan to destroy a Soviet oil tanker. "While we could probably find a way to overtly stop the tanker from loading/departing, it is our judgement that destroying the vessel and its cargo will be far more effective in accomplishing our overall goal of applying stringent economic pressure. It is entirely likely that once a ship has been sunk no insurers will cover ships calling in Nicaraguan ports." Top secret memorandum from Oliver North and Constantine Menges to Robert C. McFarlane, "Special Activities in Nicaragua," National Security Council, March 2, 1984.

50   mines in the harbors had killed: UPI, March 29, 1984; *Newsweek*, April 16, 1984; Alma Guillermoprieto, "Mines in Main Port Imperil Nicaraguan Economy," *Washington Post*, April 2, 1984.

50   *Wall Street Journal* revealed: *Wall Street Journal*, April 6, 1984; "CIA Reported Directing Mine-laying in Nicaraguan Waters," UPI, April 6, 1984.

50   "If the country whose ports are being mined": Philip Taubman, "Latin Debate Refocused," *New York Times*, April 9, 1984.

50   "We cannot permit": Speech by Jeane Kirkpatrick before the American Bar Association and the American Society of International Law, April 12, 1984 (Kornbluh, *The Price of Intervention*, 231).

50   "Those were homemade mines": President Reagan in interview with Irish television as reported by Helen Thomas in "Reagan Defends Mining of Ports," UPI, May 30, 1984.

50   "Illegal, deceptive, and dumb": *New York Times*, April 11, 1984.

50   "It is an act of war": Philip Taubman, "Mine Fields," *New York Times*, April 15, 1984.

50   House and Senate voted to censure the Reagan administration: The censure occurred on April 10–11, 1984. Kornbluh, *The Price of Intervention*, 52–53; T. R. Reid and Joane Omang, "House Joins Senate to Condemn Participation in Minelaying," *Washington Post*, April 18, 1984; UPI, April 18, 1984; Philip Taubman, "Mine Fields," *New York Times*, April 15, 1984.

50   World leaders condemned the mining: *Newsweek*, April 16, 1984; Philip Taubman, "Mine Fields," *New York Times*, April 15, 1984; Reuters, April 10, 1984.

50   brought suit at the U.N. International Court of Justice: Stuart Taylor Jr., "Nicaragua Takes Case against U.S. to World Court," April 10, 1984; "U.S. to Ignore World Court Ruling," UPI, April 10, 1984.

50   United States . . . would not recognize the court's jurisdiction: Text of Secretary of State Shultz's note to U.N. Secretary General Pérez de Cuellar, April 6, 1984.

On April 10, 1984, the U.S. House of Representatives and Senate passed a resolution deploring the Reagan administration's decision to withdraw U.S. acceptance of compulsory jurisdiction of the International Court of Justice over disputes involving Central America. The document says Congress was concerned about damage this action had done to the position of the United States in the world community as a proponent of international law and the peaceful resolution of conflict.

The document stressed that the United States was instrumental in setting up the United Nations (including the International Court of Justice), had criticized the Soviet Union and other nations for indifference and flagrant disregard of international legal restraints and for lack of support for the International Court of Justice, and had turned to the International Court of Justice when U.S. diplomats were illegally seized in Iran "to bring international pressure and world opinion against violaters of international law."

51   joined the company militia: Luis Mendoza, interview by author, Managua, September 16, 1987.

51   "All INE got to know him": Merizalde, interview.

51   "It is fun to have such an absurd skill": Ben's letter to Alison, June 1, 1984.

51   he joined because he enjoyed the contradiction: Rebecca Leaf, interview by author, Managua, July 24, 1988.

52   Ben . . . planted a garden: Millie Thayer, interview by author, Managua, January 6, 1988; Mendoza, interview.

52   "Whenever the clown appeared": Ana Quirós, interview by author, Managua, October 20, 1987.

52   chachalaca: Bruning, "One American Life."

53   "It's Ben's fault": Ana Brooks, interview by author.

53   "He was trying to be": Levidow, interview.

54   "It is amazing to see the man in robes": Ben's letter to parents, January 9, 1984.

54   "puffy white balls": Ben's journal, January 28, 1984.

54   "I introduced Ben to my husband" Ana Brooks, interview by author.

55   Bill Stewart: Ricardo Gonzales, interview by author, Managua, November 11, 1987; also Diederich, Somoza and the Legacy of U.S. Involvement; Bruning, "One American Life"; Reuters, June 20, 1979; Karen DeYoung, "Somoza Guard Kills American," Washington Post, June 21, 1979.

56   "an act of barbarism": President Jimmy Carter, quoted in Karen DeYoung, "Somoza Guard Kills American," Washington Post, June 21, 1979.

56   Ricardo . . . decided he would take care of the park: Nancy Hanson, interview by author via cassette from Presidio, Tex., November, 1987.

57   "Ben said Ronald Reagan was crazy": Ana Brooks, interview by author.

57   "Over many games of chess": Ben's "Dear Gang" letter, August 14, 1984.

58   "The weather here is getting hot": Ben's postcard to Jain Rutherford, March 1984.

58   "It was a wonderful four days": Ben's letter to parents, April 25, 1984.

59   "the school promoted Zionism": Elisabeth Linder, interview, Managua.

59   "I think Ben actively wondered": Miriam Linder, interview by Larry Boyd, Portland, Oregon, August 9, 1988.

59   "For Ben, it's who he was": Lifflander, interview, Managua.

Chapter 5: El Cuá

61   "Las Campesinas del Cuá": "Cantos de la Lucha Sandinista," Editorial Vanguardia (Man-

agua), 1989, 11.

61   group of women in El Cuá: In 1968 twelve women, wives of Sandinista guerrillas, fled a training camp in the mountains of Zinica when it was discovered by Somoza's National Guard. The Guard "grabbed all the women while they climbing down out of La Lana, and two men, who were accompanying the women, died in combat. All their family members were guerrillas; husbands, fathers, and uncles. The families involved were the Garcias, Hernández, and Guetes. The Guard took the women to the command post in El Cuá, and threw them into jail. They were tortured, and the Guard raped the young ones; Emelina, Arerelia, Julia, Candida. The older ones, like Petrona and Maria Venancia, weren't raped, but were beat every night. Matilde had a miscarriage, seven months pregnant, a boy. She lost the child because the Guard raped and beat her. In spite of all the things the Guard did to them—raped them, hit them—they never told them where the guerrilla camps were. Esteban and Juan Hernández—the same Hernández as the Hernández of the women of El Cuá—were loaded into a helicopter by the Guard, and they threw them out over the hill at Chachagona, near Abisinia, near the road that goes to El Cuá. Since I was free, I worked with a lawyer and because of our pressure the Guard did not kill the women of El Cuá , but relased them after three months. I went to pick up the women. They had 12 children with them, but the Guard had given the children away to families. About five months after the women of El Cuá were captured, I went to look for the children. I recovered three—no more—and we gave 400 córdobas to the families to give back the children. Not all of the children were given away; only the smallest ones were. Two or three died." Benigna Mendiola, interview by author, Managua, March 17, 1993.

62   "I'm musing on graduate school": Ben's letter to Peter Stricker, May 5, 1984.

62   "He is nice enough": Ben's letter to parents, April 28, 1984.

62   "Larisa and Bertil work": Ben's letter to John Linder, September 26, 1984.

63   ride to El Cuá: Author's notes.

64   "It's a war zone": Ben Linder, interview by Larry Boyd, Managua, February 28, 1985.

65   "The history of El Cuá is a sad one": Letter to John Linder, September 26, 1984.

66   "It has a dusty main street": Ben Linder, interview by Harris.

66   "The town is basically one street": Ben's letter to parents, April 25, 1984.

66   "I'm the secret weapon": Ben's letter to parents, April 25, 1984.

66   El Cuá had been carved out of the wilderness: History of El Cuá gathered from author's interview with Ezekiel "Checo" Rivera Hernández, El Cuá, May 18, 1988; Piers Lewis, interview by author, San Francisco, Calif., October 15, 1993.

67   "There was one plantation": Ezekiel "Checo" Rivera, Ibid.

68   "Go to the village": Finnigan, interview.

68   "May in Seattle": Ben's letter to Peter Stricker, May 5, 1984.

68   first rains of the year: According to Nicaraguan journalist Emigdio Suarez, you had to drench yourself in the first rainstorm if you wanted to live another year.

69   "It is amazing to us": Ben Linder, "Bringing Light Where There Was Darkness," *Through Our Eyes: The Bulletin of Committee of U.S. Citizens Living in Nicaragua (CUSCLIN)*, spring 1986.

69   "Draftsman, surveyor": Ben's journal, November 13, 1984.

69   "one of those people": Ben's letter to family, September 28, 1984.

69   Sandino was born in 1895: Diederich, *Somoza and the Legacy of U.S. Involvement*; Neil

Macauley, *The Sandino Affair*.

71   organized the Frente Sandinista: The history of Sandinistas in El Cuá is told in author's interview with Luis Kuán, El Cuá, May 18, 1988.

71   National Guard launched an offensive: Diederich, *Somoza and the Legacy of U.S. Involvement*.

72   "If the Contras attack again": Cosme Castro, interview by author, El Cuá, May 19, 1988.

72   engineers' salaries plummeted: Rebecca Leaf interview, Managua, July 24, 1988.

73   "Engineers down here": Ben's "Dear Gang" letter, August 14, 1984.

73   "I found out why": Ben's journal, August 22, 1983.

73   "You could tell he was thinking": Moore, interview.

73   "The FSLN betrayed its supporters": Ben's letter to parents, January 29, 1985.

73   "Adíos cirquero!": Contreras, interview.

74   "Everybody talked about this little man": Redman, interview.

74   "Ben told me that 90 percent": Jamie Lewontin, interview by author, Managua, April 29, 1988.

74   "When they got there, several soldiers ran up to them": Ben's letter to Alison, June 1, 1984.

74   "The outer perimeter": Ben's letter to parents, June 2, 1984.

Chapter 6: Little Ant, the Clown

75   Contras attacked Ocotal: UPI, June 1, 1984.

75   "Freedom Fighter's Manual": The 16-page manual was published by the CIA around October 1983, and instructed how to do sabotage using "simple household tools." Nicaraguans were advised to neglect equipment maintenance, arrive late for work, and call in threats to employers. The manual recommended wasting energy and water, stealing food, and destroying communications systems, office equipment, typewriters, and books. It included instructions on how to make bombs and Molotov cocktails, and advised young men to become draft evaders.

        The family in Ocotal who found the ragged manual showed it to Peter Olson, a Witness for Peace volunteer, who passed it on to Witness for Peace headquarters in Washington. Robert Parry, "CIA Publishes Nicaragua Sabotage Manual," AP, June 29, 1984; Ed Griffin-Nolan, *Witness for Peace: A Story of Resistance*, 120.

75   "Assassination Manual": The 134-page manual "Psychological Operations in Guerrilla Warfare" was based on a 1968 Vietnam-era army manual and written by a CIA contract agent, "Tayacan" John Kirkpatrick. The manual recommended assassination, kidnapping, blackmail, and mob violence. The recommendations on "selective use of violence" and "neutralizing" government officials explicitly violated a legal ban on CIA involvement in, or encouragement of, assassination. The manual was cleared by officials at CIA headquarters around October 1983. According to Lt. Col. Oliver North, "scores" of copies were "inserted into Nicaragua by balloon and airdrop." (Iran-Contra Chronology, pp. 34-35) Later, when Associated Press reporter Robert Parry disclosed its existence, a major scandal erupted, since assassination is prohibited by presidential order. Joel Brinkly, "Playing by the Wrong Book on Nicaragua," *New York Times*, October 21, 1984; "How to 'Neutralize' the Enemy: A Shocking CIA Primer Jolts the Administration," *Time*, October 29, 1984; "A CIA Bombshell," *Newsweek*, October 29, 1984.

75   "The attacks on the borders": Ben's letter to Alison, June 16, 1984.

76   "The tension grows": Ben's letter to parents, June 17, 1984.

76   "These last months have been very tense": Ben's letter to Alison, June 16, 1984.

76   fifth anniversary of the Sandinista revolution: *Barricada,* July 20, 1984; UPI, July 19, 1984; IPS, July 19, 1984. Author's notes.

76   "The offices are in the only two-story building": Ben's letter to Alison, July 21, 1984.

76   "Amongst the smelly stalls": Ben's letter to parents, July 23, 1984.

77   "And so now I'm the little ant": Ben's "Dear Gang" letter, August 14, 1984.

78   "Alfredo goes off to war": Ben's letter to parents and journal entries about the send-off, August 4, 1984.

78   "looking so young": Ben's "Dear Gang" letter, August 14, 1984.

78   "I went over to see if I could help": Ben's letter to parents, August 4, 1984.

79   "We jump out of buses": Ben's "Dear Gang" letter, August 14, 1984.

79   Tapasle: Robert McCartney, "Nicaraguan Villagers Report Rebels Killed Noncombatants," *Washington Post,* August 7, 1984. One of the first major newspaper articles on Contra atrocities, the attack on Tapasle marked the beginning of a significant debate in the U.S. regarding the Contras' human rights record. Nancy Nusser, "U.S. Backed Rebels Wage War on Private Producers," UPI, September 1, 1984; Reuters, July 31, 1984. Author's notes.

80   Ben met Mira at the diner: Mira Brown, interview by author and Millie Thayer, El Cuá, May 17, 1988.

80   U.S. solidarity groups: Author's notes.

81   TecNica: According to TecNica documents, the average age of their volunteers was thirty-five, and they had an average yearly income of $35,000. TecNica press release, late April, 1987; background on TecNica from David Creighton, interview by author, Berkeley, California, March 15, 1988. Although there are no reliable statistics, it is estimated that more than 100,000 Americans visited Nicaragua during the 1980s, and some 1,500–2,000 lived there. Most of the Americans who went to Nicaragua were motivated by altruism, compassion, and a desire for justice. William Branigin, "Americans in Nicaragua Undeterred by Killing; Linder's Death Spotlights Volunteer Brigade," *Washington Post,* May 3, 1987; Joanne Omang, "U.S. Groups Counter Contra Aid with Private 'Quest for Peace,'" *Washington Post,* April 19, 1987.

81   "If the volunteers didn't have": Shelley Sherman, interview by author, Managua, November 6, 1987.

81   "He explained how things would shut down": Wigginton, interview.

82   "They were so delighted": Creighton, interview.

82   "He called me on the phone": Kellogg, interview.

83   "I'm very sad at the idea": Ben's journal, November 11, 1983.

83   "England would be nice": Ben's letter to Alison, April 6, 1984.

83   "if I saw you in July or August": Ben's letter to Alison, May 1, 1984.

83   "I've thought a lot about what I'm doing": Ben's letter to Alison, October 6, 1984.

84   "on forming our life together" Ben's letter to Peter Stricker, May 5, 1984.

84   "The Sandinistas seem always to have been anti-Semitic": President Reagan's July 20, 1983, speech at a White House public diplomacy forum. Reuters, July 20, 1983.

84   "one of the reasons": Ibid.

84   "The evidence fails to demonstrate": Report by Ambassador Quainton, July 16, 1983 (Kornbluh, *The Price of Intervention,* 174). In response to an inquiry from the State Department on anti-Semitism in Nicaragua, the U.S. Embassy reported that it "has no knowledge of any incidents of terrorist acts against Jewish individuals or institutions in

Nicaragua in the past twelve months. In the four years since the FSLN seized power, several members of the country's small Jewish community have been among those Nicaraguans who have had their properties confiscated by the GRN [Nicaraguan government]. However, there is no evidence that these confiscations resulted from a policy of anti-Semitism, as the great majority of those who lost their properties were Catholics." "Anti-Semitic Incidents" U.S. Embassy in Managua report, July 15, 1983, attained by author; Ilana DeBare, "On Nicaragua's Jews," *New York Times*, September 13, 1983; Edward Cody, "Managua's Jews Reject Anti-Semitism Charge; Sandinistas, U.S. Embassy Dispute Rabbi's Widely Circulated Report," *Washington Post*, August 29, 1983.

84   "One of the more common lies": Ben's letter to Alison, September 12, 1984.

85   "When justice burns within us": Ben's journal, October 5, 1984.

85   "We certainly do not condone": Jeane Kirkpatrick, quoted in UPI, September 12, 1984.

85   Boland Amendment: "Iran-Contra Chronology," National Security Archive. *The Making of a Scandal, 1983-1988*, 38; Anne Manuel, "U.S. Congress Strikes Heavy Blow at 'Secret War' in Nicaragua," U.S. Congress, "Public Law 98-473," (Boland Amendment II), Section 8066[A], **October 12, 1984; Inter Press Service** (IPS), October 10, 1984; Reuters, October 10, 1984.

86   performed the play in front of the ... U.S. embassy: CUSCLIN, "All 'Bout Communism: American Foreign Policy as Jeane Would Have It, or For Whom the Big Stick Clubs," *Through Our Eyes: The Bulletin of Committee of U.S. Citizens Living in Nicaragua* (CUSCLIN), November 1984.

86   campaigning began in Nicaragua: Author's notes.

87   "I asked around among the conservatives": Ben's journal, November 1984.

87   Arturo Cruz Sr. . . . . withdrew from the ballot: On July 2, 1984, Lt. Col. Oliver North met with Arturo Cruz Sr. at North's office in Washington. According to North's diary, they discussed the upcoming elections, and North wrote, "erode credibility if they do not." North diary, July 2, 1984.

The *New York Times* reported that CIA agents worked with Arturo Cruz Sr.'s Coordinadora Democrática [Democratic Coordinator] coalition during negotiations with the Sandinistas over electoral laws "to ensure that [the Sandinistas] would object to any potential agreement for his participation in the election." One U.S. official said, "The administration never contemplated letting Cruz stay in the race . . . because then the Sandinistas could justifiably claim that the elections were legitimate, making it much harder for the U.S. to oppose the Nicaraguan government." *New York Times*, October 21, 1994; Holly Sklar, *Washington's War on Nicaragua*, 193.

Years later, in an interview with the *New York Times*, Cruz stated that pulling out of the 1984 elections "was a fundamental error," and that he believed that the Coordinadora coalition (who nominated him) never had any intention of going through with the election and only sought to embarrass the Sandinistas by withdrawing him at the last minute. Cruz said he received a $6,000 salary by the CIA for a twenty-six-month period. Stephen Kinzer, "Ex-Contra Looks Back, Finding Much to Regret," *New York Times*, January 8, 1988.

88   FSLN closed its campaign with an outdoor rally: Jane Bussey, "Ortega Reiterates Warning of U.S. Invasion," UPI, November 2, 1984; Reuters, November 2, 1984; cable from Ambassador Harry Bergold to Secretary of State George Shultz, November 1, 1984.

88   "He touched his eyes": Marlene "Chile" Rivera, interview by author, Managua, September 3, 1987.

89   "The whole process went fairly smooth": Ben's journal, November 1984.

89   votes were counted: Cable from Bergold to Shultz, November 4, 1984; Denis Volman, "Nicaragua Vote Seen as Better Run Than Salvador's," *Christian Science Monitor*, November 5, 1984; UPI, November 5, 1984; Stephen Kinzer, "Sandinistas Hold Their First Elections," *New York Times*, November 5, 1984; Gordon Mott, "Sandinistas Claim Big Election Victory," *New York Times*, November 6, 1984; Robert J. McCartney, "Sandinistas Winning in Nicaragua," *Washington Post*, November 6, 1984; Stephen Kinzer, "Sandinistas Win 63 Percent of Vote in Final Tally," *New York Times*, November 15, 1984; John Oakes, "Fraud in Nicaragua," *New York Times*, November 15, 1984.

        "Generally speaking," states a report from the Latin American Studies Association (LASA), an organization of U.S. professors based in Pittsburgh, Pennsylvania, "the FSLN did little more to take advantage of its incumbency than incumbent parties everywhere (including the United States) routinely do, and considerably less than ruling parties in other Latin American countries traditionally have done." "The Electoral Process in Nicaragua; Domestic and International Influences," LASA report, November 19, 1984.

89   "farce": AP, November 5, 1983.

89   "false, Soviet-style elections": "Nicaragua—the Facts About the Armed Resistance," draft memorandum for Otto Reich, Public Diplomacy Coordinator for Central America and the Caribbean, by Constantine Menges, September 21, 1985.

89   Soviet ship was delivering . . . MiG fighter jets: UPI, November 6, 1984; Reuters, November 6, 1984; Philip Taubman, "U.S. Warns Soviet It Won't Tolerate MiGs in Nicaragua," *New York Times*, November 8, 1984; Stephen Kinzer, "Nicaragua Says No Jet Fighters Are Being Sent," *New York Times*, November 8, 1984; Kornbluh, *The Price of Intervention*, 148, 149; "The Peril of the Missing MiGs," *New York Times*, November 15, 1984; "Newspaper Accuses Reagan of Alarmist Tactics," Reuters, November 15, 1984; "There is no ship of any nationality," cable from Bergold to Shultz, November 7, 1984.

89   Hind helicopters: Stephen Kinzer, "Nicaragua Says Soviet Ship Carried One or Two Military Copters," *New York Times*, November 9, 1984; Richard Halloran, "U.S. Officers Play Down Moves in Nicaragua," *New York Times*, November 10, 1984.

        On December 4, 1984, Oliver North met with retired British special operations major David Walker and discussed how to destroy the helicopters. Walker was hired to conduct sabotage operations inside Nicaragua, including the possible destruction of the Hinds. Walker suggested that the Contras obtain surface-to-air missiles to use against the helicopters. National Security Archive. *The Iran-Contra Affair: The Making of a Scandal, 1983-1988.*

89   American warships were dispatched: On November 11, 1985, the U.S. ecumenical group Witness for Peace began a round-the-clock vigil in the port of Corinto. In a rickety wooden fishing boat, about two dozen Witness for Peace volunteers and several journalists set sail from Corinto to confront a U.S. warship. As the fishing boat approached the warship, the Witness for Peace spokesman addressed it with a megaphone, "Ahoy, U.S. warship.... Leave these waters" The ship moved away from the coast—temporarily. Author's notes.

89   SR-71 reconnaissance planes: Cable from Gibson to Shultz, November 1, 1984. From "Nicaragua: The Making of U.S. Policy, 1978-1990," National Security Archives microfiche collection, edited by Peter Kornbluh. At a dinner party in late 1984 given by *Time* magazine correspondent June Carolyn Erlich, a U.S. embassy official remarked that "it had been a beautifully clear day—the kind of day where you could see the purple humps of

mountains on the other side of Lake Managua—yes, a perfect day for gathering aerial intelligence." Author's notes.

89   "Reagan's re-election is bad news": Ben's letter to Alison, November 7, 1984.

89   fears of a Managua invasion: "Nicaragua Puts Force on Alert for U.S. Invasion," AP, November 13, 1984; Hedrick Smith, "How the Big MiG Scare Flared up and Died," *New York Times*, November 18, 1984. Author's notes.

90   Ortega held a news conference: November 10, 1984. Author's notes.

90   "My dear Alison, I'm not sure how to tell you this": Ben's letter to Alison, November 7, 1984.

Chapter 7: Working in El Cuá

91   "Bertil speaks almost no Spanish": Ben's letter to Alison, September 22, 1984.

91   "After Larisa's [last] trip to El Cuá": Ben's letter to parents, August 30, 1984.

92   "I feel very good here": Ben's letter to family, September 28, 1984.

92   "When I got to El Cuá": Ben's letter to Alison, September 22, 1984.

92   "to find himself in El Cuá" Ben's journal, November 13, 1984.

92   rural health care system: *Recursos de El Cuá-San José de Bocay, Documentos de la Sixta Region* [VI Region Official Documents, Government House], Matagalpa, Nicaragua, 1990, courtesy of Piers Lewis. Dr. José Luis "Don Chepe" Delgado, interview by author, Jinotega, January 7, 1988.

93   Albrecht Pflaum: Reuters, May 1, 1983; Reuters, May 13, 1983; Bernd Debussman, "Border War Brings Danger for Civilians," Reuters, July 20, 1983.

94   "I see the kids": Ben's journal, November 14, 1984.

94   town's only school: In 1990, El Cuá, San José de Bocay, and Bocaycito each had one three-room schoolhouse. There were 46 teachers, only one of whom held a teaching degree. Enrollment for the region was: first grade, 513; second grade, 126; third grade: 81; fourth grade, 34; fifth grade, 16; and sixth grade, 8. *Recursos de El Cuá-San José de Bocay, Documentos de la Sixta Region* [VI Region Official Documents, Government House], Matagalpa, Nicaragua, 1990, courtesy of Piers Lewis.

94   "One day in 1979": Casilda de Rizo Castillo, interview by author, El Cuá, July 5, 1987.

95   "Up at 5:30 a.m.": Ben's letter to Alison, November 14, 1984.

95   "Either welded something to it or drilled a hole": Ben's letter to Alison, September 28, 1984.

96   "I'd be lying if I said": Ben's letter to parents, October 17, 1984.

96   "I drove down the main street": Interview with Ben Linder by Larry Boyd, Managua, February 28, 1985.

96   "She was full of such life and happiness": Ben's journal, November 13, 1984.

97   "I saw that, for the National Guard": Oscar Blandón, interview by author and Larry Boyd, El Cuá, July 5, 1987.

97   "He's very smart": Ben's journal, November 13, 1984.

97   "He never treated us like a *patrón*": Federico Ramos, interview by author and Larry Boyd, El Cuá, January 4, 1988.

98   "For this cash they sold themselves": Ben's letter to Miriam, April 16, 1987.

98   Aldo Rivera Rodríguez: The director's killing is reported in a cable from Bergold to Shultz, October 1, 1984.

98   attacked the government coffee farm of La Sorpresa: At 6 a.m. on November 14, 1984, Salamon Rivera Alvarez, a worker on the La Sorpresa state farm, was collecting wood

when the Contras attacked. He returned fire, then retreated. "Climbing a hill, I could see below a group of 30–40 men who set fire to the hacienda, houses and machinery. When . . . the Contras had left, we found 13 companions, militiamen, dead, their faces unrecognizable, because the Contras had put guns in their faces and shot them off. The women had been sliced in the stomach with bayonets.

"My wife is dead. There she died. Her name was Chamulex Sevilla Portino. We have no children. The first we were going to have; she was four months pregnant. They put a gun in her mouth and shot her, and also used their bayonets on her stomach. Not only to her, but to others as well. A woman working in the childcare center had been shot in the arm, killing the 14-month old child she was holding.

"By 5:00 p.m. everything had ended. We were only gathering the dead. The houses were still burning; only a few houses remained. What they really went after was the warehouse. We lost 190 quintales [19,000 pounds] of basic staples, including corn, beans, rice, oil, soap, salt, and other goods. They burned the two-story coffee processing building with all its machinery. The houses of approximately 700 people were destroyed and new houses were left in ashes." Interview with Salamon Rivera Alvarez by Witness for Peace volunteers Peter Olson and Larry Leaman, Jinotega, December 1, 1984; UPI, November 16, 1984; Anne Marie O'Connor, "Nicaragua Accuses CIA of Attempts to Sabotage Harvest," Reuters, November 17, 1984.

110   attacked . . . employees of . . . TELCOR: "We were going to a state farm in San Juan del Río Coco to harvest coffee. Leaving Telpaneca, a pickup with three people went ahead while the rest of us (26) followed in a Ministry of Industry truck used for carrying sand. After approximately six kilometers, the Contras ambushed us.

"There were some of us that carried guns. . . . In the truck were 11 guns. Those that had guns were around the edge of the truck, on watch. Only two companions shot back. The rest lay down in the truck with the rest of the civilians in the middle. The Contras began to shoot at us from the front with an M-60 machine gun, and then with another one from behind. They also attacked with LAW rocket launchers and hand grenades.

"For about half an hour I was in the truck, during which time the enemy was continuing firing and advancing along the road toward the truck. I was able to return fire. Many of us were already seriously wounded. Those in the back had the lightest wounds, while those on top were perhaps dead. Not all were dead; the majority were injured. When the M-60 had finished a band, I took advantage of the lull to jump out the right side of the truck. By this time I was wounded in both legs. I tried to head off into the mountainside, but the Contras were waiting for me and shot two rounds at me. Three or four bullets hit my right arm, and two more hit my left forearm. I still had one clip full of shots in my gun, so I also shot at them and several of them fell. I also fell there in a ditch.

"After some 15 minutes, two Contras who were collecting their dead came and took my gun. I knew I had to play dead to survive. Another short, fat, dark man came to where I was lying face down and opened my eyes to see if I was alive. It took all my effort not to groan in pain. He left me there. Then I heard the leader ask him if I was dead and he answered, 'Yes, he's dead.'

"Then they began to leave, and I returned to the truck to take out other wounded companions. I grabbed one who had a bullet in the left side of his ribs and dragged him to a ditch about ten meters from the truck. The truck was burning because the Contras

358/The Death of Ben Linder

had punctured the tank and spread diesel on the four tires, setting them and the tank on fire. When I took him out, he was groaning loudly and I told him to be quiet because, if the Contras heard him, they'd come back and kill him. But he couldn't help it, and continued groaning. So I quickly left him to search for help. Down the mountain I could see a little house about two and a half kilometers away.

"When I returned, I saw that the Contras had seen that the one I pulled from the truck was still alive. A Contra with a Chinese AKA machine gun went over and took out his bayonet and stabbed my companion in the chest. Then I left, rolling down the mountain the best I could with all my injuries. In the middle of the road I saw five Contras who were following my bloodstains. They opened fire on me again with an M-60, hitting me in the finger. I hid behind some rocks, and they passed by, shooting at the rocks, but they didn't see me.

"After a while I continued walking. There wasn't even a path, only mountainside and forest. Eventually I arrived at a river, where I rested a while before crossing. On the other side, I came upon a small house. There was a woman there with some children. She was too scared to hide me in the house, and she had a right to be; it was frightening. So I saw a cattle water trough which I lay down in to rest. Again the Contras detected me and opened fired with their M-60 machine gun. Quickly I jumped out the other side behind a rock. Their next round ripped into the middle of the trough, right where I had been lying. There I was lying behind the rocks for about an hour until the owner of the house came back. He took me inside where he helped me and gave me a strong cup of coffee. Then he put me on a horse and took me to Telpaneca where they began to treat my wounds." Interview with Agenor Gonzalez, a seventeen-year-old TELCOR worker from San Fernando, by Witness for Peace volunteers Doug Spence, Larry Leaman, and Jeff Hendrickson conducted at the hospital in La Trinidad, December 6, 1984; see also UPI, November 6, 1984; Robert McCartney, "Rebels, Sandinista Ambushes Viewed as Intensifying War," *Washington Post*, November 6, 1984.

Several TV news shows, including ABC's *Nightline* and the *MacNeil-Lehrer Report*, carried stories about the Contras' killing of civilians and discussed the attacks on the La Sorpresa coffee farm and the TELCOR coffee pickers. Some journalists called the Contras "freedom fighters;" others portrayed them as ruthless killers.

99   "He showed his culture shock": Quam, interview.

99   "we try to do so much with so little": Ben Linder, interview by Harris.

100   "he only found closed doors": Quam, interview.

100   "go crazy over a pot roast": Elisabeth Linder, interview, Managua.

100   "Ben said to me, 'Can't you get your neighborhood' ": Ibid.

101   "culturally strange": Ibid.

101   "I wish you were here": Ben's letter to Alison, January 11, 1985.

101   "The last several days in the States": Ben's "Dear Gang" letter, November 1, 1985.

102   "Feeling the old familiar bumps": Ben's letter to parents, January 29, 1985.

102   "Wellcome back Ben": Ben's letter to parents, January 29, 1985.

102   "Everyone is either picking coffee": Ben's journal, January 31, 1985.

103   "What is it all about?" Ben's journal, January 31, 1985.

103   "He talked about how outsiders": Mira Brown, interview by author and Thayer.

104   "Each success leads to new problems": Ben's journal, February 13, 1985.

104   "What I'd give to stay up here": Ben's letter to Alison, February 12, 1985.

104   two teachers who were killed: Stephen Kinzer, "War's Cost in Nicaragua; Two Mothers Pay in Grief," *New York Times*, January 15, 1984; Ben's letter to Alison, January 26, 1985.

104   piping specialist took one look: Mira Brown, interview by author and Thayer.

105   Aguacate hydroplant: Leaf, interview, Managua.

Chapter 8: A Decision About Alison

107   "I was appalled": Leaf, interview, Managua.

109    $14 million in military aid: Lt. Col. Oliver North's secret channel to supply weapons to the Contras was operating smoothly. In two airlifts, delivered in February and March 1985, the Contras received ammunition, hand grenades, rifles, RPG-7s (rocket-propelled grenades), mortars, C-4 plastic explosives, fuses, and detonators. In April and May, by sealift (which would have probably been unloaded in Honduran ports and trucked to the Contra camps on the Honduran border), more weapons shipments arrived, including SAM-7 surface-to-air rockets and launchers and Claymore land mines. FDN Expenditures and Outlays, April 9, 1985. Cable from Nicaragua: *The Making of U.S. Policy, 1978–1990*, National Security Archives microfiche collection, ed. by Peter Kornbluh.

109   news conference: ABC reporter Sam Donaldson asked the president hard questions at the conference on February 21, 1985, in Washington, D.C.; Reuters, February 21, 1985; UPI, February 21, 1985. Months later, Oliver North drew up a three-phase plan to overthrow the Sandinista government. "U.S. Political/Military Strategy for Nicaragua," July 15, 1985: *The Iran-Contra Scandal: The Declassified History, A National Security Archives Reader*, ed. by Peter Kornbluh and Malcolm Byrne.

109   "the moral equal of our Founding Fathers" speech: Pres. Reagan spoke to the Conservative Political Action Congress on March 1, 1985. Gerald Boyd, "Reagan Terms Nicaraguan Rebels 'Moral Equal of Founding Fathers,'" *New York Times*, March 2, 1985; UPI, March 1, 1985.

109   "brutal dictatorship": National radio address, February 16, 1985. Bernard Weinraub, "President Calls Sandinista Foes Our Brothers," *New York Times*, February 17, 1985; Lou Cannon, "President Denounces Sandinistas; Reagan Urges Funds for 'Freedom Fighters,'" *Washington Post*, February 17, 1985.

109   "turn Central America into a Soviet beachhead of aggression": Ronald Reagan spoke to a group of Central Americans in Washington, D.C. UPI, March 25, 1985; Don Oberdorfer, "Reagan Renews Drive for U.S. Aid to Rebels in Nicaragua," *Washington Post*, March 26, 1985.

109   joint military maneuvers with the Honduran army: UPI, January 10, 1985; "Nicaragua Protests Military Maneuvers," UPI, March 29, 1985; Bill Keller, "U.S. Military Is Termed Prepared for Any Move against Nicaragua," *New York Times*, June 4, 1985; UPI, August 26, 1985.

109   FBI admitting conducting . . . "interviews": "Retreating on Rebel Aid," *Time*, April 29, 1985; David Burnham, "Foes of Reagan Latin Policies Fear They're Under Surveillance," *New York Times*, April 19, 1985. Throughout the years of the Reagan administration, Americans returning from Nicaragua were harassed and intimidated by U.S. government agencies. FBI director William H. Webster admitted that the FBI interviewed 100 Tec-Nica volunteers who returned from Nicaragua, often showing up unannounced at work-

places. High school electronics teacher Deborah Menkart of Washington, D.C., was warned by two FBI agents, "It is in your best interests to talk to us—you are not in trouble yet." *Washington Post*, April 28, 1987. Agents also visited returned TecNica members in Chicago, San Diego, Los Angeles, and Kingston, Wash. *Miami Herald*, April 8, 1987.

110   House of Representatives rejected Reagan's request: Steven Roberts, "House Decisively Defeats All," *New York Times*, April 25, 1985. On June 6, 1985, the Senate approved $38 million in non-lethal aid for the Contras. Helen Dewar and Joanne Omang, "Senate Approves Aid to Nicaraguan Rebels; $38 Million in Nonmilitary Help Voted," *Washington Post*, June 7, 1985.

110   trade embargo against Nicaragua: Doyle McManus, "Reagan Embargo to Halt U.S. Trade with Nicaragua," *Los Angeles Times*, May 1, 1985.

110   "constitute an unusual and extraordinary threat": *Dept. of State Bulletin*, July 1985.

110   "Instead of designing a piece of equipment": Ben Linder, interview by Harris.

111   "Customs said he had to search luggage": Mira Brown's letter to Gordon Scott, May 12, 1986.

111   "John and Miriam": Ben's letter to family, August 30, 1985.

111   "a more grown-up Ben": Ben's letter to parents, October 23, 1985.

112   land mines: At first, many people, including journalists, thought it was safest to follow the tracks of previous vehicles while traveling the northern mountain roads. This myth was debunked when J.B. Pictures photographer Arturo Robles took a photo of Contras planting a land mine in the tire track of a vehicle. Stephen Kinzer, "Land Mines in Nicaragua Cause Rising Casualties," *New York Times*, July 19, 1986; Terri Shaw, "Rights Groups: Contra Mines May be Targeted at Civilians," *Washington Post*, December 21, 1986.

112   "This short little Yank": Don Macleay, interview by Larry Boyd and author, Managua, November 29, 1987.

113   "There is a great job at Yale": Ben's journal, June 17, 1985.

113   "Unfortunately, our interests": Ben's letter to parents, June, 1985.

113   "how much I was willing to give": Ben's journal, June 17, 1985.

114   "I have been doing a lot of soul-searching": letter to parents, June, 1985.

114   "There is a whole world out there": Ben's journal, June 17, 1985.

114   "I want to be reasonably sure": Ben's letter to parents, June, 1985.

114   "Given my plans": Ben's letter to parents, October 23, 1985.

114   "I think that by June '86": letter to parents, August 30, 1985.

115   "Maria tells me to have courage": Ben's journal, June 17, 1985.

115   "Ben was inexhaustible": Mendoza, interview.

115   Contras increased attacks: In a Secret Memorandum, Lt. Col. Oliver North wrote "There are more combatants actively in the field than at any time in the last 12 months.

      "For the first time in the war, the FDN [Contras] succeeded in interdicting the Rama-Managua road, launched simultaneous operations in the Boaco area less than 60 km. from Managua, and inflicted heavy losses on Sandinista troops in the vicinity of Siuna-Bonanza. These operations were conducted in response to guidance that the resistance must cut Sandinista supply lines and reduce the effectiveness of the Sandinista forces on the northern frontier . . . "

      "In short, the political and military situation for the resistance now appears better than at any point in the last 12 months. Plans are underway to transition from current arrangements to a consultative capacity by the CIA for all political matters and intelligence, once

Congressional approval is granted on lifting Section 8066 restrictions. The only portion of current activity which will be sustained as it has since last June, will be the delivery of lethal supplies." Memorandum from Robert C. McFarlane from Oliver L. North, on The Nicaraguan Resistance: Near-Term Outlook, National Security Council Secret Action Memorandum, May 31, 1985, p. 1–3. From *Nicaragua: The Making of U.S. Policy 1978–1990*, National Security Archives microfiche collection, edited by Peter Kornbluh.

On August 2, 1985, the Contras carried out one of the most brutal attacks documented by human rights groups. It was later debated in the U.S. Congress. In an attack straight out of the CIA assassination manual, the Contras attacked the village of Cuapa, 100 miles northeast of Managua, went house to house, gathered residents into the town square, forced them to point out Sandinista leaders and town officials, then marched 11 leaders out of town and executed them. An army truck full of soldiers rushing up the only dirt road to the town was ambushed, and some 32 recruits were killed. John Lantigua, "Contra Attack Said to Kill 51 Nicaraguan Soldiers; Local Officials Describe Assault, Ambush," *Washington Post*, August 8, 1985; Robert McCartney, "Contras Address 'Errors'; Rebel Units Set up to Foster Rights," *Washington Post*, August 23, 1985. Author's notes.

116   attacked La Trinidad: In a July 1985 meeting in Miami with Contra leaders Enrique Bermúdez and Adolfo Calero, Lt. Col. Oliver North emphasized that the Contras should cut highways and move the war into the cities. The La Trinidad attack was planned after that meeting. See "Report of the Congressional Committees Investigation of the Iran-Contra Affairs," p. 60. On the attack, see *Barricada*, August 3, 1985; Vincent Schodolski, "Rebel Raid Kills 18 in Nicaragua," *Chicago Tribune*, August 2, 1985; Oswaldo Bonilla, "U.S.-backed Rebels attack Nicaraguan town," UPI, August 3, 1985; "Traffic Delayed as Contras attack Vital Nicaraguan Highway Bridge," *Los Angeles Times*, August 2, 1985; John Lantigua, "Sandinistas to Mobilize Against Rebels; Copters Take Role in Defense Tactics," *Washington Post*, August 22, 1985.

116   "hoping to living hell": Interview with Don Macleay, November 26, 1987, Managua.

118   "I began to realize": Quam, interview.

118   "engineering in Nicaragua": Ibid.

119   "We decided that although we loved": Ben's letter to family, August 30, 1985.

119   "Back at the Chinese Dive": Ben's journal, September 4, 1985.

119   "Now that I'll be here": letter to parents, August 30, 1985.

Chapter 9: Electricity Comes to El Cuá

121   earthquake . . . rocked Mexico City: *New York Times*, September 26, 1985, October 30, 1985; *Los Angeles Times*, September 22, 1985, September 24, 1985.

121   "solidarity fair": Author's notes.

122   "Do you think" : Interview with Mira Bown, February 6, 1988, Jinotega, Nicaragua.

122   "He told me that he's feeling very sensitive" : Mira Brown's letter to NICAT, October 19, 1985.

123   "Basically, I guess I'm happy": Ben's letter to parents, October 23, 1985.

123   "I am finally going back" : Ben's letter to Anne Lifflander, October 1985.

123   "Gradually, Ben's chair": Creighton, interview.

123   "Has anybody in Nicaragua": Mira Brown, interview by author, Jinotega, February 6,

1988.

124   Jacinta's kidnapping by Tigrillo: Author's interview with Jacinta Cortadero, El Golfo, Nicaragua, May 22, 1988.

124   "Scared isn't the word" : Ben's "Dear Gang" letter, November 1, 1985.

125   "I'm sitting on the stoop": Ben's "Dear Gang" letter, November 1, 1985.

125   "After spending many hours": Ben's letter to Alison, November 3, 1985.

125   took Ben hiking in the jungle: Ben's journal, November 3, 1985.

125   "It was incredibly pretty": Ben's journal, November 3, 1985.

125   "I'm writing from my favorite godforsaken corner": Ben's letter to Peter Stricker, October 30, 1985.

126   puzzling over the vibrating pipe: Interview with Jamie Lewontin, Managua, April 29, 1988.

126   "Hopefully a truck will come by": Ben's letter to Alison, November 3, 1985.

127   "about the time you start shitting your pants": Don Macleay, interview by author via telephone, Managua–Richmond, Va., February 10, 1988.

127   "looked pretty squalid": Macleay, interview, November 29, 1987.

127   "Rigo and I": Don Macleay, interview by author, in cab of Sergio's truck, El Cuá to Jinotega, November 26, 1987.

128   Julia and Rosa Amelia Chavarría, two widowed sisters: Julia and Rosa Amelia Chavarría, interviews by author, El Golfo, January 4, 1988.

128   "I feel like I'm stepping back": Ben Linder, interview by Larry Boyd.

129   "I was extremely outraged": Macleay, interview, 1988.

130   "I didn't like it": Macleay, interview, November 26, 1987.

131   "Everyone was laughing and happy": Jenny Broome, interview by author, Davis, California, March 21, 1988.

132   "I was readjusting levers": Macleay, interview, November 26, 1987.

132   "It was too loud to talk": Broome, interview.

132   "Friday, November 22": Ben's journal, November 22, 1985.

132   "Written by the light": Ben's letter to family, November 22, 1985.

133   "Ben told us he was worried": Broome, interview.

133   "Tonight I went up to the penstock": Ben's journal, November 22, 1985.

133   "Hey *compas*": Macleay, interview, 1988.

133   "One militia man on guard": Ben's journal, November 22, 1985.

134   had poisoned his tortillas: Ramon (Freddy) Cruz, interview by Larry Boyd and author, Managua, January 28, 1988.

134   "That was the most critical day": Rigoberto Gadea, interview by author, Jinotega, February 8, 1988.

134   "crank it up": Macleay, interview, November 26, 1987.

134   "Ben was the color of death": Gadea, interview by author.

135   "At that time it became a question": Macleay, interview, November 26, 1987.

135   "the voltages were strange": Macleay, interview, 1988.

136   "At eleven-thirty": Gadea, interview by author.

136   "And then the lights came on": Macleay, interview, November 26, 1987.

136   "Ben said to me, 'Well, little brother,' " Oscar Blandón, interview by author and Larry Boyd, El Cuá, July 5, 1987.

136   "These are bullets of happiness": Gadea, interview by author.

136   "They arrived running down the hill": Macleay, interview, 1988.

136   "They'd been out there": Macleay, interview, November 26, 1987.

136   "It was very emotional": Macleay, interview, 1988.

136   "Ben said he felt like a father": Gadea, interview by author.

136   "November 25, 11:32—the lights went on in El Cuá": Ben's journal, November 25, 1985.

136   "I've spent many tortured hours": Ben's letter to Alison Quam, November 25, 1985.

136   "This woman was bitching": Macleay, interview, 1988.

136   "I wish you all could see the project": Ben's letter to family, November 25, 1985.

Chapter 10:The Next Goal–San José de Bocay

139   "He looked like a child": Mendoza, interview.

139   "We were the victorious group": Macleay, interview, November 26, 1987.

139   "When the plant went on line": Ibid.

140   "Drinking, tired, and high on it all": Ben's journal, December 6, 1985.

140   "I was amazed at how simple": Macleay, interview, November 26, 1987.

141   "Most development people": Ben's journal, December 10, 1985.

141   "all young and very sharp": Ben's letter to Alison, November 22, 1985.

141   "We realized how ridiculous": Macleay, interview, November 26, 1987.

141   "The idea is not just to put electricity": Ben Linder, "Bringing Light Where There Was Darkness," *Through Our Eyes*, Bulletin of the Committee of U.S. Citizens Living in Nicaragua (CUSCLIN), spring 1986, Managua.

142   Purísima: Ben's journal, December 2, 1985.

142   "Next step—video": Ibid.

143   "tried to play down the danger": Wigginton, interview.

143   "I thought, it would be so easy": Moore, interview.

143   "He put emphasis on the plant": Wigginton, interview.

144   "El Cuá seemed to me": Moore, interview.

144   "When night fell": Hart, interview.

145   "I thought, I would not want to live in the boondocks": Moore, interview.

145   "I'm caught up and keep going": Ben's journal, December 10, 1985.

146   "He said that he would send me a telegram": Macleay, interview, November 26, 1987.

146   "It is the first time such sophisticated equipment": Tracy Wilkinson, "Charge U.S. Is Giving Rebels Sophisticated Missiles," UPI, December 6, 1985.

146   "The United States is stimulating a wave of international terrorism": Ibid.

146   use of ground-to-air missiles: In early May, 1985, Lt. Col Oliver North met with Contra leader Adolfo Calero, and Richard Secord and John Singlaub to discuss new weapons for the Contras. Some two weeks later, Calero bought $5 million worth of new weapons, including surface-to-air missiles. They were delivered to Central America on July 8, 1985. National Security Archive, *The Iran Contra Affair: The Making of a Scandal, 1983–1988.*

146   "fine" and ... "all for it": Tracy Wilkinson, "Charge U.S. Is Giving Rebels," UPI, December 6, 1985.

146   They marched to the U.S. embassy: Ibid.; Matthew Campbell, Reuters, December 7, 1985. Author's notes.

147   FSLN hymn: Carlos Mejía Godoy, "Cantos de la Lucha Sandinista," *Editorial Vanguardia* (Managua), 1989, 36.

148   "I think most people at that demo": Mira's letter to parents, December 7, 1985.

148   "We left Managua": Francisco Chavarría, interview by Larry Boyd, Managua, March 3, 1988.

149   "The whole place fell apart": Francisco Chavarría, interview.

149   "They had never seen a clown": Merizalde, interview.

150   "We all crammed in there": Francisco Chavarría, interview.

151   "Any development project": Mira's letter to Gordon Scott on pivotal role of NICAT, March 13, 1986.

151   "He told me": Leaf, interview, Managua.

152   Reagan asked Congress to authorize $100 million: David Shipler, "Reagan Asks $100 Million for Contras," New York Times, February 26, 1986.

152   Reagan . . . forcefully lobbied: Robert Shogan, "Reagan Effort for Contras Toughest since MX," Los Angeles Times, March 19, 1986.

152   "With the vote on Contra aid": Patrick Buchanan, Opinion Page, Washington Post, March 5, 1986.

152   "ever greater repression": Joanne Omang, "U.S. Accuses Sandinistas of Rights Violations; House Opens Contra Aid Debate Today," Washington Post, March 19, 1986.

152   Reagan pleaded for Contra aid; "must never become a base": Helen Thomas, "Reagan: United States under 'Mortal Threat' Unless Communists Stopped," UPI, March 16, 1986; Thomas, "Reagan Raises Specter of Marxism across Hemisphere," UPI, March 16, 1986; Bernard Weinraub, "Reagan Condemns Nicaragua in Plea for Aid to Rebels," New York Times, March 17, 1986.

153   opposition to Contra aid: In a comprehensive assessment of his experience working with the Contras for Lt. Col. Oliver North, Robert Owen wrote North that the United Nicaragua Opposition (UNO) "is a creation of the USG [U.S. Govt.] to garner support from Congress," and that Adolfo Calero and the FDN continued to dominate the movement. The leadership, he wrote, are "liars, and greed- and power-motivated. They are not the people to rebuild a new Nicaragua." Humanitarian assistance funds, he wrote, were being sold on the black market, then the profits were "divided up between the Honduran military, the suppliers and the FDN." Owen concluded "I care and believe in the boys and girls, men and women who are fighting, bleeding and dying. But the reality as I see it is there are few of the so called leaders of the movement who really care about the boys in the field. This war has become a business to many of them." Cable from TC (Robert Owen) to BG (Oliver North) in The Iran-Contra Scandal: The Declassified History, A National Security Archive Reader, 53–57.

153   "This Contra war": Gerald M. Boyd, "Reagan Defeated in House on Aiding Nicaraguan Rebels; President Turns to the Senate in Fight for Bill," New York Times, March 21, 1986.

153   House of Representatives voted 222–210: Ibid.

153   "He said to me, 'What would you say' ": Mira Brown's journal, March 27, 1986.

154   Sandinista army battalions . . . attacked main Contra training bases: Robert J. McCartney, "U.S. Helicopters Airlift Hondurans; Two Sandinista Prisoners Presented to Reporters," Washington Post, March 27, 1986; "U.S. Moves Hondurans to Border as Combat Said Continuing," Reuters, March 28, 1986; "U.S. Senate Approves Aid for Nicaraguan Contras; Sandinista Raid in Honduras Disputed," Facts on File World News Digest, March 28, 1986; James LeMoyne, "Amid Signs of Battle, Questions about Its Scale in Honduras," New York Times, March 29, 1986; Dan Williams, "U.S. Reportedly Pushed Honduras to

Complain; Ally Wanted to Ignore Incursion but Found It 'Hard to Disagree,' Officials, Envoys There Say," *Los Angeles Times*, March 29, 1986.

155   "I sat sipping grapefruit daquiris": Mira Brown's journal, March 27, 1986.

155   Daniel Ortega's news conference was held March 29, 1986. Author's notes.

155   "Apparently [Ortega] was asked": Mira Brown's journal, March 29, 1986.

155   Senate Contra aid vote of March 27, 1986: Milton Coleman, "Senate Narrowly Approves Modified Contra-Aid Plan; 11 Democrats, 42 Republicans Join to Give Victory to Reagan," *Washington Post*, March 28, 1986.

155   "sure to send": Ibid.

155   "certainly no mandate": Ibid.

155   "We thought Americans were immune from attack": Leaf, interview, Managua.

156   Regine Schmemann: Reuters, July 4, 1985; July 5, 1985.

156   captured twenty-nine Americans: On August 7, 1985, members of the ecumenical group Witness for Peace carried out a "peace vigil" on the San Juan River, which forms the border between Nicaragua and Costa Rica. At the halfway point of their trip, the Americans disembarked and presented Costa Rican border guards with bouquets of flowers. I interviewed the group's director, Ed Griffin-Nolan. "Any trouble?" I asked. "Well," he said, wrinking his forehead, "a little rain." The next morning, two warning shots were fired across the bow of the boat, and the 44 Americans were kidnapped by a group of Contras directed by Edén Pastora, who called the Americans "wolves in sheep's clothing." The Contras ordered the Americans off the boat, and forced them to spend the night at a hut in the jungle. The next day the Americans were released on orders from U.S. embassy personnel in Costa Rica, including the U.S. military advisor, Col. Lent. Author's notes; Reuters, August 10, 1985.

156   Maurice Demierre: Author's notes; Reuters, "Swiss Demonstrate after Death of Aid Worker in Managua," Fribourg, Switzerland, February 21, 1986; Anthony Lewis, "Abroad at Home; Freedom Fighters," *New York Times*, April 10, 1986; Reuters, "Swiss Seek Explanation from U.S. of Contra Attacks," Berne, Switzerland, June 10, 1986.

157   "When he came down to Managua": Leaf, interview, Managua.

157   "with a feeling of life and activity": Ibid.

160   "Much of my life has been up in the air": Ben's letter to parents, May 18, 1986.

Chapter 11: Don Moves to El Cuá

161   "The only thing": Macleay, interview, November 26, 1987.

163   "How often have I written about survival?": Ben's journal, April 28, 1986.

163   nine families . . . formed a cooperative: Community profile from Witness for Peace documents, Witness for Peace office, Managua, 1987.

163   Kaliman . . . opened fire: Cecilio Rosales Seas, interview by author and Larry Boyd, San José de Bocay, July 31, 1987.

164   Children played "bowling": Community profile from Witness for Peace documents.

164   "I have known war since I was fifteen": Interview with Sorida Blandón, *Newsletter of Veterans Peace Action Teams* (Santa Cruz, Calif.), September 1987.

164   "Somehow the corn and beans are planted": Ben's journal, May 1, 1986.

165   "Tomorrow is May Day": Ben's journal, April 30, 1986.

166   "Well, it looks like the Contras": Ben's journal, May 1, 1986.

166   "Always the pit-pit-pat of tortillas": Ben's journal, May 1, 1986.

166   "I reach into my change pocket": Ben's journal, April 28, 1986.

166   "I think I walked into the wrong set": Ibid.

167   "The exploration goes in front": Ben's journal, May 1, 1986.

167   "Family. Part of my not writing earlier": Ben's letter to parents, May 18, 1986.

168   "I got materials": Macleay, interview, November 26, 1987.

168   "It was like a German shepherd": Don Macleay, interview by author, Albany, Calif., May 9, 1990.

170   "Last night I returned to my barrio": Mira's letter to Gordon, April 19, 1986.

170   "While I haven't heard any of this": Mira's letter to Gordon, April 25, 1986.

170   "If they can get a driver": Mira's letter to Gordon, May 12, 1986.

Chapter 12: Mira Visits El Cuá

171   "When the vehicle stops": Mira Brown's journal, May 17, 1988.

171   Contras had blown up two bridges: Mira's journal, May 22, 1986.

171   "We climb and climb": Ibid.

173   "Hilda thought I was crazy": Mira's journal, May 28, 1986.

175   "El Cuá is done": Ben's journal, May 24, 1986.

176   "One of my companions": Dr. Sergio Chavarría interviewed by Witness for Peace volunteer Mary Ramos, November 30, 1986, Matagalpa. Witness for Peace documents, Witness for Peace office, Managua, 1987.

176   "It's about 7:00 a.m.": Mira's journal, May 25, 1986.

176   Ambrosio Mogorrón: *Barricada,* May 27, 1986.

177   "The layers build up slowly": Mira's journal, May 28, 1986.

178   "It was awful": Marlene "Chile" Rivera, interview.

179   "I saw him working here": Sonia Rodríguez, interview by author, Managua, September 1, 1987.

180   "Nothing is certain": Ben's letter to family, May 18, 1986.

180   "I need an unconditional relaxing relationship": Ben's journal, April 28, 1986.

180   "He was shy about making his interests clear": Redman, interview.

181   "He moved heaven and earth": Sonia Rodríguez, interview.

183   "the reality of a Soviet military beachhead": Linda Greenhouse, "House Votes, 221-209, to Aid Rebel Forces in Nicaragua; Major Victory for Reagan," *New York Times,* June 26, 1986.

183   "Let's end the vacillation": Edward Walsh, "House, in Reversal, Backs Reagan Plan for Aid to Contras," *Washington Post,* June 26, 1986.

183   "proxy war": Ibid.

183   "We are being asked to vote": Ibid.

183   "The Contra program has been rotten": Greenhouse, "House Votes," *New York Times,* June 26, 1986.

184    $100 million in military aid: Walsh, "House, in Reversal, Backs Reagan Plan," *Washington Post,* June 26, 1986.

184   "More tax dollars for war": Statement of CUSCLIN, Managua, June 26, 1986.

184   government would no longer tolerate internal groups: Author's notes of Ortega's speech, June 25, 1986, Managua; Nancy Nusser, "Ortega Condemns New Aid to Contras; Nicaraguan President Assails Reagan as 'a New Hitler,' " *Washington Post,* June 26, 1986.

184   U.N. International Court at the Hague ruled: Brian Cathcart, "World Court Rules U.S. Aid to Contras Is Illegal," Reuters, June 27, 1986.

184   *repliegue:* Author's notes; Millie Thayer's letter to friends, June 30, 1985; Mira Brown's letter to friends, June 30, 1986; *Barricada,* June 28, 1986.

185   "unjust, brutal and criminal": Daniel Ortega, speech at *repliegue.* Author's notes, June 27, 1986; Matthew Campbell, "Nicaraguan Leader says Reagan's Friends should Leave," Reuters, June 28, 1986; Tracy Wilkinson, "President Ortega Leads March, Calls Contra Aid a Declaration of War," UPI, June 28, 1986.

185   "50,000 of us": Ben Linder's journal, June 2, 1984.

185   "just for the occasion": Sherman, interview.

186   "4:30 a.m. in a park in Masaya": Mira Brown's letter to friends, June 30, 1986.

186   "This march has been one more repudiation": Daniel Ortega, author's notes, June 28, 1986, Masaya, Nicaragua; Mira Brown's letter to friends, June 30, 1986.

Chapter 13: Classes Begin

187   asked [Hilda] to be a plant operator: Hilda Granados, interview by author, El Cuá, May 20, 1988.

189   "My fear of heights": Macleay, interview, November 29, 1987.

189   Don's classroom: Description from Mira's journal, October 18, 1986.

190   "I was amazed at how low their academic levels were": Macleay, interview, November 26, 1987.

191   "We're from the phone company": Don Macleay, interview by author, Berkeley, Calif., September 20, 1991.

193   "chelones grandotes": Teodoro Arauz, interview by author, El Cuá, May 19, 1988.

195   "He came to my office": Juan Tercero, interview by author, El Cuá, January 7, 1988.

196   "You walked in": Sherman, interview.

196   "He told me he wanted it to be": Sonia Rodríguez, interview.

Chapter 14: The War Closes in on El Cuá

199   "Liberty Weekend": Robert McFadden, "On Day of Record Heat, Liberty Weekend Ends," *New York Times,* July 7, 1986.

199   Nicolas Castilblanco: Castilblanco, interview by Jan Howard-Melendez and author, army tent hospital, San José de Bocay, July 4, 1986.

199   mass burial . . . in San José de Bocay: Author's notes, July 4, 1986.

200   "I was stunned": Lou Dematteis, interview by author, Managua, February 20, 1990.

202   "I am reeling, trying to absorb it": Mira's letter to friends, July 4, 1986.

202   "Five was stay put; don't move": Macleay, interview, November 26, 1987.

203   "Ben and I did a speaking tour": Mira Brown, interview by author and Thayer.

205   "In the evening": Joel Schmidt, interview by Bob Malone, Washington D.C., December 8, 1987.

206   "I heard a big roar": Delgado, interview.

206   Dr. Chepe Luis drinks for two weeks: Tom Carson, "Ben Linder, 1959–1987," *Village Voice,* May 12, 1987.

206   "It was unsettling": Ingrid Bauer, interview by Larry Boyd, Seattle, August 16, 1988.

207   "Sonia was jerking him around": Moore, interview.

207   "He asked what he should do": Lois Wessel, interview by author, Managua, September 12, 1987.

208   "the most important thing": Sonia Rodríguez, interview.

208   "It was painful for him": Redman, interview.

209   "They could easily see that he was unarmed": Carlos Lazo, *Barricada*, July 30, 1986.

209   Five civilians had been killed: Author's notes; Douglas Hamilton, "U.S. Shares Guilt for German's Death in Nicaragua, SPD Says," Reuters, July 29, 1986; "U.S. Contra Aid Denounced in German Hometown of Rebel Victims," Reuters, August 2, 1986.

209   "He came into my office": Mira Brown, interview by author and Thayer.

209   "It was a shock": Macleay, interview, November 29, 1987.

210   El Cuá was defended by the civilian militia: Adolfo Zeledon, interview by author, El Cuá, May 19, 1988; Maximilian Merlo, interview by author, El Cuá, January 4, 1988; Macleay, interview, 1988.

211   Contras had kidnapped eight West German volunteers: According to declassified U.S. embassy cables, Lt. Col. Oliver North communicated with the Contras during the Germans' abduction. After the eight West Germans were released, Secretary of State George Shultz described the aid workers as "military combatants," which provoked an angry response from West German envoy Hans Juergen Wischnewski, who called the accusation outrageous. He said the eight West Germans were "politically engaged idealists" who were neither armed nor in uniform when kidnapped. Shultz later said he misspoke. Stephen Kinzer, "Contras Release 8 West Germans Held for 24 Days," *New York Times*, June 11, 1986; "Shultz Withdraws Charge West German Hostages Were Combatants," Reuters, June 13, 1986. Author's notes.

211   "any foreigner who voluntarily aids": Frank Arana, quoted by Gerald Caplan, "A Uniquely Canadian Dilemma," *Maclean's*, August 25, 1986.

211   Belgian development worker: Author's notes, July, 1986.

212   Swiss and West German governments officially urged: Matthew Campbell, "Contra Kidnap Highlights Plight of Volunteers in Nicaragua," Reuters, June 12, 1986; Caplan, "A Uniquely Canadian Dilemma"; Douglas Hamilton, "U.S. Shares Guilt for German's Death in Nicaragua, SPD Says," Reuters, July 29, 1986

212   "Everyone agreed": Mira Brown, interview by author and Thayer.

212   August 15 relocation order: Julia Preston, "Foreign Volunteers Ordered to Quit Nicaraguan War Zones; Move Follows Contra Attacks on West European Workers," *Washington Post*, September 21, 1986.

213   "I said, How am I going to share a house with you": Sonia Rodríguez, interview.

Chapter 15: Ben Goes to the United States on a Fundraising Tour

216   "He was a man": David Linder, interview, Managua.

216   "When he got out of the car": Jim Levitt, interview by Larry Boyd, Seattle, August 16, 1988.

216   "I felt he'd been hardened": Brian Toal, quoted in Eric Scigliano, "The Last Days of Ben Linder," *Seattle Weekly*, May 4, 1988.

216   spent the summer wiring 140 houses: On August 24, 1986, Oliver North's notebook, in notes about Nicaragua, made references to: "Collect intelligence on airport–refinery–Puerto Sandino–electric system–telephone system."

218 "Someone was yelling 'I'll kill them'": The conflict between the government branches described in an interview with Don Macleay, 1991.

220 "He mentioned people in his letters": Elisabeth Linder, interview, Managua.

221 "This trip, when he said he was 'going home'": David Linder, interview, Managua.

222 "The lawsuit included four other Americans": Reed Brody, interview by Larry Boyd, Managua, January 30, 1988.

222 "I plan to remain in Nicaragua": Ben Linder's deposition. It was notarized in Portland, Oregon, September 7, 1986.

223 "I didn't think we would win": Brody, interview. The case was dismissed by Judge Charles Richey in U.S. District Court in Washington, D.C., on February 6, 1987.

223 "It was hard to change the relationship": Quam, interview.

223 "I've read and reread your letter": Ben's letter to Alison, September 24, 1986.

224 "I actively did not involve myself": David Linder, interview, Managua.

224 "dressed head to toe like a nerd": Creighton, interview.

225 "The trip was very good both work-wise": Ben's journal, December 12, 1986.

Chapter 16: An American Contra is Captured in Nicaragua

227 Eugene Hasenfus: Testimony at the Hasenfus trial from author's notes.

228 "It was the fourth time I had flown": Mira Brown's journal, early October 1986.

229 "I met him the first day I returned": Barbara Francis, *Red, Black . . . and Green Newsletter* (Managua), April/May 1987.

230 "I ran after him": Sonia Rodríguez, interview.

230 "My dearest friend": Ben's letter to Alison Quam, October 29, 1986.

231 "No one wants to play the role of diarrhea": Silvia Valdivia, interview by author, El Cuá, January 5, 1988.

232 "Justo, a student in the class": Mira's journal, October 18, 1986.

233 $100 million began to flow: Danilo Galeano ("Tiro al Blanco"), interview by author, Jinotega, March 12, 1993; Sandra Dibble, "Inside Nicaragua: With the Contras," *Miami Herald*, May 17, 1987; Sam Dillon, *Comandos: The CIA and Nicaragua's Contra Rebels*

234 new graffiti appeared on buildings: Mira's journal, November 17, 1986.

235 "I told him that a mini-plant": Quirós, interview.

235 "He made jokes": Ani Wihbey, interview by author and Larry Boyd, Managua, July 22, 1987.

236 secret trip . . . to Teheran: *Al-Shiraa*, November 3, 1986; Nora Boustany, "Beirut Magazine Says McFarlane Secretly Visited Tehran," *Washington Post*, November 4, 1986.

Chapter 17: First Anniversary of the Plant

237 "Forty trucks, a crane": Mira's journal, November 17, 1986.

239 "It was good to have him": Mira's journal, November 25, 1986.

239 "we found Ben going crazy": Mira Brown, interview by author and Thayer.

239 "I told him I didn't ask": Macleay, interview, November 29, 1987.

240 "Don was so annoyed": Mira Brown, interview by author and Thayer.

240 "We didn't talk our way out of it": Don Macleay, interview by Larry Boyd and author, El Cuá, July 4, 1987.

240 "Don wasn't supposed to speak": Mira Brown, interview by author and Thayer.

241   "Don orchestrated the show": Ben's journal, December 12, 1986.

241   "I told him, 'Mucha mujer'": Oscar Blandón, interview by author and Larry Boyd.

242   "Ben rode his unicycle": Mira Brown, interview by author and Thayer.

242   "It's hard to describe how I feel": Ben's letter to parents, November 25, 1986.

Chapter 18: El Cuá Graduates Four Local Electricians

245   "Your books": Ana Brooks, Interview by Barbara Stahler-Sholk, June 10, 1987.

245   "Culturally, in El Cuá, a person felt isolated": Macleay, interview, July 4, 1987.

246   "It was a relief to have Don": Mira Brown, interview by author and Thayer.

246   "Don moved up to El Cuá": Kruse, interview.

246   "I like working with Don but": Ben's journal, April 28, 1986.

246   "Not that I expected any trouble": Macleay, interview, November 29, 1987.

248   "He'd pick up his briefcase, calculator, and gun": Mira Brown, interview by author and Thayer.

248   "I ask the peasants to repeat themselves": Mira's journal, December 11, 1986.

249   "Oscar seems to be Hilda's owner": Ibid.

249   heard gunshots: Attack on El Cuá described by Wilfredo Montes, interview by author and Larry Boyd, El Cuá, July 5, 1987.

251   "tag-alongs": Macleay, interview, November 29, 1987.

252   "We both felt odd": Mira Brown, interview by author and Thayer.

252   "He told me 'stop supervising, and start working'": Tercero, interview.

252   "When the revolution occurred": Montes, interview.

254   "Later, I went to his store to buy cigarettes": Macleay, interview, November 29, 1987.

255   Doña Chica . . . ironing her shirt: Valdivia, interview.

255   "everyone got their box of materials": Macleay, interview, July 4, 1987.

255   "I walked through four houses": Macleay, interview, November 26, 1987.

256   "I told them, 'I'm going to see if I can put in these lights' ": Justo Pastor Rivera Benavides, interview by author, El Trebol, May 19, 1988.

Chapter 19: Three Americans in One Small Room

259   "It became suffocating": Macleay, interview, November 29, 1987.

259   "and she asked me, 'Why does a generator'": Macleay, interview, 1990.

259   "Ben and Mira were constantly turning to me": Macleay, interview, November 29, 1987.

259   "Ben and Mira resisted that extremely": Macleay, interview, November 26, 1987.

260   "He was a goody-two-shoes": Macleay, interview, November 29, 1987.

262   "[Don] gives silent, grudging answers": Mira's journal, November 25, 1986.

262   "Don hated us being in his house": Mira Brown, interview by author and Thayer.

262   "They just wouldn't shut up": Macleay, interview, November 26, 1987.

262   "Ben didn't really appreciate the fact": Mira Brown, interview by author and Thayer.

262   "I've been sharing a room": Ben's letter to Jain Rutherford, January 2, 1987.

262   "Here I am in El Cuá": Ben's letter to Alison, December 28, 1986.

263   "The table just so": Ben's journal, December 15, 1986.

263   "Corn, beans, coffee, bananas": Ben's letter to Alison, December 28, 1986.

263   "Lived on each side of the holler": Ben's letter to Alison, December 16, 1986.

266   "It was the first time": Leaf, interview, Managua.
266   "La gran fiesta": Ben's journal, January 10, 1987.
267   "Christmas '86 comes and goes": Ibid.
267   "get some other place to live": Macleay, interview, November 26, 1987.
267   mule stepped on a land mine: Witness for Peace documents, Witness for Peace office, Managua, Nicaragua, 1987.
267   New Year's song: Author's notes.
268   "But the light grows slowly": Mira's journal, January 1, 1987.
269   "Not a bad meal": Ben's letter to family, January 4, 1987.
269   "I told him that Ben was a nice person": Rizo Castillo, interview.
270   Cosme's guerrilla camp: Cosme Castro, interview by author; Captain Miguelito Castro, interview; Mendiola, interview.
271   "I'm going to build a room at Don Cosme's house": Ben's journal, January 10, 1987.
271   "He stands my height with my build": Ben's letter to family, January 4, 1987.
271   Ben's room in Cosme's house: Author's notes; Stephen Kinzer, *Blood of Brothers: Life and War in Nicaragua*, 330.
271   "I rolled over": Ben's letter to family, February 21, 1987.
272   "There is peace at certain times": Ben's letter to Miriam Linder, April 16, 1987.
272   "It's 7:30 A.M.": Ben's journal, February 21, 1987.
272   "For some reason we get along": Ben's letter to family, January 4, 1987.

Chapter 20: Working in Bocay

274   Information on San José de Bocay: Author's notes.
275   "Working completely alone is for the birds": Mira's journal, January 15, 1987.
276   "He died over by Kilambé": Mira's journal, January 23, 1987.
276   "He was ignoring a very real problem": Mira's journal, January 24, 1987.
277   "Ben was really like a mule": Tercero, interview.
278   "When we least expected it": Ibid.
278   "Today I had my first real-life, close-up, face-to-face look at a dead person": Mira's journal, January 24, 1987.
279   "He stayed at my place": Kruse, interview.
280   "Ben didn't know a thing about horses": Lillian Hall, interview by author, via cassette from U.S., January 1988.
280   After six years of war: Description of Managua in 1987 from author's notes.
280   "Being here in Managua": Ben's letter to parents, March 6, 1987.
281   "the type of project": Leaf, interview, Managua.
281   American radio reporter: That is, the author.

Chapter 21: Attack on the Hydroplant

283   "He wasn't difficult to spot": Tim Takaro, interview by Larry Boyd, Jinotega, February 6, 1988.
285   "I'm sitting here writing by the flickering light": Ben's letter to Alison, February 27, 1987.
286   "They brought the guy into the Health Center": Mira's journal, March 4, 1987.
287   "only to wound him": Merlo, interview.
287   "I was talking to a friend afterwards": Ben's unmailed letter to parents, April 10, 1987.

288   "There is nothing romantic at all about this war": Mira's letter to family, March 10, 1987.

288   "Greetings from Bocay": Ben's letter to parents, March 14, 1987.

288   "Don was a tough act to follow": Kruse, interview.

289   "Don will leave and I'm slated to take his place": Ben's journal, December 12, 1986.

289   Contra attack on El Cedro: Witness for Peace volunteers Cathy Thomas, Gary Hicks, and Karen King interviewed the cooperative's residents in El Cedro on March 22, 1987. In the attack, the health center was destroyed for the third time. Witness for Peace documents, Witness for Peace office, Managua, 1987.

290   "The attack on El Cedro hit me particularly hard": Ben's unmailed letter to parents, April 10, 1987.

291   Ben ... wandered down to the creek: Ben's letter to Alison, April 4, 1987.

291   "He said that someday these people would arrive": Clifford Brown, interview by author, El Cuá, May 21, 1988.

291   Radio 15 de Septiembre: Author's notes. Radio Liberación, a 50,000-watt radio station featuring Contra propaganda, music, and sports coverage, began broadcasting in January 1987. *Los Angeles Times*, January 19, 1987. The stations were funded by the CIA.

292   "Ben told me that I sang like an angel": Valdivia, interview.

292   "When Don left for good": Broome, interview.

292   "It was happy and sad": Granados, interview.

294   Attack on the plant: Oscar Blandón, interview by author and Larry Boyd; Granados, interview; Mira Brown's letter to Cuá-Bocay Support Group, April 21, 1987; Ben Linder's letter to parents, April 10, 1987.

       Information about the attack has been obtained from declassified top secret CIA documents. After the attack, the Contras informed Contra headquarters in Honduras of their successful raid, and this news was forwarded to Washington D.C.

       "On 24 April 1987, at ???? hours [sic] local, a group of unified Nicaraguan opposition/Nicaraguan democratic force (UNO/FDN) combatants under the command of 'Mapuchin' attacked the El Cuá electric generating plant, one kilometer from El Cuá. The plant, which supplies lights and electricity to El Cuá, was completely destroyed; two Sandinista soldiers, one UNO/FDN combatant, and one U.S. citizen were killed in this attack ...

       "The following items were captured: one recorder, two communication radios, two military ponchos, a large number of photographs which were taken by mostly German workers at the plant, one radio tester, one pair of military boots, seven cassettes containing political propaganda, one Suzuki guitar."

       In an interview, Danilo Galeano said, "I don't know [who attacked the plant at El Cuá]. Maybe it was a special sabotage group that left from one of the bases. Since it was in an area where a lot of troops passed, it could have been any one of those groups."

295   "It was horrible": Granados, interview.

296   "Ben didn't believe me": Oscar Blandón, interview by author and Larry Boyd.

297   "He was thinking about Hilda": Kruse, interview.

Chapter 22: Ben and Mira Build in Bocay

299   Burial of the construction crew: Letter from Ani Wihbey, March 25, 1993.

300   "We couldn't do much to prepare the bodies": Wihbey, interview.

300   "Miguel dead": Ben's unmailed letter to his parents, April 10, 1987.

301   "Truly, she'd like to leave now": Mira Brown, interview by author.

302   "I am the Measles Monster": Valdivia, interview.

303   "The show must go on": Mira Brown, interview by author.

303   met Dr. Anne Lifflander: Anne Lifflander, interview by Larry Boyd, New York, August 24, 1988.

304   "He got defensive": Wessel, interview.

304   interview with John Lantigua: Lantigua's notes from interview with Ben Linder. Also John Lantigua's story "Risking It All in Nicaragua: The Life—and Death—of an American Idealist." *Washington Post Magazine*, May 31, 1987.

305   "I was filthy dirty": Juliet Thompson, interview by author, Matagalpa, December 6, 1987.

305   "When there are others here undressed": Mira's letter to parents, April 9, 1987.

306   "The smell of shit that pervades the town": Mira's journal, November 25, 1986.

307   "looking sheepish": Takaro, interview by Boyd.

308   "Perhaps [war] is the hardest part": Ben's letter to Miriam Linder, April 16, 1987.

309   "We were convinced": Takaro, interview by Boyd.

310   "Ben and I spent yesterday getting the jeep repaired": Mira's letter to parents, April 19, 1987.

310   massive counteroffensive against the Contras: CIA documents. Richard Boudreaux, *Los Angeles Times*, April 26, 1987; June Carolyn Erlick, *Miami Herald*, May 18, 1987.

311   Another dozen children would likely die of waterborne diseases: open letter from Norman Brown quoting Mira Brown, May 1, 1987.

311   "broken people": Enrique Morales Suarez, interview by author, San José de Bocay, July 30, 1987.

312   "If we build this week": Mira's letter to Cua-Bocay Support Group.

Chapter 23: Ambush

315   "To stand with the people" and biblical verse: Griffin-Nolan, *Witness for Peace*.

315   a dozen Contras marched south: CIA documents; U.S. embassy official's debriefing of Contras, Tegucigalpa, Honduras, May 1, 1987; Galeano, interview; Ramon Herrera Palma ("Estrella") , interview by author, San José de Bocay, March 9, 1993; Santiago Giron-Meza ("William"), interview by author, Agua Zarca, Nicaragua, July 26, 1995.

316   Gaunt farmer: Mira Brown spoke to Fidel Molinaris about this. Mira Brown, interview by Barbara Stahler-Sholk, Managua, May 21, 1987.

316   "It is a zone of combat": Alcide, quoted in James LeMoyne, "Contras' Killing of American: Doubt Cast on Rebel Account," *New York Times*, June 16, 1987.

316   Tiro al Blanco: Galeano, interview. Tiro al Blanco ("Bull's-eye") commanded the Juan Castro Castro, a Contra task force of some 1,200 troops.

316   training . . . in North Carolina: Tiro al Blanco studied with Spanish-speaking American instructors who taught military tactics, map theory, and use of artillery and explosives. Galeano, interview.

316   Mapuchin: Galeano, interview; Martin Cruz Huete ("Sommer"), interview by author, Matagalpa, February 23, 1993.

316   William: Giron-Meza, interview.

316   Background on Contras: Affidavits from Contra Human Rights Association, May 1,

1987; CIA documents.

316   a smooth ambush: CIA documents. U.S. embassy officer E. Briggs, stationed in Teguci-
        galpa, Honduras, commented, "an excellent ambush set-up." Herrera, interview; Giron-
        Meza, interview.

316   Ben's early-morning activities: Center for Constitutional Rights, *The Killing of Benjamin Lin-
        der*; Bruning, "One American Life."

317   dropped in at the house of . . . Antonio Chaw: Antonio Chaw, interview by Larry Boyd,
        San José de Bocay, July 23, 1987.

318   First arrivals at the scene: Pablo Arauz, interview by author and Larry Boyd, San José de
        Bocay, August 23, 1987.

319   "Pobre gringo, pobrecito gringuito": Ibid.

319   He removed Ben's clothes: Dr. Miguel Garcia, interview by author, San José de Bocay,
        July 30, 1987.

320   Gary convinced Cecilio to jump into the truck: Gary Hicks, interview by author, Man-
        agua, August 2, 1987.

321   "I cried because I felt like he was my brother": Rizo Castillo, interview.

322   "I felt so sad": Granados, interview.

322   "My heart is heavy for Benjamin": Ana Brooks, interview by Barbara Stahler-Sholk,
        Managua, June 10, 1987.

322   "No, no, no, that can't be": Sonia Rodríguez, interview.

323   "I was . . . stunned, just stunned": Macleay, interview, November 29, 1987.

323   "Not to be opened": Ben's letter sent to Alison Quam on November 21, 1983.

325   "Certainly understood that they put themselves in harm's way": UPI, April 29, 1987.

325   Candlelight vigil in Portland, Oregon: *Oregonian*, April 30, 1987.

325   some 300 demonstrators: Author's notes.

326   "He felt he belonged here; he wanted to help people": David Linder responding to
        author's question, April 30, 1987, Managua. Author's notes.

326   "Someone who paid someone": David Linder to author, April 30, 1987, Managua.
        Author's notes.

326   "The body is being moved around": Alberto Fernandez, April 30, 1987, Managua.
        Author's notes.

327   Ben Linder's funeral: Author's notes.

327   "In the book of Isaiah": Miguel d'Escoto, April 30, 1987, Matagalpa. Author's notes.

327   "It is clear that many people here love him": David Linder, Managua, April 30, 1987.
        Author's notes.

328   "He came here because Nicaragua represents hope": John Linder, April 30, 1987, Mata-
        galpa. Author's notes.

328   "Because of the beauty of his life": Alison Quam, April 30, 1987, Matagalpa. Author's
        notes.

328   "'For whom the bells toll,' Hemingway wrote": Daniel Ortega, April 30, 1987, Matagalpa.
        Author's notes.

Chapter 24: Finishing Ben's Work

331   "My way of keeping myself together": Mira Brown, interview by Stahler-Sholk.

332   "The conflict between": Letter from Mira Brown to the Linder family, May 21, 1987.

333   "There it sat, a cubic meter": Letter from Mira Brown to her family, July 7, 1987.

333   "There is a profound change": Letter from Mira Brown to the Linder family, May 21, 1987.

334   "Hoy vino Donaldo": Plant logbook, June 15, 1987.

334   "He spent time": Letter from Mira Brown to her family, July 7, 1987.

334   "Standing in the spot": Ibid.

Epilogue

337   "Someone, I believe": David Linder, news conference, May 5, 1987, Managua. Author's notes.

337   "This is murder": John Linder, news conference, May 5, 1987, Managua. Author's notes.

337   Contras' actions after the killing; CIA documents; FDN documents and communiqués; Cruz Huete ("Sommer"), interview; Herrera, interview; Galeano, interview; Giron-Meza, interview; correspondence of Marta Patricia Baltodano; *Los Angeles Times; Dallas Morning News; New York Times;* documents from the Center for Constitutional Rights, New York.

338   "Halt! Surrender": Contra affadavits.

338   investigation aided by the Center for Constitutional Rights: Documents from the Center for Constitutional Rights.

339   U.S. Congress held hearings: Testimony from the Subcommittee on Western Hemisphere Affairs Committee on Foreign Affairs, Washington D.C., U.S. House of Representatives, May 13, 1987.

339   whether Ben was a Communist: William F. Buckley Jr., *Washington Post,* May 21, 1987.

339   "a man whose intent was to make life better": Editorial by Richard Cohen, *Washington Post,* May 5, 1987.

339   "We really cannot spare many more Americans like Ben Linder": Mary McGrory, *Washington Post,* April 28, 1987.

339   Anthony Lewis: *New York Times,* May 15, 1987.

339   "a national hero": Peter Kostmeyer, testimony at the Subcommittee on Western Hemisphere Affairs Committee on Foreign Affairs Hearings. *Washington Post,* May 14, 1987.

339   "The Central Intelligence Agency is very much in control": Statement issued in Washington, D.C., by former Contra leader Edgar Chamorro, April 30, 1987.

340   "Ben Linder, Presente": Interview with Bob Malone by author via telephone, Washington, D.C.–Managua, May 10, 1987.

340   Ben Linder Peace Tour: Documents from the Linder family, 1987.

340   Contra attack on San José de Bocay: "Big Raid by Contras Produces Casualties But No Visible Gain," by Stephen Kinzer, *New York Times,* July 1987; Kinzer, *Blood of Brothers.*

340   Arias Peace Plan: *"Esquipulas II" Procedimiento para Establecer la Paz Firme y Duradera en Centroamerica,* Guatemala City, September 7, 1987. Author's notes from Guatemala.

340   additional $270 million in U.S. aid: *New York Times,* September 11, 1987; *Los Angeles Times,* September 12, 1987.

341   $3.5 million in "humanitarian" aid: *Washington Post,* September 24, 1987; *New York Times,* September 24, 1987, September 26, 1987.

341   Nobel Peace Prize: *New York Times,* October 14, 1987.

341   Reagan's request for $3.6 million: Tom Kenworthy, "House Rejects Reagan's Contra-Aid Request, 219–211; President's Central American Policy Suffers a Potentially Fatal Blow,"

Washington Post, February 4, 1988.

341   last time Reagan would sign a bill on Contra aid: Sara Fritz, "Congress Passes Federal Funding with Contra Aid," *Los Angeles Times*, October 1, 1988.

341   Linders filed suit: Spring docket, Center for Constitutional Rights, New York, February 1994.

341   Daniel Ortega lost: February 26, 1990, Managua. Author's notes.

342   war was finally over: Michael Molinski, "Contra Chief Hands in Weapon; Declares End to the War," UPI, June 28, 1990. In the town of San Pedro de Lóvago, Nicaragua, on June 27, 1990, Contra commander in chief Israel Galeano "Franklin" and 200 other Contra leaders handed over their guns to Nicaraguan president Violeta Chamorro, thus signifying the end of the war.

342   made by two machinists: National Union of Farmers and Ranchers (UNAG), *Nicaragua Farmer's View*, June 1994, 12.

Glossary of Organizations and Spanish Terms

Agencia Nueva Nicaragua (ANN): The Sandinista government newswire service.

APSNICA (Architects and Planners in Nicaragua): A U.S. solidarity group that built houses. They, like many solidarity groups, disappeared after the Sandinistas lost the elections in Nicaragua.

brigadista: Volunteer, usually from the city, collaborating with the Sandinista government in health or education.

Casa de Gobierno: Building in Matagalpa where all the government offices were located.

CDS (Comité de Defensa Sandinista): Sandinista Defense Committee.

Centro de Cultura Popular (CCP): People's Culture Center. Sponsored by the government, the Centro offered workshops and supported plays and other arts in poor neighborhoods.

CISAS (Centro de Información de Servicios de Salud): Center for Health Information Services; health training organization begun by an American woman, Maria de Zuniga.

compañero, compañera: Friend, companion, person in solidarity with the revolution.

Coordinadora Democrática (Democratic Coordinator): Coalition of anti-Sandinista political parties that ran Arturo Cruz as their presidential candidate in 1984 elections.

CUSCLIN (Committee of U.S. Citizens Living in Nicaragua): The "gringo club" of Americans who supported the Sandinistas. They met weekly in Managua and sponsored a Thursday-morning demonstration in front of the U.S. embassy.

cususa: A homemade cornmeal liquor.

despedida: Traditional farewell party.

FDN (Frente Democrático Nicaragüense): National Democratic Front; the Contras.

Flor de Caña: Nicaragua's premium brand of rum.

Frente Patriótico de Madres (Patriotic Front of Mothers): A group of pro-Sandinista women whose sons were fighting in the war.

fritanga: Deep-fried foods, including cheese, plantain, and meats, cooked over open fires in the street in the evenings. Served on banana leaves.

FSLN (Frente Sandinista de Liberación Nacional): Sandinista National Liberation Front; the Sandinistas.

gallopinto: Rice and beans fried together; the Nicaraguan national dish.

INE (Instituto Nacional de Energía): National Institute of Energy, the government-owned utility company in Nicaragua.

July 19 Sandinista Youth (Juventud Sandinista 19 de Julio): A national youth organization named for the day on which the Sandinistas overthrew the Somoza government, in 1979.

La Chiquita: El Cuá's jail during the Somoza dictatorship.

MICONS: Ministry of Construction.

MINSA: Ministry of Medicine.

MINVAH: Ministry of Housing .

National Guard (Guardia Nacional): The Nicaraguan national army under the Somoza dictatorship. Created by the United States in the 1920s, the National Guard became loyal to the Somoza family, who ruled Nicaragua for fifty years.

NICAT: The Nicaragua Appropriate Technology Project; a solidarity group, headquarted in Washington State, founded by Mira Brown to finance appropriate technology projects in Nicaragua.

oreja: Spy or collaborator with the enemy.

patrón, patronas: Bosses or masters, mistresses. A term frequently used during the Somoza dictatorship.

Radio 15 de Septiembre: Contra radio station, broadcast from Honduras.

Radio La Voz de Nicaragua: An official radio station of the Sandinista government, broadcast from Managua, known as simply "La Voz."

Radio Liberación: Contra radio station, broadcast from Costa Rica.

Ron Plata: The cheapest store-bought rum.

TecNica: A U.S. solidarity group that brought skilled professionals from the United States to Nicaragua on work brigades.

UNAG (Unión Nacional de Agricultures y Ganaderos): The Sandinista-affiliated National Union of Farmers and Ranchers.

Bibliography

Interviews

Altamirano Flores, Aran. "Zanate." Interview by author. San José de Bocay, March 9, 1993.

Altamirano Lopez, Alejandra. Interview by Beth Stephens. San José de Bocay, July 27, 1987.

Arauz, Pablo. Interview by Beth Stephens. San José de Bocay, July 28, 1987.

———. Interview by Beth Stephens. El Cuá, August 25, 1987.

———. Interview by author and Larry Boyd. San José de Bocay, August 23, 1987.

Arauz, Teodoro. Interview by author. El Cuá, May 19, 1988.

Atkinson, Barbara. Interview by author. Berkeley, Calif., March 30, 1988.

Bauer, Ingrid. Interview by Larry Boyd. Seattle, August 16, 1988.

Bereano, Phil. Interview by Larry Boyd. Seattle, August 15, 1988.

Blandón, Oscar. Interview by author and Larry Boyd. El Cuá, July 5, 1987.

———. Interview by Larry Boyd. El Cuá, January 5, 1988.

Blandón Montenegro, José. "Siete Mares." Interview by author. San José de Bocay, March 8, 1993.

Brody, Reed. Interview by Larry Boyd. Managua, January 30, 1988.

Brooks, Ana. Interview by author. Managua, November 11, 1987.

———. Interview by Barbara Stahler-Sholk. Managua, June 10, 1987.

Brooks, Franklin. Interview by Larry Boyd. Managua, August 29, 1987.

Broome, Jenny. Interview by author. Davis, Calif., March 21, 1988.

Brown, Clifford. Interview by author. El Cuá, May 21, 1988.

———. Interview by Larry Boyd. El Cuá, August 27, 1987.

Brown, Mira. Interview by Beth Stephens. El Cuá, August 26, 1987.

———. Interview by author. Jinotega, February 6, 1988.

———. Interview by author and Millie Thayer. El Cuá, May 17, 1988.

———. Interview by Barbara Stahler-Sholk. Managua, May 21, 1988.

Calderón, Armando. Interview by author. Matagalpa, November 17, 1987.

Cardenas Olivas, Fermin. "Cain." Interview by Maritza Peña. Plan de Grama, October 19, 1988.

Cardenas Olivas, Pedro. "Deglis." Interview by Maritza Peña. Estelí, October 12, 1990.

Castilblanco, Nicolas. Interview by Jan Howard-Melendez and author. Army tent hospital in San José de Bocay, July 4, 1986.

Castro, Cosme. Interview by Larry Boyd. El Cuá, January 1988.

———. Interview by author. El Cuá, May 19, 1988.

Castro, Captain Miguelito. Interview by author. Matagalpa, March 12, 1993.

Castro, William Lt.. Interview by author. Matagalpa, November 16, 1987.

Centeno Garcia, Evaristo. Interview by Beth Stephens. San José de Bocay, July 28, 1987.

———. Interview by author and Larry Boyd. San José de Bocay, July 24, 1987.

Chavarría, Francisco. Interview by Larry Boyd. Managua, March 3, 1988.

Chavarría, Julia. Interview by author and Larry Boyd. El Golfo, January 4, 1988.

Chavarría, Lucas. Interview by Beth Stephens. San José de Bocay, August 25, 1987.

Chavarría, Dr. Sergio. Interview by Witness for Peace Volunteer Mary Ramos, Matagalpa, November 30, 1986.

Chavarría González, Rosa Amelia. Interview by author. El Golfo, January 4, 1988.

Chaw, Antonio. Interview by Larry Boyd. San José de Bocay, July 23, 1987.

———. Interview by Beth Stephens. San José de Bocay, August 25, 1987.

Christov, Alice. Interview by author. Managua, October 28, 1987.

Clements, Steve. Interview by Larry Boyd. Seattle, August 15, 1988.

Colton, Larry. Interview by Larry Boyd. Portland, August 11, 1988.

Contreras, Celia. Interview by author. Managua, November 4, 1987.

Cookson, Susan Dr. Interview by author. Managua, August 23, 1987.

———. Interview by author and Larry Boyd. Jinotega, July 8, 1987.

Cosgrove, Serena. Interview by author. En route to San José de Bocay, November 25, 1987.

Cortadero, Jacinta. Interview by author. El Golfo, May 22, 1988.

Costa, Michelle. Interview by Bob Malone. Washington, D.C., October 1987.

Creighton, David. Interview by author. Berkeley, March 14, 1988.

Cribb, Gayle. Interview by author. Managua, October 1, 1987.

Cruz, Ramon (Freddy). Interview by Larry Boyd and author. Managua, January 28, 1988.

Cruz Huete, Martin. "Sommer," Interview by author. Matagalpa, February 23, 1993.

Dematteis, Lou. Interview by author. Managua, February 20, 1990.

Dormo Centeno, Bertilda (widow of Sergio Hernández). Interview by author and Larry Boyd. San José de Bocay, July 24, 1987.

———. Interview by Beth Stephens. San José de Bocay, July 28, 1987.

Downing, Allison. Interview by Larry Boyd. Managua, December 15, 1987.

Delgado, Dr. Jose Luis (Don Chepe). Interview by author. Jinotega, January 7, 1988.

Driggs, Sarah. Interview by Larry Boyd. Seattle, August 16, 1988.

Echeverria, Victor Rene. Interview by Larry Boyd. El Cuá, January 6, 1988.

Equale, Tony. Interview by author. Matagalpa, November 16, 1987.

Escorcia, Miguel. Interview by Beth Stephens. San José de Bocay, August 25, 1987.

———. Interview by Larry Boyd. San José de Bocay, July 24, 1987.

Evaristo, Santos. Interview by Larry Boyd. San José de Bocay, August 24, 1987.

Fabersune, Mikos. Interview by author. Managua, October 1, 1987.

Fernandez, Alberto. Interview by author. Managua, April–May 1987.

Finnigan, Dave. Interview by Larry Boyd. Seattle, August 13, 1988.

Fley, Luis. "Jhonson." Interview by author. Managua, March 18, 1993.

Folen, Rod. Interview by Larry Boyd. Portland, August 12, 1988.

Forero, Amanda. Interview by author. Managua, September 3, 1987.

Francis, Barbara. Interview by author. Managua, October 21, 1987.

Gadea, Rigoberto Interview by author. Jinotega, February 8, 1988.

———. Interview by Larry Boyd. El Cuá, September 2, 1988.

Galeano, Danilo. "Tiro al Blanco." Interview by author. Jinotega, March 12, 1993.

Gannon, Joe. Interview by author. Managua, December 9, 1987.

Garcia, Dr. Miguel. Interview by Beth Stephens. San José de Bocay, July 27, 1986.

———. Interview by author. San José de Bocay, July 30, 1987.

Gessel, Beverly, Director of Office of Public Exercises. Interview by author. Univ. of Washington, Seattle, March 1992.

Giron-Mesa, Santiago. "William." Interview by author. Agua Zarca, July 26, 1995.

Glaser, Lenor. Interview by Fred Bruning. Portland, Oregon, 1987.

Gonzalez, Agenor. Interview by Doug Spence, Larry Leaman, and Jeff Hendrickson. La Trinidad Hospital, December 6, 1984.

Gonzalez, Juana. Interview by author. El Cuá, May 20, 1988.

Gonzalez Lopez, Douglas. Interview by author. El Cuá, May 21, 1988.

Gonzales, Ricardo. Interview by author. Managua, November 11, 1987.

Granados, Hilda. Interview by author. El Cuá, May 20, 1988

Gupta, Anil. Interview by author. Mountain View, Calif., March 20, 1988.

Hall, Lillian. Interview by author. Via cassette from U.S., January 1988.

Hanson, Nancy. Interview by author. Via cassette from Presidio, Texas, November, 1987.

Hart, Jeff. Interview by author. Managua, August 27, 1987.

Hernández, Marta. Interview by author. Managua, October 20, 1987.

Herrera Palma, Ramon. "Estrella." Interview by author. San José de Bocay, March 9, 1993.

Hicks, Gary. Interview by Beth Stephens. San José de Bocay, July 16, 1987.

———. Interview by author. Managua, August 2, 1987.

Hirshon, Sheyla. Interview by author. Matagalpa, December 6, 1987.

Hooker, Socorro (Coco). Interview by Larry Boyd. Managua, November 23, 1987.

Jarquin Reyes, A. Interview by Beth Stephens. San José de Bocay, July 28, 1987.

Kellogg, John. Interview by author. Managua, September 4, 1987.

Kozobolidis, Niko. Interview by Larry Boyd. San José de Bocay, July 24, 1987.

Kruse, Tom. Interview by author. Managua, August 29, 1987.

———. Interview by author. Managua, April 27, 1988.

Kuán, Luis. Interview by author. El Cuá, May 18, 1988.

Kurtz, Carl. Interview by Larry Boyd. Managua, March 11, 1988.

Lantigua, John. Notes from interview with Ben Linder. Managua, March 1987.

Leaf, Rebecca. Interview by Barbara Stahler-Sholk, Managua, July 1987.

Leaf, Rebecca. Interview by author. Managua, July 24, 1988.

———. Interview by author. San José de Bocay, July 25, 1995.

Levidow, Nancy. Interview by author. San Francisco, March 29, 1988.

Levitt, Jim. Interview by Larry Boyd. Seattle, August 16, 1988.

Lewis, Piers. Interview by author. San Francisco, October 15, 1993.

Lewontin, Jamie. Interview by Bob Malone. Washington, D.C., October 1987.

———. Interview by author. Managua, April 29, 1988.

Lifflander, Dr. Anne. Interview by Larry Boyd. Managua, 1988.

———. Interview by Larry Boyd. New York, August 24, 1988.

Linder, Ben. Interview by Scott Harris. WPKN Radio, Univ. of Bridgeport, New Haven, Conn., December 20, 1984.

———. Interview by Wally Priestley. Portland Public Cable TV, January 9, 1985.

———. Interview by Larry Boyd. Managua, February 28, 1985.

———. Interview by John Lantigua. Managua, March 1987.

Linder, David. Interview by author. Managua, February 15, 1989.

———. Interview by Larry Boyd. Portland, August 9, 1988.

Linder, Elisabeth. Interview by author. Managua, February 15, 1989.

———. Interview by Larry Boyd. Portland, August 9, 1988.

Linder, John. Correspondence with author, 1987–1994.

Linder, Miriam. Interview by Larry Boyd. Portland, August 9, 1988.

Lopez, Eugenio. Interview by Larry Boyd. El Cuá, January 6, 1988.

Macleay, Don. Interview by Joe Gannon. El Cuá, July 30, 1986.

———. Interview by Larry Boyd and author. El Cuá, July 4, 1987.

———. Interview by author. In cab of Sergio's truck, El Cuá to Jinotega, November 26, 1987.

———. Interview by Larry Boyd and author. Managua, November 29, 1987.

———. Interview by author via telephone, Managua-Virginia, February 10, 1988.

———. Interview by author. Albany, Calif., May 9, 1990.

———. Interview by author. Berkeley, Calif., September 20, 1991.

———. Interview by author. Berkeley, Calif., February 29, 1992.

Malone, Bob. Interview by author via telephone, Washington, D.C.–Managua, May 10, 1987.

Marin, Anne. Interview by Larry Boyd. Portland, August 12, 1988.

Mejía Gonzalez, Douglas. Interview by Larry Boyd. Managua, December 4, 1987.

Mendiola, Benigna. Interview by author. Managua, March 17, 1993.

Mendoza, Luis. Interview by author. Managua, September 16, 1987.

Merizalde, Jaime. Interview by author. Managua, September 6, 1987.

Merlo, Maximiliano. Interview by author. El Cuá, January 4, 1988.

Montes, Wilfredo. Interview by author and Larry Boyd. El Cuá, July 5, 1987.

Moore, George. Interview by author. Managua, October 28, 1987.

Morales Suarez, Enrique. Interview by Beth Stephens. San José de Bocay, July 28, 1987.

———. Interview by author. San José de Bocay, July 30, 1987.

Moray Cornejo, Eulogio. Interview by Beth Stephens. San José de Bocay, July 28, 1987.

Morin, Anne. Interview by Larry Boyd. Portland, Oregon, August 12, 1988.

Mourad, Desiree. Interview by author. El Cuá, November 26, 1987.

Nicaragua, Manuel. Interview by author. El Cuá, January 4, 1988.

Parkinson, Carol. Interview by author. Managua, October 30, 1987.

Petschek, Bruce. Correspondence with author, Cambridge, MA–Managua, September 21, 1988.

Pittman, Jim. Interview by Larry Boyd. Seattle, WA, August 15, 1988.

———. Interview by author via telephone. Seattle–Berkeley, March 7, 1993.

Quam, Alison. Interview by Larry Boyd. New York, August 20, 1988.

———. Correspondence with author. 1987–1994.

Quirós, Ana. Interview by author. Managua, October 20, 1987.

Ramos, Federico. Interview by author and Larry Boyd. El Cuá, January 4, 1988.

Reasoner, Don. Interview by author. Managua, November 28, 1987.

Redman, Dina. Interview by author. Managua, September 9, 1987.

Reyburn, Ria. Interview by author. Managua, November 28, 1987.

"Rigoberto" (Tirzo Ramon Moreno Aguilar). Interview by Larry Boyd. Honduras, August 1988.

Risacher, Mary. Interview by author. Matagalpa, November 20, 1987.

Rivera, Marlene ("Chile"). Interview by author. Managua, September 3, 1987.

Rivera Alvarez, Salamon. Interviewed by Peter Olson and Larry Leaman, Witness for Peace volunteers. Jinotega, December 1, 1984.

Rivera Benavides, Justo Pastor. Interview by author. El Trebol, May 20, 1988.

Rivera Hernandez, Ezekiel ("Checo"). Interview by author. El Cuá, May 18, 1988.

Rizo Castillo, Casilda de. Interview by author. El Cuá, July 5, 1987.

Robinson, Circles. Interview by author. Matagalpa, November 16, 1987.

Rodríguez, Salvador. Interview by Larry Boyd. Managua, December 1, 1987.

Rodríguez, Sonia. Interview by author. Managua, September 1, 1987.

Rosales Seas, Cecilio. Interview by Beth Stephens. San José de Bocay, July 28, 1987.
———. Interview by author and Larry Boyd. San José de Bocay, July 31, 1987.
Rutherford, Jain. Interview by Larry Boyd. Seattle, August 15, 1988.
Saenz, Sergio. Interview by author. San José de Bocay, July 30, 1987.
Sanchez, Lt. Diovigildo. Interview by Beth Stephens. San José de Bocay, July 29, 1987.
Santiago, Mirna. Interview by author. Albany, Calif., May 9, 1990.
Santo Vallejos, Jose (Chepe). Interview by author. El Cuá, May 19, 1988.
Schmidt, Joel. Interview by Bob Malone. Washington, D.C., December 8, 1987.
Sherman, Shelley. Interview by author. Managua, November 6, 1987.
Smith, David. Interview by author. Managua, October 30, 1987.
Solis, Franklin, Interview by Larry Boyd. Managua, December 4, 1987.
———. Interview by Larry Boyd. Managua, May 12, 1988.
Solis, Tomas, Interview by Larry Boyd. Managua, May 12, 1988.
Souter, Annie. Interview by author. Managua, November 16, 1987.
Stricker, Peter. Interview by Larry Boyd. Seattle, August 14, 1988.
Suarez Lopez, Socorro. Interview by Larry Boyd. Managua, May 12, 1988.
Takaro, Tim. Interview by Larry Boyd. Jinotega, February 6, 1988.
———. Interview by author and Larry Boyd. Jinotega, July 8, 1987.
Tenerio, Edie. Interview by Larry Boyd. Wiwilí, June 22, 1988.
Tercero, Juan. Interview by author. El Cuá, January 6, 1988.
Thayer, Millie. Interview by author. Managua, January 6, 1988.
Thompson, Juliet. Interview by author. Matagalpa, December 6, 1987.
Tiffer, Pablo. Interview by author. Managua, September 10, 1987.
Valdivia, Silvia. Interview by author. El Cuá, January 5, 1988.
Vallejos, Ileana. Interview by author. Managua, September 16, 1987.
Wands, Curt. Interview by Bob Malone. Washington, D.C., October 1987.
Wessel, Lois. Interview by author. Managua, September 12, 1987.
Wihbey, Ani. Interview by author and Larry Boyd. Managua, July 22, 1987.
Wigginton, Barbara. Interview by author. Managua, August 27, 1987.
Zamora, Antonio. Interview by author. El Cuá, May 19, 1988.
Zeledon, Adolfo. Interview by author. El Cuá, May 19, 1988.

Sworn Declarations

Bowman, Carol. Deposition. Managua, July 1986.
Centeno, Evaristo. San José de Bocay, August 19, 1987.
Cook, Mark. Deposition. Managua, July 24, 1986.
Goff, James. Managua, July 24, 1986.
Linder, Ben. Portland, September 7, 1986.
Moran Cornejo, Eulogio. San José de Bocay, August 20, 1987.
Norwood, Susan. Deposition. Managua, July 21, 1986.
Price, Sandra. Deposition. Managua, July 23, 1986.
Rosales, Cecilio. San José de Bocay, August 18, 1987.
Declarations from Contras' Human Rights Association.

Books, Articles, and Documents

Americas Watch. *Land Mines in Nicaragua and El Salvador.* New York: Americas Watch, 1986.

Atkinson, Barbara. "Remembering Ben," *Earth Island Journal,* summer 1987, 25.

———. "U.S. Engineer Slain by Contras Remembered," *Daily Californian,* May 4, 1987.

Bereano, Phil. *Eulogy for Ben Linder.* Eulogy delivered at University Christian Church in Seattle, May 10, 1987. Transcript published in *Technology and Society,* Vol. 16, no. 2 (summer 1997): 3–4.

Bourgois, Phillippe. "Running for my Life in El Salvador," *Washington Post,* February 14, 1983.

Boyd, Gerald M. "Reagan Defeated in House on Aiding Nicaraguan Rebels; President Turns to the Senate in Fight for Bill," *New York Times,* March 21, 1986.

Brody, Reed. *Contra Terror in Nicaragua: Report on a Fact-Finding Mission, September 1984–January 1985.* Boston: South End Press, 1985.

Bruning, Fred. "One American Life: The Killing of Benjamin Ernest Linder," *Newsday Magazine,* December 6, 1987.

"Cantos de la Lucha Sandinista," *Editorial Vanguardia* (Managua), 1989.

Cabezas, Omar. *La Montaña es Algo Más que un Enorme Estepa Verde.* Managua: Editorial Nueva Nicaragua, 1982. (Published in the United States as *Fire from the Mountain: The Making of a Sandinista,* translated by Kathleen Weaver [New York: Crown, 1985]).

Carson, Tom. "Ben Linder, 1959–1987," *Village Voice,* May 12, 1987.

Center for Constitutional Rights. *The Killing of Benjamin Linder.* New York: Center for Constitutional Rights, 1988.

———. Spring Docket. February 1994, New York.

Chamorro, Edgar. *Packaging the Contras: A Case of CIA Disinformation.* New York: Institute for Media Analysis, 1987.

Colton, Larry. "Ben Linder Stands Tall in Memory of Adams High," *Sunday Oregonian,* Portland, Oregon, May 31, 1987.

Cruz, Arturo Jr. *Memoirs of a Counterrevolutionary: Live with the Contras, the Sandinistas and the CIA.* New York: Doubleday, 1989.

CUSCLIN. "All 'Bout Communism: American Foreign Policy as Jeane Would Have It, or For Whom the Big Stick Clubs," *Nicaragua Through Our Eyes: The Bulletin of Committee of U.S. Citizens Living in Nicaragua (CUSCLIN),* November 1984

———. *Nicaragua Through Our Eyes.* Managua, March 1986.

———. *Nicaragua Through Our Eyes.* Managua, May 1987.

———. *Nicaragua Through Our Eyes.* Managua, July 1987.

Davis, Peter. *Where Is Nicaragua?* New York: Simon & Schuster, 1987.

Dickey, Christopher. *With the Contras: A Reporter in the Wilds of Nicaragua.* New York: Simon & Schuster, 1985.

Diederich, Bernard. *Somoza and the Legacy of U.S. Involvement in Central America.* New York: Dutton, 1981.

Dillon, Sam. *Comandos: The CIA and Nicaragua's Contra Rebels.* New York: Henry Holt, 1991.

Everett, Melissa. *Bearing Witness, Building Bridges: Interviews with North Americans Living and Working in Nicaragua.* Philadelphia: New Society, 1986.

Foster, Claire. Transcripts of video footage. May 1987.

Francis, Barbara. *Red, Black .. and Green Newsletter* (Managua), February 1987; April/May 1987. Edited by Frances Tyson.

Garvin, Glenn. *Everybody Had His Own Gringo: The CIA and the Contras.* New York: Brassey's, 1992.

Gonzalez Vargas, Dr. Bayardo. Forensic Pathology Report from German Pomarez Ordonez Hospital, Apanas, Nicaragua, May 2, 1987.

Griffin-Nolan, Ed. *Witness for Peace: A Story of Resistance.* Louisville, Ky.: Westminster/John Knox Press, 1991.

Gutman, Roy. *Banana Diplomacy: The Making of American Policy in Nicaragua, 1981–1987.* New York: Touchstone, 1988.

Hart, Jeff, and Barbara Wigginton. Video of El Cuá hydroplant. December 1985.

Kinzer, Stephen. *Blood of Brothers: Life and War in Nicaragua.* New York: G. P. Putnam's Sons, 1991.

Kornbluh, Peter. *The Price of Intervention: Reagan's War against the Sandinistas.* Washington, D.C.: Institute for Policy Studies, 1987.

Kornbluh, Peter, ed. *Nicaragua: The Making of U.S. Policy, 1978–1990.* National Security Archives microfiche collection.

Kornbluh, Peter, and Malcolm Byrne eds. *The Iran-Contra Scandal: The Declassified History, A National Security Archives Reader.* New York: The New Press, 1993.

———. *The Iran-Contra Affair: The Making of a Scandal, 1983–1988.* National Security Archives microfiche collection.

LaFeber, Walter. *Inevitable Revolutions: The United States in Central America.* New York: W. W. Norton, 1983.

Lantigua, John. "Risking it All in Nicaragua: The Life—and Death—of an American Idealist." *Washington Post Magazine,* May 31, 1987.

Lifflander, Dr. Anne. "Remembering Benjamin Linder," *Washington Peace Center Newsletter,* June 1987.

Linder, Benjamin. "Bringing Light Where There Was Darkness," *Through Our Eyes: The Bulletin of Committee of U.S. Citizens Living in Nicaragua (CUSCLIN),* spring 1986.

———. "Desarollo Eléctrico." Unpublished paper. Managua, June 1985.

Linder, Benjamin, and Mira Brown. Script for slide presentation on the Cuá/Bocay Integrated Development Project. August 1986.

Macauley, Neil. *The Sandino Affair.* Chicago: Quadrangle, 1967.

Millet, Richard. *Guardians of the Dynasty: A History of the U.S.-Created Guardia Nacional de Nicaragua and the Somoza Family.* Maryknoll, N.Y.: Orbis, 1977.

National Security Archives. *Nicaragua: The Making of U.S. Policy, 1978–1990.* Alexandria, Va.: Chadwyck-Healey, 1991.

National Union of Farmers and Ranchers (UNAG)."Electricity on the Nicaraguan Frontier," *Nicaragua Farmer's View.* June 1994.

Petschek, Bruce. Audiotapes and videotapes of Ben Linder. Boston, MA, 1988.

Portland Central America Solidarity Committee. "Ben Linder, Presente." Portland, Oregon, June 1987.

Robinson, William, and Kent Norsworthy. *David and Goliath: The U.S. War Against Nicaragua.* New York: Monthly Review, 1987.

Scigliano, Eric, "The Last Days of Ben Linder," *Seattle Weekly,* May 4, 1988.

———. "To Die in Nicaragua," *Seattle Weekly,* April 27, 1988.

Selser, Gregorio. *Sandino.* New York: Monthly Review, 1981.

Sklar, Holly. *Washington's War on Nicaragua.* Boston: South End, 1988.

U.S. Congress, "Public Law 98–473" (Boland Amendment II), Section 8066[A], October 4, 1984.

Vandermeer, John, and Peter Rosset, eds. *Nicaragua, Unfinished Revolution: The New Nicaragua Reader.* New York: Grove, 1986.

Veterans Peace Action Teams Newsletter (Santa Cruz, Calif.), September 1987.

VI Region Official Documents, Government House. *Recursos de El Cuá-San José de Bocay, Documentos de la Sixta Región,* Matagalpa, Nicaragua. Courtesy of Piers Lewis, 1990.

Walker, Thomas, ed. *Nicaragua: The First Five Years.* Boulder: Westview, 1986.

Walsh, Lawrence. *Iran-Contra: The Final Report.* New York: Times Books, 1993.

Wisconsin Coordinating Council on Nicaragua (WCCN). "Benjamin Linder; A U.S. Martyr for Peace," *Update,* April/May, 1987.

Witness for Peace. *Bitter Witness: Nicaraguans and the "Covert War."* Santa Cruz, Ca.: Witness for Peace Documentation Project, 1984.

———. *Witness for Peace Newsletter* (Washington, D.C.), July/August 1987.

———. Witness for Peace Documents. Witness for Peace Office, Managua, 1987.

Woodward, Bob. *Veil: The Secret Wars of the CIA 1981-1987.* New York: Pocket Books, 1987.

Index

About the Author

Joan Kruckewitt is a journalist who lived in Nicaragua from 1983-1991 and covered the war between the Sandinistas and the U.S.-backed Contras for ABC Radio. She did graduate work in Latin American Studies at Stanford University, and reported from Latin America and Europe for various radio networks (Pacifica, RKO, Mutual, NBC, Monitoradio, Canadian Broadcasting Company, National Public Radio) and newspapers. Kruckewitt is currently writing a book on the U.S.-trained death squads in Honduras in the 1980s. She lives in Northern California.